The Last Red Stick Warrior?

By Ghost Dancer

Ghost Dancer and Shungamanitou, NW Territory 1995

Collected and Transcribed By

Lynda M Means PhD

authorHOUSE®

AuthorHouse™
1663 Liberty Drive
Bloomington, IN 47403
www.authorhouse.com
Phone: 1-800-839-8640

Published by AuthorHouse 6/26/2012

ISBN: 978-1-4685-8853-8 (e)
ISBN: 978-1-4685-8854-5 (sc)

Dedicated To

All of My Relations

That All People May Live

With a Better Understanding

Among All Beings

And To Contribute To

Peace and Harmony

In Our Universe

"We Are All One"

Symbolism of the Drawing on Front Cover

The picture of the alligator, snake, and eagle is to represent the struggle that is in protecting Mother Earth and myself as a guardian. Both the alligator and rattlesnake are very symbolic to us, for each are guardians, and represent protection and power. Many might think they are fighting each other, but that is not what this means. The picture represents me, fighting to protect what I love and as my spirit is tied to these powerful beings, the snake and the alligator, I call upon them with the eagle for justice in protecting all that I love and believe in.

Symbolism of Back Cover Drawing

Mama Eagle in the drawing represents all the eagles. It is representing the symbols of justice, protection, duty and responsibility, honor, trust, respect, courage, and compassion that all should have for Mother Earth. And since most Native Peoples know their own heritage and know that we are the keepers and guardians of all of Mother's children, (all life from creepy crawlers, four-legged ones, winged ones, those who live in the waters, plant peoples, stone peoples, those that live in the ground) and all two-legged ones as well as those that crawl upon her; that as her guardians, who keep in trust and honor for the next seven generations, we each have the duty just as Mama Eagle, to do whatever we have to do to preserve all these lives, and protect them from those who are greedy and have no respect for all life. We all (native peoples) were once called the Eagle Peoples in the ancient times and have this duty and responsibility from our birth right! For each generation must Preserve and Protect for the next seven generations, their right to life! And just as anyone should know, you don't mess with the children of any Mother, because Mother will always fight and protect her young!!

Both of these original drawings are by Ghost Dancer.

Foreword

"The Last Red Stick Warrior?" is an opportunity for everyone who is ready and willing to take a journey like no other, travel to the stars and learn where you truly came from, learn of the ancient ones and live as they live, transform your body, mind and spirit to the awakening that has been prophesied for millennia, take part in the new beginnings, of the new world that is coming. If you are willing to open your mind, heart and spirit to the truth of your own self, then come along and begin your transformation as the Mayan, Aztec, Cahokians, Ani-yun-wiya, and so many others have spoken of and did themselves.

Do you feel lost, out of balance, confused and just plain nowhere to go, and no one seems to understand you, no one can answer your questions because you feel there is more, and you know inside of yourself there is more? Then this is your time, time to know who you really are, what you are, and what you shall become! But it is up to you! All it takes is you opening your heart and mind to come take this journey and let your future begin now.

These stories are a spiritual journey into our self to truly believe in ourselves, our spirit. Our world is alive, and must be balanced with pure love. Love is what will create the new world, the new bodies we will have, because our vibrations will change as Mother Earth changes. We will bring light to the next generations as our minds and spirits realize that into the light of love flows the essence of life, so powerful, that energy of love flows throughout everything.

These pages carry messages of your own struggles in life just as was mine. For even though you did not go to my jungles, and swamps, you live in your own. Just a little different is all; for monsters are in all of us, and all around us. And we create them as well as others even when we don't realize it. Our own thoughts are pure energy and what we think we program and bring into existence.

It is the path to the highest form of transformation of the physical body and the mind and the spiritual growth that will be needed to walk into the future of the world. Only those who are truly willing to let go of their pre-programmed self and are open-minded can take this journey that is awaiting all, when the prophecy unfolds. We are just the messengers bringing in a new consciousness, and creating this into the new world that will be available to all who are on this higher consciousness of thinking and living!

This is what this is all about, new transformations for us all!

Ghost Dancer April 2, 2012.

"We are our own devils and gods,

We walk where their feet had trod,

So in our minds and hearts we bring,

All these things into being just the same,

So free your thoughts and hearts,

Fill them with love and you will see,

The true you that is free.

Because you create all you will ever be."

An Ancient Prayer

Table of Contents

SECTION 4-COMMENTARY

SECTION 5-MEDICINE STORIES

SECTION 6-SPIRITUAL EXERCISES

SECTION 7-ENGLISH/MUSKOGEE DICTIONARY

Ghost Dancer and Lynda Means, 2005

Introduction

As a professor of Native American Studies for the past eighteen years, I became disenchanted by the sources of information available to teach about real Native Americans or First Nations Peoples. Knowing that there were some 500 plus distinct Native groups in North America, I did my best to choose books and videos that best showed Native Peoples today and yesterday.

In 2003 I met a man at a Powwow who changed my way of looking at Native People from this continent. I explained that I was a professor at a local university and that the information I used was inadequate to paint a true picture of the Natives of this land. I was tired of reading of the Bering Strait theory, and finding that the scientific community discounted the oral tradition of the Native Peoples of the Americas. Thus began my friendship with Ghost Dancer.

My students, as part of their class work were required to go to Cahokia Mounds and write a "research" paper. They were instructed not to tell me the information they learned but how they felt as they toured and learned about Cahokia, an inner research paper. Then almost at the end of the quarter, I would give them the paper handout (at that time, now a chapter in this book) by Ghost Dancer. Many said they wished they had had the handout first, but I assured them they could certainly return to Cahokia with a whole different mindset. Thus began my own personal journey into the life of a man who lived what most people have only heard or read about.

I have learned that life is all about the journey, not the destination. I have learned who I truly am. I have learned that oral tradition, even though it may have changed over the many thousands of years, is still based on truths. And I have learned that I am, as well as everything, and every being around me, LOVE.

After a certain point in our relationship, Ghost knew that there would be more to his writing than just teaching university students. His words were for the whole world. The writing was first done on legal paper, handwritten in English, not his first language. I then transcribed them onto the computer just as he wrote them adding only punctuation and grammar corrections. Since his first language is Muskogee, his English sometimes leaves out words. Muskogee grammar is quite different than English. I added nothing but to clarify a sentence, many times asking him directly to get exact answers. The more recent writings were done the same way although he did send them via email rather than hand writing them.

Also Ghost speaks the old language, not the modern language that combines the dialects. His dialect is used in this writing. It is common now for the language of Oklahoma and Florida to speak the same! Ghost does not! The old language is the language he was brought up speaking, the language of the stars, and the language of the spirits. The language of Hvfvne'lke Jerv is the language of the ancient ones. There are maybe five people left alive who speak it. He is the youngest!

The language he speaks is the Mvskoge Cvssvtv (Cussutta) Upper Red Stick from the Warrior River, at High Rock, Flint, and Mulberry rivers. This area is where they all come together and causes a big white water current.

He realizes that most of the Seminole tribe still speaks Miccosukee, Timmacu, Yucchi, Mvskokee, and Mvskogee, but is it the old language, or is it modernized, or mixed? Ghost knows that there are no more than six that speak the old dialect, and no more than five that speak the language of the spirits, and maybe only three that speak the language of the stars.

The time is right to share this information. Our world, our Earth Mother, is in need of our help. Only we can choose our destiny. Please read the following pages with Love in your hearts for Love is the answer to all things. In Love all things can be done! We hope you feel the Love that has been put into this book and pray that this new book brings further enlightenment and understanding to all. This book is about the Message: how each person can apply it in their own lives, how we can all live better lives in the new "jungles" of our society.

I have come to learn that there are no coincidences in

the messages, wherever we each may find them. Some folks call these messages, synchronicity. Whatever you call them they are out there all around us in the lyrics to a song, the words of a child, or in the assigned homework for the week. I pray that you are all open to them!

This book has one source, chapters written in Ghost Dancer's own words including the stories and essays from the author's first books, "A Gift To The People: A Collection of Writings by Ghost Dancer" first published in 2006 and revised in 2008, plus all newly received writings, drawings, and photos.

In 2012 as this book is being written, Ghost Dancer is about 70-71 years old. Most of his contemporaries have already crossed over. He is probably one of the last men alive that was raised in the true Red Stick warrior tradition. Today many American Indians tend to live much shorter lives than their European brothers and sisters. As such, he is one of the last of the Red Stick Warriors that learned from the Old Ones.

Sadly, Ghost feels, most of the all the tribes, and clans, have forgotten the old ways, old practices, and therefore have forgotten who they really are. Because when you act like other people, talk like other people, and take on their ways, their customs, then who are you? Today many of all native peoples are acting and becoming members of gangs, acting like these other cultures of people. Many of them are dressing, and talking like them, and making their lives like them. Then what have they truly become?

It is sad that many of these are just native by enrollment number only. The beliefs, customs, religion, language and practices and even the way we think is what truly separates us from other peoples. This applies to any culture! And this can be a full blood, half-blood, or mixed. You are what you are! Which part of a person is his/her blood part? None of the old ones ever used any blood lineage to make a person. When you know your history, you know that all tribes, all nations, married and had children from different nations, either through capturing, war, trade, or just plain out of love. Every single tribe did this to keep their blood pool from being inbred, and it was used even when the Europeans came, and the Asian, African, and every other culture. This blood thing was a creation by the government to "divide and conquer" all tribal nations.

As Ghost states, "I guess you could call Tshunka Wikto (Crazy Horse) a half breed, or mixed blood then? Why? Because he was a real pale one, with long curly blond hair, and blue eyes! He grew up around the fort and was called Curly for years. Or Osceola himself was born of Scottish/Irish/Muskogee people. He was one of the great leaders of the Seminoles. Or Mangus Coloradas, the Apache, who was a giant amongst all men, white, black, or native. But what makes them who they are, are their customs, beliefs, religion, and practices. Another prime example would be Blue Jacket of the Shawnee. He was Tecumseh's war leader of the whole nation. He was born a white man, raised to be a minister, and was captured as a young missionary man. He was adopted by the tribe and rose to the position of war leader! There are many, many examples of this. If you think like the other people then you have part of them as you."

That is why Ghost believes that the thinking is also a part of the way of life. If you think like the other people, then you have part of them as you already, and when clans forget their obligations to teach, and instruct their members in the old ways, they have taken that from the next generation. And this applies to all tribes and clans.

It is hoped that this new book will fill in some areas not covered in the original texts, much more of his personal life not included in the earlier books, some of his Peoples' Medicine Stories, more Spiritual Exercises, and some of his personal photographs.

We hope you enjoy this new book! Welcome to the Journey!

Walking in Love and Beauty Always
Lynda M. Means PhD

American Indian Basics

Now what type of religion did the Etowah practice? Do you have any idea? Well, the individuals who all participated in the tribe's ceremonial practices, recognized the solar solstices, lunar solstices, equinoxes, the fire, the sun, and all living things. They had royalty, kings and queens, musicians, artists, doctors, priests, teachers, warriors, government administrators, messengers, historians, orators, actors, etc. They used the stars, planets, Mother Earth. They used herbs, teas, amulets, crystals. They recognized that Mother Earth was a living being, the universe was alive; that everything in the universe affected their lives each and every day. They understood that every thought they had created an entity, that everything had power. Every attitude affected everything around it, like a ripple in a wave.

See, unlike modern man, or even the invaders of the 1400s-1800s, the Native People understood that their every action, every feeling even, affected everything that existed. They prayed every single morning giving thanks for the rising sun, giving thanks for the gift of life, giving thanks for the water in which they bathed and purified their bodies to start the new day, giving thanks for the beauty that was all around them, for they lived their lives in beauty and harmony.

Since water was so plentiful around the Etowah People, different types were used for different types of ceremonies. The rivers, streams, fresh springs, hot springs, sulfur springs, lakes, creeks and the ocean, represented and was the life blood of the Mother Earth. Going into the water was going into the womb of our Mother Earth, to be cleansed and purified and reborn. When we drank of this water, we were drinking the sacred blood of the Sacred Mother/Grandmother, like a babe suckles at his mother's breasts for life. Lying on the bottom of these waters, we feel the heartbeat of the Mother throughout the entire flow of the water and through our own bodies. Our hearts become one. We were One.

Each plant had a purpose, a use, a power of its own.

Never would anything be picked or used, or consumed without first the proper prayer and the prayer of thanks for the plant. Some plants such as corn (maize), cedar, ginseng, datura, etc. were so important that ceremonies were done during planting time and harvesting time, for these were so important to the peoples' everyday life.

Unlike most western tribes, females were truly Blessed Ones. Beloved Women were Sacred to every person of the Nation. Clan Mothers had control of the clan. Clan Mothers took the needs of the people to the Nation's council. The council told these needs to the kings and queens. Then the needs were met.

Every single person had a purpose and was guided and helped to ensure that they achieved their specific purpose. Some children were selected for their memories, to start training to be historians. Some were selected to be artists or sculptors. Some were chosen for musicians, actors. Some were chosen for their ability to be leaders. As a child was born, he was watched by all to see the character and nature of the child. Each child demonstrated as it grew its natural abilities and interests. These were respected and promoted by the Clan Mothers to insure each child would receive the best training and teachers in that particular area.

The Sacred Fire was and is a most important aspect. The Sacred Fire Keeper dedicated his or her life to the Sacred Fire, for the gift of fire came from the sun as a gift to the people. The Sacred Fire Keeper had many who also were Fire Keepers, who worked and learned from the older ones.

Each year, the Fire Ceremony would commence with the coordination of the Green Corn Ceremony as well. When every fire in the Nation was extinguished, fasting and purification was done while preparations were being made. The Sacred Fire had to be cleaned and all redone. Special wood was prepared that had been previously selected for this purpose. The High Priests had been in the Sacred Temples, fasting and on spiritual journeys to receive the visions and guidance for the people from their specific spirit helpers. The High Priestesses were all glorious and had danced with Grandmother Moon for the full cycles of the moon. They had danced with Sister Datura and danced the Water Dances in the waters (streams, rivers, waterfalls etc.) bringing the power of the moon to themselves for the people. They had used their spirit bowls (bowls specifically designed) to journey back to the past to visit the High Priestesses in the ancient past, finally, to visit the true Mother, Mother Earth. There they would talk to her and receive her gifts and be shown what they needed to do.

All these things took place for three days in preparation for the final day which would be the fourth day, the Day of the Fire. On this day, all would gather as the Sacred Fire Keeper would lead the procession to the Sacred Fire, followed by the High Priest and Priestesses, Clan Mothers, The King and Queen, Prince and Princesses, and the people. When all was ready, the Sacred Fire Keeper would unwrap the Sacred Crystal, sing his special prayer song to the Sun and using the powerful crystal, light the Sacred Fire again for the people. Then, each female by rank and position would come forth and take a burning ember back to her own home to bring this sacred gift from the Sun to their home hearth. Then feasting and the Fire Dancers would commence.

Now, in explaining some of this to you I have given you a basic group's religious practice. But, understand, this was an example of one Nation's group ceremony. In understanding Native American Traditional Religions, one must understand that each person must find and connect to the spirits in their own way, using their own individual spirit helpers, their own special songs and chants, a special place where they go, and what they do. Some may use the plant dog fennel, a hallucinogen, to help. Some may run; run until they are totally exhausted and dehydrated. Some may use snake (poison) venom to go to the spirit world. Whatever method that a person uses, it is his or her own special beliefs or practices. It does not belong to anyone but that one person. Each person's own method is respected and never, never put down or even suggested as being wrong or should be good for anyone else. See, in Native American

Traditional beliefs and practices, there is no specific way, no laws, and no books, that say you must do it this way! For in doing something like that, then a person has no special direct connection to the Spirit, or even to the Spirit of all living things, there would be no individuality.

I hear and read about people claiming that this belongs to this Tribe or Nation, or it was given to this tribe only. When I hear things like that I laugh! For it is totally hogwash to even think that way. Some of their claims are so ridiculous; they even go against the tribe's true history. Many have combined the newcomer's (European) religions to their beliefs, so that they are like the religious dogmas of the European Churches. Many are reflecting these acts of these other peoples' practice as putting themselves or their tribes as the only right way, or the only true way, or as the originators of a certain practice. But all you have to do is search the true history of the tribe to see and know the truth.

From the beginning of time, there have been people, Tribal Nations, here on this continent. Certain practices are tens of thousands of years old. Sharing knowledge and customs was common. So some tribe that wasn't even known, say for instance 10,000 years ago, how can they then lay claim to practices that have been used by others for 100,000 years? Then there are tribes who have forgotten where they actually came from, before they grew prosperous, or became a large Nation, because other tribes had been devastated by disease and war with the white invaders. Some tribes moved to these areas after the Nations and People were all but wiped out and took on many practices and customs of the people who survived, and now believe and proclaim these as their own teachings and that these teachings belong only to them.

They sound just like those who came across the waters 500 years ago claiming they own this, they are the only ones, and all must believe as they do. All of this is caused by ignorance. And then you must look at the motive. For a true Spiritual person understands no one can claim anything they did not create themselves, for only can the Great Spirit,

Manitou, Great Mystery, Master of Breath, God, the Creator, lay claim to creating all. We as humans are pitiful and mostly only create problems, destruction, and our own deaths.

Historical records of a tribe, along with archaeological artifacts, and museum pieces, all can open your eyes to the truth. It is like the coming of the white invaders' mentality. It has assimilated into the very people of a tribe, now thinking they are the best and the only right ones, and all others got their beliefs from them. When a person claims these things or a tribe claims these things, there is a strong motive. Money! Religion of any kind can never be true if it is based on money, fame, power, or control of a people or any one individual.

Then it is sad to see people proclaiming to be Holy Ones, drinking alcohol, using drugs, cursing and doing bad things, for a true sacred person does not do these things. And how can one of them help someone when they need help themselves. No one can tell you how to pray. That is foolish. How you pray, what you say and do is between you and the Creator. I realize that a lot of people are lost and confused in the world. I realize that many people are searching for their connection to the Spirit. And there are those in the world who will try to sell you religion for their own personal gain. Or even sell you so-called Sacred items or Sacred Ceremonies as well. But remember this: if it is really truly Sacred then you know it can't be sold! So stop and think!

These things cannot be taught in a book or even a series of books. They must be learned by living and experiencing these things. It is sad today to see all these different ones who buy a book, read it, and then decide they are Teachers of these things. What is even sadder is all of the people who believe these people. Books like this one can give us a start, but we must find a true teacher to continue from here if we are to understand fully, much less teach!

Now let's study what is truly Tradition. We hear all the time Tradition is this or that. Native Tradition is a deep, buried in the heart, spirit being, of specific customs. Also Natives always learned to be adaptable; to co-exist with their environment.

This is important because, as I have said, many tribes moved from place to place, either out of necessity or by being forced or driven from their lands. And True Tradition always respects other's beliefs and customs. If it suited them, or they saw something that they liked or enjoyed, then they adapted it to themselves.

Native Tribes may have used many, many different ways, or items, or even nature, but it was and is a way they all understand as part of themselves. Every Native knows you must watch all of Nature: plants, water, animals, birds, clouds, season changes, storms, insects, to learn how they live, what they do, their character and rituals. All things have Nature within them, and we as humans do as well. It is Nature, and we are all a part of it. No matter if you are butterfly, eagle, frog, deer, oak tree, blackberry bush, a trout, snake, or human, each living thing is a part of you, just as you are a part of each of them. You sometimes act like them. Sometimes they act like you.

We are all part of the Sacred Circle! If you attack the tree people, you attack all the other life forms as well. If you hate a people, then that hate radiates from you and causes an effect in others around you, even plants, animals, birds, etc. Just as in Nature, the young challenges the old. The strong devours the weak, old, and injured. This is the force of Nature. Those that conquer will be conquered. Those that rule will later be ruled. For everything we do will get returned to us many times over.

Most people don't observe Nature anymore. They watch television, VCRs, DVDs, computer games, etc. So, therefore, they take on the same things they are watching. They watch a violent, evil person in a movie; they take on some of the character and nature of the evil one. If they watch killing, they want to kill. If they watch a sad depressing movie, they become sad and depressed. If they watch these types of things most of the time, then they are programming themselves to become exactly as those they are watching. It is the same with music, schools, government, parents, relatives, and religions.

That is why we have what are called senses. Our senses give us these things to see, hear, smell, taste, and feel. So it is our senses that are being programmed by all these things. That is why it is important to be careful what you watch, hear, taste, smell, and do. That is why so many Native Americans have taken on and become just like the whites, blacks, Asians, etc. They have taken on these peoples' lifestyles, habits (drugs and alcohol), and characters. They have become disrespectful, deceitful, etc. Why? Because they have been surrounded by these people, forced to go to their schools, and take on their way of life.

But <u>NO</u> it is not traditional to act or live this way. This, again, is all caused by ignorance. Ignorance of the Native People's past for allowing themselves to forget their true religion, history, customs; their own virtues of truth, honor, humbleness, generosity, love, giving, respect, and pride. It is the ignorance of the others to not look at themselves and where they came from and possibly learn from the Native Peoples how to live in Beauty and Harmony with all living things.

Ignorance causes all pain and suffering, ignorance of who you are, what you are, and what you are to become. This applies to all living things. And there is no excuse, no one to blame but the individual personally. No one should allow anything or anyone to control their life, thoughts, beliefs, or actions. You cannot blame anyone for your mistakes, faults, habits, troubles, problems, etc. except your own self. You can and probably will want to make excuses or lay the blame on others. But that is false. You are responsible for your own self. If you haven't taken the time and put forth the effort to learn who you are, what you are to become, then it is your own lacking! If you haven't connected to the Spirit of all living things, then you have to blame your own self. If you don't know the true history of your family, ancestors, clan, tribe, nation, then blame yourself. If you are ignorant to the Truth of the Universe, Mysteries, and the Spirit World, then blame your own self! For these things are not hidden or lost. You just haven't looked or tried hard enough.

No person can give you the answers you seek but only the Spirit can do this for you. A great teacher always lets the students find the answers themselves. That is true knowledge, for when the student finds the answer, they will understand it. If a teacher gives an answer, then the student won't truly know, because they never truly experienced it by realization. That is where wisdom and knowledge comes from.

The beliefs, customs and practices of the Zuni are different from the Huron, just as the Aleuts are different from the Iroquois. The Pawnee are different from the Shoshone. The Lakota are different from the Apache etc. And, each person of a tribe is different. What is right for one is not right for another. And don't let anyone tell you that their way is the only true way or the oldest way. Or, that a specific teaching was only given to them. Ignorance breeds more ignorance. And, if you are going to learn from someone, make sure that someone lives that life, not just speaks about it.

Visit established museums. Study the artifacts they have displayed. Ask questions. Ask for additional informational sources. Many journals by Spanish, French, English, and others about what they saw, heard and experienced, will be helpful. Research these different tribal Nations. Learn their history, as the old ones of their people say it was and how it happened. Check and cross check your information with all the different sources and evidence. See what other tribes said about their histories along with other tribes involved with their own histories, such as wars, alliances, disasters, etc.

Go to these locations. Look for the written history painted on stone, or hieroglyphics or pictographs. Check out the actual sites of some of these places, such as Cahokia, Serpent Mound, Window Rock, Jicardah Rock, Ruby Falls, Stone Mountain, Cliff Dwellings etc. Always try to find a native of the people in that area. Ask them to go with you and explain these things. This is done out of <u>Respect</u>. And always offer them a gift out of Respect. By doing these things you will notice the attitude change because you have given respect to them. There are thousands and thousands of places here still in North America and the histories of these people still exist. Every single state has some documented places, but many more exist known only to the Natives in that area.

Go to cities such as:

St Augustine, FL
Atlanta, GA
Tuscaloosa, AL
Mobile, AL
Biloxi, MS
Cedartown, GA
Tallahassee, FL
Apalachicola, FL
Perry, FL
Window Rock, AZ
Painted Rock, CO
Roanoke Island, VA
Cherokee, NC
Allegany, NY
Crystal Rock, WI
Cahokia, IL

Serpent Mounds, OH
Castle Rock, TN
Devil's Lair,
Horseshoe Bend State Park,
Vinemont, AL
Hot Springs, AR
Rickwood Caverns, AL
Bangor Cave, AL
Crystal River, FL
Juniper Springs, FL
Silver Springs, FL
Salt Lake, UT
Mystic Lake, MN
Blue Feather Falls, NY
Moundsville, AL

Most towns on the east coast were built on the cities of the Native Peoples of Ancient times. What wasn't understood was destroyed. Never take anything from these places but the spiritual blessings, experiences and beauty. Learn to see it, feel it, taste it, hear it, know it as it truly was, and is. If allowed to sleep there, in silence, listen to the voices of the spirits. Absorb the senses from all living things. Open your heart, mind, and spirit to these to see them as they were. Always come in truth, love, respect, humbleness, and generosity. Offer offerings of tobacco, something that means something of value to you. Offer cedar and cedar smoke, a piece of your food, and most of all yourself. Do all these things in sincerity, respect, truth, and love, and you will be rewarded. For the Spirits always watch and know your every thought and feeling.

Never make messes or leave trash or litter. Clean up after yourself. Thank all of the things there: plants, flowers, trees, grasses, insects, rocks, animals, birds, etc. Send out messages of love, respect, beauty, truth, gentleness, and friendship to all things. Thank Mother Earth and walk upon her with respect. Lie down upon her and hear her heartbeat and make it your own, as one with hers. For those only truly willing to learn and experience can truly experience these things. And, they in turn, can truly become teachers because they know it in their own hearts and have lived it.

Remember to Walk in Beauty and Love Always!

Section One

The Red Sticks

Chapter One

Red Stick Muskogee History and Life

My whole family was Red Sticks.

I will tell you what I know of the history of the Red Sticks as it was told to me, from my ancestors, as was passed down from generation to generation, and this was as it was said in the old days, by those of the old times.

The people were grouped by their clan blood and allegiances to each other. Some clans were stronger in numbers, some in honor, some in religion, some in orators, crafts, or organizers, and some were just naturally great in warrior status. Some were great hunters, some could build anything, and some were devoted to medicine and cures, but each was necessary and complemented the other. Towns were divided so that no one area would have to support more than it could handle.

Farming, and cultivating crops, was a primary source of food for any town; growing beans, corn, squash, tobacco, melons and numerous other crops. Berries, nuts, and fruit crops needed to be harvested too, but under the responsible understanding between the plant people and the two legged people, never take more than necessary, never take all, and always give in return, ask before you take, respect what you have been given, and give thanks for everything. The crops were all treated this same way. There had to be balance for all. So dividing the towns into smaller towns was done out of respect, love and understanding. And it was out of this necessity that the Red towns and White towns came into being. All were equal. All shared in the common good for all and all of life, not just the two-legged but to include every form of life!

The Red towns consisted of those of warrior status clans, those of traditional religious teachings, those of crafting weapons, those who taught all these skills, those who conjured up spirits, those that walked between the worlds, and those that were great at hunting, tracking, running, and scouting.

The White towns were set up to build and teach building skills, to organize all the foods for the whole nation, to store and supply the foods that were harvested, great farmers and those who knew each plant and its uses and gifts, those who were great weavers, artists, speakers, historians, politicians, keepers of the laws, administrators, etc.

Each town worked in harmony with each other and the nation as a whole! Each town was noted for its distinct qualities.

Also traders were a very unique part of the people! They were of a status that all nations welcomed them, and their knowledge of lands and different nations was always shared! Traders from every nation known came here to trade and share stories, knowledge, and goods. Some came from other lands so far away it would take months to arrive by boats. Some who had traveled by foot, had been gone for years from their people just to get this far and would one day travel home with stories and trade goods, that would make their elder years filled with eager ears, and shocked faces on young ears that were filled with wonder and awe!

Traders were a very special breed of people. They had to have courage and skills in bartering, and commerce of all nations that he or she would travel to. They had to have the restless spirit that loved to see new things, places, people, and experience aloneness. Most traders had to enjoy their own company, because traveling was mostly alone, unless you were training someone, or being trained yourself. This was generally considered an apprenticeship to the trader who was your teacher in all the business. Or you went into a partnership to work together with someone. This would normally be a blood relative since traders were a close group of people who didn't share their wares, or techniques without a reason or cost!

Red towns were responsible for protecting all the people, and the territories', hunting and fishing grounds, and they did this very well. Young warriors were trained, taught, and put in responsible areas to see how they would do!

All day every day you were pushed and encouraged in wrestling, strength training, (using wooden clubs some bigger than others in size and weight). The wooden clubs were used to strengthen your shoulders, arms, and back. You would need this in fighting hand to hand using war hatchets, war clubs, knives, or spear, or just fighting bare handed. Warriors were taught to dodge arrows, spears, and the blows of war clubs and hatchets. You had to run and keep running, up and down the mountains, through the rivers, mud, heavy brush, rocky grounds, or through heavy thorns.

You may run for three days, running all day, and only stopping briefly to relieve yourself at sunset, and eat a small portion of your warrior rations (these rations usually consisted of dried and smoked venison jerky, dried corn, herbs that not only were used as food but as medicine and rejuvenators, sort of like a big energy boost). The rations could be eaten as they were or added to boiling water for soup. Drink some water, and you were running again. Once you got to the area you were supposed to be, other older warriors would attack suddenly, and you must fight just as in a real battle. The elder warriors did not take it easy on you. Your life and the life of those you love or those you were protecting may depend on you to be prepared, so you fought, wrestled, and kept on. You may have to fight for hours with no rest. This was the warrior conditioning.

Because if and when you were called on to take the war trail by the Clan Mothers, (clan mothers were the only ones who could ask the warriors to pick up their war hatchets and avenge their honor or the deaths, theft, or the violation of one of the blood laws) you must be ready to leave once all the proper ceremonies were done and completed. That preparation may require you to fast, purify yourself, by drinking the black root drink, eating the datura roots, holly berries, snake venom, or other lesser acts, then dancing all night, and seeking your medicine, your power to come to you, then taking your war club and striking the war pole that was covered in red from the poison berries of the holly plant and the blood of our enemies, and even some of the blood of your flesh offering you may have given to offer the spirits for help.

Once all this was done and all proper ceremonies were completed, the warriors took off at our famous warrior trot, which we would maintain as long as we needed to get to where we would attack. Then redo all your war paint and medicine faces (either a mask or painted on) this was done and used to frighten your enemies and hide your identity from the spirits that may want vengeance against you, spirits of the dead, of their ancestors or their spirit helpers.

War faces were unique to each person, as each has its own medicine and uses. Warriors were also ranked; those who had leadership of a small group, or ones that commanded at least 50 warriors, those that commanded 100 warriors and the ones who led the war party. This person was chosen by the clan mothers and carried the honors and medicine items in a sacred bundle, the war bundle. This was his to carry only. No other was ever to touch it, unless the leader was killed or under attack himself, then a young warrior who was usually a clan relative in training would handle it until he was relieved or dead. War bundles were power and enemies would go for it to break your medicine. This was just the beginning for a Red Stick warrior!

In the old times, young warriors were pushed hard to build up their stamina, endurance to fatigue, and going without sleep (Any warrior caught sleeping at a post, or at any teaching, or training session would be severely punished in front of all other warriors. This is to instill in all, the consequences.) These training methods were necessary so that you would be able to do whatever was necessary in battle or in life.

When I was a young boy and was in training I thought I would be alright, for I was anxious to become a warrior as all young ones are. I was a Red Stick and all my family were Red Sticks, meaning we all came from the Red Towns of the old ways. My grandfather's father, and his grandfather, and all our great, great grandparents, were Red Sticks. The name struck fear in everyone's eyes. My people were the same ones who had fought the Red Stick wars. When our Nation became divided, the White towns decided that they wanted the goods and religion, and schools of the white people. The Red towns, who were all traditional religious practitioners, warriors, conjurers,

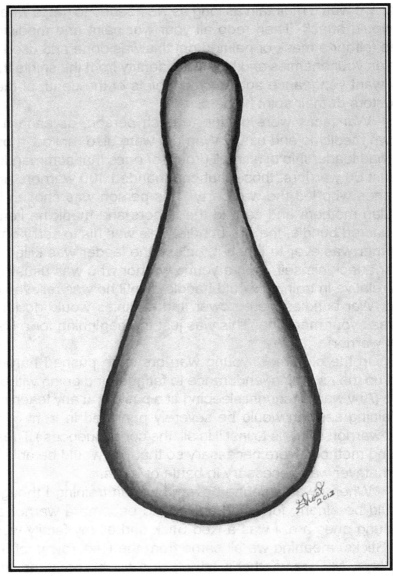

Wooden Club

The wooden club or pin as some call it is hardened oak, cypress, or hickory. The sizes vary from 10 pounds to 40 pounds. One practices swinging, slicing, and blocking using it backhanded as well. It is used to build stamina, strength and speed, and can be practiced for at least an hour with another person.

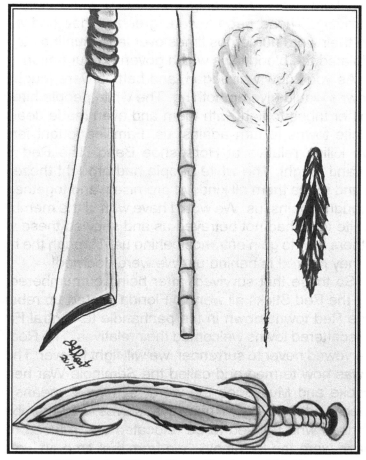

Machete, Blow Gun, Dart, and Knife

The machete is ½ inch thick at the point, weighs 12 pounds, is 9 inches wide at widest point and is three feet long.

The blowgun is bamboo river cane, sectioned into two pieces each 3 feet long. It is about ½ inch inside diameter and can be used as one or two pieces, depending on the target, that could total 6 feet long overall.

The dart is either a bamboo sliver or bone and is ridged and serrated to hold the poison. The average length of a dart is 12 inches. The fluff is made of cattail bulbs or feathers.

The throwing knife is obsidian and is 3 inches by 8 inches.

The hooked knife is 5 inches by 16 inches.

spirit walkers, wanted nothing from these white people, not even trading. These people were greedy. They had already broken their word numerous times over land, hunting etc. They had violated the blood laws which governed our nation.

As you know war began, and battles were fought! The Red towns would give up nothing. The white people hired and paid other tribes to fight with them and even made deals with the White towns to turn against us. Families fought families, relative killing relative at Horseshoe Bend. The Red Sticks fought and fought. The white people had brought these other tribes and made them all kinds of promises, and together all of them fought against us. We would have won, if the members of the White town had not betrayed us and showed these whites and others how to gain entrance behind us. Through the hidden cave, they poured in behind us. We were doomed!

So those that survived, after being outnumbered forty to one, the Red Sticks all went to Florida to start up rebuilding with the Red towns down in the panhandle to central Florida. These scattered towns welcomed their relatives. The Red Stick people vowed never to surrender, we will fight forever. The Red Stick was now termed and called the Seminole War because in Mvsoke and Muskogee the word "seminole" means "wild, untamed, and runaway". Runaways, slaves, and members of other tribes who refused to be relocated and refused to give up, these were the Seminole, and from that time on we never surrendered.

We never were conquered, and we never will be! In all the wars fought against all the tribal Native nations, the Seminole wars were the most costly, in every way! It was the longest war in American history. Even today the Seminole Nation not only fought the Americans, but the Spaniards, French, British, and all the foreign so called warriors who thought they could come and defeat us. Those came from Germany, Russia, Italy, Sweden, and just about everywhere else. But none who came defeated us. All lost and we remained free; the only tribal nation that did.

Anyway all my family members were all Red Sticks and

we were a proud people! So for me going to my warrior training was a dream come true as each of us wanted to be great warriors.

My training started before dawn. We were grouped into different areas, and given wooden clubs, and shown how we were to loosen up our muscles in our shoulders and then in our back, finally our arms. We were asked were we good and loose and we all said yes, and our uncles smiled. We should have known something was up when they smiled. They had us pick up those heavy clubs and now act like we were hitting each other as they paired us up. Swinging that heavy club as hard as we could time after time, my arm almost fell off. They felt like they were boulders. My shoulders, back and my whole body was covered in sweat as if I had been swimming. We were told to put our clubs back where they belong and come right back. We started walking and we were yelled at to do it now. So everyone took off running, trying to put their club up. And you know how chaotic that was! When we all got back two different uncles stood before us and told us to stretch our legs real good because we were going to need them. Well this is what I was real good at, running. So I smiled. I would impress my uncles now with my long legs. I could really run. My grandfather had taught me, and he had sent me to one of his friends he met in the Great War, a Yaqui Apache, and that man put me through some of the worst torture my poor body ever went through at that time. So I was confident that I could do this real good and catch my breath while others struggled, because that old Apache, taught me to run like a wolf.

He trained me to run a wild horse down, because the horse can only run for so long, and if he can see you, he will continue to run. But a horse needs to feed. He needs to drink and catch his breath, and to rest his body, because he uses too much energy. That was something a warrior didn't need to do. So you wear the horse down constantly chasing him until he is so exhausted he can't run any more.

Then you walk up to him talking to him, for he or she

is a relative, telling the horse of the courage and beauty the horse has, and you are honored to have run with him. And you tell the horse how exhausted you are and you make sure the horse sees you breathing hard, how he ran you to death, and that you are honored that such a fabulous horse beat you. The horse has been listening to you this whole time, his ears are the key to his thoughts, as he moves them you see the sparkle in his eyes as he accepts the praises from you. He stands up straighter, and relaxes his breathing and now accepts you and respect for him.

If it is your plan to ride the horse you must first win his respect of you, and that comes from your respect of him. Disrespecting the horse and making him lose his honor is not the way of the people, and not the way to make a friend. The horse can be a friend or he can be an enemy you never can trust or let your guard down. It was never my intention to ride the horse at that time, but I did with others. This is just one way to catch a wild horse. I prefer a lot easier ways of my own people.

Anyway my uncles had us all stretch and we did, thinking we would all be running for a long time. Boy, were we in for a surprise as our uncles began walking and signaled us to follow. We did and when we saw where we were headed, my mouth dropped. This wasn't what any of us was expecting at all. Before us were numerous heavy war canoes. These are built heavier, by burning out the middle of the tree, and chopping and shaving it down. These were very heavy and could hold 20 warriors. These war canoes were used when we were traveling through rough waters, swirls, white water, drops and lots of rocks. The sides were higher to give you better protection, and it was a lot harder to sink, or even be harmed by arrows. Only flaming arrows would bother you. Since we didn't go on war travels like in the old times, these now were used in training us and boy did they.

Our uncles had us group up to each canoe placing ten of us per canoe. Then they called the elders to come, and had three elders sit in each canoe. Then we were told to lift our canoes. We were told that our elders need help getting home and we would carry them there. We recognized the elders and they did not live anywhere near us. We knew then that we must dig deep inside for any who could not do this would disgrace not only himself, but his family, relatives and his clan. Failing, giving up, or quitting was not a Seminole way. It was not a Red Stick way either.

So we all lifted these elders up and our uncles set the pace. Up the hills, sometime almost straight up, we went, we followed no trail because our uncles were making their own. Going down the hills was just as bad, always keeping the canoe balanced, keeping our elders safe, as they sat tall in their places, and enjoying their sightseeing trip. What a joy to just sit back and ride, with smiles on their faces!

We kept the pace of our uncles, down the hills, through the woods, and into the swamp we went. Now if you have never been to a swamp, you will never appreciate its wild beauty. It is untamed, raw and deadly; water moccasins, alligators, quicksand, and the muck. Muck is like a big hunk of dirt clod mixed with concrete and water. It sticks to you, and drags you down, pulling on you. It is wet, it is heavy, and it is very, very hard to run in. Imagine trying to carry someone in water up to your waist and trying to run against the current and you might be getting close to what it is like. And run we had to!

We ran and ran. Finally I think the elders took pity on us and asked if they could relieve themselves. We all let them down. They all had a twinkle in their eyes. We thanked them silently with our eyes as well. As each of us took time to stretch our muscles in our shoulders, and backs, we decided to rearrange ourselves so that we could change up our positions so as we could now rest the shoulder we used before. This would help us continue a lot better. We ran the whole day long, finally sitting our elders down and helping them out of the canoes. Our uncles told us to all relieve ourselves and make camp. We would be here for a while and rest a little and eat.

We all immediately did as we were instructed. After

bladders and bowels were emptied, we discussed amongst us who would take up positions as lookouts and how our rotations would go. We didn't have to ask our uncles, because this was expected of all our people always. We didn't trust outsiders, and people of other nations. We all stood alone. We each may look a little different, black Seminoles, half breeds, mixed breeds, and full bloods. We were all one. We are Seminole. And we knew that for us to remain a free people we must always be a strong people.

Now this may shock you but our women are warriors too. They train in warfare and survival, just as men do. For at any time they may have to defend themselves or others of our people. If you have ever faced a female grizzly combined with a female African lion and a female alligator, all of them protecting their young, you just might get a taste or idea what it would be like to face against one of our Seminole women. You never want to do that. You would last a lot longer and better against the bear, lion and alligator!

Sculling Boat with Pole

Carrying the canoes was done to build our strength as well as our stamina, also teaching balance, for in war and in survival, your reflexes, your balance, your stamina, and strength could mean the difference between living and dying. We also were trained in the water, swimming, on top of the water and lots of underwater swimming. Swimming makes you use all of your muscles and conditions your body. Carrying loads of weight on your back while you swim, rowing the canoes, hour after hour, climbing the palm trees, like a squirrel, swinging in the limbs of the giant oaks, and magnolias, sweet gums, and others. Even our daily work, was a training; throwing our cast nets, for fish and shrimps; poling our small dugouts or scull boats, through the sloughs, and bogs, then to the canals; wrestling the alligators; and working our fields with hoes, rakes and picks; using our machetes; hunting the wild pigs, in our daily life.

Being a Red Stick meant always practicing all the traditional ceremonies, and religion. This requires lots of fasting, purging your body (throwing up and making your bowels empty) by drinking the black drink, using the datura, holly berries, and snake venoms. These were all prepared by those who are trained in such matters, and are very skilled and knowledgeable in what they do. The clans themselves each had their own ceremonies as well. And your war clan had its own ceremonies as well. And you must learn all the old ways, because you are entrusted to pass this down to the next generations.

We were entrusted to protect the land, and to take care of all our relatives that lived on the lands as well! It is our duty because the lands are our future generations' life as well. It is why we protect the panther, manatee, alligators, the fish, birds, plants and everything. Even the quick sand is alive and must be protected. Our land is in balance, because in balance of nature it is the balance that determines its health as well as yours. We today even make sure we try to preserve and protect all from modern society, and civilization. We have cattle and run a cattle business, but we are the only ones who guarantee all of our beef, and products are all natural and organic. It is this respect for nature that has made all Seminoles, a strong and prosperous people, who still practice the old ways and still live and work with modern life as well. We still have a generous heart and help all the surrounding communities, schools, children and even tribes and tribal nations across this nation and even in Central, South and North America.

Now days many don't do this type of training, but they do have the opportunity to learn martial arts, body building, and all athletics and sports, since the people live in an area that offers such numerous sports, colleges and schools that thrive on sports. All Seminole members, especially the young ones, to the high school graduates can and do go to these colleges.

Even though they don't do the things of the old ones, doesn't mean they don't care. It is just times have changed. Today they would charge one of us with a crime of child abuse or endangerment or something. Because society says oh no that is so wrong!

Now days people think that things such as our training was cruel; just as our test of courage against the alligator, or our test of fear with the snakes in the pits, we all went through as a child! But each of these things was for a reason and purpose, and they were truly necessary to help us as a people to survive. It was a world filled with beauty and dangers everywhere. And it still is today. Whether you live in the city, suburbs, country, deserts, mountains, or swamps, people think that now you are safer have more laws! Yet murders, rapes, child molestation, child abuse, spousal abuse and every type of crime there is, is everywhere today. Plus natural disasters, such as Katrina, tornadoes, floods, can happen anytime and anywhere. Then we have such atrocities as 9/11, and the school shootings, and the drug wars, and the gang problems.

So you stop and think real hard people, do you need such laws that restrict you from teaching your children, family, community, to protect itself? Do you feel safe and secure that you would know what to do in any situation? Could you take care of yourself? What about your kids or you grandparents? Every time I see these disasters I see fear in the peoples' eyes and actions. When disasters strike people always panic, starving because they have no food, no electricity, no heating, or cooling systems, no water. It is a shame for people that this continues constantly. How many times does it have to happen before your eyes get opened and you say I have the right to train my children, my family to survive no matter what happens.

No government should ever be allowed to pass laws that restrict parents or guardians in the proper upbringing of their children. Any one that pushes for laws like this does so for totally selfish reasons. Such as political favors for those who will profit from your tragedies! You might see a big change in children's behavior, and it would affect the attitudes of teenagers and adults as well. When you can teach an arrogant loud mouth that is disrespecting you the consequences of that type behavior and you put him or her on their butts with a good smack in the mouth they will learn real quick to keep it shut, or have it happen to them again. No I don't believe in striking a child, no native does. Our children are precious to us. But we must have our respect from them, so at an early age in their life they are taught very quickly that there are consequences to their actions, and they won't like what it is! So really think about this. Maybe you'll want to make some changes?

Being a Red Stick Seminole was being very proud yet humble as well. Our numbers were small due to all the wars and disease. So it was very important that we procreate! Many people ask me "how could you possibly have that many wives and children"? I noticed you didn't ask how many husbands a woman could have though! Ha ha ha! Yes procreating was vital to our survival as a people. The clan mothers in their wisdom understood these things and made sure each woman got pregnant, and after having the baby or babies, she was given a chance to recuperate and heal. Then given the drink to help her ovulate and got pregnant again. This was vital to keep our population growing. And I was a healthy young male, therefore my service was needed and I made sure I helped as every warrior did.

We never had a problem with it. Only outsiders did, and the church people. Yet after reading their old testament old Solomon had a 1,000 wives, plus concubines. He must have been some warrior plus his people must have been almost out of males. So I never could figure out why it was wrong for us and not wrong for the church people's religion to do so. I had one preacher argue with me that it was a sin. I looked at him and said since I have learned about your religion and can read; maybe you need to read your own Bible because Jesus himself said he didn't come to change Moses' law, but to fulfill it. And everyone that can read knows that under Moses' law numerous wives were okay. So please people get off my back. I love my wives equally, and I love all my children and grandchildren and great grandchildren all equally. Try it you might just find that it is good for everyone!

Now in understanding my Red Stick ways, you had to really understand our people. Our women were our leaders in all things. If someone violated their honor all they did was call the warriors and their honor was restored. If someone violated our hunting, fishing, or fields of our crops, well you already know the warriors are coming. Our women represent our souls. They give us our blood lines to each of our clans, and teach us the meaning of love. They give us everything a man could possibly dream or fantasize about. Our women are respected beyond outsider's understanding. Why? When your own histories speak of all the great leaders of old times like Queen Sheba, Katherine the Great, Joan of Arc, Nefertiti, Mary, mother of Jesus, plus Mary Magdalene (Jesus' wife) and of course Queen Cleopatra! Then there is Queen Elizabeth, Queen Mary, and numerous others. Even in Russia and in other countries. Don't let a belief deprive you of the facts of life itself.

Now, being a Red Stick Seminole, a people who was still technically at war with the US, we didn't feel we should ever let our guard down. And even today main stream media (TV, newspaper, radio) do not cover the ongoing atrocities with tribal nations by the government, large corporations, and state governments. And the mainstream media knows the American public really wouldn't care to know this anyway. But if any of you truly want to find out what is happening, just go online to "Indian Country Today" news magazine, or any tribal newspaper, such as "Black Hills News", "The Lakota Times", "The Navajo Times", or just Google for all the tribal news and you will get a very good idea if the wars are still going on.

So we trained every day, for emergencies, for safe getaways, routes that every child, every person must know. For if we were attacked, by whoever, we expect every person to do what they are supposed to do! Young kids would automatically grab smaller ones and babies and help the elders, or those that were handicapped or disabled. Warriors are to guard and protect the women and the children as they make their getaway. We never had large groups of us living together anymore. Only small camps, always ready to move at any time.

This applied to everything, hurricanes, tornadoes, severe lightning storms, flash flooding, wildfires, drunken groups of people who wanted to get some kind of kicks. A lot of the Ku Klux Klan attacks were just crazy, because on the law books it still wasn't against the laws to hunt and kill Seminoles or any wild Indian that could be found.

Even though we didn't hate or seek trouble, sometimes it found us anyway. Not all, or in fact most peoples we saw, didn't do dumb things towards us. It was always those who were drunks or KKK peoples, or some young fool trying to prove how bad he is in front of his girl, or friends. We did business with many people who lived around the areas. Most of them lived in towns. We tried to avoid the towns as much as possible. We did trade and business with stores for our handcrafted goods, selling vegetables, fish, shrimps, and things to supplement our needs. We hired out to fishing boats, or work crews. We stayed to ourselves, and only ate what we could catch or gather or kill that was around in our area. And there is always something around if you really look.

During these times we had to be real careful because it is against the law to hire any Indian as we were called then. By the way there are still many states that have laws such as the one I just mentioned still on their books. That law that states no Indian can own land and it is illegal for you to sell any Indian any land. It is against the law for any Indian to work on your property, with the confiscation of all your lands and property if you are caught doing so. There are various laws that are still in effect even today. So we as native peoples know that even though there is no declared war, the war still goes on by the government, and corporations, to annihilate all native peoples. What they started all those decades ago, Manifest Destiny is still very much in their eyes. President Obama has for the first time put together a native council to bring these things to light and he has said that we would be having changes, and things would get better for us. There has been some change, but for most it's the same old story. We will see though, and wait.

I hear people all the time claim they are discriminated against because of their color of skin, or sex, or religious beliefs. Now before the 70's and 80's even, yes that may have been, but it is nowhere to what it used to be, and none of you that are living can say you would be hanged or killed for your religion or practicing it. But even today all native nations still face these problems and we aren't even listed as being human. Check the facts on any census by the government. Check your law books, on federal laws pertaining to criminal law. Native Americans have a totally different law book, with different sentencing.

What if your religion was to have an eagle feather and you got caught with one? Now only recently were we given protection of the law for our eagle feathers. But we must get our feathers from guess who? The government! And there is a waiting list and all kinds of legal paper work to obtain them.

Now you understand why we had to train and still train as warriors! Water, mineral rights, and land, big corporations still want. Which we have! Now we all know how those in congress and the senate get into office. It is through campaign funds, and those who finance their positions. So these same corporations will get their bought and paid for politician to vote to take our minerals, water, and land. So you still think we don't need our warriors?

Wake up and pay attention in life to more than just yourself. Whatever befalls the weakest, smallest of peoples or any life whether it be plant, animal, fish, whatever, if you take away one, you will destroy the balance of everything. It has happened time after time with nature and bad things always happen. Yes I am a Red Stick and very proud of that fact, and I will remain so as will others. Oleha! (At last)

Remember to Walk in Love and Beauty Always!

Chapter Two

Living in a Red Stick Matriarchy

I would like to explain to you how I grew up. Growing up traditionally under the authority of the Clan Mothers is a lot different than growing up the way today's society is. When I was growing up, Clan Mothers' words were law. Whatever they decided was the way it would be. No warrior, no headman, no war leader, did anything without the Clan Mothers' say so! No wars, no raids, no marriages, no planting crops, no harvesting, nothing unless the Clan Mothers decided that was to be. The reason for this is that we get our blood clan from our mothers. It determines which clan we belong to. This clan is now our entire family. Your clan is responsible for everything that comes to your learning, living, marrying, everything. Your father has no say so regarding you whatsoever. Only your clan does. Your uncles, cousins, aunties, all from your mother's blood are there to teach you, or have others teach you. Your Clan Mother, who is generally the oldest female of the clan (or a very specially gifted female who has proven her great wisdom or other things that the eldest Clan Mothers feel earns her that title), directs your life in all matters.

All males are born for protecting, providing, pleasuring, and procreating purposes only. Males are treated with high respect and can become headmen, leaders (mikko) chiefs, kings! But they still live under the authority of the Clan Mothers. When the Clan Mothers see or hear that there is a problem they discuss it and make a decision. Now in minor problems this stays only within the particular clan, and is taken care of by the Clan Mother after she has heard from all the females of the clan. Yes even young maidens have a say so. But it is the Clan Mother of the clan who will decide what is best for all concerned. Now if it affects the whole tribe or band, then all the clan mothers meet and make a decision. They in turn speak to the headman, who in turn tells the council, who then addresses the warriors, and that is the way it will be.

Men are very honored by the women though. Men have the duty to provide for the whole band, protect the whole band, and to pleasure all the women (their wife or wives) as women may have a husband or husbands. Yes it works both ways. The main thing to remember is the respect. Men are expected to provide children so breeding is very important. And a man who is known to be very potent in making babies will always have numerous wives, because the children belong to the mother and her clan. Now this may offend some, but <u>survival of the tribe and band is depending on the continuation of children.</u>

A man will naturally love his children, and the children will love their father. You would be able to have time with each other naturally. But another reason your uncles are your instructors is because they will not go easier on you or harder on you. They all want what is BEST for you. All homes, all property belongs to the females. Males only own their own weapons and what they have on. All food, trade goods, possessions are property of the women by tribal law and under the blood laws of the nation, traditionally.

And a woman can divorce a man at any time for whatever reason she chooses. To divorce him all she does is place his weapons outside the home, and maybe some clothing if she is generous. A man can't divorce a woman though without the woman and the Clan Mother's approval, because all marriages are made by the Clan Mother and must be arranged through her. All marriages are made with the benefit of the clan and tribe ALWAYS in mind; what good it must be for the clan and for the tribe as well.

No woman, no clan, no tribe would ever want a no good man, a lazy man, a drunk, or a poor hunter. The man must bring some good benefit for this wife to be, because when a man married he moved to the woman's house. Men don't have a house or home. Bachelors live in a bachelor house. But even being a bachelor, you are still under the rule of the Clan Mothers, and the women of the band or tribe.

This is a traditional Mvskoge and Mvskoke Traditional Blood Law. It is still my way of life. I know the rest of the world may live differently, but I'm my own man and I live by these laws willingly because they are good and for the right reasons. See men have egos about themselves and I'm no different. We have our pride, our tempers, and our own interests. It is why Creator gave women the gift of bearing the child, not a man. She is chosen by the Creator and I accept that. Men have only themselves that are important while the women all think of their children first.

There is your reason! Women think of the children and the next generations, and for all the people, while our temper or ego will make us do something dumb. That is truth, I accept my way of life!

Remember to Walk in Love and Beauty Always!

Chapter Three

More Than One Wife

Over the years I have had numerous people ask me about having more than one wife. Some have asked if you have them all at the same time. Do you have one, leave her, or she leave you, and you get another? Do you sleep with more than one at a time? Do they all live in the same house? Don't they get jealous of each other? How can a woman allow you to have another or in your case so many? There were questions upon questions about something they have only read about! So to answer everyone that has questions about this matter, I decided to answer these questions for all. But first you need to know why this was so common for those of the old time. And yes it was practiced even in the times of ancient Egypt, biblical times and even practiced today by other cultures, and countries!

So to understand the purpose is to understand why it was so practical to all those who believed in the act itself. The main purpose in the very beginning was to produce more children. Because the more numerous the people, the stronger the band, tribe, nation. This act of producing children was an act to also produce more workers, more laborers for your crops, your fishing, your hunting, those to manufacture more clothes, trade goods, more help for the household. Also this helped produce more strength in numbers for protection, also to replace those who are lost to disaster, accidents, violence, war, disease, health issues, and old age. More people entitled you to more territory, more land, more water, more food, more crops, more hunting and fishing areas, and less likely to be attacked and robbed, killed or enslaved.

Now these reasons not only applied here in America, but also around the world since the beginning of time for people to live. Also men were more likely to be killed, either by animal, accident, or war, attacks of others robbing or plundering, and generally lived a shorter life. Women, usually in the old days, became a woman after her first moon time (bleeding time) and were ready for marriage, or the more common practice, of being mated. Times were different in those days, and didn't change until around 1970's and 1980s in this country, especially in the southern and mid-west states. In the southern states a girl unmarried at the age of 15 was considered an old maid!

To get straight to answering your questions about this matter! In the old times, many men had numerous wives to help strengthen the tribe or band. By constantly having the women pregnant, this kept a steady supply of people to the tribe or band. A man who was known for his powerful seed planting in women was a popular man. Why? Well every woman wanted children, and the children always belong to the mother and her clan. Because the blood line comes from our mothers, and the bloodline determines which clan you are born to.

Now having the numbers once again comes into play. The larger the number to a clan gives more authority, more status to a clan and the number of votes. See every person has a voice, and every person has a choice in what they decide. But every person is also loyal to her or his clan. So the clan with the strongest voice has the more say so in the decisions of the tribe or band, and male and female children are loved by the clan the same.

Only the females can own any property though. The home and all the possessions belong to the females only. Males are only entitled to their weapons and medicine bundles, etc. Only the females are owners of the land, plots of gardens, etc. Men have a simple life: provide, protect, pleasure and procreate. That is their main function in life. Now I was born in a time when very few of us were still alive and living free, wild and untamed, living as we were born to live, and trying our best just to survive! I was young and powerfully built, and once I became a warrior I was ready to start my duties as a warrior. And that meant providing, protecting, pleasuring, and procreating.

I was very fortunate to have a very good and powerful Clan Mother, who was very wise and understanding as well. My first wife was chosen by her and all arrangements were made.

She was a lot older than me and very beautiful as well. I did my duty as a good husband. Being a male I was fully aware of the laws of my people and our Nation, and I also knew that the advice my Clan Mother had given me would be valuable to me for the rest of my life.

I was trained in the art of pleasuring as all males born to the people were. Both male and female are taught the pleasures of love making; to make the act always sacred and always fulfilling. The process is much like that described in the "Earth's Children" books of Jean Auel. I made sure always to have my wife pleasured beyond her expectations. I have practiced this all my life. I know that any woman, who is satisfied totally and completely until her whole body is alive with pleasure and she is floating in paradise, will always welcome you to her home. And this applies with every woman. All she wants is respect, truth, honor, love, humbleness, generosity, and understanding. You must listen to every part of her. To her words, her spirit, her body, her heart, her mind, her beliefs, and her dreams!

To make any relationship work there has to be a balance; a balance that is equal. All must understand exactly what that means. Equal means just the same in giving and getting. Today and in the past too many have been influenced by those who wish to control the truth and bend it to their own needs. Women were told they had to be silent and serve men and that they were beneath men, and must submit to men's authority. What a bunch of crap! I can't believe that they honestly went for that load of BS! I'm sure glad they never tried to tell any of my ancestors that, and none of my people's Clan Mothers! The Clan Mothers would have demanded that the war cry ring throughout the land, because they would demand their honor and respect be restored! And you all question my beliefs and practices. Wow what a joke! Because any woman who willingly denies herself pleasure in life never has ever lived.

Life was meant to enjoy the beauty of all that was created. How can a woman truly love if she has never been loved? Love is unconditional, not asking for anything in return, not expecting anything in return; just giving because it feels so good and natural to give your love so freely! When I love I give everything I am. I feel every sigh, every vibration that flows within her. I want to feel her heart beat as one with mine, as she flies into the clouds of total blissful pleasure. Any man should want to pleasure a woman until she can't make up her mind: stop and don't you dare stop, until she can't stand it, and purrs like a large tiger with total contentment. A woman who is always satisfied beyond her own imagination, that you continuously surprise, excite, and pleasure, will give you the world. She will make you feel like you just made her feel. She will do things to you that only those in love truly experience. The saying "ladies first" should be every man's motto. Never leave a woman behind!

Now you asked me how, I just told you. Is there jealousy? No! When a couple decides that they should be together, then they should know and understand how each one is. I had several wives before I was even 15 years old. Were they jealous of each other? No! They each loved me. I loved each one of them equally. Remember this! The laws of my people states that only the women own the homes, lands, etc. Each has their own space, their own home. A woman must have her own castle so to speak, where she fixes it up to her liking. It is hers, not yours. You just happen to be lucky enough to enjoy the comforts of her home and benefits therein.

Some women may be sisters that was and is a common practice. To take the sister as a wife also, especially if the man is good to his wife, then she looks out for her sister to have this good man as well. Sometimes it is best friends, because she wants her friend to have something this good for life as well. Or a cousin, distant relative, or the woman in mourning whose husband crossed over and out of your friendship with him you make arrangements through the Clan Mothers to look after her for your friend who took the journey (died). Love is power. But also no woman wants any man that is lazy. A woman is like any other female in existence. She is looking out for herself, and any children she may have or hope to have.

A man has to be a good provider, responsible, and

most of all dependable. There can be no excuses. Today too many people always have excuses. No excuses! Do what you are supposed to do! Take care of your household! Provide, protect, pleasure and procreate! Always I hear men tell me oh wow that must be great having that many! Really? Now that depends on if you are a man! A man takes his responsibilities very seriously! He must provide as a good husband should. He must protect as he should. He must pleasure as he should, and he must procreate as he should! Now if you can't take care of one, how do you think you would do with more? You only get what you can do. And in today's society some men can't even take care of the one right? And don't blame it on the other. You should never have gotten together if you weren't ready to meet your responsibilities, and that goes both ways.

People didn't get divorced hardly ever in the old days. That is something that just came around really recently. It shows also how people really try to get to know one another first, doesn't it! To be honest, today is not the past. We can't live in it, and most who have any sense don't want to either! It was hard back then. I know! I lived that way! Really hard! Women need to be what they are: the gift that gives life through the love of their hearts and from that love they can change the world in which they live.

Because their love is so powerful it can humble any man, and make him act like a man should act. And their love must be for themselves first, because most women today really don't love themselves from what I have seen and witnessed. If they did, they would treat themselves like they truly deserve, and lift their heads up to be equal to any man, and quit accepting the way they are treated. And also heal the hearts of their men, because when you love the men the way you should, he'll act right or he isn't worth your time or trouble.

Each woman has to have her space, she has to have her dreams too, and the man needs to respect her space and support her dreams, and make them come true for her. Yes the children belong to the mother and her clan, but as her man you must make sure you support her and those children as well, not only with money but your time, your love, your understanding. Children need that security from you even if you're tired, sore, sleepy, or you have other plans. Your duty as a man as a husband and as a father is to be there in every way, not just in thought or on a piece of paper.

So you still think it is easy having more than one wife? You think it's cool because you sleep with numerous women? Be a real man then and step up to the plate, and let's see how you do when there is sickness, accidents, health problems etc. As a man you stick and hold the course old boy, through good times and bad times, for better or worse! Women all seek a man that is real, a man that can be trusted, a man that will love her in those bad times, who'll love her when she is upset, sick and puking her guts out because of the child inside of her. She is looking for that man who'll tell her how beautiful she is even on her worse day, and truly mean it from his heart.

Yes the old times having more than one wife was a big challenge, and a bigger responsibility. But the Clan Mothers usually were very good at choosing the right man for the job. And those men who were chosen were honored to be chosen and rewarded with this treasure of love and respect, and he never forgets this in his life. For to love this way takes give and take on every person involved and no it is not easy. No it is not fun. No it is not something to just try to do. People's lives and hearts are involved and you never ever play or mess with someone's heart, love, or their life, because if you do then you have no respect, no honor in you and you never, ever deserve to ever have any love, as a punishment for disrespecting love!

I hope I have explained this well enough for all of you. Maybe it was not the way you expected, or not what you wanted to hear, but it is the truth. And for those who still practice the old way I know you know this all to be true because you live it as well. There is much honor in these matters for all parties.

The women have a special place for each one of them amongst themselves. There is always the one who is the first wife, second wife etc. but that does not mean who was married first. This comes from them, the women, as they accept each other as sisters and help each other in all matters and help with each other's problems as well, as well as the children. They all grow up as brothers and sisters and they have lots of mothers and aunties as some now call themselves, and the children treat each other with respect and their mothers all with respect.

Hopefully this has answered most of you questions and satisfied your curiosity!

Remember to Walk in Love and Beauty Always!

Section Two

Ghost Dancer's Life Stories

Chapter Four

A Short Biography of Ghost Dancer

Thunder Eagle Ghost Dancer: the literal Muskogee translation-Pvyfek'lktv Opvnknv Lvmhe Terrvmhrv means "he who dances with the spirits and speaks as eagle with the power of thunder"! Now to understand the true meaning of this name, you have to understand fully the meaning of each part. Pvyfek'lktv means ghost, spirit, while Opvnknv, means dancer. Just to understand these two parts is important. Dances with the spirits, means just that and then some. It also means in his life walk, spirits will always be speaking to him, working with him, helping him, because in our lives it is a dance, the dance of life as the old ones say. It is intertwined in the thunder and eagle. Lvmhe, Eagle is a powerful being to us. To speak as the eagle, means to speak with authority, of truth, justice, loyalty, honor, etc. While Terrvmhrv, thunder is a power of the thunder beings, it represents in the meaning in this name, as a powerful voice of the thunder beings, because as thunder shakes the ground, his voice will shake those around as he speaks out about the injustice, the lies, betrayals, deceit, theft, that is being done to our people and some done by our people.

My name came from the spirits while during a long fast and purifying of my body, mind, and spirit. My original name was Eagle Ghost which traditionally would actually be Ghost Eagle. I had been fasting, seeking help for someone who was very ill, and we couldn't figure what was wrong. I decided to fast and seek help for her. I went to the spring and did a washing of my body with the pure clean spring water, then prayed, drank the black drink, drank some datura tea, and went into the special place in the swamp that I used, and started my prayers and chants. We do things different than a lot of people do; those who talk to the spirits that is. We do things sometimes that don't make sense to others, but makes sense to us.

Bear is a medicine spirit for helping us with healings. But sometimes Bear will just be Bear; she won't pay attention to you! See the Bear spirit I speak with is Grandmother Bear. But she likes to ignore people sometimes because she is always eating or looking for play time. Anyway I had to get her attention. Now when dealing with any of the spirits sometimes you have to do things that can be strange, and to an observer, you'd think we might be crazy.

Anyway while I was trying to get her attention, my spirit helpers spoke to me and said that I needed to refocus because some ancient ones wanted to speak with me. I focused again and some very old spirits said I was being given a new name. They told me the name and I told them thank you but I didn't want that name because it would cause me trouble. They asked why and I told them. They said yes, but it is your name regardless, and it will help you as you grow. See all these spirits work with you anyway. And by accepting the name and wearing it, it will only help strengthen you even more. I asked them again to please understand and give me a different name. They called me by my new name seven (7) times and shouted it. I had my new name to wear, and that is how I came by the name.

And when I shouted my new name Grandmother Bear turned and came to me smiling and gave me the help I needed for my friend.

See traditionally we are given a name at birth by a holy one who talks to the spirits and brings forth a name for you. That name changes as you grow. When you fast and pass your warrior tests and become a warrior, you get another name by a holy one who does this and performs the naming ceremony and presents you to the people, introducing you once again to the people. Every time you get a new name you go through this.

We never kept the same names like people do now, and you usually always have four names. One that only your family calls you, one that only your people call you, one that outsiders call you, and one that is your true spirit name (Our spirit name you must know to be able to go through the door that Brown Eagle guards when you cross over [die]. If you don't know your name you can't go through and are stuck here in your spirit form until you learn your real name.) All of us seek our spirit names from the spirits when we are young, as we seek our medicine, and we never give that name to anyone. It is our key to the doorway to the Stars of the Milky Way!

From the time I got my name, my entire time was spent training not only as a warrior but as a spiritual person. I was learning from grandfathers (extended) and his many friends around the country, learning different ceremonies and rituals, from various different tribes and their spiritual leaders. All of this would never have happened if not for my maternal grandfather Edgar Beaver, and my paternal grandfather Big Snake. They were the motivators in my life, the ones that pushed me to learn as much as I could. They always told me the world was changing and changing fast, and that so much had already been lost to so many nations.

Since my early youth I had always basically been a loner anyway, trusting my animal and winged friends more than any two legged ones. It was just so much easier to just learn all the time. I spent time with all the elders as much as possible, for they were the ones that had the knowledge and it was up to me to seek it, which I did. I didn't have time much for anything, but work, learn, and take care of all who I was responsible for. It seemed that everything was always already planned for my life.

I was a husband and father for many already and still had clan elders who I must always take care of as well. I did not sleep much most of my life, and still don't. I still have too much to do. I never have depended on others to do what should be done. I just always went and done it myself. That way I knew it was done, and I never put things off that needed being done either. That is how you always have things piling up on you. And I have always had the habit of always finishing everything I start, and I applied that to everything in my life.

Our moments here in this life are numbered, and we have the duty and responsibility to do as much as we can to lessen our load for when we come back. Because I believe as all my ancestors believe, that we continue to come back until we have experienced and evolved ourselves to earn the right to be a true spirit to always help others. But as long as we lack in any area of personal spiritual enlightenment and advancement we will have to come back to work on that until we get it right. But of course we can still choose to come back as well. Many do so because they wish to always help their people and love life because their nature is to love. So all my life until I joined the navy was this way, and no I don't regret it for one moment! It was great! The only regrets I have are the mistakes I've made in life and those I will make before I take my journey (die).

Ghost was born about 1941-42 in a sugar cane field in "The Frogs Return Moon", between the end of April, and the beginning of May. He is a member of the Santa Rosa Muskogee Band and the Florida Seminole Tribe, Wind Clan. He is also Ani-yun-wiya (Cherokee) Bird Clan through his mother. He has two full sisters. Ghost was born first, then Judy, and Jackie. His half siblings are Greg and Teresa, and step sisters Linda, Vicky, Patty, and Cindy.

Living with his grandfather, Big Snake's Muskogee family in Florida, he spent very little time with his mother and siblings.

He was able to enjoy the company and teachings of his grandpa Beaver from the time he was three until he was about 15 when Grandpa Beaver crossed over.

As there are different warrior levels to achieve, by the time Ghost was inducted into the navy he was a senior warrior with rank to lead others.

Ghost Dancer was inducted into the US Navy in 1958 at the age of about 17. He was recruited by men in suits who came to talk to the Clan Mothers and Elders. He worked in underwater demolition and was later recruited to the SEALs in 1962 serving in SEAL 1. He served in Indo-China, the Philippines, Italy, Guam, Japan, the Middle East, and Russia. He then served in Viet Nam from 1965 until 1972 when he was discharged from service.

In the 1970s he was recruited to help AIM, the American Indian Movement.

Today he teaches, conducts ceremonies, and works, making beautiful beadwork, jewelry, and art. His artwork, and photos of a few jewelry pieces, is on the front, back, and inside of this book.

Remember to Walk in Love and Beauty Always!

(Note: Hurricane Katrina did destroy most of Ghost's memorabilia, photos, art, religious items, family heirlooms, etc.)

Chapter Five

Growing Up Muskogee

My life as a child was not an ordinary life. My people back then were scattered and struggling to survive with all the encroachment of other peoples. They (government) were trying to dredge the whole state of Florida, and take away the swamps that were our homes. Bears and panthers were still plentiful. Alligators averaged over 30 feet in length, unlike today at around 14-18 feet. Crocodiles were still present both fresh water and salt water. I tell you this so you can better understand my world as a boy. The swamps were thick with trees, so thick that it was dark as night in places. Huge giant oaks, cypress, hickory, magnolias, and sweet gum branches made canopies over the swamps. Quicksand, muck, snakes, leeches, sand fleas, and chiggers were just as plentiful.

Now picture all this in your mind, and see it, as it really was, in beauty, full of life, vibrant with power, full of danger and pleasure. See, my whole world was the swamps. There was no electricity, no civilization in the swamps. You walked or sculled or ran. Sculling is a method of using a long pole to push yourself in your dugout (boat) through the swamps. Or, you could use a paddle.

My daily life started with chores while it was still dark. I had to haul water home to be used for drinking and cooking. Now, it wasn't as hard when I got older, but for a small boy, it made you very tired carrying all this water on poles across your shoulders. After I carried water, then I went to the bean, corn, and squash field to weed our family's ground for the garden, then to the tribes' plots to hoe and work the fields. Then, about an hour before sunrise, I would go to the river and purify myself and offer my prayers of thanks to the Creator and to Mother Earth for all she gives us. Diving down to lay on the bottom, letting all the air out of my lungs, I lay down there on the Earth Mother's bosom, and felt her heart beat filling my soul with vibrating love.

Then it was off to the house to eat. Now, many of you wouldn't understand what we eat or when we eat this, but this was and is our world. We had fresh fruits, cattail bread with hunks of meat, either wild boar, venison, or gator, boiled in our hominy grits, fresh potatoes, sometimes fish, shrimp, or crab even. We eat what we have, but eating is a true pleasure. Because we help the plants grow, watching them and praying for them, then protecting them from other life forms (all our relations) who want to eat them as well. Or we caught or hunted the food, so we had bonded as one with all we ate. And we always gave thanks to them for allowing us life by eating them.

See, as a child we are taught and must develop this understanding of our relationship to all things. You may be instructed by a Clan Mother to go and watch an ant, learn everything that the ant does, follow it, become the ant. Eat drink, crawl, everything as an ant. See the world as an ant. Then, come back and report to your Clan Mother what you had learned about the ant. By doing this with all that was in your world: birds, insects, reptiles, animals, fish, plants, and trees; you develop a true understanding of life, and you learn there is nothing to fear. Life and death are part of a cycle that never ends, just changes forms again and again.

Many of the things we were taught would be considered today as cruel or abusive, but the Ancient Ones knew what they were doing. Many children today are in fear in darkness, or encounters with wild animals, or left all alone somewhere. But, in my days it was part of life's training and teachings. Life is a constant struggle. There is pain and there is suffering. So, as children we were taught these things to survive and make us strong, not only physically, but mentally, and most important spiritually. Usually, each child has something to learn every single day, so our elders always used each day to give us that lesson. Children are always silent. You were taught silence before you ever walk, or even crawl. You must listen to hear what is said by all life, whether it be 2-legged, 4-legged, winged or crawlers. All life has language. It must be heard first, so you must be quiet.

Life for me was hard because of my father. My father

was banished for drinking alcohol and never to return, which automatically put bad medicine on me. My mother was half Ani-yun-wiya (Cherokee) and half white. That put more bad medicine on me because I came out looking more like my mother's white part. When I was small I used to think I was cursed with a bad medicine, because of all that had happened in my young life. Other kids put me down because of the way I looked and my father being banished. Kids will be kids, so I had to learn to fight really soon, and fight to win or at least survive. But always the kids got bigger, and more of them than just me. I grew up fast. By watching the rattlesnake, I learned how to strike fast and hard. By watching the panthers I learned how to ambush. By watching the red wolf I learned how to be patient and stalk. With all the hard work of carrying water, swinging in trees, carrying huge Congo melons, cast net fishing, and wrestling alligators, my muscles and body developed fast, and others learned to leave me alone.

I sat with my grandfather and used to listen to him talk of all the old days, and I learned to be silent while he talked with all his old friends and brothers, listening to all their experience, knowledge and wisdom. My grandfather saw my sincere interest in the spiritual world, and, since I was of the Wind Clan, I naturally had my birthright in the Spiritual Society. So, I learned to be patient and watch and help them in their spiritual practices and ceremonies. I had a good voice so I began singing with them the Sacred Songs, and I learned of the Fire.

Now I must go back some in time to add what every child must undergo in the Red Stick Customs. When a child turns four years old, the child is placed in a pit with a rattlesnake, water moccasin, and copper mouth. The snakes are made angry by tapping them with a feather. The child must be bitten by all three snakes. The child must not panic or have fear, because the snakes are our brothers. They will now give us their powerful medicine. This medicine will help us with our vision of life and death and take us quickly to the Spirit World. If our Spirit is strong, we will know that snake brothers and sisters will always help us. If we are weak, have fear, and panic, we will surely die, because our people and the spirits need those that are strong-hearted. This was the old way, what is called "Hofunv'lke Nen'ne" the Way of the Ancient Ones. Once this is done, children continue to drink the snake venoms. This not only helps for the visions, but also builds anti-bodies, or immunity to poisons. And, in the world in which we lived, filled with snakes, spiders, leeches etc., there were poisons everywhere.

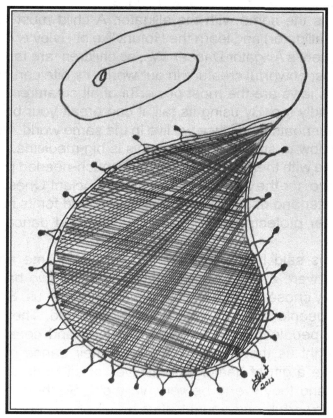

Cast Net

The cast net is a 6 foot one. There is a braided line that runs completely around the outside making a total of 28 feet. The end is tied to the person. It is cast out, stones around the edge allow it to sink to the bottom and the person draws the net closed like a string bag and hauls the net back.

Now many of you would think this is cruel and too dangerous, but stop and think. Snakes, spiders etc. were everywhere. As an adult or parent you could not possibly watch your children continuously to prevent them from being bitten by some poisonous snake or spider. Children will be children; you know that kid is going to take off when you least expect it. So, this was necessary: plus it helps take away fear, which is what kills most people - the fear of the snake.

It is the same with the alligator. A child must learn of Hvlpv'tv (alligator) and learn the Hofunv'lke of Hvlpv'tv Opv'nkv (The Ancient's Alligator Dance). We, as children, are taught this is the most powerful creature in our world. Its bite can bite you in two. Its jaws are the most powerful of all creatures, and its tail is deadly too. By using its tail, it can break your body and crush your boats, and since we live in the same world, we need to know how to survive. But also, this is big medicine. To fight and dance with the alligator gives you a much-needed powerful confidence, for the alligator is one of the Ancient Ones. It lives under water and on dry land. It builds a mound for its nest and the mother protects her young. They sing and dance all the time.

It is said by the old ones that a long time ago, the alligators were a great people who walked on two back legs when they chose to. This is what the ancients tell us. So these alligator people are very important in our world. They taught us, as a people how to build our mounds and ceremonies. They taught us their dance of life and their dance of death. They have a gift of healing themselves of all kinds of mortal injuries, and they live to be very, very old. So their medicine is very powerful, and sought after by all of our people. Yes, we eat the alligator, not only for its delicious meat, but also because of all the medicine (power, gifts) they contain, that we seek in ourselves. To be strong, have no fear, to ambush, to strike quickly, heal ourselves, to produce numerous children, to protect our territory, to live in both worlds of land and water, and to pray to the sun.

Yes, alligators do pray. I know you probably don't believe

this, but your understanding is different than ours. Alligators and crocodiles all love to lay in the sun. They do this to warm their bodies, but more important, they draw energy from the sun. This energy they absorb into their bodies. This is then stored for when it is needed. And yes, they talk. When this is going on, the alligators communicate with the sun. Their vocal language you probably wouldn't understand, but they do talk. They even sing. We never disturb their ceremonies of prayer.

Anyway, when its time comes, a child must dance with the alligator in the dance of life and death. The child has been taught by his elders how to do this. If the child has been paying attention, and learned as it should, then the spirits will be with the child. The child is taken in a boat to a particular spot where a large grandfather bull gator is waiting in the water. The child has been prepared ceremonially for this: by purification, drinking the black drink, by prayers, fasting, and singing. Now it is time to earn its honor.

The child dives out of the boat and swims under water to the gator. It must attack the gator from underneath, grabbing the mouth with one hand and holding tight while it wraps its legs around the alligator. The alligator will immediately go into a roll and thrash over and over. You must know the alligator. Alligators and crocodiles have muscles that close the mouth very powerfully, but to open their mouth, that is their weakness. A young child can hold an alligator's mouth shut with one hand easily. The trick is to catch the mouth right by placing the fingers at the "V" of the mouth or better put right behind the jawbones. Then hold it tight. By wrapping your legs around the alligator, this gives you protection from his tail. This ride is a true ride of life and death. A mistake can truly kill you or at least cost you dearly. The gator must breathe air just as you must, so when placing your hands on the mouth, you are partially blocking his nostrils. This tires the alligator faster, until eventually the alligator will lie still or roll over on its back and lie there. Now you must release the gator and get away very fast. His reflexes will be slow at first, but his sensors pick up every vibration in the water. His sensors are on his mouth, so release and get away. This is the one for the water and then there is the dance with him on the land.

On land he is still deadly and powerful. Never think or believe he is slow, for in truth, he is very fast. The dance on land is slightly different, for an alligator is captured and taken to a pit. There he is released. You must go into the pit and dance with him and defeat him by putting him to sleep. This is done by grabbing the mouth, wrapping your legs around him and rolling him over. We always rub his belly to gently coax him to go to sleep. Being upside down the blood drains away from the brain and causes unconsciousness. This gently puts him to sleep and now the child has earned honor and respect, not only for its clan and its family but for itself as well. Pride fills the heart, and strength and confidence in the child develops quickly to understand defeating fear, and defeating something that is greater and more powerful than you.

As I said earlier, these old ways most of you would consider cruel, dangerous, or abusive, but not only were these things necessary for survival, they developed true character in a child. A character of courage, honor, truth, generosity, humbleness, compassion, and loyalty are the seven virtues of the warrior and of the people. These things are lacking in today's society and even amongst Native Peoples. You must understand that all these old customs were for important reasons, to help the child develop and become a True Person; one that is connected to every living thing in existence, and knowing and understanding that connection. Plus, one learned that life and death is the same, only new beginnings, new shapes. This is repeated as long as is necessary or when we choose not to. That is the Law of the Universe that never changes and has always been. We know our Spirit comes back, time after time, what some call reincarnation. It is what we call the Circle of Life.

So I knew then, that day, why I was back, and why I would have a hard life this time. Understand, we as a people, know we are truly spirit before anything else. We know that we come into this world to experience its beauty, harmony, and all the lessons to experience in a physical form. In my last life, the one previous to this one, I had developed a hatred for the white man, and had brutally killed numerous white men, sometimes killing them just for being white. In that life, I had forgotten the true nature of the Spirit. Not to say it started out that way, but behind the anguish of my family and loved ones murdered by whites, I forgot my true Spiritual Teachings of Life and took the path of vengeance and hatred under the Blood Laws of my People until it consumed me. That was why Spirit, in his wisdom, brought me back this time looking like what I hated and despised in my past life. It is why I had to feel the pain of hatred; my own people despised and disgusted because of the way I looked on the outside.

Ironic, isn't it to see the laughter on Spirit's face at what he decided I must learn again, and to have to learn that I must just be my spirit for all to see. Understand that as a child I felt I had to fight, and felt and thought that I had to be stronger, faster, more cunning, and more Indian, than my full-blooded brothers. I pushed myself to think I had to do this to gain their respect and approval. Spirit showed me how wrong I was, and I was so sad. I felt so ashamed and foolish. But Spirit explained to me that this too had its purpose, for in time I would understand why. I could be an example for others. And, because I was so sincere, then I would have those put in my path to help, teach, and guide me in this path, that for our people, I would become respected and loved, and that I would be able to help others on their paths too.

After this experience, my life changed, for I knew now for certain why I was here. I dedicated myself to my people, especially to all the old ones, to learn and memorize all they said. I would learn all the songs, stories, and ceremonies that I possibly could and to participate in every activity. But mostly I dedicated myself to Spirit.

My true father I never saw again until later in life, but my mother I saw quite often. My mother was a half-breed who remarried to a white man. My mother was still Ani-yun-wiya, a member of the Bird Clan, and her father, my grandfather was

Edgar Beaver. He was blind and had been for years before I first met him. He was a full-blood, a large powerful man, yet gentle and quiet, and even though he could not see with his eyes like you or me, he saw everything. At night when staying at my mother's, I used to sit with him outside. He loved the night because it was his world now. He told me all the old stories, the customs, the history, the beliefs of the Ani-yun-wiya.

He told me that I was not like the rest of his grandchildren; that my spirit was totally native, unlike the others who had mixed blood, but lived and thought like white people. Then he handed me his personal crystal. Boy was I ever surprised to hold this powerful stone that my grandfather had used all of his life. It was just as much his spirit as it was the spirit of the stone. It pulsed and vibrated in my hand, sending energy throughout my body. I remember him laughing and saying, "You know, you have always had the gift, as did your great-grandmother who was a powerful stone person". He asked to feel my left hand, so I gave it to him. He ran his fingers over the entire palm of my hand and fingers reading the lines the way you would a trail, explaining to me the sign that was in my hand to show that I was marked by the Spirits for this path.

But, he went on saying that he would help me by showing me the true meanings of reading lines in people's hands, eyes, their ears, their bodies. He explained that these were maps, history of a person's past lives, their experiences, their strengths and weaknesses, their health and so much more. What was strange to me was that as he said all this, I knew it; knew that I had known these things all the time. I just had never sought this from inside myself. Oh, I had done things as a child, and as a kid, that made the old ones look at me strange or shock the other kids, but I never really thought that much about it. My grandfather went on telling me all he knew about his ancestors and all that they had experienced in life.

My time with my grandfather Beaver was very important in my life, for it opened me up to more knowledge of the Ani-yun-wiya way, but it also showed me the differences in different tribal nations, beliefs, and customs. He also told me to seek out certain ones he knew who would help me learn more. Some of these older ones were of other tribes as well, such as Choctaw, Shawnee, Chickasaw, Micmac, and Potawatomi. That was so true. I was like a sponge, wanting to absorb all I could, learn all I could, and most of all experience these things. Later on I would relish these important times.

Back in Florida, my true home, I was steadily growing and learning. I helped my people by going in groups as a worker. Boy did we do some work. Ha! Ha! My people made money by whatever means. We worked on white people's homes, learning to become stone masons, brick masons, carpenters, roofers, on fishing boats, working on building roads, and whatever was available. All the money that we made was made for the People, to better ourselves in securing our lives. But to me the most enjoyable was working the real wealthy people's horses. These were Thoroughbred horses, very valuable to their owners. To us, these were still relatives and we were good with them, and we knew how to work with them.

But of all these memories, my times in Silver Springs, Ocala area, were the best. There was a place built that tourists would come to see the world famous Silver Springs, and they had people come and build a village. Oh, it was built before I got there, and these people had been there for a while, but they still were relatives. We did alligator wrestling for shows, but the real work was snake handling. Ross Allen had built a place there for poison research where they made anti-venom. I saw snakes from all over the world. I loved handling the snakes, for they were good medicine. Their knowledge of the secret places and the secrets of Mother are highly sought by my people.

This is also where they filmed the Tarzan movies, "Creature of the Black Lagoon", etc. I had a lot of fun there, especially scaring innocent tourists who are so scared of anything they don't understand or fear. Boy, did we have lots of laughs. We put on Booger masks (masks made from a hornets nest) cutting holes for eyes and mouth, putting gator and shark teeth in them, and using coconut hair, and then we wore them. We would wait until they were in the glass bottom boats deep in the forest, then swim underwater and come up at the bottom of the boats where they were watching, looking down. You should have seen their scared faces!

The mask is called a booger mask. They are designed and made to frighten away evil spirits, for use during ceremonies, and for war to frighten the enemy. This hornet's nest booger mask also has a rattle snake, gator teeth, sharks tooth (middle one) with a turtle shell and a frog hanging from different antlers shaped in different directions. Masks are designed this way because spirits know that frogs, turtles, and rattlesnakes aren't supposed to be in the air and it scares them.

Or, we would steal a ride on the boats, wait until they got to the area with all the alligators, then stumble and fall off the boat, in with the gators. People would be screaming and crying thinking we would surely die and be torn to bits. Not us though. We would dive down to the bottom, holding our breath, hiding in the swaying grass. The water is crystal clear and you can see a hundred feet deep to the bottom very clearly. Once we were safe, we would swim under water slowly to the shore and yell at the tourists to get their attention. They would be shocked with amazement that we were okay. This was not planned by the owners or the tour, just something we did, because it was fun for us. Our elders would scold us for causing these poor people distress, but they scolded us with a smile in their eyes. Then they would have us tell them everything that happened. We would all be rolling with laughter.

During this time I was growing into a man. Not like today's society though. I was a first rate warrior before I was ten years old, had already fought in battle and killed a grown man when I was eight summers old. This was in self-defense though. It was not something planned. It was a strange feeling, because first I was saddened, because I took his life, but then proud because I had defeated a large enemy who had attacked me. We, a couple of young ladies and three of us boys who were carrying the baskets for the young ladies, had gone to town. There, the ladies would have sold their items and we would have gone home. But we were attacked while there. I guess they figured three young boys could not protect the women from them. These men did not have the knowledge that these young boys had been training in warfare and fighting since they could walk. Another boy and I were taken into custody. They kept us locked up like animals and studied us. Finally, after a long, long time, we were released to return back to our homes.

What I mean as a man is that we had developed mentally, spiritually, as well as physically, as most men have. We were of marrying age, the right to have a woman as a mate, listened to and respected. To take a life is not something that anyone should be proud of, because we are all taught that life is Sacred.

But, in life, the struggle of survival and life or death is part of the circle in all things. To become a real man, one must learn that you have nothing to prove to anyone. You are as you are, to be respected, loved, etc. Just be yourself. The struggle you have with these things is within you.

I have told you of this early life so you can get a better understanding of me. It is not all of my life. It's just to give you a small part of myself to know who I am and experience it as I did. I didn't go into all the religious ceremonies, for that is Sacred. It is for those who truly walk the path and seek that path.

I have been blessed in life with a large family. I have two full sisters, Judy and Jackie, one half-sister, Teresa, one half-brother, named Greg, and four step-sisters named Linda, Vickie, Cindy and Patty. I have been blessed with many beautiful ladies in my life. The first one was a sad story ending in her death and the death of my son, when they were murdered. Yes, I do have children and grandchildren, not by all the same mothers though. I married very young in life and I married often. I am a strong man, full of life, and spirit blessed me to breed like a bull gator. I was born in the time of the Frogs Return Moon - the last of April through the first part of May. I have no birth certificate. I was born in a sugar cane field.

On my father's lineage, it goes back to the time of the Ais Nation and Etowah Nation that I know of. My great-grandfather was the sole survivor of the Locust Fork Massacre. That took place at High Rock on the forks of Locust Fork River, Warrior River, and the Mulberry River in Central Alabama around the year 1817 (a guess). His name as a boy was Red Hawk. Escaping in the river, he fled from the Georgia Militia who were violating the law and killing his people. He hid in the woods and later was taken in and hidden and raised by a family of whites named Johnson. When he got older, he went to Oklahoma, got a woman of his Nation and brought her home to live in the High Rock area. Later, his sons moved to Florida because of the whites removing and hunting all Muskogee people. My father's lineage goes to the Red Stick Band of Muskogees, what you call Creek, but became known as the Seminoles which mean: "wild ones."

Red Sticks are those that were Traditional who would not convert to the white man's ways or anything of his world. The battles against them later became known as the Red Stick Wars. These people fought rather than be removed and never surrendered. What was truly sad was that our great Nation split and fought against each other. Some chose the path of the white man and other Tribal Nations who came with the white man to destroy my people. Bitter feelings developed for all others who turned against us.

My grandfather was named Elias Johnson-native name Big Snake. My great grandfather Elijah Headley Johnson-native name Two Heads. My grandfather's friends and my Clan Mothers: Ruby Osceola Tiger, Black Hawk, Wildcat Fixico, Bullhead Ellis, John Sands, Ma-ma Jaybird, Nan-tay-shay, Art Solomon, Big Tree, Gray Eagle, Chief Dan Etohama, Heals With Water, Sees in Smoke, White Crane Woman, C. L. Ellis, Bearsheart, Anthony Tiger, John Grass, Grandmother Grass, Red Hawk, Aunt Wohoe, David Beaver, Aunt Inez Barns, Mary C. Doty, Aunt Leethee Doty, plus numerous others over the years. These are all elders who taught me all they could.

Many escaped African slaves joined our people. Many indentured Irish, French, and Scottish servants joined our people. They fought side by side with us against all European Nations and their Indian Allies who attacked us, until after years and years of war which the whites could not win, which cost them a fortune in material and lives, they just quit.

It is still the longest war in the history of this country. The people of my Tribal Nation are the only tribal nation that has never been conquered or defeated. And it all goes back to the way we were taught and believe as a people. Many of these others who joined our people intermarried and had mixed-breed children such as myself. But inside we are all One People and proud of our heritage, our people and our values of life.

The Ancient Ways in which I was brought up have kept my People strong, not only spiritually, but also mentally and physically. We retained our language, history and culture and remain an independent Nation. We don't ask for help, don't beg or expect anything to be given to us. We work. Laziness is a shame for any person. Laziness is a disgrace amongst my people. Weaknesses such as alcohol and drugs are for other people, not my people. This would call for banishment for life for any offenders. Begging is disgraceful. No Seminole would ever stoop so low as to beg, even for his life! We fear no man, no government, and no beast.

We are a peaceful people until we are threatened or attacked, then the laws of our People must be upheld. There are no sexual assaults, rapes, child molestation, or incest among my people. This would automatically be a painful, tormenting death sentence that not even a Seminole would relish to be put through. There is no disrespecting anyone. There is no degrading or abusing a woman. Our women are loved, honored and respected above <u>any</u> man. They are the heart of our people: strong, independent, resourceful, spiritual, courageous, and very wise and protective of all the young ones, just as mother bear, mother wolf, and mother alligator would do. Never disrespect a Muskogee woman, for her wrath is a match for even a grizzly bear.

I hope and pray that each of you finds something in what I have said to apply in your own life that might help you. I'm no one special, just a simple man really, who lives a very simple life. I know who I am, what I am, and what I am to become. It is how I live this life that is important. I've made mistakes, as each of us has and all of us will make more mistakes as we continue to live and experience this life. The important thing to remember is: do not keep repeating the same mistake!

Now I have questions for you, questions you really need to ask yourself:

1. What are you truly looking for in life?
2. Is it only material things that won't last?
3. Who are you?
4. What are you?

5. What will you become later on?
6. What have you truly experienced with power?
7. When have you ever felt truly as one with all living things?
8. Do you know true love?
9. Do you give true love in all that you do?
10. When have you gone out into the wilderness all alone and just watched and listened to all that is there?
11. In reading this you are studying. Will you truly seek to understand, feel, and think freely with an open mind about what you are studying?
12. Will you try to use this later on in your life to teach others or even yourself?
13. Do you seek your own understanding of this knowledge or will you use other people's words?

I ask each of you to answer these questions yourself. Write them down. Then when you have finished your studies, later on, answer these questions again. You will come to understand that life changes. We change as we grow older. Our way of thinking and perceiving things changes as well. What we thought was important in one part of our life, we will find later on to have been not so important after all. What is truly important is your seeking the path of your own spiritual growth. This will also reflect into your mental growth and physical growth.

I am not a young man by anyone's standards, but I also still compete athletically with all the young ones and can still win in every sport with the best around. Why, because of my spiritual growth that has reflected in all of my life and body. I know, even with all the broken bones, bullet wounds, and burns that my body has suffered, that I can still hold my own in this world. I know I can jog non-stop for 200 miles in the old warrior run. Yeah, I smoke tobacco to pray; have since I was a small boy. I do not believe in modern medicine for they are not healers any more. They just work for the pharmaceutical companies and for money. Many times doctors have said that I was legally dead, yet here I am. Many times they say they must amputate, yet I still have all my original parts. Many times they have said that I would never be able to use that part again, yet I still do. So much for modern medicine! I say this because I want you to understand that all academic scholars are not always correct or right, and this applies in all things.

So, may you all walk in Beauty and Harmony and surround yourselves with Spirit, for Spirit is the true teacher of all things.

Remember to Walk in Beauty and Love Always!

Chapter Six

Muskogee Boy's Training

When a Muskogee boy is around five years old, he begins learning how to use a blowgun. Now many of you might not understand why, but bear with me and then maybe you will understand. The blowgun is made from bamboo usually, but also sometimes made from hickory or willow. These both have a soft center that is easily bored out. It is treated by steaming. Then it is fire hardened. This is done to make it stronger and for it to last. The darts are usually made from quills, wood, or bone. One of the best sets that I used was all made from bone, and serrated so that the poisons would hold better. These then had feathers attached to them.

Young boys and even girls begin practicing using these blowguns. Small leather balls, bark, leaves (palmetto), or saw grass are rolled and dried out to use for target practice. This starts out as a game for youngsters. The ball is thrown or rolled and the youngsters all try to hit it. Naturally every child knows his or her own darts. Each dart made has specific markings just as arrows and spears do.

This is very competitive. The elders, clan mothers and all members of the tribe encourage, praise and even wager on the youngsters. Naturally every kid wants to be the best. During certain ceremonies such as the Green Corn Ceremony, these youngsters will be selected to compete against other tribes of the Nation. It is an honor to be selected by your clan to represent the clan, and even more so to represent your particular town.

See, in the old days, there were White Towns and Red Towns. White Towns were for clans that were administrative; politicians, orators, scholars, artists, craftsmen, distributors, etc. The Red Towns were for warriors, war clans, spiritual leaders, medicine people, and even what you would call sorcerers (wizards) today. These towns kept the Blood Laws, and they all had a large post that was red with blood. When warriors or a spiritual leader made a vow for blood, justice, or war, the hatchet was struck into this post.

These towns competed at the ceremonies, and these youngsters strutted around like young turkey gobblers, all proud to represent their People. Towns wagered all kinds of things on these games. Now most of you wouldn't have wanted the responsibilities of the wealth and pride of your clan and entire town on your shoulders as a young child, but any Muskogee child looked forward to this. This is a game of life, so you see and learn the lessons of life very early. If you lose, your People will lose all they have wagered and that was usually quite a lot. But, you have also disappointed your clan and People.

See, these practices taught youngsters the importance of their lessons, practice, and dedication to the People, because even though it was a game, it was a War Game. A youngster will become a warrior and the skill and dedication he or she learns might save the People or cause them to lose their life. So, instead of a game competing against other members of the Nation, they are protecting the People by killing enemies who are attacking the People.

In using the blowgun, it is silent but also very, very deadly. No grown man can survive the poison mixture. It will kill a bear, panther, deer, or whatever living thing you hit. A Muskogee child is taught to be silent, and to stalk, to be one with the land. The art of camouflage is a way of life. A child could single-handedly take out an entire war party by using a blowgun. The poisons that are used are very fast and will immediately take effect. Different poisons are used for different things.

Now, imagine just for a moment: Here you are with a bunch of your friends walking in the woods of the South. Gnats and mosquitoes are everywhere. You feel the bite, and slap yourself where you are bitten. You think nothing of it. You are dead! What just hit you was a tiny poison dart. You were last in line behind your friends. They don't know you just collapsed eyes bulging, and totally unconscious. As you hit the ground, another of your friends is already dropping, and the rest of your friends still don't know that a little five or six year old is taking you all down.

Oh, but you say, it would be different back then. All of us would be trained, ready, alert for this kind of attack. Really! Check your history. No Army, no Combined Army, no Tribe, or combination of Tribal Nations could defeat my People. Not even when the White Towns of my Nation joined with the US Army, 60,000 Cherokees, 100,000 Iroquois, 40,000 Nakota/ Lakota, along with the French Army, and Spanish Army; all attacked the Red Town People. This is known in your histories as the Red Stick War! It is what gave us the name Seminole (The Wild Ones or the Untamed Ones). To this day, the Muskogee still feel this split of the most powerful Nation.

The White Town People were traitors to the Muskogee Blood Law and attacked the Red Town People because they would not take on the religion or anything of the white man. All of these armies would have been totally wiped out if the White Town People had not given them information and fought against us too. To this very day, no Red Stick member will ever forget this treachery by the White Town Muskogee.

Read your history on this war. You will find out that it is the longest war in American history and the most costly. And never could my people be conquered by anyone. Why? Because of our religion, our culture, and practices! Just as the youngster started with the blowgun, the life of his or her people depends on it.

The blowgun is also used for hunting. Every member of the tribe is needed and expected to provide; to help the entire tribe. Children are important people too. They hunt squirrels, rabbits, birds, fish, deer, possum, raccoons etc. These children provide meat for the tribe and families, just as the adults do.

After a boy had mastered the blowgun and the poisons, he next begins to learn the bow and arrow. This too is started as a game and advances; with serious injuries as the boy grows older. What starts out with a blunt arrow later turns to real hunting and war arrows. There are different arrows for different purposes. War games are promoted and encouraged; if you let any part of your body be exposed, you will surely be hit. To this day, my left leg has the scar from the wounds. Ha! Ha!

Groups are set loose to hunt you. Hunt you they will. Shoot you if they can. Boys and girls both participate. No mercy is shown. Believe me. Every one of them wanted a chance at shooting me. It seemed like every time I was selected to be hunted, every Muskogee, even from neighboring bands, would be like hounds on a scent after me. I guess it was how I looked. Ha! Ha! For some reason, the older I got, the more and more I was selected to be hunted. Until you've been hunted by a Muskogee, you don't know the meaning of dedication and persistence.

Sometimes these games might last for two weeks straight before it was over. Running, hiding, shooting, burying yourself; I even slept in a gator cave several times with the gator in it to win. They never did figure that one out. Ha! Ha! (A gator cave is where an alligator has dug out a cave under a bank of a river, lake, or swamp and he takes his food in there to rot. Alligators and crocodiles like their meat soft, very soft; because it is easier for them to digest.) How many of you would have done that just to survive? Ha! Ha!

Yeah, I'm just a tad bit on the crazy side or maybe I would risk the gator before I would chance my brothers and sisters beating me. See, in this game, it teaches you the skill of eluding enemies, endurance, patience, and determination, shooting on the run, ambushing and stalking. And I am hunting them too. Everyone I hit must return home. If they get me, then I would be beaten as an enemy, and then taken back in disgrace to my People. This applies to everyone and the rules apply the same. I just believe they rather enjoyed hunting me more than any other.

I remember one time when they were really, really close, and many of them were older boys who I had fought and beat up. Naturally, I knew that if they got me, I would really suffer a beating before I made it back home. Anyway, these guys were really hunting me hard. For two days straight they had been getting closer and closer. I knew I had to do something drastic to get away.

Do you know what muck is? Muck is a deep black mud almost like quicksand. Well, I found a four to five foot rotten hollow log, and then went to the muck. I covered it with muck. Then I covered myself in muck. I mean the only thing not covered was when I opened my eyes. I laid down in the muck and pulled the hollowed log over my head and shoulders, to my chest, and laid in the muck about eight feet from the shore bank. I laid in this muck for three whole days, until they figured I slipped away somehow and had gotten by them. I waited until the early morning hours of the fourth day before I crawled out. I was starved, dehydrated, filled with fever, and had leeches on me that I had to get off. But I had won.

This is what my people used to teach. It was a way of life. Now days, it would be called a crime. But it made the character and heart of the People. All boys must be taught to endure pain, for life is full of pain. To live, you must perform through the pain so there is life! This now days would be called cruel and even a heinous crime. Every boy in the past was honored to pass these tortures and pain. He did it for family, clan, tribe, and his Nation. It gave him pride and confidence. If you move, cry out, give any emotional sign, you fail! And then you have disgraced your family, your clan, your tribe, and the People.

No one wanted to fail. For if one did, everyone knew it, for all of these tests were viewed by all of the People. If one did fail, he had to wait one whole year to try again. Usually they didn't survive the next year. The disgrace ate at them until they were like walking dead people, until they did something that took their life. Some even took poison because their disgrace tore them up. I knew several who didn't pass the test at first, then passed it the next year. But during this time, it really hurt them and their families.

It was really important to pass these tests. Some of them were minor compared to others. Others were very, very painful, and once you went through it, you never, ever wanted to have to do that again. That is why some never made it to the next year if they failed. They knew they did not want to face that again. I will not tell of these pains for none of you would believe or understand. But just know this, it is the way we tortured an enemy if an enemy was captured. And the women were noted for their skills at torture. Believe me when I tell you, you never, ever want to have to go through all of that.

Boys also must train for the water. We hunt in the water and travel in the water as well. It helps develop muscle growth, strength, and endurance, and allows you to move differently than on land. Many attacks or stalks can come from the water. Even battles are fought in and under the water. That is another story.

Remember this: most of you pay money for your knowledge and skills to live. In my world, you pay with your flesh, blood, and your life. What I learn I will never forget. And I will survive and live. Now most of you and most Native People believe that these are different times. These things are not necessary or do not apply. Well my answer to that is "you are wrong." The skills, knowledge, responsibilities, and character I have learned will always be to react and survive in any situation. I will always eat well and live well, no matter what. I can still compete with men thirty and forty years younger than me and win! Ha! Ha!

I don't get sick. If I hurt or have a pain, it doesn't stop me. Most of the young Natives do not understand because they try to live as other peoples. I see grown men cry because they twist an ankle and can't work. It is just an excuse to be lazy. I've worked on even with broken bones. Or they say they can't do something because it's cold, or it's raining, or it's too hot. That's just another excuse because they are lazy, have no pride, honor, or respect.

What really gets me is when one says "I can't pick that up, it will hurt my back" or "that's woman's work!" Boy, they better be glad my grandmother wasn't around! Ha! Ha! Women have always had a hard life. And pain - ask any woman who has given birth what pain is! So men, quit being a wuss! Women have always had it rough. That is why my People always honor our women, and we treat them all as queens, for they are the true warriors, and the life of the People. I've known women who would beat you silly and make you look foolish for even thinking you could fight them. And <u>most</u> women work real hard; those women that <u>don't</u>, well, who wants a lazy woman, or a weak one either? When I say weak, I mean of heart and spirit! I've known men who were giants, big as trees, strong, bulging with muscle, who were babies and cowards! Strength lives in the heart and spirit!

Think on these things. Look into your own heart, and at yourself. Do you really like yourself, your character, your strengths, your responsibilities, your dedication, your respect for yourself?

Understand this. Females will always be drawn to a strong dominant male! Why? It is an animal maternal instinct! Why? For the offspring to be a strong breed; for protection and survival!

Understand this. Males are always drawn to True Females - dedicated, strong, skilled, mysterious, compassionate, and independent. Why? Because a male wants a partner, friend, an extension of himself, lover, someone he can trust. Why? A man doesn't truly want a woman who he has to think for, raise, take care of, and tell what to do! He wants a woman who can take care of herself, make decisions, act on any situation, and do what needs to be done.

The problem today with men and women is that they don't know who they really are or what they really are, or what they really want in life. Therefore, they don't want responsibilities, honor, or respect. They settle for whatever they can get for as long as they can get it, or until they get tired of it.

Learn from the animals, plants, birds, and fish. They will teach you how to truly live and enjoy life. But remember to always do everything in Honor, Truth, Respect, Humbleness, Generosity, Courage, and Love! If you do, you will truly notice a change in your life.

Remember to Walk in Beauty and Love Always!

Chapter Seven

Dancing With the Dolphins

Growing up in Florida offered me many opportunities. One that is surely remembered is swimming with the dolphins. Now, first let me say what most people call dolphins aren't dolphins. Dolphins are a fish. What people usually call dolphins are really porpoises, usually bottle-nosed porpoises. But just not to confuse you I'll use the term you are more familiar with, dolphin. Dolphins are mammals. They are unique in many ways. They are highly intelligent and have always been our friends. Their language and characters are very beautiful and very much like our own. They use a vibration and frequency, and like whales, they do sing as well.

When I was a young boy, the waters of the Gulf were full of dolphins. I would go out with others while they were fishing (cast netting and gigging) and we would sing to the dolphins. Then, when they answered us we would dive in and swim with them. Boy was this fantastic! They would let us ride by hanging on to their fins and dive us down real deep. As kids, this was magical to us.

We played games with them, and they loved us as much as we loved them. We always gave gifts of fish, shrimp and crab to them. Dolphins really love to eat mullet. Mullet is a fish that is very delicious and they swim in schools. Dolphins attack them like water wolves; herding and eating the mullet. This is fun to watch as well.

When we are swimming with the dolphins we never have to be on the lookout for sharks either. Dolphins will attack any shark that comes into their area. They use their noses and their speed to swim real fast and ram the sharks with their noses. I've seen sharks knocked completely out of the water by dolphins, so they are our protectors as well.

Swimming with them at night under the stars and moon is something I wish everyone could experience. The water caresses your body with the heartbeat of Mother, and

Grandmother Moon dances upon the water and shines down upon you, while the stars are all talking to you. The dolphins would circle us and dance. It is a beautiful dance, filled with many intricate movements all in sequence with each other. Their bodies flash in and out of the water, silvery and sparkling in the moonlight, and they are singing as they do this. They flash by in bursts of speed barely touching you with their flippers as they invite you to join them.

Just so you know, we all "became" dolphins! Oh, I know the dolphins all laughed at us, but we were having the time of our lives. We tried to leap our bodies out of the water like they did, and they were all laughing and clapping their flippers to encourage us that much more. Swimming was part of our lives and we could do very well under the water, but nothing like our friends. They felt pity for us and gave us help. When we tried to propel our bodies out of the water, they would give us a boost. They would do this by swimming fast and using their noses, pushing us up into the air. We were all flying now, and we tried to mimic their language. This really caused them to laugh at us, so we started a water battle with them. Now, if you think for one minute that you can out-splash a dolphin, you are sadly mistaken. They can use their mouths and squirt you with water dead aimed at fifteen lengths from you, or they'll use their flippers and spray you all over with water. Their best stunts are turning upside down and using their tails to splash you with giant waves of water that knock you backwards. It is lots of fun and everyone has a good time.

Dolphins have remarkable memories too. They know each one of us is different. They can tell us all apart. What is sad though is when you hear one in pain or calling for help. Several times we had to help our friends. Many of the foreign fishermen who came to the waters used huge nets, and would get the dolphins caught in their nets. These people didn't care about what they caught in their nets. They were only interested in money. We have had these people shoot at us for cutting their nets. We didn't care. Our friends needed our help. We always came.

Commercial fishermen were the cause of most of all the dolphins leaving or disappearing from the Gulf. Most of these were fishermen from foreign countries. Now, many of our friends are back, for the simple fact that people made a fuss about this type of fishing, especially in protecting our friends. It does my heart good seeing our friends plentiful and back in our waters, on both the east coast and the Gulf coast. This helps restore the balance. It's not quite good enough yet though. See, with the dolphin population devastated, sharks became more numerous, and moved into the waters. That is why so many have been attacked in the coastal waters of Florida now. Hopefully in the years ahead with more dolphins coming back, the shark populations will leave the area, and once again people will be safer, for the dolphins are our friends, relatives, and protectors of the waters.

Another concern is the US Navy secretly experimenting with their underwater frequency, which is harming our friends. This is being done now and has been going on for some years now. This frequency is distorted and messes up the dolphin's delicate senses. This frequency destroys part of their brain and motor senses. That is why so many of them are beaching themselves. Once again, our friends are in trouble. The Navy denied this for a long time, yet finally had to admit to this. Now, they claim it is for National Security to detect foreign subs. That is pure garbage. The Gulf is too shallow to hide submarines from government satellites, planes, and so on; plus the Coast Guard and Navy ships are plentiful. There is no excuse for this, so we are told lies again.

My friends, your friends, need our help. We must pray that Mother Earth and Spirit help us in this matter, for the dolphins are here for all of us to enjoy. Every man woman and child should experience the love, beauty, and dance of the dolphins.

The best way to call dolphins is by singing in the water. They love shells and crystals too. And they each have a frequency just as does each one of us. All over the world the dolphins have saved human lives, throughout all time, since man and woman were first here. We as humans have disrespected them by

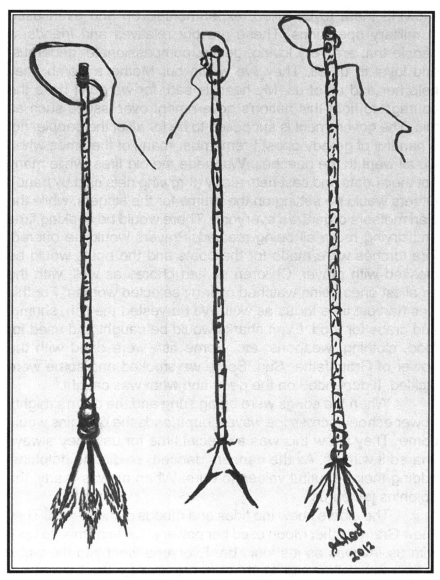

Fish and Frog Gigs

The gigs usually are around 5-6 feet in length and have different amounts of points. Points are made from bone that is boiled then shaped and carved out. Or it could be from fire hardened wood or split bamboo slivers, sharpened and made jagged to trap prey so they can't come off easily.

allowing them to be killed, experimented on and even used in military operations. These are our relatives and friends, a people that are very loving, gentle, compassionate, generous, and loyal to us all. They live within our Mother's womb; they help her and all of us. My heart is sad, for we don't have the courage to fight this nation's government over issues such as this. The government is supposed to be for all of the people, not a handful of greedy ones! I remember many of the times when we all went to the beaches. We made the big fires, while many got their boats and cast nets ready (throwing nets cast by hand). Others would be setting up the drums for the singers, while the clan mothers organized everyone. There would be cooking fires and drying racks all being readied. Prayers would be offered. Fire torches were made for the boats and the boats would be blessed with prayer. Children all had chores as well, with the smallest ones being watched over by selected women. For this was harvest time for us as well. We harvested the fish, shrimp, and crabs for food. Even sharks would be caught and used for food, clothing, weapons, etc. Some fish were dried with the power of Grandfather Sun. Some we smoked and some were pickled. It depended on the need and what was caught.

When the songs were being sung and the drum's mighty power echoed across the waves, our friends the dolphins would come. They knew this was a special time for us. They always shared it with us. As the dancers danced, so did the dolphins, adding their beautiful voices to ours. When all was ready, the dolphins joined us.

The elders knew the tides and moods of the waters. They knew Grandmother Moon used her power at certain times to work with us. All was as it should be. Everyone went into the water to sing and talk to our Mother, and to sing for the lives of our relations who we prayed would help us by coming to our nets.

The dolphins would lead the way as the boats all left, scattering out. They would help drive the fish and shrimp to us so we could cast our nets, and from each cast of our nets, we gave gifts to our dolphin friends. It was beautiful and wonderful to see these friends come up out of the water and take our gifts from our hands.

When our boat was full we would paddle back to shore and hand the bucket of fish, shrimp, etc. over to those on shore and then paddle back out again. Crab baskets we tossed into the water would be picked up later. Crabs really loved our baskets. That is why they always come inside and fill them up. Many of the younger boys would be with a few elders who showed them how to spear or gig flounders. Flounders are really flat fish with eyes on top of their heads. They like to lie on the bottom on the sand and feed near shore. They are easily seen using the torches at night, and you can walk right up on them. You just have to be sure it is a flounder and not a stingray. Many of the young girls were scooping up oysters from the sand. As I said, there were times when everyone was busy, but everyone had a wonderful time. It was a time to be happy and enjoy all the wonderful life we had.

Shrimp and mullet was a joy to catch. It was funny because we all danced a stomp dance. The shrimp swim in schools, millions of them, jumping up out of the water, while the dolphins chased the mullets that were also jumping up out of the water. We chase after the dolphins to help drive the mullet into the shallows, then surround them and throw our nets. It was exciting to see and do all of these things. The dolphins would circle in like a barrier keeping the shrimp and mullet all bunched up. This is what you really call teamwork. The paddlers kept the boats moving, the net throwers were casting their nets; all flashing in the moonlight. This is a dance of life.

We would do this for four days. Afterwards we would have a feast and special ceremonies were done for our friends the dolphins, the fish people, and the shellfish people for they gave us their lives so we could have life. Storytellers would tell us all the old stories. And new stories would be told of the deeds that were done during this harvest. Stories would be told about our dolphin friends and they would clap their flippers and dance in the water with delight accepting our praise of them.

Remember To Walk in Love and Beauty Always!

Chapter Eight

The Ani-yun-wiya-The Beginning

In writing this, I wish to thank my grandfather who passed this on to me when I was a little person, and to my Ani-yun-wiya ancestors who passed it down generation to generation. It is an honor to know these gems of knowledge, and it has taken me a long, long time to even consider telling others these things. But, I meet so many who are confused, lost, or seeking, with nowhere to find answers. The Spirits have approved for me to tell the things I know; that I have been shown and taught.

Many will scoff or doubt the things I say. I expect that is because it goes against the way scientists, organized religions, and even scholars will ever admit. But there are many things that are supporting in fact that none of them can answer. For those of you who seek the ancient knowledge and ways, this will only help you to understand yourself and who you truly are.

I only wish I could relay this story the way it was given to me. But that is not possible today, for most of you have not been taught the Ani-yun-wiya breath of chant, to dance with Spirit, and to leave your body to travel and experience firsthand. I am not there with a special power stone to open things up for you, nor are there many left here who truly know the power of the stones, much less how to truly use them.

That is the reason I have been telling these stories to you, for I know there are those amongst you who have the gifts, who can learn, and teach others. So, this is the way I can reach you. Some of you I have seen in my dreams, some in my spirit form, others I have met in my travels, yet those have not stepped forth to claim their birthright.

So, before you go any further, please take some water, and wash your face, hands, feet and heart. I would prefer you wash completely your entire being in water, but this will help to some degree before we go further. Now take some tobacco, corn meal, corn pollen, and start a smudge to smudge yourself.

(Smudging is lighting sage, letting it smolder and using it to purify yourself in the smoke.)

If you have a crystal, please smudge it too; hold it in your left hand and place it above your eyebrows in the center of your forehead. Sing to your crystal to harmonize your vibration frequency of energy to the crystal. If you do this correctly the crystal will respond by vibrating in your hand. It will grow warmer and warmer. You will feel a tingling in your head and it will flow throughout your body. Become one with the crystal.

Remember this: all the Traditional and ancient Ani-yun-wiya used the crystals. It is why they had so many doctors, artists, sorcerers, speakers, musicians, engineers; because of the power of the stones.

Throughout North Carolina, Tennessee, South Carolina, Georgia, Alabama, and some of Kentucky, there are places which archaeologists, scientists, and scholars cannot explain the stone formations, the ancient civilizations, mounds, cities, or even the ancient writings.

I am not a scientist or even an educated person. I am just a simple man, part Ani-yun-wiya, part Muskogee, and part Irish, but I know who I am and what I am, and what I will become. So bear with me and now try to learn what you can. I have not tried teaching this way, so I don't know how it will affect you. I normally teach hands-on to those that truly seek. One day I hope to be able to teach more and more hands-on with those of you who truly seek.

I pray and ask that Spirit guide my words so that the message and lesson will open the knowledge for those who seek the Truth. I pray that my Spirit Helpers will lend me their power and help me reveal the paths of knowledge, wisdom, and understanding. I pray that the Star People look at me and guide my words to be power for the children to learn who they are, and that all may learn the path of Beauty and Harmony.

On a rainy night in Florida many, many years ago, my Ani-yun-wiya grandfather was sitting outside. The sky was talking with thunder and lightning and my grandfather had his face pointed to the sky. I quietly stood for a while waiting to be acknowledged, just watching the different expressions on his face. My grandfather was blind and had been for over fifty winters, but he could still out see anyone I had ever met. His body and face always let me know that he was traveling, not like most people, but like a true Ani-yun-wiya. My grandfather knew the old ways of letting his spirit loose from his body and go wherever he sought to. Finally, after a long time, he motioned for me to sit. I did and he said: "Do you know who you are?" I said "yes", and then went on reciting my Ani-yun-wiya lineage, then my Muskogee lineage, clans, etc. He just laughed. And I looked at him, not believing he was laughing at me. He smiled and said: "I'm going to tell you the story of the Ani-yun-wiya; of who they really are. Not many have known the beginnings for many, many, generations. Few know the whole story, even before the coming of the white man to this land.

"The only ones who knew were the ones these things were passed down to: those of the Wind and Bird Clans who were chosen and gifted with knowledge and with the stones. This story goes back before the story of First Man and First Woman, K'aniti and Selu. It goes back before Water Beetle and Buzzard. I'm entrusting you to keep the story of the Ani-yun-wiya alive and not forgotten. Because of your blood and clans is one reason, but most of all it is because of the gifts you were born with. I have spoken to the Spirits and they direct me to pass this on to you.

"One day you will use this knowledge. You will know when. But, until then, you must remember all that you hear, see, taste, feel about this knowledge. You can always call on your true relations to help you and teach you. You, I have watched. You, I have seen truly have the gifts. You are not better than anyone else, as you know. You are just more sensitive and open with your heart than many or most in these days that I have met. You are my blood as well. But, unlike the others of our family, you live in the old ways. You seek more and feel more than they do. Oh, they all have gifts. They have the blood, but they are taking on more and more of the ways and thinking of others. So, go get my pipe from over next to my things and bring it to me.

We will smoke and I will tell you what you must see, feel, hear, and most of all, come to know about who you are."

I was excited, as any little person would be. I literally ran to get his pipe. My mother and the rest of my family was sound asleep in the house, so I moved quietly as a butterfly through the house and got his pipe and tobacco bag, then got his corn meal and corn pollen bag. I handled them with proper respect, for these were his personal items (and naturally they were medicine items) and I took them to him.

While he loaded his pipe, he offered the corn meal and corn pollen to all the directions, and he was praying. He sprinkled me with the corn meal and pollen and then himself. He got out his crystal and I took the one from my neck that he had given me previously. We covered the crystals with corn pollen, corn meal, and tobacco. Then, he lit his pipe and offered it to the directions, then to the crystals. Then, he started to sing in his beautiful voice and I added my voice to his to harmonize our voices to the powers of the crystals, and to the pipe, and to the entire universe. The rain harmonized with us, as did the thunder and lightning. Then, he smoked his pipe. When he finished, he said: "Now we must breathe the way of Spirit, and the way we've been taught to harmonize our entire beings into relaxation, so we can let go of this world. You must breathe slowly through your nose deeply and then exhale through your mouth.

"Beginning with your left foot, relax your toes, and foot, letting your muscles, aches and pains totally relax. Then relax your left calf muscle and knee, relax your left hamstring and thigh. Now do the right foot, leg and thigh, just as you did the left. Relax your left bottom, and your left side, now your right bottom and your right side; now your lower back and lower stomach.

"Now relax your shoulders and your chest, then your neck, now your left hand and fingers, moving up to your shoulders. Now relax your right hand and fingers moving up to your shoulder. Now, begin to relax your face, your eyes, and then relax your mind. Release all thoughts you had. Empty your mind. Picture a hole in the top of your head, and all your thoughts, worries, problems, fears, pouring out of your head like water pouring from a gourd dipper.

"Picture in your mind a large bowl with spiraling designs going down to inside the bowl. This bowl is the universe and you are in the universe. You are totally safe here and are loved. Now with your crystal, touch it to your spirit eye and hold it there; feel it harmonize with you and the universe." (This method of meditation of the Ani-yun-wiya is a traditional method used in many ways; for healing, for hypnosis, spirit travel, training a little person to enhance their memories etc. Sometimes a spirit bowl is used, sometimes a secret place, using mountains, trees, waterfalls, etc. In the old days the Ani-yun-wiya knew this technique. It is also listed separately in the Spiritual Exercises in the back of this book.)

"Now listen closely, little one, for you are about to learn powerful knowledge. You will hear my voice and travel to an ancient time. Let your spirit loose from your body and come with me. We are going home to where we came from - far, far, into the sky, into the Stars themselves, for that is where we came from, for we are the 'Pleiadeans'. We are from the stars. We are all star children. And we will return with the help of our relatives, the crystal stones. The language is the language of Elati (The ancient language or Star Language). It is the language of True Power and Being. The sounds you hear will be the sounds of Power." My grandfather chanted and I felt myself vibrating; so light I could feel my spirit leaving my body. I looked and saw my grandfather leaving his body. He turned his face towards me and his eyes sparkled like black coals, and I knew in this form, my grandfather could see. It made me very happy to know he could see like me now.

We traveled through the stars to the Pleiades stars. Then we traveled to the one he pointed to as our home. My grandfather pulled me close and there was a popping sound and all went black. Then we were in a beautiful chamber. This chamber was huge; solid rock, but the rocks were all precious stones. The floor, I noticed, was all green stones, which I recognized as jade. The walls were some of the most beautiful stones my young eyes had ever seen. There were blue ones, black ones, red ones, yellow ones, and purple ones. Today you would name them as topaz, onyx, jet, beryl, ruby, amber, citrine, garnet, jasper, etc. The ceiling was magnificent. Huge crystals hung down in the formation of east to west. (Note: crystals grow from east to west towards each other.) Amethyst crystals larger than any man were at specific points of the ceiling.

Then my grandfather nudged me and nodded his head to the other side of the chamber. I stood next to my grandfather and watched in total wonder, for there walked a woman like no other I had ever seen. Her clothes were sparkling with crystals and amethyst. Around her necklace was a beautiful tiny crystal skull. Her face was sparkling in a mask like the face of a spider, and her headwear was an amethyst crystal covering her head. She was so beautiful and she was singing in the most beautiful voice as she approached towards the center of the chamber. She lifted her left arm, and the stones on the floor shot forth a light. In the center was the most beautiful of all that I had ever seen.

A large Amethyst Crystal Skull was surrounded by twelve crystal skulls with crystal power wands in between them, forming the cardinal points of directions. She entered the circle and spoke to the crystal skulls and the Amethyst Skull, and the skulls were chanting and singing. I was scared. I mean truly scared. I had never even heard of anything like this. My grandfather squeezed my hand and I knew he meant everything was alright; but no matter how much he assured me, this was Power. Power I could feel all over. Tears ran down my cheeks, for I was truly standing in a most Sacred Place. I felt unworthy to see all this, to feel this.

Who was I to think I should ever witness something so beautiful and sacred? Then I felt someone talking to me. I looked around, but saw nothing. Then I felt a pulling in my head, directing me to look at the Amethyst Skull. I did, and was immediately overwhelmed with love. This beautiful stone was talking to me. And then I felt the other skulls talking to me. Images flooded my mind, showing places, other stars, other peoples, and all had the circle of the skulls with them, all welcoming me to be with them. They sang, and nothing in the universe could ever touch you the way this touched me. Now you must understand that this wasn't telepathic (or mind) communication. This was sound communication, and the jaws on all the skulls moved. Their beautiful voices filled the chamber with such harmony that my very being was charged with this energy of love. I stood still for a while, and then I knew instinctively that I had to enter the circle. I did not know why, but just knew. I let go of my grandfather's hand and walked into the circle. The beautiful lady with the Spider Mask turned towards me and spoke.

"Welcome my child. I am known as Spider Woman, First Woman of Dreams and Power. I am the Keeper of the Sacred Chamber and of the Sacred Skulls. I am glad you have come home to know who you are and where you came from. Your grandfather came here when he was your age. Give me your left hand now."

She took my hand and guided it to the Amethyst Skull and then I was bombarded and overwhelmed with images, designs, feelings, and everything that was and would be. She lifted my hand and knelt down and looked into my eyes. She touched my face and it felt like a gentle fern leaf brushing against me.

She said: "Many, many lifetimes ago, all the people known now as the Ani-yun-wiya lived here and on other stars. Huge towns and buildings of marvelous designs were everywhere. Then, an explosion in the universe happened, and comets and meteors poured into us. Many, many died or were injured severely. Yes, many survived, and still do to this day. There are twelve planets that we live in. The one you now live in is known as the Planet of All Star Children, meaning that children from each of the twelve were sent there to live and grow, each to evolve spiritually and physically at their own pace.

"Each of the twelve planets had sent children with skulls of crystal and amethyst to the Planet of the Children of the Stars. Each had knowledge and gifts to help themselves grow spiritually. None are better or worse than the other. All are equal and were given equally in knowledge and power. Now, most have destroyed themselves and others, because they forgot who they were and what they were. They quit listening to their spirit and listened only to themselves. What started out as beauty has turned into ugliness.

"Because of this, throughout the planet's history, messengers have come to teach and bring back the children to the Sacred Way. Some have listened, most have not. Ask yourself. Where are the Atlantians, Lemurians, Mayans, Incas, Ais, Etowahs of yesteryears? No, they are not gone, only became others. In your time you will see much and hear much of further people's destruction and disappearance. The Children's Planet has lost the Sacred Way. But do not fear or grieve. All will be as it should be. When you are older, you will see people confused, lost, turning from one belief to another and another seeking answers, yet never finding it in the majority. What once was forbidden will become acceptable and sought after. What was once ridiculed will become acceptable. What once was hated will become loved.

"This is not your only time experiencing this there. You, like everyone else there have experienced this time after time. Each time you have returned you have evolved a little bit more. Only when you have learned and experienced all these different things and have truly evolved spiritually will you then come home, or you can choose to return again. Many think they can explain or prove with their silly science the true history. Oh, how foolish they are. It is because of these who think they have the answers or are the ones in power that most of the children suffer in ignorance. And the more someone who is truly spiritual and trying to bring back the old ways will that person or persons be persecuted and ridiculed.

"Understand this, blood of my blood, heart of my heart, your life will be very hard. You will suffer not only from your own people but from others as well. For ones like you will always be hunted by those who fear the truth and do not want others to know the truth. But remember also: you asked to go back this time. Remember your own vows to do so. It is a lesson you had to learn as well. For ego, pride, and self must never overcome the Spirit of love. At times in your life you surely will be tested. I warn you that you will suffer dearly. But if you do as you are to do, then your reward will be here awaiting you. I am your Mother, your Grandmother, and have been throughout time. You will make mistakes because your heart will lead you to do things. But no matter what you do, if you ask humbly and truthfully from your heart, all will be forgotten and you will be embraced once again.

"Now I must tell you how your people went to the planet, so that when your time comes you will know inside all that you see. It is not exactly as some have recorded it, nor is it the way most will believe. Understand this: believing is very powerful. So when others persecute you for your beliefs, you will be able to stand strong against them."

She then placed my hand on the Amethyst Skull and I saw things before the children left to go to the planet I now live on. I knew the Traditional Story of Spider Woman and the Creation. But this was not like this. The twelve planets representing the children all had ships.

My home was represented by Spider Woman. Our ships were huge ships shaped like a giant spider, with a large body connected to a smaller body with long legs out the sides, so I could now see where the story of Spider Woman could be misconstrued as being a spider. In the ships, thousands of children with adults were loaded. Since we were a people of simplicity using the power of the stones, and living in Harmony and Beauty with all life, we did not need to take a lot of things. We were told that all we needed would be provided by the planet, and since we had stones, we knew we could communicate with all the other children, home, and with the plants and animals. We did bring many different plants and animals with us. Each planet sent some as well.

Animals were treated at home like they are on this planet. All animals and plants are our relatives. We lived together, communicated together, just as two-legged ones do with each other. We were no better or worse than any of them, and we certainly didn't enslave them, hunt them for sport, or kill them just because we could. It was the same with the plants.

Plants are very emotional beings, and they love to talk. They love to sing and dance. The winged ones are a very unique people because they all are true singers, and their voices and characters are very strong. Plus, they remind us of back home where we can all fly. Yeah, in the home of the Pleiadeans, we can fly. No, we don't have wings; it is just that we are harmonized so fully that we ride the air because our energy is the same. Oh, it can be done here on this planet as well - it just takes more harmonizing and mental discipline.

Now, when the children came here, they scattered all over the planet. I won't go into all the places, not at this time, but will speak only on the Ani-yun-wiya children.

In Traditional stories of the Ani-yun-wiya, Water Beetle dove into the water and brought up mud on his back and Buzzard flew down because others couldn't fly that far and back. I can see why this part was told that way after generations had passed and others had come and gone.

But what happened was that where the Ani-yun-wiya wanted to live was covered in much water, and what the adults did was to lower a submersible that could maneuver in the water and drill. This submersible would look something like a beetle. Instead of Buzzard flying down and shaping the Smokey Mountains, it was aircraft that had thrust burners to help dry out the lower valleys. See, the people all wanted the beautiful mountains and trees for their homeland. This covered a large area of the southeast United States. Oh, by the way all my Muskogee, Ais, Jeru, Timacua, and Yucci brothers and sisters all came from the Pleiades system as well! In fact, you came on the first load and you landed in the areas south of the Ani-yun-wiya.

Anyway, K'aniti and Selu known as the First Man and First Woman were the two leaders responsible for the children and the growth of the People. K'aniti was also the keeper of the Animals and Winged ones. Traditionally, the story goes that Wild Boy released all the Winged ones and animals after seeing K'aniti release a few for food. Then, Wild Boy wanted to be like his father, a great hunter, and Wild Boy couldn't roll the stone back into place to keep them inside.

Well, the truth is a little different. The People had been here for some time now, and children had been born here. K'aniti and Selu were now much older and children had grown and had children for generations. Selu was considered a powerful witch. Yeah, she had power as all Ani-yun-wiya do. K'aniti had been releasing animals and winged ones periodically for a long time. He wanted to make sure they all had plenty of room, and food, to multiply and spread out. He was in communication with the other children, therefore he knew when they were releasing and into which areas.

To protect the genetic pool of blood, he only released certain ones to areas where animals from others of the twelve planets were not yet directly related to the ones in his care. One of the children found abandoned and adopted by K'aniti and Selu was called Wild Boy. Wild Boy did release all the animals at one time to see if K'aniti was a good enough hunter to get them all. What Wild Boy did not know was that K'aniti would not hunt them. What Wild Boy did was release all the winged ones too, such as mosquitoes, gnats, flies, dragonflies, all birds, etc. That is why in the south and southeast until this very day, there is an abundance of flies, gnats, mosquitoes, etc.

Now, in understanding what I was shown, I can better appreciate the Traditional Stories. No, they are not wrong! Only interpreted the way the People saw it at the time, when stories were told generation after generation. As in any story told over thousands and thousands of years, some interpretations by the storyteller can change a story. When these stories were passed down over thousands of years, the original people's knowledge deteriorated - from their true Home in the stars and their new beginnings here.

When Spider Woman removed my hand from the crystal, I was saddened. She said "Why is your heart so sad?"

I said, "Because so much was forgotten and because the children have all suffered so terribly."

She took my face in her hands and said "Yes it is sad,

but it won't always be so! Your life is just beginning this time and you too will make mistakes. You will do foolish things, which will tear my heart, but still you will be loved, and hopefully, one day, you will make your place and teach what you have been taught and shown. Your grandfather, standing there, will return home here in the near future.

"He has done well by you, and I encourage you to learn as much as you can, for one day in the future, most will be lost and forgotten. Learn from other children of the stars as well. Your grandfather here will help you and your grandfather of the Muskogee also. There are other ways to learn from them all. What most have forgotten is that we are all one and the same. The messengers who continue throughout time to bring gifts, and knowledge from the People of the Stars, have brought it to them as the People would accept it. It does not mean that it was given to them only or that it only belongs to them.

"Messengers will continue to come for all the children and no one child is better than the other. There are no royalty bloods, true bloods. We are all the same blood. All are equal. That is why you look the way you do. It is why you will suffer from your own people, and especially from others, for it isn't what is seen outside but on the inside. It is your heart, their heart, our heart that is all the same. Just as the knowledge of history, events, messages, sciences, are etched in the crystals, and you children have etched these things in other stones, so it is truth etched into each of your hearts. It is only when the children of the stars learn the Truth of themselves and each other that they will truly begin to evolve spiritually. It has hurt us all to witness the atrocities that the children have done on that planet, and they will commit even more and more atrocities in the future.

"Hopefully in your lifetime, you and others like you will stand up and be heard. Make your energy touch those that will listen and are seeking the Sacred Path of Love, Truth, Generosity, Humbleness, Loyalty, Respect, Honor, and most of all Spirituality. Then will these things begin to change. The lessons you must endure will give you strength, knowledge, and experience to be able to do this.

"Just as a warrior trains for battle, you too must first train in life for your battle, and remember the greatest enemy you will ever have is your own self, your doubts about yourself, your fears of failure, your fears of acceptance, your worry and doubt of what others will say or think about you. You must believe in your own self if you are to become what you are to be. Your gifts will become more evident to others as you grow, but your beliefs will only strengthen and multiply them. And, when you have made your mistakes, if you feel doubt or feel unworthy, then you will be unworthy; only because you believe that. If you are to heal someone, then it is on your belief; not on the one who is being healed.

"So, my child, you see it all comes down to you: how strong you believe in yourself and in the Sacred Circle of Life.

"When you conquer your fears, it makes you stronger. I know you have already gone through many of the old customs of your tribe. Your fear was conquered; it made you strong and gave you more confidence in yourself. The world you live in is covered in fears by the children - fear of who they are, what they are, what they will become.

"Because they have lost their true ways they live in ignorance. Fears run rampantly wild on your planet. When people live in fear - they strike out in fear, they kill and destroy in fear, they hate in fear. Why? Because of their ignorance of who they are, what they are, what they are to become. Ignorance they have lived in for thousands of years now; ignorance in which each one is their own blame. That's right. They can only blame themselves, for if they seek the truth sincerely they won't quit until they find it. If they put other things in front of the truth, then they are truly not seeking. If material things, wealth or social status, are more important to them than the truth and the spiritual path; then they will stay ignorant and can only blame themselves.

"I listen and I hear their cries and prayers; their outbursts of rage at others, blaming their parents or ancestors, blaming someone else always for their problems or mistakes. If they would only look inside themselves and listen to themselves, they would see that the problem is themselves. No one can control anyone's spirit or free will. We all make choices in life. Sometimes they are good. Sometimes they are bad, but you live and learn from each of them. When you make a mistake, admit the fault as your own. Accept the responsibility and learn from it.

"There is no excuse for anyone who is ignorant. If they want to change then they must put forth the effort themselves. You cannot make a person change, nor can anyone else. They must want to do so themselves. Civilizations progress with many things. Many things can be beneficial or destructive. But, in order for it to work, then the minds and the hearts of the people must evolve spiritually higher, for power without compassion and wisdom is dangerous.

"What I have seen on the planet is people who are greedy for power; people who want to enslave the people and all life to their own gains. What I don't understand is how the Children of the Stars' own hearts have allowed these ones to enslave them. Oh, I know they use fear propaganda against the children, but the children should listen to their own hearts. If they did, then these types of people would not be in power. I have watched civilization after civilization fall because of one thing, greed; those who want to rule the world or hold things over peoples' heads as a threat. And just as all the other civilizations have fallen, so too will those in existence now and in the future. And it will continue until civilization is compassionate, humble, respectful, honorable, and truthful; in every form.

"When it gets bad, the planet on which you now live will call upon her sisters and they will answer her call, as they always have in the past, and civilizations will be destroyed again. Yes, little one, your planet is a living being, just as all life in the universe, are all part of the whole. She has a heart full of love but she has a wrath to match it. If the people don't respect her, if they continue to mistreat her and all she gives, then she will strike back. Now it is time for you and your grandfather both to come to the Amethyst Skull."

My grandfather came and stood by me and she placed both of our hands on the Amethyst Skull. The Amethyst Skull vibrated powerfully and all the crystal skulls began chanting, and the eight powerful crystal wands glowed brilliant blue light to us, through us, all around us. The Amethyst Skull burst forth a powerful energy burst of purple light that flowed into us and filled us. My mind filled with songs of the universe, songs of healing, songs of beauty, and songs of love. I felt so much love that I did not think I could hold it all. Then it all stopped and my hand was tingling.

The Amethyst Skull released us from its power and Spider Woman said, "It is time for you to go back now. Your bodies are getting very weak and cold. You must return to them. But, know this: anytime you seek you can come again. Do not forget what you have been shown, and remember: believe in yourself."

We returned swiftly back to our bodies. We sat there for a long time, unable to move. When I opened my eyes, I noticed that I saw things differently than I had before. I looked at my grandfather. He was smiling, so I smiled too. It was now morning and we sat there waiting and listening as all life was waking up. I saw the birds fluttering, shaking the rain from their feathers. I watched as the leaves on the trees lifted themselves up toward grandfather sun. I watched as the grass rose to sing as well. I was full of wonder and energy with a purpose.

My grandfather sensing my energy said, "Go on boy. See the world now. I will rest for a while and we will talk later. But say nothing to anyone about this. You know how your mother and stepfather feel about you and me and especially about our beliefs. So run along and I'll see you later on this evening."

Boy, I was gone in a flash. Now from my mother's home to the swamp was no more than one hundred yards and I was there in a flash. As soon as I was there, I dove into the water but was aware of Hvlpv'tv (pronounced hulpu-tu), the alligator people, all around. I dove down to the bottom and dug up two cattail bulbs (they are natural tubers like potatoes) and brought them up to the surface. I washed them off as I walked up out of the water and began eating my breakfast.

I wanted to go to my special place. It was in the very center of the swamp. It was an island surrounded by water, quicksand, alligators and snakes. It was my sanctuary when I wanted to be alone. No one could find me there. This was a place I had found when I first came there to visit my mother and two sisters. This was in the area of what is now called Ocala, Florida. I was staying at the Seminole village in the Ocala Forrest at this time. Anyway, it took me a long time to get to know the hidden passage to the island. Quicksand is a real danger to anyone, and much of the quicksand areas were covered with two inches of black water on top of it. If you made the mistake of thinking there was only water there, you would be in big trouble.

I had developed a ritual game with the Puca Hvlpv'tv (grandfather alligator), a contest to see if he could get me before I reached the island. Now in those days there were really big gators still plentiful. This one was huge, still the Bull of the swamp. He was as wide as a gigging boat and a lot longer than a boat. We developed this game, him and me, on our first encounter. I found a path that was only maybe twelve inches wide. It was barely covered with water; mostly with lily pads. The path went in a round-about way to the island. The only problem was that I had to figure out where grandpa gator was waiting to ambush me.

The path was maybe three hundred yards long where the danger would be or could come from. Snakes and leeches I never worried about. But this contest between me and the grandpa was something else. Two times in the past he had come very, very close to getting me. He was very, very, sneaky. He once had used the tip of his tail to raise a lily pad thinking I would think it was his head. I almost went for it, but something didn't fit the water pattern, so when he lunged out of the water I was gone faster than a wild pig can slip through your fingers.

Oh, most of you probably don't know this, but an alligator can outrun a horse in a short distance. Never ever underestimate their speed.

On remembering where I had just been with my grandfather, I grasped the crystal hanging on my chest and started singing. The crystal responded to me and I opened my mind to the crystal, sending energy and a mental image of the grandpa gator. I then opened my mind up to the crystal and let the crystal use my energy with its own to locate him. Before long, I got my answer.

The crystal showed me where he was waiting. Boy, grandpa was getting very sneaky. He had burrowed out a part of the bank next to the path right on the island. He had dug it out under water, and had pulled lily pads, limbs, dead bamboo, and driftwood up to it to conceal his hideaway. He had apparently used his tail to splatter mud on it to help conceal his ambush. I thanked the crystal and began my journey down the path. I knew where he was yet I still couldn't see him. When I was halfway there I paused and looked behind me, like I was looking for him. Then I lay down in the water gently so as not to disturb the water.

See, alligators and crocodiles have sensors on their mouths that pick up vibrations in the water. I pictured in my mind that I was water, just floating along, and let the current be me. I lay there floating on top of the path motionless, watching and waiting. Now I knew he felt me when I first started on the path, so he must be getting confused as to why I had not continued. Patience is a developed gift. Some creatures are born with it, others have to practice at it and boy was I practicing now. Finally, I felt movement. Then I saw his mouth and head appear, hardly above the water. He was about twenty feet from me. I watched him as he turned his giant head side-to-side looking for me, wanting his small snack.

Still, I lay there. If I moved now, I would be his. Lily pads, algae and muck covered my body lying there so I knew that unless I moved and disturbed the water, he would not see me. Then, he disappeared under the water. Still, I could not move.

This game was now taking on a new life; a game of life and death. In my mind, I kept seeing myself as black water, still and motionless. Over and over I repeated this to myself while I waited.

I don't know how long I actually lay there, but it sure seemed like a long, long time. Anyway, I finally saw him near the middle moving towards the bank. I guess he figured I decided not to come and went to wait in ambush for the wild pigs that always came to drink. Anyway, I slowly moved one inch at a time using only my toes to push myself towards the island.

Upon reaching the island I was exhausted, yet filled with exhilaration. I had used my gifts and I had believed in them, and I was happy. Using some moss and fern leaves, I cleaned myself up. Then I went to the middle of the island where the fresh water spring was. It only was a small spring but the water was ice cold and very good. When I had finished drinking I walked over to a muskodine vine to pick the wild muskodines (This is a wild grape that grows throughout the south) and ate some of them.

Then I went to my spot. My special spot here was secluded even for the island. I had been there many times already. It was surrounded by tall bamboo cane and had a large old cypress there. There was a small pool of water surrounding this like a miniature pond; but it was very shallow. It was fed by the small spring. Bullfrogs, leopard frogs, and rain frogs all loved this place with the giant elephant ears, palmetto, cattails, bamboo, and the fresh water. A large osprey mother had her nest in the cypress tree. She loved eating snakes; and all the snakes knew she loved feasting on them and the fish that were plentiful in the swamp. The only snake that the osprey never ate was the king snake. The king snake looks almost like a coral snake, which is deadly. The king snake is non-poisonous and eats poisonous snakes.

Anyway, this was my special spot here. I had others in other places near my village and the village at Silver Springs, and one very special place deep in the everglades in the Big Cypress. Here I could let my spirit roam and think about all I had just witnessed and experienced. I wanted to be ready for when my grandfather talked to me next; for I knew it was his custom to always talk to me about things after I had time to "chew on them" as he would say.

I opened my mind up to Mother Earth and crawled inside of her. I needed her now and I needed to just be held by her. So I just lay there and enjoyed her loving embrace. I woke up about noon time, guessing by the location of the sun directly above me, and figured I better go see my mom. Not that she would ever worry about me in the swamp; she only worried about all the other creatures in the swamp. Ha! Ha!

After I made it back to the path leading from the island, I looked for grandpa gator. I spotted him way up on shore sleeping in the sun. He must have already eaten earlier because he doesn't sleep until he has eaten. (Mostly gators and crocodiles don't immediately eat their kill. They take it down and wedge it under a log or in a gator cave, which is dug out in the side of a bank. They take their kill here to soften it up and rot so they can digest it easier.)

I made it across the path to shore without waking up the grandpa gator and then went to my mother's house. Mother was hanging up her laundry after doing the washing, between two large water oak trees with lines wrapped around them. I smiled at her and went and got my water poles and jugs to go fetch water. It was a good half a mile to get the drinking and cooking water. I used seasoned cypress wood limbs to carry the water jugs on as they dry out light as a feather but they are very hard and strong. This way I could carry a lot of them at one time and I would only have to make four trips to fill all the water barrels up.

When I had finished, I went to the garden that I had spaded. (Spading is when you use a shovel to dig and flip the topsoil upside down, wait fourteen days, and do it again.) I had spaded four acres this way for her to make her a garden. (She didn't have any mules or plows; although later I used to hook myself up to a plow while my sisters steered the plow.) I had planted corn, green beans, squash, peppers, melons, potatoes, cabbage, cucumbers, eggplant, carrots, celery, radishes, collard greens, spinach, turnips, butter beans, and black-eyed peas for her, so I had to weed and check on all the plants.

After finishing with the garden, I went fishing. Fishing for me has never been a sport. I enjoy it, but I don't fish like most people. I use fish traps, ones that I made, that start out with a big circle with a hole and get smaller as the fish goes inside. I also use a dust that paralyzes fish when I dam up a stream or river long enough for me to gather what I need. As soon as I get enough I un-dam the stream, creek or river, and the water flow then revives the fish quickly. This is a method that my people have used for thousands of years. I won't name the source we make this dust from lest someone use this in the wrong way. Yeah, it is very powerful.

I cleaned the fish I gathered and took them to my mother's sink outside the house, and poured some water over them to clean them off. Then I put the cork stopper in the sink and poured some more water over them. I did a few more things for my mom and then went to get me something to eat.

The swamp is my home and has an abundance of food supplies, so anywhere you are, you can find something to eat. I was already trained using blowgun, darts, bows, spears, slings, throwing sticks, and making snares, so it wasn't very long before I had me a cane cutter.

Now, cane cutters are a giant swamp rabbit. Actually, it is a hare, but these rabbits are fast, sneaky, and can swim real fast. They are four times bigger than a cottontail, and they can really jump, so you have to stalk one, spot it out, and catch it before it even knows you are there. I said a prayer for him. He was a buck, and I offered some corn meal from my pouch to his spirit and then cleaned him. I saved his hide so I could make my mom a nice bag. I gathered a few wild onions while my fire was burning in its hole. Then I went and got me some wet clay.

When I got back to the fire it was burning real good and I added more dead oak pieces to the fire. I put the onions inside my cane cutter and used sticks I had sharpened to hold his stomach together, and then I covered him in the wet clay. I put him in my fire and covered him with the hot coals, then, put a few more pieces of wood on.

While my cane cutter was cooking, I fleshed up the hide and began to stretch it over a piece of hickory that I found and bent to make a hoop. Using the bark, which I stripped from the hickory, I slowly stitched the hide over the frame and left it to dry. When my cane cutter had cooked long enough, I raked back the coals and using a forked stick, pulled my meal out of the fire. The clay was now like a brick. I picked up a rock and cracked open the clay, and began enjoying my meal. (The clay is a way we use to pressure cook many food items. It traps the flavor of all that is inside as well as tenderizes all that is inside, including the bones, which has marrow in it that we eat. This method of cooking in clay is used for almost any type of game, fish, birds, pig, snake, turtle, squirrel, rabbit, and even deer.) Now, we don't always cook everything in clay but we do cook a lot in clay.

After eating all I wanted, I wrapped the remainder up in a palmetto leaf which I had first soaked in water and then wrapped the food. I would share this with my grandfather later.

I sat and thought about all I had seen and experienced with my grandfather and all that Spider Woman had told me; mostly that I was my own worst enemy. And I thought about all that the Amethyst and Crystal Skulls had shown me. I knew my grandfather would help me understand a lot of this, or at least put questions in my mind to make me find the answers myself. I had grown to know that all the grandfathers and grandmothers had a habit of never really answering a question, but only giving you a question to think about an answer. So I thought about that for a while, and then realized that they did this for a purpose. Knowledge and wisdom come from understanding.

If you truly understand something, then that is power as well. If they give you the answer, you won't really understand the answer, because you didn't make the connections and figure it out. It would be like trying to track a cane cutter and losing its trail in the water. If you turn to your uncle for help and he shows you the trail, you would never look for yourself.

It all made sense to me now and I began to go over the questions my grandfather had been giving me all this time. I was proud and happy with myself. I could hear Spider Woman talking to me about myself, my doubts, my fears, and all. This too applied in believing in myself; this was truly a power. I instinctively touched my crystal power wand, giving thanks to all those who were helping me, and I would now make a vow to learn all that I could, especially from the stone people.

I already knew that there were many types of stones and that even amongst them they were different just like us. Some were teachers, some were record keepers, some were power wands, some were keys, some were generators, and some were double pointed (meaning they were positive and negative and could reverse anything to its opposite). But I knew I had to know more so I vowed to talk to all the stone people and ask to learn from them.

I went back to my mother's home and sat down next to a big water oak tree and waited for my grandfather. My grandfather came a little later and sat down on one of the stumps next to the tree. He patted my head, letting me know he knew I was there. I handed him the wrapped cane cutter and just sat there while he ate. I loved my grandfather and was very proud of him.

He had made it through life, which was very hard. He was a full blood, yet struck down in early life by being blinded in an accident. No one would give him a job, plus he was a savage in their eyes. He was a large man, powerfully built, with skin that looked like leather dyed mahogany. His hands were strong, yet he could feel things and identify them by touch. He never complained and never made excuses for himself. And what I truly loved about him was his independence.

Even at his great age now, he wanted no help in getting around. He made me proud of him always. I sat in silence, just thinking about all the things he had told me, shown me, and about all I had watched him do. He never ever said anything bad or otherwise about my mother's mother or about her leaving him and taking his children away from him. I knew it had to hurt him. All of his children were grown and had children of their own, and now he visited with his children, something he could not do when they were growing up. He loved them dearly, for children are a blessing to any man or woman, and all are cherished. I could feel some of his pain, for I did not know my own father. He and my mother split up when I was about four springs old. I did not know my mother either, not like other kids know their parents. My father was a full-blooded Muskogee, a member of the Red Sticks and my mother was a half-breed, half Ani-yun-wiya and half Irish.

My mother had remarried at this time to a hard working German man. He provided for her kids and for his four daughters. I was a person that was accepted only because of my mother. My grandfather knew this as well. That was why we timed our visits so we could be together. Being Native was not accepted around this house, never spoken about nor allowed to be spoken about. Don't get me wrong, my mother's new husband was a good provider. It wasn't easy in those days, much less for a half-breed with three children, so my mother put up with a lot, never saying hardly anything. She knew that I knew she loved me and that's all that counted.

My grandfather then got out his makings, which was cornhusk and tobacco, and he rolled himself a smoke. He offered the smoke to Corn Maiden, Mother Earth, and all the directions. He then smoked his smoke. When he finished he crumbled the remains in his fingers and blew it to the winds. We just sat for a while. Then he asked me what I had learned today. So I told him of my discovery about knowledge and wisdom, and about believing in myself. He just nodded his head and smiled. He said later on tonight, when all had gone to bed, we would continue with the story, for my mother's husband would be home soon. He told me to run along and come back later.

I did, and as I walked away, watching him sitting there, picking up all the sounds, smells, and feelings of all that was all around him. Sometimes he would remind me of a snake sticking out his tongue, testing the winds.

I left and went to my tree. Yeah, I lived in a tree. It is

not safe to sleep on the ground in the swamps. There are too many things that like to bite, eat, or suck on you. I climbed my tree, way up near the middle, where I had woven and tied vines to make my shelter. Using palmetto leaves, branches, limbs, and leaves, I had a nice shelter. A family of squirrels lived above me and they all hollered at me when I climbed up. I slept for a while waiting for the time I should leave to see my grandfather. I lay there listening to the night, the time when all predators love to hunt. I could hear the roar of bull gators all around, the bullfrogs, the leopard frogs, the owls and monkeys. Whippoorwills were singing tonight and there was a taste of more rain in the air.

As I lay there picturing all these relatives and what they were doing, I sensed silence come. All the little creatures were silent. Something was near that was a hunter. I silently moved a palmetto leave and looked out. The swamp is a dark place in daylight. It is much darker at night. I could see nothing yet I knew and felt that danger was still close. All hunters are dangerous until they are fed. When they are fed they don't bother you unless you intrude or bother them, so I waited and waited. Finally I heard a scrambling down the path, then a cry of death, then the scream of a panther. The panther had made his kill. He would enjoy a careless young pig tonight. I waited another thirty minutes and then climbed down to go see my grandfather.

While walking back to my mother's home I picked some wild plums and enjoyed their sweetness. It was raining softly and I raised my mouth to the sky and drank my fill of water. The cool rain washed my body of the sweat that always covers you in the swamps. It felt good walking in the rain, yet you are always aware of everything around you. This was my world, a world I knew. I knew all that existed in my world. If I made a mistake I would be like the young pig that the panther just got earlier.

Where my mother lived at this time was more civilized than where I lived and had been growing up, yet it was still full of dangers and one mistake could be your last. But I was not careless and never will be because of my training and the way I lived. It goes with me everywhere I go.

Even in a large city now days, those lessons of life are valuable for there are predators who walk on two legs. There are dangers everywhere, but when your senses are attuned to these things you will be ready, and two-leggeds cannot hide their thoughts like a four-legged. A two-legged concentrates too much, releasing energy that your body will quickly identify and prepare you for. A true hunter never stares at his prey. It looks next to or around the prey. It never thinks about it. It is totally natural for it to eat. There is no hate, no greed or lust in its heart. Instead it respects and even loves its victim. Not so with two-legged ones. So, yes, there is a difference. The rain felt good coming down; hitting all the leaves and branches singing a song as I walked. The cool breeze that pushed the wind brought untold thousands of smells to my nose for me to sample.

I arrived before I realized that I was there. My grandfather was sitting down waiting for me. I knew he knew I was there so I walked closer and then stopped, waiting to be acknowledged. Now many of you probably aren't familiar with this custom but to traditional people, it is out of respect that this is done.

To the Ani-yun-wiya it is a great offense to disrespect anyone's harmony or balance. By boldly intruding on someone, this is an act of disrespect to that person and all they are harmonizing with. Not even a little person was allowed to disregard this code of conduct. To disturb anyone, no matter what they were doing, either with a group, a couple, or individually, was disrespect. If an emergency had occurred, then a simple shuffling of the feet or a cough would alert that person or persons that something was urgent or important. Otherwise you never interrupt or intrude on someone's privacy. Today very few know this custom. It is why so few sense when someone approaches and why so many intrude on people's conversations, privacy, etc. They have lost respect!

So I waited on my grandfather until he was ready to acknowledge me, and when he did, I approached respectfully and sat down. I handed him some wild plums that I had. I knew that he could smell them and how much he enjoyed them. He thanked me and began eating his plums. When he finished, he pulled out his makings and rolled himself a smoke. He offered the smoke to all the directions and then smoked it. He pulled out his corn meal pouch and corn pollen pouch and sprinkled himself and me. He pulled out his crystal and took mine from my neck. He sat for a few moments and cleared his mind, then said: "What have you decided boy?" I told him I wanted to know more, especially about the places the crystal skulls were and the other locations of some of the Children of the Stars.

He thought for a moment than said: "We will have to journey to the places you seek. Which ones do you want to know first?" I told him I wanted to see the old places of the Aniyun-wiya, the Etowah, Ais, Jeru, Maya, and Aztec.

He asked me: "Why do you choose these first?"

I told him that the Tradition of the Muskogee makes it important that I witness the Ais, Jeru, and Etowah, and since the Maya and Aztec are still close relations to the Muskogee and have been for generations, with an exchange of knowledge and ceremony, it was important that I understand these groups as well as all the others. But these were closest to my tribe, so I decided to see them first.

(The Etowah were Ani-yun-wiya and had temples, pyramids, arts, music, and healers. They also had monarchs that passed down by blood. The Ais, and Jeru were tribal nations in south Florida that were also assimilated into the Muskogee. These were very fierce people who had a vast civilization that went to the islands of the Caribbean and they traded with the Aztecs and Mayan peoples. The circle found in Miami a few years ago is of the Ais People. What was discovered under water off the coast in Cuba and in the Gulf are actually Ais and Jeru ancient cities. And no, the so-called archaeologists and scientists haven't figured it out yet. Etowah is not correctly pronounced today. The correct pronunciation is E-toh-wa, and they spoke Elati, the language of the stars.)

My grandfather nodded his head and said: "Very well, but you do realize that you will still need to see them all?"

I said I understand that, but I only want to visit a few at a time so I have time to experience and learn at each place. If I went to them all at once I would be rushed and miss the heartbeat of these places. I also know that I can only stay away for short periods of time lest I let my physical body go, which I have not strengthened myself or disciplined myself enough to do yet.

He nodded his head and said: "You are thinking boy. It is your decisions in life, those moments that you must choose and live with, that are important. So let's begin again the Traditional breathing and relaxation method so we can begin our journey again."

(For those of you who have never tried this, please do so. It will be important that you are comfortable. Don't begin unless you have used the restroom lest you have to interrupt yourself or have an accident. You should be sitting down. You can use a chair for back support, but do not lie down to begin to learn this. If you do, you will most likely just go to sleep. Do this in a quiet area where you will not be disturbed. Get rid of all phones, pagers, or anything that will distract you or interrupt you. See the Ani-yun-wiya breathing method in the Spiritual Exercises at the back of this book. It is a great stress reliever.)

When we left our bodies we went to the Etowah center plaza. In the center was a huge rectangular type pyramid with steps leading up to the flat top. The top had a small opening in it and I could see plumes of smoke coming out. I smelled the air and could detect the aroma of cedar, oak, holly, and dogwood. I knew these were incenses being used by these People.

(In olden times, many of the descendants of the Etowah were called People of the Holly, and bands of the Ani-yun-wiya and even Muskogee also were called this because it was part of their inherited traditions passed down to them. Holly is a very special plant. In my language it is called Es' se fv' ske, pronounced Es-see Fu-skee meaning leaves that are sharp or with a keen edge. There is a reason that they have sharp points. It is because it is a powerful medicine, only to be used by those trained in these matters and methods.)

The People were all beautiful and filled with laughter. Their clothing was beautiful, intricately woven with fibers of bark and long grass leaves. Some had skirts. Some had long swaying skirts. Each was decorated with dyes and shell works.

I noticed the dwellings were circular and had been done in mud plaster form. Some were even done using limestone, which naturally made them white. The homes formed a circular formation around the plaza. The highest societies were closest to the plaza, and lower castes surrounded these.

I saw artists at work intricately carving green soapstone. I saw knappers inspecting flint to become one with the stone before knapping out the stone for blades, spear points, tools, etc. I saw huge fields all cultivated with crops. This was a thriving city, beautiful with lush green valleys and mountains surrounding them, with all different types of trees. A beautiful river was to the south of the town, and I could hear children laughing and playing. I could hear flutes playing and beautiful voices coming from the pyramid. I closed my eyes and concentrated on being inside, and I was there.

It was built going downward as were our mounds. These types spiral down with chambers on each level. I saw numerous beautiful ladies down below and I wanted to see what they were doing, so I walked down to the area where they were. These women were all singing in harmony; no words, just a chant, their voices going high and then lower and lower before the chant started again. The flutes I had heard were matching the women's voices. On a marble table lay a man injured. I could not tell what had happened to him because the women surrounded him. An older woman stood beside him with a beautiful power wand crystal in her hand. Also placed on different parts of the man's body were different types of crystals. The crystal wand in the older woman's hand was now moving over the man's body, and the women's voices were sending their energy to the crystal wand as well. The older woman was sending her energy too. I could feel the power in this room, and I knew the man would be healed. My grandfather and I left and continued my journey. But first, I must see something here. I did not know what it was I was to see, but something was pulling at me. So, I let my spirit be pulled and my grandfather followed. We were outside again and I could still feel a pull, so I followed it.

We were leaving the city but within sight of it. I was being drawn to a mountain. I knew this now. This mountain I could see was being attended to by men and women. The only difference between these women and the ones in the city were that these women had more stone necklaces and all wore crystals around their necks.

Midway up the mountain I could see two very old women sitting proudly and directing people. In the lap of one was a crystal skull just like I had seen back home in the stars. I understand this was to be the place for the chamber of the skull. It was being carved out of the mountain. I looked around in every direction; looking for markers that I would recognize later on in life or when I needed to. I know that the skull crystal had pulled me to it so I would know this. My grandfather smiled and I knew he knew this as well. My grandfather led the way back down and we sat in a beautiful field and released our mind to go to the land of the Ais Nation.

We opened our eyes and were in a large jungle and swamp. I know this land. I grew up here. The only difference now was that the swamp was more covered in vegetation, huge trees, and the creatures of the swamps were more plentiful. I could hear the drums and I knew we were on the path, but something had pulled me to this spot. So I just stood still and let my spirit pull me to what I must see. I was being pulled towards a small path leading to the dense woods. I let myself be pulled until I came to a clear-running stream.

The water was beautiful, clean, and it was cold. I knew this spring. I had played and swam in it most of my young life. I knew whatever was pulling me was very near. So into the water I went. I felt the heartbeat of Mother Earth strong in this water. I let myself be pulled onward, across this large beautiful stream. There was another path here all lined with shells and coral stones. I noticed crystal and rose quartz hanging from several trees along this path as I followed it. The fragrance of magnolia blossoms and morning glories filled the air. I noticed a dense growth of cedar trees forming a wall. I parted the branches of the cedars and continued on the path.

It opened into a clearing. Here in the center was a beautiful stone Medicine Power Wheel. In the center where the altar was, there was a giant alligator skull. In its mouth was a large crystal wand. The Medicine Power Wheel was laid out beautifully, with different colored stones. There were pearls of all colors (fresh water), red coral, pink alabaster, green agate, green soapstone, chert, copper (raw), red sandstone, blue agates and small crystals everywhere. I studied these patterns and also studied the poles at each point. These poles were decorated with animal amulets and bird amulets. I stood back and just waited to see everything in my mind, looking at it as a whole and individually.

The crystal on my neck was vibrating strongly and I felt pulled to the gator skull. I went and examined the skull closely. On the skull was painted in detail the symbols of the stars, moon, and sun. It showed an arrow pointing down to the figure of a man. This was the message I was being shown. The Ais knew they came from the stars and this was their sacred way of communicating with the skull and the Star Nations. I let my eyes take in everything and I touched my crystal to the crystal power wand of the skull. (Crystals all love each other, and they know each other.) I thanked the Spirits for bringing me here and left with my grandfather.

I still wanted to see the Ais People. I wanted to know them as they truly were. So we crossed the spring water again, and took the path to the village. This was a large village. The Ais People had a fierce warrior reputation and I wanted to see how they looked and how they truly lived. Their sentries were posted well up in the trees, with platforms built for them. Up that high, they could see any movements coming from their areas. These were lean built people, but you could see they were lean only in size, not in muscle. The heat of the swamp makes everyone sweat, so it is hard to have excess body weight. I noticed some of the spear points were coral shell, which is extremely sharp; others were flint. They wore only loin cloths. Arm bands were mostly of beaten copper. Some arm bands were of shells and they were very pretty. Some had necklaces of gator teeth others had panther or bear claws. A few of them had shark's teeth necklaces. I let my spirit pull me to go inside the village.

The women were lean and strong like the men. All wore skirts, some long some mid-length. Most were dyed and woven from plant fibers. Others were of tanned hides. Shells, pearls and stone beads were their jewelry. I watched and felt the flow of energy of these people. These were relatives but their enemy was aggressive. The only laughter I could hear was from children. Everyone was busy. Foods, hides and crafts were being done everywhere. In the center of the village was a large fire. I knew instinctively that this was the heart of the village. It would be the Sacred Fire of the village, and these would be the Sacred Fire Keeper and his apprentices, who took care of it.

The homes and structures were pretty much the same. They were all built solidly, with posts sunk into the ground and framed in a round shape. There were woven mats of palmetto used to make the sides and roof. All were raised about four feet from the ground. I heard a commotion and followed the sound of the noises. People were shouting and cheering, all grouped around something. I went to see, and what I saw, I had experienced myself. A young boy was naked facing a huge bull alligator. The boy was circling him, making the alligator follow his movements. Every few minutes, the boy would take his hand and smack the alligator on his mouth, which was opened. I knew this method. It is used to make the alligator close his mouth. The alligator spun and swung his powerful tail at the irritating boy, but the boy easily dodged it. I could see that he had trained well.

The boy rushed in and smacked hard on the alligator's mouth again. (The alligator and crocodile's mouth opens very slowly. The muscles are mostly for closing the mouth and it is always the top jaw that you slap, for it is the top jaw that moves, unlike the two-legged whose bottom jaw moves.) The bull alligator closed his mouth, and in an instant the boy rushed in and grabbed his mouth with one hand and wrapped his other arm around the jaws, and jumped on the alligator's back. The alligator's feet are dangerous as well, but the boy positioned himself correctly and the alligator couldn't use his claws or his feet to hurt the boy. The boy pulled back on the alligator's mouth and neck and the gator rolled over. The boy maintained his grip and held on for dear life. The alligator was rocking side to side. The boy now wrapped his powerful legs around the alligator's upper body. The alligator struggled for a little while longer and then went to sleep.

The crowd cheered and were all praising him for his courage, strength and skills. His eyes were sparkling with pride when he released his grip of hands and legs and scooted away from under the alligator. He quickly ran over to his family and clan members, accepting their joy and praises to him. Several men rushed in and tied strong braided vines on the gator's mouth and tail. Then several more did the same. Others rolled the gator over and waited. In a few moments, the gator was awake and very angry and went to thrashing his body in different directions. The men were prepared for this and they pulled hard. The gator struggled at this new nuisance for a while before he tired of the game. I knew this would continue with other boys, and yes, other gators would be used as well.

My grandfather and I left and made our way back to the Sacred Fire. I knew that the dwelling of the Holy Ones would be near the center. I just wanted to see a few things. So I let my spirit guide me to where it would be. I saw what I expected: spirit bowls, crystals, herbs, and the circular beaten copper discs. Each disc was about the size of a large plate. I was searching for it because I knew that this was part of the oral history my people spoke of. We, my own tribe, have these discs. I examined it closely to see what all it would say. It was slightly different from ours, yet it was very similar. (These discs are sacred items. The Muskogee, Ais, Cahokians, Mayans, Aztecs, Incas, Anasazi, Egyptians, Atlanteans, Lemurians, and Tibetans all had discs of this nature. Scientists and archaeologists have failed to explain these as in many other things. The Ani-yun-wiya also have these discs and still do to this day. They are hidden well.) These discs are a symbol of who we all truly are. They are a symbol of the universe: that we are all connected or related, that all arrived at the same time, and all are equal. The faces in the centers are all female, for it is the symbol of birth and of love. Throughout the universe, the female is the most powerful in energy and especially love. Why on this planet all the Ancient Ones of all civilizations were controlled and ruled by females? It is because of their hearts and their natural powerful energies. The Universe gives birth to planets, stars, moons, meteors, etc. These planets, stars, etc. give birth to others. The reason this planet is being destroyed and polluted is because men have seized power and authority and have no love or respect for her or for women in general now days.

Even the women have so long been subjected to this that they accept these things. If women were in charge again, then you could bet that all this foolishness by governments would cease, for women are creators of love, beauty, harmony, life, and joy. They would not allow the forests to be destroyed. They would not allow the waters to be garbage dumps and polluted. They would not allow the Mother to be dug in and bombed, or experimented with. They would not tolerate the war on children and elders. They would not allow children to starve or elders to be forgotten.

Men are only guardians and providers for women, to provide even in breeding, but that is all. Everything that has ever been created has a role and a purpose. Men have forgotten theirs and women have forgotten as well. This is why Mother Earth will call her relations to come to her aid and correct the wrongs committed by men.

It was time to continue our journey so grandfather and I let our minds clear and pictured our next destination. Quickly, we were there in the lands of the Jeru (pronounced Jah-roo).

This too was in my homeland: the central west coast of Florida. This was not a large nation, but they were extraordinary in their crafts and water travel. Oral traditions I had learned said that the Jeru traveled across the waters great distances, that they knew the waters extremely well, and were great hunters. (They are said to have secret locations under the coral reefs where ceremony was conducted.) We had arrived. We recognized the river immediately. We were on the Crystal River.

Manatees were swimming everywhere and the eagles and other birds were numerous. Flocks and flocks of them filled the trees, the skies, and even the water. Many boats lined the shores, and many were different sizes and shapes. Some were burned out elm trees. Some were like flat bottoms, and several were designed for open sea. These are the ones I wanted to see closely. These were canoes, yet built also like an outrigger, which meant they had arms swaying out to help with balance and stability. These arms were fashioned beautifully. They were made from bamboo and bent while heating them over a fire.

I looked inside the boats for items, and saw spears with lines of leather attached and coils of braided vines, nets, catch baskets, and several large clubs with stones protruding from them. And then I noticed an item that caught my eye. Yes, I knew this is what we measured waves with. It is designed with bamboo into an oblong sphere with circles within circles. Each circle is a measurement. It floats on the water when you place it there, and depending on where the waves hit it and the distance or time between waves, it lets you know how far from land you are. With these devices you could travel the waters to other islands, nations, even continents. With any knowledge of the stars, weather patterns and reading water, you could go anywhere.

We turned and went to the village. Fish racks were everywhere, sun-drying the catches. Shark skins were on frames and large sea turtle shells as well. Seaweed was drying on poles to be eaten later as well. Throwing nets, drag nets, and driving nets were on hanging poles all around. Everyone was busy, doing whatever their responsibilities were. Oyster shell jewelry that had been drilled and shaped was on all the women, making flash and glitter in the sun. They wore mostly grass woven skirts and their hair was pulled forward and "bunned" to shape like shade for their eyes. The men were wearing only loin cloths, with different amulets hanging from their necks and ears. Some had discs piercing their chest and lips. A few had these oyster shell discs hanging from pierced noses at the bottom of the nose.

I noticed the beautiful woven baskets next to the homes. These baskets were woven from grass or bark. I checked them out closely, for their baskets were highly prized by all tribes according to oral tradition. I could see they had split grass after soaking it. Instead of the usual wrap technique, they had braided them using five strands of grass. Then they had started their coil, then the wrap. These could then be added to. Of course many were dyed using roots, berries, clays and even stone, to get the pigmentation they desired. Their pattern work was beautiful though. It was somewhat similar to our known patchwork techniques, but these were different. The hickory bark and palmetto bark baskets were just fantastic. A lot of work went into them as I could see. I had watched the grandmothers working in my own village and I could tell these people took great pride in their baskets.

It was now time to move on and continue our journey so we walked back to the river; saying goodbye to our manatee friends, and clearing our minds.

This was real beauty. There were stone-laid pathways all over the mountains as far as the eye could see. We were in the land of the Maya. Much of the Mayan and Aztec cultures were very similar to the Muskogee. The astrology and geometry were very close. Most of the religious practices were very similar. The Sacred Fires were identical and the use of crystals was universal. The fact that they used pyramid mounds was identical to all the mound builders, something the scientists and archaeologists still haven't connected the dots to understand.

We were in Maya land at a time they were building, not at the close of this mighty Nation. Runners passed by us every few minutes as we walked toward the beautiful city. I love to see beauty and this was a beautiful city. The stone structures were true craftsmanship, true works of art. What scientists still haven't figured out in every major ancient city where huge tons of stone are laid and precision cut, is how. Yet even a small boy like me knows how. It is done by the Sacred Crystals!

Scientists now know that crystals are holders of energy and they amplify energy, yet in the scientists' and scholars' minds, which are boggled with garbage, they miss this key point. Artists of stone are holy people. The crystal power wand can be used as a laser! That is right, a laser for precision cutting. Yet, scholars think all aboriginals are ignorant savages and would scoff at the idea of native aboriginals having knowledge of medicine, astrology, physics, mathematics, theology and on into quantum physics, and time travel. Yet once again they miss another key science: zero gravity. They have no concept of using a crystal generator to alter the energy fields of matter around something and make it zero in weight. Nor are they familiar with an energy field pulse wave. They can figure many things, yet never figure that a Native person is naturally aware of these things.

I haven't met a scholar yet in my life that can feel or understand any of these things. They just look at me with shock on their faces. When a stone person, one who knows the stones, can make a generator stone, alter all energy and matter around it and using a power wand plus the energy the stone person channels into the crystal and then can lift a forty ton stone like a feather. It is how the little man in Florida built a coral castle. He was a stone person, and the energy at that point is a crossing of magnetic fields. With all of scientists' machines and technology, they haven't discovered the power of their own true mind. Each of our minds is extremely powerful. It has enormous energy, if one trains in using and developing his own mind. Each person's mind is a muscle. If you don't exercise it, and push it, then it will grow weak. Just as if you didn't use your legs, then you would lose all the strength in your legs. People now days let machines do their thinking for them.

They are destroying the most powerful computer that exists in the universe.

As we walk into the plaza, the aroma of all the food sent a variety of delicacies to us. I wanted to go into the pyramid to see the ancient skull. I knew it was here. I could feel it as it pulled on my spirit. So I cleared my mind and let spirit guide me. We were in a subterranean chamber. It was all stone, but beautiful in all the work. Priests were all around and most had masks on.

Now most of you don't understand, why a mask? Why do almost all ancient cultures use masks? What is their significance? In doing a lot of ceremonies, especially involving the spirit worlds, you encounter bad spirits, bad energy. The masks are worn to hide your true identity and to represent a powerful spirit to them. This keeps the Shaman, Holy Person, Priest, Sorcerer, Witch, etc. protected from being followed back to this world and having bad things start happening or bad spirits coming back with them. In Spirit work, the power of a name, word, or person's identity, is having that power to use! That is the reason spirits generally give you a false name for you to call them. They don't want you to have power over them, just as you don't want them to have power over you.

The priests were being instructed by the crystal skull. Its power was strong and filled the room; touching all of their minds, giving them the information that they needed. The information on the planets' movements and alignments was being given to them. (To this very day, scientists have no technology that can match any of the ancient civilizations' knowledge of astrology, measurements of distance of planets and stars, without a telescope or even satellite images they still can't explain how any of them did these things.) This skull of crystal could always tap into all the other skulls and power wands for more information. Also the crystal skulls are all capable of tapping into any planet, star, meteor, comet, and even a black hole.

If any of you have doubts about this; go to the ancient sites and examine the histories written in stone. For instance, the Hopi tablets, all written in stone, tell of the different worlds and the Red Star and the Blue Star. The problem with all archaeologists and historians is that they don't live the life they proclaim to be an expert on. That is why their interpretations get all messed up. And even modern day Native People have not followed the ancient ways, and they haven't a clue either as to what certain signs, hieroglyphs, pictographs represent.

Only those who have been brought up the old ways, practice the old ways, and believe in the old ways have the true knowledge. It is a way of life incorporated into everything you do, see, hear, smell, feel, taste, wear, or want in life, and it makes no difference how old you are or how much you don't know. You can always begin to learn and open up yourself to knowledge: who you are, what you are, what you will become, and to the gifts you were born with. That is another of those choices in life only you can decide. We all have choices to make. No one can make them for you because all choices must be done freely; so you get what you choose, or what comes for that choice.

I listened to the harmonic pitch and tones, seeing the energy it produced in the chamber. This is another example of archaeologists and scientists not understanding the importance of the stone's structures because they are designed for acoustic sounds; for harmonic frequencies in order to harmonize everything in the whole chamber. I felt my body responding in spirit to the energy of the musical notes. I felt wonderful and at peace with everything. That is the power of sound and energy flowing in perfect harmony.

My grandfather touched me, and we left.

We were back outside of the pyramid and just walking when my grandfather said we must hurry. So we cleared our minds and let our spirits free. We were now in the land of the Aztec. The cultures of the Nations were so similar it was as if we hadn't left any of them. This was a mighty Nation. Prosperity was evident everywhere. Workers were busy as bees. The people were all doing something. Everyone was smiling though, which is always good to see. The colors of brilliant flashes of cloth, jewelry, and feathers were truly beautiful to behold.

Artists were busy everywhere: potters, sculptors, carvers, silversmiths, coppersmiths, goldsmiths, weavers, cooks, and leather masters. People were everywhere. Never had I seen a Native civilization so crowded.

It brought tears to my heart, knowing what was to happen to all these millions of people, murdered, enslaved, diseased, tortured, robbed and raped of their very being. I never have come to grips with modern civilization's excuses for these acts.

Talk about genocide, and holocaust, how can anyone excuse the mass annihilation of over 200 million people? War crime charges against Spain, England, France, The Catholic Church, Portugal, Italy, Russia, Germany, and the United States all must come to pass. All the governments and Churches were financed using the robbery and murder of all these millions. And it is still being done today.

I notice that many people and governments have been tried, convicted, and had their monies and properties seized and returned to the original owners for other peoples; but never has any such thing ever been done for any Native Nations in North, Central, or South America. But I know in my very soul that justice will be served to all the people who still do this, all those who allow this to be done, and those who have extorted and still profit from their greed over the Native Peoples. And when the time comes, and it will be soon, the Native People will once again protect and cherish the lands, and all their relatives as in the old days.

I felt the pull of the skull. It was near and it wanted me to come. My grandfather and I cleared our minds, and then our spirits went to the energy pulling us from the crystal skull.

We were instantly in a deep underground chamber. It was so beautiful that tears of joy came to my eyes. The walls were all covered and sculpted from jade. There were also inlaid mica tiles, turquoise, onyx, gold, silver, and crystal. Sculptures were everywhere. The floor itself was all inlaid with stones. Something pulled me to look at it clearly, so I studied it intensely, memorizing the layout.

Yes, there was a message. A story was laid out in code. This I knew. Then I realized it wasn't completely in the floor: it was a coded message in the walls, the ceiling, and the floor. Yes, I could see that it was very well designed. Only a few would know the code. Others would never be able to decipher it. It did openly speak of the stars, star travel, and the events of the future. That was the message all could see. But the other messages were the real treasures, and I knew the crystal skull wanted me to see this, for one day, a time would come when that information would be needed by the descendants of these people.

A tall female, beautiful in every sense, came into the chamber. She was extraordinarily beautiful, for her spirit radiated beautiful rainbow colors from her. She moved like a jungle cat, so graceful, yet perfect in silence and motion. I knew she was a gifted one, the moment her eyes turned to us. Normally no one can see us unless we ground ourselves there, or we allow someone to see, or as in this instance, the person is truly gifted with spiritual awareness.

She greeted my grandfather first as respectful custom required. She was so calm about this that I knew she saw spirits on a regular basis and was used to this. My grandfather, as was custom, did not look directly at her; or as some would say, lock eyes. That is not good manners. They spoke to each other about family, weather, and about their Nations, and even time events. This is the correct way. You never start speaking about what you really want to say until the host invites it. It is always good to ask about family, conditions and such, to show respect, compassion, gentleness, and honor. This relaxes everyone, and gets people speaking from their hearts. Not once had she even acknowledged that I was there. It would not have been proper.

But, she was aware. I could feel her power, seeking out answers. I knew she knew and was aware of my gifts, for we all feel the energy and vibration of energies from each other. That is why most gifted people always know the other gifted ones. Many times you see them in visions, long before you ever meet them, or you'll feel a particular energy and you will recognize that energy whenever you encounter it. Many people might call one like her a sorcerer or high priestess or such. No title like that means anything. She knew she was a gifted one, chosen, and accepted that.

Titles, names, and labels are what other people use for their own concept of gifted ones. That's like calling a Holy Person a Medicine Man or Woman, or a Shaman. Each of these has different meanings, yet one can be all at the same time. And, no matter how many people you help, people will always treat you as different, yet never let you close, and still have a fear of you no matter what because they don't understand. And anything they don't understand, they always have a fear of inside of them.

After they went through the respectful greetings and acknowledgements, she asked my grandfather about me. He smiled and told her. And then told her she could talk to me. (Children always have the most powerful energies because their spirit is still new in the physical form, and their spirits are more powerful than their fleshy body shells. Their minds and hearts are pure and uncorrupted. In all ceremonies, in all civilizations, Children have been used and invited so the work being done is guaranteeing that it will be perfect.)

I was glad for her to talk to me. I was on my best behavior, totally respectful and humble. She was a woman and therefore the true power, I being here for the purpose as a guardian and helper for the true power. Women are the true gifted ones. Men, such as I are only gifted for the purpose of guardians, helpers, keepers of the knowledge, and to keep the Truth Alive. We help the young and old alike to understand their true powers and how to develop their own powers and knowledge.

Being a gifted one is not easy. You have a heart that is of love and beauty, very emotional, because you feel everything so strongly. Your senses are bombarded with things constantly. You are always attracted to women and women are always strongly attracted to you, for you are never truly like other men, and other men will always have resentment toward you, jealousy of you, and fear you, for they can never understand why and how you do the things you do. And your heart will get you into trouble because others don't understand your heart. Most gifted ones are always hurting inside. Because their hearts are so full of love, it pours out to others. This causes jealousy amongst most women because they treasure the love and support they get and don't want to share this with anyone else. That's why being a gifted male does have downfalls and pains. I was here to serve the Power, and I could see that this truly gifted one knew this. When she touched my head I felt her in my soul. Here was a young woman who truly understood her purpose in life. She was a daughter of the Stars, daughter of the Earth Mother, daughter of the Moon; daughter, mother, and sister to all that existed. Her heart touched me like that of a sister who missed me for a long time. She lifted my head up to look into my face.

She was smiling. And then she told me: "So young yet so old. You have been through this many times, young brother. You were born a gifted one, yet this time you have brought a gift most gifted ones only dream of. You are gifted with the sacred stones and skulls. I feel your connection to them. Even I am not that connected. Your gifts are very strong and developed for one your age, but I can see why with your grandfather here and I also see that your other grandfather is a very powerful one. You will be wise to learn from them as much as you can; and never forget what they teach or show you.

"Your life will be very hard, with much trouble, and you will suffer. You will lose much, but in the future you will be blessed and will be one with many Nations. Many will fear and hate you, for none understand us, and most men want our attention always yet they don't understand that we have to serve the True Power before anything else. When we are needed, we answer the call. But it has always been that way for the gifted ones, female or male. Our lives touch many people, yet we are always lonely for understanding and acceptance. The love we have is never the love we are given in return.

"So just remember to trust your heart. It will cause you to

suffer, but it will also cause you to become stronger and more capable to survive what you will endure. But also remember this: don't let what will happen to you harden your heart. Your heart must have compassion for all living things. Love is what your heart must always strive for. Now you must go to the skull; it is calling for you. We will meet again someday, young brother, I feel this. Dimensions in time are still full of energies. We will talk more, one day. Now, let us go."

She walked over to a stone wall and touched a certain stone. There was a "pop" and the wall moved inward. She walked through and we followed. As we entered, the chamber was lit with the glowing light from the crystal skull. Other crystals surrounded it, including a beautiful tabby crystal. This chamber, I recognized, was set up for a powerful power source with the tabby crystal, a key crystal, two double terminated power wands, two teachers, two record keepers, and four beautiful long narrow power wands.

The crystal skull sat upon a beautiful large jade stone. The crystal skull was programming all the other crystals. The vibration was pure joy to me. I was here to observe and remember, so I began looking intensely at everything. The walls, the floor, the ceiling; every detail I programmed into my memory. Then the beautiful lady touched me and the vibrations in the chamber gentled down.

I felt pulled to the skull, so I allowed my spirit to be drawn to it. I looked intensely at the skull and then placed my left hand on the skull. I was to receive a message that the skull wanted me to have. My mind was flooded with images, smells, feelings, and sounds that were programmed into my mind. After a while I was feeling very, very weak and my grandfather touched my shoulder and said we must hurry back. The lady was gone. We cleared our minds and let our spirits return back to our bodies.

My body was very, very cold. I was so weak that my grandfather helped me sit up and told me to get nourishment into my body fast. He would see me later and we would continue my education. So I got up and began walking down the path, picking wild plums and eating acorns as well. I knew I needed food and rest so I must be cautious because sometimes you have a tendency to make mistakes when you are weak, sick, or exhausted and the swamp lands are no place to make mistakes lest it be your last one. I made my way down to the water and looked for crawdads and mussels. Finding several, I ate them raw. This was good protein my body needed.

I kept walking until I came to several of my fish traps. I was fortunate. They all had fish inside. I emptied them, placed the traps back and walked back to my home in the trees. After eating and drinking plenty, I let my body relax to get the rest it needed.

Remember to Walk in Beauty and Love Always!

Chapter Nine

The Ani-yun-wiya-Part 2

I had eaten everything I could to replenish my body. I was so tired and weak. After eating, I went to sleep. It was late afternoon, close to evening time, when I woke up. I never had been so exhausted. I climbed down from my tree, stripped naked and went to bathe. Diving into the crystal clear ice-cold water will surely wake you up. I swam for a while just to loosen up my body, stretching all the tension out. Then, I got out and walked to find soap root, buttercups, and dandelions. I used the soap root to lather and wash my body. Then I rubbed the buttercup juices from the flowers on as deodorant (smells good). Not too many predators eat buttercups. Ha! Ha!

The dandelion I used to make tea. Why? Well first my body needed a cleaning out, but mostly it was for any type of cold. My body temperature had dropped so dramatically that I risked getting a cold. The dandelion root and petals would take care of that for me. Sure there are other plants I can use, and I do use them as well, but the dandelion is handy here where I bathe, so I used it.

When I finished, I went and unwrapped some of my fish from the palmetto leaves I had placed them in. I dug my hole, cleaned my fish, and using some wild onions, I covered them in clay and started my fire. While it was burning I went and gathered me some cattail tubers, saving the tops for flour. Yes, cattails make good bread. Then I went and picked some fresh poke for salad and some good moss and mushrooms. This would make my meal.

After eating I wanted to offer my prayers of thanks to all of the spirits who help me and protect me. (I have made a commitment to Spirit, and all of the spirits of things, to offer my prayers of thanks and respect to them always. I pray this way at least four times a day unless I'm preparing for a special ceremony, then it's seven times a day.) It is very important that anyone who prays should always make gift offerings. By this I mean that if you pray to bear spirit, you make offerings to the bear that the bear would enjoy having, such as berries, honey, fish, or such. If you are praying to the wolf spirit, you would offer things to the wolf spirit that the wolf would enjoy, such as rabbit, venison, mouse, etc.

If you want something specific from a spirit, then you must show your sincerity and willingness to honor that spirit for what you ask. Sometimes this requires sacrifice of your own self. Sometimes you must make something very special and offer it as a gift. Sometimes you must sacrifice all your food, water, even sleep, to the spirit or spirits. It all depends. But you must always offer gift offerings of thanks. And, if you are blessed by a particular spirit, then make sure you always honor that gift and pay respect and gratitude to the spirits.

The problem I have noticed over the years of my life is that hardly anyone wants to truly give of themselves to learn something. Even if they have a natural gift and don't know how to use it, they would rather forget about it than put forth a serious effort to develop it to help. People always tell me they want this or that, or they know this, but don't have the time. Then there are those that seek power, thinking they can get it from you, or that you can give them power. This shows they don't know who they are or what they are!

And a teacher is always responsible for what and who they teach. Then there are those who want to shortcut this or that, never wanting to go through the full process; just wanting it now. It doesn't work that way. You develop slowly, just as you grow slowly. You develop your power, your gifts, your knowledge, by practicing, learning, and experiencing this each and every day. And you never quit learning. Every day there are things to learn. A child can teach you. A butterfly can teach you. Everything that exists can teach you if you are truly trying to learn. Even when bad things happen, you can learn things from this. Your whole existence here is a learning experience.

Most important in life is a constant prayer. Your thoughts, your actions, what you see, what you say, what you hear: these should be a constant prayer. Be thankful for all that you see, hear, feel, taste, enjoy, touch, know, learn, desire, and even dream about. No matter how hard life gets, if you truly understand Spirit then you will be giving thanks.

After my prayers and offerings, I needed to just relax and reflect on all that I had seen, learned and experienced. Truly think on every detail. Why? Well, because if you truly reflect on all things, many insights, messages, answers, even things you don't automatically recall, will come to you. Always remember: wisdom comes from understanding, knowledge, and experience.

I walked down a path to a beautiful spot that overlooks a natural crystal clear ice-cold river. I dove in and swam, feeling the icy cold shock and refreshed my body. I dove down to the bottom, letting all the air out of my lungs and letting the heartbeat of Mother Earth harmonize to my heart. (This ancient water ceremony goes back to the beginning. When we are in our mother's womb, we breathe water. We feel her heartbeat and our little heart beats in harmony with her. That is why when the European Christians came over here and talked about baptizing in water, we said okay; because the water ceremony was ours before there were Christian beliefs. Only our water ceremony is a lot more intense and pure. It heals the heart, spirit, and body every time.)

The way the water ceremony affects you is dramatic. The calming effect is automatic, letting all your thoughts, worries, and feelings loose and floating in the water. The water has a vibration as well. This vibration touches your vibration, until they become one. Your mind empties into the water. Water is a conductor. It is a power; a truly great power. Your body is made of mostly water. You feel everything, yet you are weightless. You are free, yet you are one with the power. Most people panic when they think of their bodies. Their minds play tricks on them. They go into shock. Shock kills and destroys from fear. Why fear water? You breathed this water as an embryo, as an infant in your mother's womb. Forget the body. Let your spirit be in control. Not your body. Not your mind, but your true inner self which is your spirit. You are a part of and one with everything in the universe.

Why fear, when you are what you fear? This ceremony is very sacred and has been used since the beginning by all the People, but it too takes time developing, just as all things do, unless you were brought up this way.

In the old days, when a child was born, it was carried to the river by the mother and clan mothers. It was cleansed, purified, and offered to the Sun and the Earth Mother:

Behold this child, which is yours.

Behold the child in Beauty, Harmony, Love, Honor, Truth, Generosity, and Courage.
Behold this child and accept it back into your womb, to feel your heart, your love, always.
Behold this child and bless it with your gifts and protection.

The child is submerged in the water after each prayer no matter how cold it was or how hot it was. This was done every single day. The morning ritual of bathing and praying was done by everyone. The women, girls, and small children went to one area; the men and boys to another area. This Sacred Ceremony served several purposes. First, it connected everyone back to the Mother and purified them as being reborn pure. Second, it paid respect to the Sun for the gift of its light, power, warmth and another day of life. Third, it harmonized the spirit and body to the Mother and to the Sun. Fourth, it conditioned the body to strengthen it for all types of conditions.

Imagine it is twenty degrees below zero. Frozen ice is everywhere. You are naked and going into this freezing water not to just bathe, but to connect and pray. Imagine yourself as an infant, not even walking yet, and this being done every day. In tremendous heat to icy water, or from freezing cold to icy water, this way helps the child withstand extreme harsh conditions of weather. Not like today's people who whimper and moan about the slightest discomfort. These are the same ones who get sick very easy. They can't work if they have a headache or their toe hurts them. Who would starve to death if there was not a store to buy food? Just look at the world today. If a storm strikes, people panic. No electricity, no communications, no heat, no food, you call this a major disaster.

I call it a terrible shame and disgrace on the people because of their ignorance; ignorance of who they are, what they are, and their connection to everything in the universe. It's like they throw up their hands and say: "I can't live without machines. I can't live if someone doesn't sell me food. I can't take being in a house without electricity." It is sickening to hear their ignorance. Why? Because their spirits are so weak, their minds are weak, and they can't see or understand the Truth. Discipline of the Spirit, discipline of the mind, discipline of the body, that is what is lacking in today's people. Yet these are the same ones who moan and complain all the time about everything. They want everything yet are not willing to do anything. And when something is given to them they don't appreciate it. They want something else. These are some of the reasons I'm telling this story.

But all these people better change, because Mother Earth is calling her relatives! Our Star relatives have been watching us all along. Some of them want to annihilate all of us. Others want to use the people as slaves. And still others want to use the people as sacrifices. Your governments have known for years upon years and have made arrangements and agreements with all the Star Peoples. They have allowed many atrocities to happen out of fear, hunger for power, and material things. The people of this planet have been used and used for centuries as experiments and amusements. What has happened time after time, when civilizations have degraded all that is Sacred and all that is Truth, is destruction. And that is coming real, real, soon. I tell you this now. Hopefully in knowing this story you can look inside yourself and make the right changes. If not, well, you will know soon enough!

After recuperating all day and getting my strength back, I was ready to go see my grandfather. I went and gathered him some wild plums, muskodines, scuffines, and his favorite persimmons. A scuffine is similar to muskodines, but does have a different flavor. My grandfather loved these wild fruits and so did I. I gave thanks to each of these plant people for their gifts of life and began my walk back to my mother's.

Now, many of you might think it strange for a young boy to be alone in the swamps or any wilderness. But that is not so with all peoples, for we were raised and taught the lessons of life and of death. That is what makes a People strong: how they raise their young ones. If you treat them wrong or just give them everything, they will always be weak: weak of body, weak of mind, weak of heart, and weak of spirit. The laws of Nature and the Universe clearly dictate that the weak shall die. Weakness breeds weakness. That is why all the old ones always pushed the young ones to be the best they can be. In actuality, my mother worried about everything else other than me! Ha! Ha! She knew I was at home anywhere in the swamps or any other wilderness because I was raised that way by my people, and it was my nature as well. Today's society is controlled by governments who want to weaken all people so they are no threat to them, and they all become better slaves. They control how they think, what they desire, how they live, and what they are to become. What is sad is that the people of this world allow them to do this.

It was already around 10:00 pm when I finally saw my grandfather that night. He still looked very tired. I realized this was taking a lot out of him. I quietly stood waiting for him to acknowledge me. When he finished his prayers he said: "Sit, my young Eagle." He knew my spirit, one of my spirit helpers was the eagle, and my being a member of the bird clan on my mother's side of my blood made it all natural. But it had a lot to do with my heart as well, for I could not be quiet about injustice nor sit by when something had to be done, and I was loyal in all things. My grandfather told me I had the heart of the eagle inside of me, and to always treasure this part of myself. It would get me into lots of trouble, but that it would make no difference as long as I was true to my heart. He said whites made their own laws to use against whoever they wanted to and would not apply that same law to themselves, so you will always have them against you, for your heart will make it so. Boy has that ever been so true. Ha! Ha! But I have no regrets. I chose this life. I chose to come back and I chose to experience all of this; just as I chose to walk this path. So I cannot complain.

My grandfather sat there quietly, and I knew he would say whatever he wanted to when he was ready. I sat there about thirty minutes before he spoke to me.

My grandfather said: "I know you want to continue because your time with me is short. But I can't go with you, so I am going to do a ceremony and I want you to pay attention to every detail. This ceremony is a dangerous one if not done correctly, but this will allow you to do many things, learn many more things, and give you the strength and energy to do them all. After I do the ceremony for you, I will stay here to help bring you back. You need to learn this. That way you may help others in their learning. This ceremony will work on any person, even other people who have not the slightest belief or understanding. It will open doorways and pathways for them and give them a truth about all things they can never forget or claim does not exist. Now, go to the cedar chest and bring me out my white deerskin pouch wrapped in a purple sash. It will be on the left side of the chest."

So I quietly got up and went to the cedar chest and opened it up, and took out the pouch wrapped with a single purple sash and brought it back to my grandfather. He took it from my hand and told me to go get a gourd full of water, which I did. He then asked me to go get his medicine bundle, but to only touch the thongs holding it. This I did as well. He then told me to go back in the swamp and to drink plenty of water and to cleanse my body and relieve my bowels and bladder. So, this too I did. When I got back he had his Star Blanket laid out. Now this Star Blanket is not what is made today. This is an old hand woven blanket with nothing but stars, planets, moons, and geometric designs all over it. It is still the most beautiful blanket I have ever seen. It was given to him by his mother, Margaret Glass, a very powerful Ani-yun-wiya woman. She was known far and wide as having the gifts. She was a true healer and was also known for her prophecies. She also used tea leaves to read what the spirits had to tell her. She was a water person, meaning she gained power using water.

Anyway, he sat there and was pounding on a gray root. I knew what this was. It was datura, a very powerful poison plant, but also a very powerful medicine plant. This was my first experience with datura. But this was Power and I was a little nervous, for I had seen people who had danced with the Sister, as it was called. You could always tell the ones who were Dancing with Sister, for they were not in this world, they were radiating power, and they would have the color of the gray root on them. I knew this was something to pay strict attention to, so I concentrated on what my grandfather was doing. I will not tell how it is prepared or how the ceremony is done because some of you might try to do this yourself, which could result in your death. Only those who are trained and knowledgeable about this should ever prepare and administer this powerful helper. So I will leave this information out.

When my grandfather was ready, he reached into his bundle and got out a leather thong about six feet in length. He tied one end around my ankle and the other to his wrist. He got out his gourd rattle and sang a medicine song, asking for the help of the Sister to help me. He then dipped his fingers into the medicine and touched my temples. He then handed me a shell with the medicine in it to drink. Then he began singing power songs. I looked at the blanket. It was alive and all the stars and planets were moving into alignments. I could hear my grandfather in my head as he instructed me as to what to do. I let my spirit free and went into the Star Blanket.

My first journey was into ancient Egypt. I arrived in a beautiful place. Tall palm trees were surrounding a walled garden. Guards were stationed everywhere. Beautiful exotic ladies, barely clothed, scurried everywhere. Then I saw why I had arrived at this particular place. Here was a pharaoh, one who lives as a god on this world, and beside him stood the powerful one. She was extraordinarily beautiful. This was a true Sorceress, a Necromancer of high power. She knew I was there, for I felt her probing with her energy trying to touch my spirit. I was not ready to let her do so, so I used the power of water and called the water spirit to shield and reflect her energies. This seemed to amuse her as I saw her eyes dance with delight and humor. The pharaoh got upset with her because her attention had not been with him, and I could see that this man was a man who was not a good person. His spirit colors were not good. You could easily see that he had let his position in life turn his heart and spirit into something ugly. He ordered the priestess from his sight.

I felt she wanted to be away from him anyway, so as she left I followed her. Oh, this one was mischievous and I guess she liked to play, as she led me in circles. And she tried various tricks to get me trapped or to actually locate me. I was having fun too. I could feel the power of the Sister flowing in me. I knew the Sister was natural at giving people power beyond their own abilities, so I rode and danced with this power, and I knew I could do this a long, long, time.

She led me down a corridor that was covered with cats. Now cats have a true gift at picking up spirits, so I veered off from that and went over the rooms and corridors to avoid them. Next she went to a chamber, but this chamber was burning lots of incense and with plenty of smoke. Not me, priestess! I am aware of the use of smoke. I sent a laugh to the priestess and saw a smile appear on her face. Then she just disappeared. One moment she was there and the next she was gone. I was looking everywhere, using my senses to feel her energy, when in my head I heard her laughing. She then said: "You should know better than to follow an illusion!"

I had to laugh. She had tricked me. I had not been following her, but only an illusion she had used to get me to follow. She had sent her illusion with enough energy of herself to fool me. It was a lesson I would not forget. I heard her in my head telling me to come, to let my spirit touch hers and I would find her, that no harm would come to me, that she wanted to just talk. So I let my spirit free and felt her immediately, and felt my spirit rushing to her. I was in her sanctuary now. This was a Temple, I knew. I could smell the incense and hear the prayer chants vibrating through the walls.

She was sitting on the floor next to a beautiful bath. She held both her hands out and said, "Come, sit, and let us talk." So I sat down next to this powerful woman and just enjoyed her company. She asked me my name, knowing I could never give her my true name. It is a test I knew, so I said you can call me Por'rv [Pohlr'hlru].

She asked me what language was that, and I laughed and told her it was of my people of my time. Then she said, "Well, what does it mean?" I told her in my language it meant that I was a sorcerer, conjuror, witch, or shaman.

She laughed and said: "Well done, then, Por'rv. Now why have you come to my time and my world?"

I told her I was learning all the connections of all the Star People and the Children of the Stars, to better understand the Truth and relationships that we all have. She nodded her head in thought and she said, "It is really quite obvious to all who truly seek the truth. For all peoples of all nations are related. We all have come from the stars. There are the twelve planets plus their moons which all have come from and will return to again and again, until we learn and experience all we can to achieve the highest form of pure love. For that is the true power.

"Every kingdom, every nation here in this time and throughout this world is now trying to keep the knowledge, power, and truth hidden from everyone. They want the power and knowledge for themselves. What these people fail to understand is that in keeping the knowledge and truth hidden, it will become distorted, lost, and even forgotten. But most importantly, they have lost the truth and understanding of even themselves. For in truth, love is given freely without conscious thought or effort. And never can one give love with any strings attached or expectations of anything in return. These same people want everyone to love them, yet they in turn do not love everyone and all that exists.

"For example, the pharaoh here believes he is a god a

vessel that the Spirit uses to speak to the people. Yet he adores his power, himself, and all his worldly material possessions. If he truly was a vessel of the Spirit then he would give freely of his love, his possessions; that all may enjoy the fruits of the love of Spirit. All these great things that are built here are built and designed by those with true knowledge. It is out of their love for all peoples that these are built. It is why they are all built out of stone. Truth is truth and knowledge is knowledge.

"Each stone, each pebble, each item has truth and knowledge if the true seeker of knowledge and truth looks with the eyes and heart of love. Just as you are here, I know who you are and I know what you are, and why you are doing this. You may appear to me physically as young, yet I know your spirit is one of the ancient ones, ones that have dedicated their entire being to guard and protect all of us, the truth, and the knowledge.

"Just as your spirit here in my world is an illusion for me to see, so is the physical form we all take on here in this world. Each individual will see something different because it is what is in each individual's heart that manifests itself.

"We all are created with the pure essence of the Spirit. All of us are composed of the dust of stars, planets, moons, and even comets. Each of us is part water, air, earth, and fire. So what makes us so different; our own selves and the hearts of others? We can do anything, and become anything we so desire to. Yet how many do this? How many put themselves down, lower themselves, hate how they look, hate and despise those around them? When they look to the stars, what do they truly see or feel? Do they even understand why they do these things? Forgive me my friend. My heart aches and is full of sadness here, and I should not waste your time with these complaints. Now, how can I help you?"

I told her she had not wasted my time. In listening to her, my heart went out to her. Yes, it is sad how quickly people forget the truth, but to know and understand that it all has a purpose. What once was will be again. Everything will come to pass and all that she had been through and would go through would not be in vain. It would make her stronger and more gifted the next time; better to help more at a later time. I told her of my world and time, and all that was being taught to the new generations about the histories and beliefs of all the different peoples.

She was shocked at first, then angered. Then she just laughed and I laughed with her. She asked me what was taught about the pyramids. I shook my head and told her what so-called scientists theorized. She didn't know what a scientist or archaeologist was but when I told her, laughter filled the room.

She said, "And these are the ones who profess to be knowledgeable and know the truth?" I told her "yes".

She shook her head and said "No wonder your world is all messed up. Is this what is done in all things?"

I told her "Pretty much so. Governments and so-called authorities dictate what is taught. Just as there are strong, established religious dogmas that dictate how people are to believe. Anyone that contradicts either the government's teachings, beliefs, or what they want everyone to do, will be either destroyed, ridiculed, or imprisoned. They wish to keep all truth and knowledge only in the hands of so-called 'world families,' who control wealth, life, belief, and everything on this planet.

"They even keep their meetings and agreements with their star nation's visitors silent and disclaim that any visitors from the stars have even come. They claim that time travel, astral projection, anti-gravity, lasers, even space travel by the ancient peoples is not only false but totally ridiculous. They even disclaim the importance of the Sun as a source of time travel. These people don't even understand it is a doorway to a black hole. They don't believe in using the power of a tornado, whirlwind, waterspout, or even a hurricane as a doorway. Their concepts of energy and matter are worse than their understanding of vibration power. They believe that Atlantis and Lemuria are only myths, so you can imagine how far away from the truth the people of my time are. They don't even know of the Crystal and Amethyst skulls.

"I know what I am telling you saddens you, but take heart my friend. Have hope, for one such as I will not let the truth be lost or totally forgotten. When I am told by Spirit to reveal the truth to all, I will. When the time comes, I will gather you and others like you from all places, and bring forth the truth and knowledge. When we are called, then I will call for the Crystal Skulls and the Amethyst Skulls to come. And then we will all call our relatives to come to us from the stars to get things right. And the truth will cover the entire Earth.

"There will be those who will try by whatever means available to them, to stop us, and to prevent this from happening, but it will come to pass. This I have vowed to see come to pass through whatever hardships I may gather. And I will do all in my power to protect ones such as you from all harm. I also know you lived in Atlantis and that you are from the planet Sirius, the same as I. But I have come to connect directly to the skull. It has gifts to share with me.

"So my friend, please come with me to where my spirit takes us, for you are part of my future as well. I also want you to know that I know you are the friend of many gifted ones. One especially will be important, your friend Nefertiti. She is truly gifted so you must guide her in her path, and with her power here, she can protect the skull for when it is time. It must not be found by others. I will call it to us when it is time. This is important. I know you have instructed her previously, but many of the secret places will be discovered in the future by those who are seeking treasures and many of the power tools. So the skull cannot be placed in any of the places where anything connected to this place can be found.

"Have her use her authority and have it shipped out of the country. Tell her that there is a beautiful continent towards the setting sun. Follow it until you find this land. There will be mountains full of trees, and rivers, and streams. The skull will guide her to instruct where it must go. I will talk to the skull and show it an image in my mind. That will be where the skull must be hidden and buried. Now, let us go, my friend."

She took my hand and we let our spirits free. We felt the

pull and then we were there, deep inside a beautiful chamber covered with stones of all types, and the walls were inscribed in the language of the Birds.

The chamber vibrated with power as the skull began to vibrate with song and touched our souls. The beauty of song, love and harmony engulfed me. I began chanting a song "Ilanti-Ilanti, Tslagi, Tslagi mani-wi-shi-go" in perfect harmony with the skull. I felt its power pull me and go through me. Holding out my left hand towards the skull, I received the gifts I would need for the future, not to be used until the power time. I then went to the skull and placed my hand on it and sent it the image of why and where it must go for the future, making sure every detail of the location was programmed into it and that the skull must touch the heart and spirit of Nefertiti to get her to help in getting this done.

I allowed my spirit to absorb the love of the crystal skull into myself and fill me with its energy and knowledge. When the skull released its hold on me, I turned to my friend who stood by watching. Her eyes were wide with excitement. A large cobra rose up and faced me. I opened my spirit to the cobra to let it know I was a brother. It danced before me and I could feel its energy harmonizing with me. Its mind touched me and told me it was a friend and sensed that I had a bond with relatives of his, the rattlesnake, water moccasin, and cottonmouth, and it would be my brother as well. I knelt down and faced my friend eye to eye. I knew what to expect, and let my spirit become one with the cobra.

The cobra gave me the kiss, its essence forever marking me with its scent, so all others of his kind would know me as well. I felt the sting then the adrenalin pumped into me. The taste of the poison was on my tongue. My mind opened up to the cobra and I vowed to always remember this. That one day in the future I would mark my body with the cobra for its honor, its love, and its gift to me. (I later had my arm tattooed with the cobra and will wear it in honor of its gift.) The cobra lowered its head and moved off to a pile of stones and gold trinkets to lay and rest.

My friend was smiling. She said "That was beautiful. How did you know it was there for you?"

I told her of my initiation as a child of four summers with relatives of his in my world at my time. The serpent people are my brothers and sisters and they too have relatives in the stars. They are children of the stars as well. Only where they come from they walk on two legs and are larger, but their wisdom is known far and wide. They too are guardians now. They guard all the sacred places and sacred items, and have given their lives to this calling to amend the past of their relatives and future relatives in the stars who took a dark path and started experimenting on children in the time of Atlantis' hey day. It was one of the many bad things that they did that caused the destruction and war to come.

She said she "wished she could remember that time of her previous existence. That way it could help her in her present world and time."

I said, "Really? Is that what you truly wish to remember?" She said, "Yes." I told her that she must be sure and that she had to ask. That's the rules. You must ask before it can be done. So she asked me and I told her to sit down and relax. Then I had her breathe the ancient way of the Ani-yunwiya, and then instructed her to empty her mind, her heart. Then I took her head into my hands, and still talking to her, sent her the energy of myself and Sister Datura. I felt her leave then.

When she returned she was in tears. I held her head in my hands and told her "sometimes the past is painful. But now you must remember. You must let the past go and live for today and the future. What you saw was the atrocities that caused the fall of Atlantis; the same will come to pass here as well. For those who try to control and keep the power and knowledge for their own selves shall fall always. Any time man takes the power for his own to hold it over others, then destruction shall follow, for the true power belongs to woman because of her heart, whereas man is flawed and the power hardens his heart.

"This magnificent city and Nation, with all its glory, will come to an end soon, and your return to the stars will happen.

I will see you in my time, but you will have come back at least seven times before that comes to pass, and each time you too will suffer because of man's heart, for most men have forgotten the great Truth and Law. And even women in your future will have forgotten their true selves. But when the time comes, you will know in your heart and you will feel my spirit and remember me. All of you like yourself will call out with those of my kind and the power of the stones and skulls will help us as we call our relatives to come.

"Those who have lived and destroyed with Darkness in their hearts will be destroyed, and our relatives will help create a new world, a better world. The circle will be complete and the Power of Woman will heal the Mother Earth and all on her. The women, such as yourself, will take their rightful places and teach the Truth and Power that will be used for all. Our relatives of the stars will stay and help in all things, and when we have achieved the perfect harmony of Beauty and Love, we can go to all the places we have been denied for so long.

"So cheer up my friend for Truth is simple and easy to see! It is the lies and deceit that cause confusion and pain.

"For now you must give love to all who will listen, for Spirit will touch their hearts with love when love is given or shown. Laws and the teachings of men will come and go. Only the Law of Spirit will forever have hold and cannot be changed.

"Now I must continue my journey and go to your former world of Atlantis. I must seek the Crystal and Amethyst Skulls that are there. You know I see all these writings in stones here, telling of the migration and relationship to the stars, and I still cannot understand how the people of my time don't understand them. Well, I guess that's another example of government and religious dogmas hiding the truth from all who are not part of their inner circles of elite power.

"Take care, my sister, and walk in Beauty, Harmony, and Love always." I cleared my mind and let my spirit free. I could still feel the power of Sister flowing through my very being. I felt the tug and heard the pops of energy clearly and then I was on my way.

Atlantis was one of the true wonders of the world. Atlantis wasn't just one city of one part of one land. Atlantis was a vast civilization, all directly from the stars. Every one of the twelve planets is represented in the Atlantian cities. The technology of the stars was brought here, and the crystals and skulls were a major part of the power source. The Ani-yun-wiya, Lemurians, Inca, Maya, Australia's aborigines, Aztec, Egyptians, Eurasian, Celtic, Himalayans, and East Indians were all from the stars. That is the reason so much of the original teachings, histories, and cultures were so much alike.

Atlantis was the scientific community where many of the science people did their work. Alchemy was the main work, but genetic research and experiments also. Using the knowledge and technology from the stars together with all of Mother Earth's resources, advanced these civilizations far beyond what is here today. Airships were in use. Submersible boats and diving equipment were obvious. Music and vibrational work was being done by everyone.

What startled me were these people's auras around their bodies. Auras are energies of each person. Energies all have colors and are visual in light and darkness, for it is the energy from within the individual, which connects to their spirit, heart, and mind. It is the energy they put out of what is inside of them. What I was seeing was not a harmonic beauty of energies, but energy of darkness. Power will do that to people.

I was always taught and truly believe that power does not belong to you. It belongs to Spirit. That you must not try to hold on to the power, but let it flow through you, around you, to all things. Yes, you can summon power. You can pull the energy and power from things into you, but only to release them as you direct that energy in and for something good; such as healing or helping someone. What I was seeing was these people gathering energy and power and not releasing it; holding it within themselves, using it for their own uses.

Crystals are holders and conductors of energies. They amplify and magnify all energy that comes into them. They then can be released with a direct purpose, such as a laser for precision cutting, or for communication, or for healing, or even for lifting something. It was obvious the use these people had for the true laws of the universe. Tension was hovering over this place. With all the beauty of these marvelous buildings and structures, it was a place of ugliness because of the darkness of these peoples' hearts. Now, not all were that way. I could see the beauty of different ones' spirits glowing brightly, but the good ones were far outnumbered by the bad ones.

I let my spirit be pulled where it was intended to go, observing all that passed around me. My heart ached at the genetic experiments, for this was wrong. Animals, plants, winged ones, fishes and even people were being experimented on. Heated arguments were taking place between the blues and the grays, authority figures that were in the laboratories.

Blues were a taller people with a bluish complexion. Their minds were always calculating figures, problems, etc. These people were from the second moon of Sirius. Grays were smaller people, with heads with large eyes. Their heads were not shaped like ours today. These were designed for their purpose. They were vegetarians. Their eyes were big like owls for their ability to see with hardly any light. But their eyes did not see as ours do. They pick up heat, elements, and molecules. These people were from what is now called the planet Neptune. Their spirits were generally gentle, but now I could see that they had been taken over by the taste of power. This was sad to me, to see anyone take on the darkness in their hearts because of power.

Machines were being built furiously. Many I have no idea what they would be used for. Many I could reason what their purpose would be, such as a transporter. Transporters are devices used to teleport anything from one place to another. This is designed with the power of crystals. By displacing matter, molecules, and even cells; to separate them, and then upon reaching their destination; bring them back together. This is done by using the crystal's natural ability as an energy field: to charge an electrical field energizes particles, with another generator crystal and a power wand used and programmed to focus the dislocation of matter. Another generator and power wand crystal produces another energy field and it is attuned to the other generator and power wand crystal with the memory encoded of the original matter. It is like two magnets that are opposite each other with two other magnets alike. Each pulls on the other one to make the teleportation work. And since gravity, or I should say zero gravity is applied because of the energy field created by the charged crystal, the speed of these energies is faster than the speed of light, which accelerates to a mass that separates each individual cell or molecule, even atoms.

It is sort of like a tornado. The outside rotates so fast that the inner particles are flung in all directions, only to swirl towards the center, which becomes a vacuum hole. The hole then allows the particles to travel to the pulling force of the other hole, and in an instant all particles are teleported to another location and in a reverse process are realigned together.

Solar domes were being designed to harvest the solar energy from the sun. This would allow them to use solar power as a useful energy in many forms. Precious metals were being worked in intricate designs, but these were also being designed for other machines or instruments. I knew then why there were so many submersible boats. They were mining and exploring the ocean floors. Shells and coral all have a high-energy memory and so are easily encoded for memory. They are also strong and light in weight.

Many volcanoes lay beneath the surfaces of the ocean floors, and the heat of the Mother is easily accessible through the vast chasms of the ocean volcanoes. I studied the walls with the maps showing immense and numerous locations where they had colonies, cities, and ports. I could see that every corner of the Mother Earth was being covered. Numerous places were at what looked to me like Antarctica, the South Pole region of today's world. On every continent, on every major body of water; the Atlantians had ports and cities sending their experiments of "people" to these locations as well. The maps showed the locations of the storage facilities and all were marked with the code of the star language.

I let myself be pulled to follow the guidance of the Crystal and Amethyst Skulls. Then I was there. The skulls were all together now, with the power wands all laid out in between the skulls for the directions, each complementing the other. The skulls were producing holographs, detailing information on all kinds of designs and calculations for those that were studying them.

I saw one that I felt familiar with; familiar with the energy radiating from her. It was the friend I met in Egypt. She was studying the astral physics of matter and particles of the universe. This would help her later on to make star and planet alignments that would have effects on all living things here on Mother Earth. I watched her for a few moments then my eyes caught the one I knew I must see.

This was the True Essence of Woman. She was dressed in a beautiful emerald green gown and had a large emerald on a pure silver bracelet that ran up her arm. A power crystal hung from her neck. It was about sixteen inches long and hung from a silver chain with links of stars that was wrapped around the crystal. The point of this crystal was like needle, and I could feel the pure energy that radiated from it. The woman was tall, extremely tall, a good six and a half feet or more tall. Her hair coiled and wrapped around her head like a crown, and tiny chains of silver with small crystals, diamonds, and emeralds hung freely in her hair. She had beautiful sparkling eyes and I knew then that she knew I was there. She looked directly towards me and I lowered my eyes, for this is proper, for I am a man unworthy of the true gifts of power.

Here was a woman whose heart was so pure of Love that the power flowed like rainbows from her. I knew she was schooling all these women to carry the gifts of power to all corners of Mother Earth letting the skulls program their memories, filling them with information. This is done by the holograph along with musical sounds radiating from the crystals that intensify the hearing of the brain to record it; as well as allowing the students to feel, taste, and smell. The eyes automatically record the image in the subconscious brain, which allows them to recall all of this when they seek the inner self of their spirits. Instant recall will occur.

This is why every civilization known to the world today that is considered ancient, extinct, etc. all has stars, planets, power wands, skulls, etc. etched in stone for all this information was known by all peoples. Yet, scholars today try to make what they represent into something else, but with all their modern technology today, they can't even come close to the calculations, precision of mathematics, planet and star movements, medicines, alchemy, physics, or anything. They can't even cut a stone with the precision the Egyptians did, much less move it if it weighs one hundred or one thousand tons. And no matter what they tell you, in your heart you will know the falseness of what they say.

When I looked up she was standing before me smiling down at me. "Well, well young friend what are you doing here?" she said. "Others here might not feel you sense you or even see you but I do. And others here will and can too. I know what you are. I can feel your energy and know you are a guardian and keeper of gifts. What I don't understand is why you are here now. So tell me why have you come here?"

I looked into her beautiful eyes, into her very soul and let her see my soul as well. I told her "that the time and world I come from was a long, long time in the future. I had come because it was my free choice to come and learn the connections of all Peoples to the stars. But my main purpose was to connect to the Sacred Skulls, for in the future the skulls would be needed again: that even this powerful place would be destroyed.

"Civilizations that come afterwards would steadily forget the Truth and destroy once again; that time after time this would happen; that even women would forget who they are, what they are and what they will become. That man would put them down and enslave not only their powers, but their spirits, minds, and bodies. That in my time women served men which I knew was wrong. The religions and governments would put down women as evil and that they must be silent; that they have to obey the men; and many, many more atrocities."

Tears were flowing down my face as I told her of all the ugliness and evilness that would cover the Mother Earth, for I was a man-child, and man had done all these things and would do more. I was ashamed of my male relatives. She, too, was shedding tears, and placed her hand under my chin and made me look at her.

With her free hand she wiped my tears away and said: "Listen, my young guardian, I have seen in your eyes the future. Your words have cut deeply into me, to all you know will happen. I understand your true purpose now and I will help you with what you must do. As you know these women here will scatter to every direction, to all regions to carry the knowledge, teachings, and the skulls to where they must go. Do you know who I am? No. Well I am the Green Sister. I come from what in your world and time would be called Venus. This is my home planet. We are the people of Love. The one you know as Spider Woman is my sister. We all belong to the True Power.

"My gift to this planet is my love, to bring beauty and love to all the star children. I know what is going on now with all those who are under the influence of power, changing genetics, using crystal energy for bad things. I know destruction will come. I have warned the Councils, but their hearts are tainted. In your path is much difficulty and I can see and feel your loyalty to Spirit. Therefore, I will give you a gift, a gift that is for women, I will give you the heart of a woman filled with love; that no matter what happens, you will have that love in your heart always, and can share that love with all who will listen."

She then took the crystal power wand from her chest and began to sing, her voice so pure, so perfect. The crystal in her hand pulsed and vibrated with power. The emerald on her wrist glowed with a brilliant green and the green energy flowed out from the emerald, engulfing me. The crystal began drawing her energy from her heart and I saw it gathering strength.

Then I felt it as it poured into my chest. Love flowed into me. Everything that existed in me was Love. Emotions I never knew I had, I now began feeling. Songs, dances, and images filled my mind. Beauty was Love, for all Love is Beauty. There is no possible way I can tell you what I felt or experienced. I can only show you, for true love is a power that is beyond the imagination.

When she was finished, she lifted me up and said: "This gift I give you will also have an effect on you. Your heart now is not like others. Your love for anyone will not be like the love they give you, for your love will be complete, whole, and pure. Many will love you, but their love will not be the love you give, for your heart is your strength and you will give it totally and completely. It will cause you to do things others will not. It will guide where others won't go, but it is the love you must have to do what you have to do. Now come with me, for you must give your love to the Circle of Sacred Skulls. You must give your heart to the entire circle."

So I followed her to where she led me; into the center of the Sacred Circle. The Amethyst Skull was vibrating. All the women stopped what they were doing and were all looking at us. Green Sister reached down next to the Amethyst Skull and picked up a beautiful crystal power stone.

She held the stone up for all to see and then said, "My sisters a young guardian has come who has a great task before him. Feel his energy. Feel his love, so you will remember when he meets you again. His purpose is love. His goal is to protect and keep alive the True Power we all serve and live for. His life will not be easy. Hardship and suffering will be his life. He will protect these Sacred Skulls and the Truth with his very life. I now give to this young guardian the Sacred Scepter of Atlantis, the Scepter of Power for a Holy cause. Sing with me now as the Scepter will attune to this young guardian."

I held out my left hand and she placed this beautiful power crystal in my hand. I began to sing and the crystal vibrated. Then all of them were singing with me, and the crystal and crystal skulls joined in. The crystal in my hand began to change form and melted itself to fit perfectly to my hand with a key embedded with my thumb. Blue light began radiating from it, and all up my arm, then began circling us all. The skulls and power wands began releasing brilliant colors of light and energy and encircled us all until it looked like a rainbow shimmering all around us.

And then the skulls all connected to me. I let them see all that I knew of the future ahead, of how the other children would change, of all the destruction and chaos that would plague this world throughout its history, and that I was here to protect them and the Truth, and that I would call them in the future to come with the Women of Truth and Love, to call upon their help in calling our relatives in the stars to help us. The Amethyst Skull spoke to me and said "that all I had said was true, and all had been sent to our relatives in the stars and they would be involved in bringing this about. They knew what was happening even now and would soon put an end to it. They would be watching and intervening when it was necessary, but the Star Children must evolve to a higher being, but for now and later, the Star Children would experience many different things.

"It was all designed by the Spirit, and that all would happen that must happen, that the skulls would always be able to reach me if I would just call upon them, that my heart was attuned to them and this would always be. Then it showed me some parts of the future that I did not know, and told me to be aware of these groups, for it is their desire to rule all. They will try to control the world. Even now they are collecting wealth and materials, and technology to use against the People.

"These secret groups will change names, signs, and symbols but you will know them by their energies. They will put puppets in place as leaders or figureheads, while they are the ones who pull the strings. They will try to act like others but they will not be, and they will always try to act like they care for others. But understand this: their goals will be for themselves to be rulers of this world. The only thing they want is the Power, which will never come to them. But, it will drive them to any lengths to try and get it.

"You will be attacked. You will be labeled and marked by them. They will do all they can to either stop you or turn others against you. You will not have a life of your own, but remember you chose to do this. Your wants, dreams, and even your desires, matter not the least. Your duty and responsibility is for the protection of all the Sacred Truths, the Women of Power, and the Circle of Skulls. The chosen one here has given you a heart of love. The chosen one of your home planet, Sirius, gave you a gift as well. The chosen ones you meet in life will give you gifts to help you in your tasks. Many will give you the gift of their own love, for you will need this.

"I know who you truly are, and will know your energy, but never forget why you are here. Power and gifts can distract even the purest of hearts. Never try to put yourself above others. Never think you are better or more loved. And never use the power or gifts for your own personal wishes. If you do, you will lose the gifts and powers. Then you will have to really make amends and suffer terribly to humble yourself and prove you are sincere enough to get them back. Remember this well, for you already know Spirit, the Creator, Yahwey, Yah-aha-hey-ya, Ra, and all the other names for the True Spirit are one and the same. Spirit is in all of us, and in every living thing that exists, and that is who the power belongs to, not you or anyone else. It is there for you to use, borrow as you will, but it cannot belong to you or any other.

"You are a young man-child now, but you will grow tall and powerful. Your spirit is an old spirit and knows the Universal Code you must live by. When you call, my friend, we will come. Others may come with us, as we will call those relatives of the stars to help put things right. Yes, I can see you realize that even those in the stars will battle as well, for what happens here affects the whole universe. Now you must speak to the hearts of all the women of the circle."

Then I sent my heart of love to the circle of women, letting them know why I chose to do this, why I would always protect the Truth and help them, and that I would call upon the women in the future to come claim their rightful place and power. That I was honored to serve Spirit, the Truth, Love, and them and all their kind; that I would protect Mother Earth and help her as much as I could until the time was called for the return; that all the animals and birds, plants, trees, and all living things were my relatives and I would do all I could to help them as well; that in their futures they would be directed by the skulls to move them to different locations and keep them hidden; that many in the circle would come back again and again to help in this cause, and that I would know them by their hearts and energies; that this Scepter of Atlantis will be with me and you will all know what it is and what it is for, and I will protect it and honor it always.

The women all gathered around me with pure love in their hearts and each placed their hands on my heart. (Till this very day I still feel their touch and will cherish their gratitude, confidence, trust and love they have given me.)

(The Scepter I still have today. I keep it hidden from most people. Many have seen it. Many have felt its love and power heal them and open their memories to the Truth! I keep it in a safe place that no one else can ever find it when I do not need it with me, for there are those in this world who would do anything to possess it, not understanding that it is programmed and is part of me only. It would not work for them, and only I can unlock the power in it. That was part of the Ceremony Green Sister did when I was entrusted with it, and it is attuned to my energy and vibrations only.)

Green Sister then touched my left ear. A hot pain of fire shot inside my ear like it was on fire then went away, only now no sound came to my left ear. I looked at her in confusion. She said "Do not be shocked my young guardian. Understand this: you will hear many things in your life, but you will need an ear attuned to the Spirit, and the spirits of all of us. You now have an ear that can hear only the voice of Spirit, and those in the spiritual realms. This way, when others talk, you can still hear the voice of all Truth. Just as you must live in different worlds, in different times, you must also hear differently than others, and you must learn to listen for Spirit or spirits all the time. Messages will come to you from many places, and in different ways. Now, come. There are things I must show you so you will remember them."

She led me from the circle and took me to another structure. It was beautifully designed and the vibration of the pure coral vibrated with the sounds of the ocean and heartbeat of Mother Earth. She touched a particular spot in the wall and took me inside. There were many, many things she had me memorize and understand: how, why, use of, etc. These were things I had never heard about, things that even today are not in existence. All I can tell you is that they will be available when the time is upon us.

After she finished, she looked deep into my eyes and said: "I know you are dancing with the power of a plant. I don't know this plant but I can see it has enhanced your gifts, power, and energies. This plant, is it near here or only in your time?"

I told her, "Yes, it was all over, just that most people don't know about it. It is a very powerful plant, a very deadly poison, yet if one is knowledgeable in its use and how to prepare it, then it can be used for other uses as well."

She asked, "Would you tell me about this plant and give me a mental image of it?"

So I did, and I knew she had seen this plant plenty of times. She asked, "Could you reveal how it was prepared?"

And I told her, "Yes." Then I showed her what I had seen my grandfather do. She said, "You have given us a better chance now. The women of the circle will learn this and use this in the work they have before them. Now you must follow your journey young guardian."

I cleared my mind and let my spirit free.

(Atlantians still live today. They are very secretive and have their caches of wealth, which they use for their own goals. There are two different groups of them. One is for the truth. The other is for their own power to control all. Most of the ones now are direct descendants of the original ones, only with genetic alterations. They are extremely intelligent and in extraordinarily good physical shape. They do not intermarry with any others. They remain close-knit and all are loyal to each other. They have many gifts and love to be near water and warmer climates. They do not mingle with others unless necessary and they move around traveling all the time; their wealth allows them to do this.

The Atlantis civilization was destroyed by the Star relatives. They came with their ships from space and destroyed the ugliness that was taking place here. This caused tremendous earth changes: tidal waves, earthquakes, tornadoes, hurricanes, and floods. Whole cities were swallowed up by Mother Earth. She opened up, swallowing them then closed back. The explosions of the technology, research, and weapons were destroyed, causing mass explosions greater than has ever been before or ever after, until this very day. Survivors were few and scattered, just as animals, plants, and birds were. Many places turned to ice, others to deserts. What was land became water, and what was water became land. Continents opened up and broke apart, all because of the corruption of man's heart.)

I had freed my spirit to travel to Lemuria, there to gather a gift for the future. Lemuria was another Atlantis, but it would be there that I gathered the other object I was destined to have for the future, and to see for myself how it was there.

Lemuria was a magnificent place, with many beautiful architectural works, sophisticated sciences and technology but a place quite like Atlantis. These too were direct children of the stars. They were building and constructing devices at this time to enhance their power here on Mother Earth. But what I had come for was in a priestess' possession. It is called the Crossed Universe Wand, but it is more than that. It is a double terminated crystal power wand that is crossed at the center with another double terminated power wand. Surrounding the center is a cluster of generator crystals with a key crystal in the center. It is a symbol of the four directions with points of generator crystals shooting out in the other directions between the four directions like a star burst. (I named this crystal wand the Morning Star and she loves her name and is very beautiful.)

I let my spirit pull me to where it was I needed to go, and there I met the priestess. She was very beautiful and stood regally before me. I lowered my eyes and head and waited. I knew she would know I was there.

"So you have come," she said. "I have known you would be coming. The stars have told me. But first I must see into your soul, young one."

So I lifted my head and let her look into my eyes. Her eyes were the bluest I had ever seen. They sparkled like blue diamonds. Her heart was very gentle and I could sense her emotions. I knew she loved the crystal she had been entrusted with, and it hurt her to part with it.

I told her, "Beloved Woman, I say this to you. I will honor and love this precious gift. I will keep it safe and use it only in love. I will only hold it in my possession for its protection until the time comes to place it once again in your hands. You know what is coming as well. This way it will be safe and not be lost or taken by the others. I will know you by your heart and energy, as you will know mine. As you know what is to happen here, you must make ready and send what needs to be sent by those of you who you can trust. Look into my eyes now and see where it is to go. It will be safe there, guarded by fierce warriors who will protect it with their life."

She looked into my eyes and I visualized the area, how to get there, and where it must be put. After she saw all of this she said: "I must show you something first."

She moved again to a large beautiful chest and brought forth a beautiful shell. The shell was intricately carved and she told me to listen. I held it up to my ear and I heard the voices of dolphins. I pulled it away and looked at her stunned. She said it was a divine gift given to her that she used to communicate with the dolphins. She said she could also talk to the whales with it. Its high frequency allowed her to even talk their language. I told her it was extraordinary and wonderful. She then reached down to the altar and handed me the Crossed Wands. It vibrated in my heart. I spoke to it with my heart, and let it feel my love, my respect, and my honor at being its keeper and protector.

The Beloved Woman touched my arm and said: "Strong guardian, walk in beauty, love, and harmony always."

I thanked her and cleared my mind. I let my spirit free.

My eyes opened and my grandfather sat there looking into my hands. Two magnificent crystals were in my hands. One was the Scepter of Atlantis, the other the Crossed Wands of the Universe. He could not see, yet I could feel the eyes that were blind feeling with his senses.

He asked me: "Boy, are you alright? How do you feel? Can you feel Sister still flowing inside of you?"

I relaxed and listened to my body. It was cold, but still strong. And yes, Sister was still flowing strongly in me. I told my grandfather that I was okay, and yes, I could still feel Sister's power flowing strongly in me.

He then said: "You have brought something back, for I can feel its power. No, it's more than one. Is this part of your path?"

I told him of all I had seen and learned and all that had happened, and then I told him of the Scepter and the Crossed Wands of the Universe. He told me I should never let anyone know what they were until the time was upon us; that as long as the secret was hidden, the safer it would be.

It was getting almost daylight now, and I knew my mother and her family would be up soon. I told my grandfather that my mother would be moving around soon and that I should go. He agreed, so I untied my ankle from the thong that was tied there and to my grandfather's wrist. I told him I would see him tonight to continue my journey. He laid his hand upon my chest and said: "You have done well boy and I am honored that I have helped you. It makes me proud of the man you are developing into. I'll be waiting for your return."

I walked quietly into the swamp in the morning fog, which was heavy this morning. My senses were alive with the enhancement of Sister. The crystals in my hands were vibrating with power, so I took them to my bathing area for a swim with me. The water was ice cold as I dove in. Crystals love the water. It is important that they are given baths in fresh and salt water. They also love to sun bathe and lay under the moon. The water came from an underground spring that fed this stream. It wasn't a fast stream, just one that flowed gently, but it was crystal clear and very refreshing. I bathed the crystals and washed them with the white sands, then laid them in the shallows to use the water to energize themselves.

Then I scrubbed myself with sand and just relaxed my body, let all my air out from my lungs, sinking to the bottom, and just let Mother's heart touch mine. Sister still danced inside of me, so I just let my senses take completely over. The water carries many messages and images of what they have seen and experienced, and I waited to hear their stories. So I let my mind and spirit merge with the water. Some stories were funny, some were exciting, but all were interesting. You can learn a lot from the water if you just listen.

When I got out of the water, I stripped naked and hung my clothes on the branches of limbs to dry. I took the crystals out of the water and laid them in the morning sun. Now crystals really love to bathe in the sun. The sun sends energy to the Mother Earth and the crystals were soaking up all this energy. They flashed brilliant colors of rainbow light as the sun covered them in energy. I, too, decided to lie in the sun and absorb its energy, and let the warmth dry my body.

While I did this, I kept thinking about all I had seen, felt, and experienced on this journey and I was thankful that Spirit had blessed me by allowing me to do these things. I knew I had a lot to learn and I prayed out loud that I would not fail or become unworthy of this trust, for anyone can make mistakes. We all do. It is part of our experience we must go through. I just prayed that I would not let anyone down. My life meant nothing to me, only to serve Spirit and those I was entrusted to protect and help.

While I was lying there a shadow crossed over my face. Instantly my eyes opened to see a beautiful eagle above. He circled for a while then flew directly over me, his piercing cry echoing in my ears. Yes, my friend, I know you will help. Thank you for coming to support me. I sent these thoughts to my brother and watched as he circled once more and then glided out of sight over the treetops.

While the crystals were sun bathing, I knew I must eat something to strengthen my body even though Sister still danced inside of me. So, I decided to eat some good fruits that were always available. Wild strawberries grow all over the swamps along with blackberries, and I love eating them. Of course my fingers always change colors. Ha! Ha! So I walked, and ate them as I walked around. I did not eat much because I knew Sister would make me sick if I eat too much. So, I went back to the water to scrub the berry stains from my hands and to drink some water.

Then I went back to pick up the crystals. They were excited and as happy as could be. They were singing to me and so I sang with them. Crystals are very emotional and they get excited very easily, and when they are happy, they will sing. The birds joined in, and then the bullfrogs, so we were having a good time. The swamps are alive with life if you listen. If the swamp becomes silent it tells me that danger or something is about to happen. Even forests are like that too, and even the deserts. Butterflies and dragonflies were dancing in the air, and the trees were dancing in the winds. Enjoying moments like this is what makes life so worthwhile.

Even though I was a loner, I was never truly alone, for all the plant people, winged ones, those that crawl or who have four legs, or live in waters, were always with me. And Grandmother Moon and all the star people watched over me. Even Grandfather Sun always smiled down at me, and sent me his warm love. And always there were spirits talking to me day and night. My neighbors may have been different than those you or others may have had, but they were better to me than your neighbors would have been to me.

We lived together in love and harmony and always respect. The flying squirrels like to play games and are always up to mischief, and I know they never just drop an acorn on my head by accident, or the blue jay who loves to scare me by screaming at the top of his voice when I am hiding or stalking something. No, he isn't just exercising his voice, or the family of raccoons who seem to think that my bed is a good place to commandeer as their own play area while they just happen to get into the things I gather and dry for bad weather days.

Then, there is my little green demon. Actually he is a lizard, but he loves to catch me sleeping, sneak down, and bite my nose. I guess he's just practicing his stalking techniques on a proven warrior. Yeah, we are one big happy family. Oh, my most interesting neighbor is the pack of wild pigs. Now for some reason they love to test their speed against me, because they sure love chasing me every chance they get. Lucky for me they haven't learned how to climb trees and swing from trees yet.

But my best neighbor is the large male panther. I never know when he is going to test me, but he sure spends a lot of time trying to stalk me. I guess he is helping me in my climbing and running skills and especially in my tree surfing lessons. I haven't seen him try that yet, but I'm getting faster and stronger all the time thanks to him

And I sure can't forget all my snake relatives who love teaching me to pay attention to where I step, place my hand, or move anywhere. The rattlesnakes are always nice enough to tell me they are near. Now the cottonmouths, well, they are real territorial, and they will jump down from trees, or sneak up out of the water, just to see if I'm paying attention.

Yeah, my neighborhood is really crowded, not like all you who have space all to yourself. And no one cares about you, to teach all that my neighbors teach me every day and night. Yeah, I live in a beautiful world, full of laughs, beauty, and love, for I love them all. I did have a stray dog pup for a while. Someone had dumped him somewhere and I happened to find him. He was a little one and I liked him, but one of my neighbors invited him for dinner and he never came back.

I spent the rest of the day making pouches for my new friends the crystals. I used some deer hide I had tanned and stretched. I used shells and wooden beads I had made to decorate their carrying pouches. When I had finished them, I showed them to my new friends and they loved them, so I put them in the pouches and let them check them out. They were busy attuning themselves to their pouches as I walked to my house in the trees. I would rest for a while before I went to see my grandfather. I said my prayers of thanks to all the directions, and to Spirit, Mother Earth, and to all the Elements. I said special prayers for all those who were of the Sacred Circle, then for my relatives, young, old, sick, injured, for the plant people, winged people, four-legged people, water people, stone people, those who live in Mother Earth, the Star People, and all those spirits who are on journeys. I prayed and prayed until I finally slept. Grandmother Owl woke me with her hunting calls. I judged it to be about 9:30 at night. I picked up my pouches with my new friends and climbed down from my house in the trees. I went to drink first because I was so dry of mouth. That is one of the effects of Dancing with the Sister. I could still feel her flowing in me. I then went to relieve myself after hanging up the pouches, then came back and bathed. I gathered my clothes that I had left to dry and put them on. I gathered the pouches and began the walk to my mother's home. I gathered gifts for my grandfather on the way. I sent thoughts of love to my new friends as I walked letting them know I was thinking of them while they rested.

I stood by a large old water oak tree near the home of my mother. I could hear a loud argument going on, so I just stood. My step-dad did not want my grandfather around. He worried my step-dad. I couldn't understand the words, but I could pick up the feelings. I knew my mother would argue for him, but this was one of the times when my step-dad was drinking the evil spirit water, the drink that makes people crazy, the drink that caused my father to be banished and my family to bust apart. This same drink caused me to be cursed by all the boys and girls of my own tribe, calling me the pale one, dead man walking's droppings, and even worse.

Why would people use something that makes them so evil and mean? I would never understand this. I could understand if it helped a person, or did not cause the madness, but never have I ever heard that it helped anyone. It only destroys and that is not good.

I heard my grandfather's whippoorwill bird call and I

went to where he was. I knew he knew they were talking about him. I could feel the energy of love going out to my mother. I knew my grandfather would never say anything, so I left him there and stalked up to the house getting as close as possible to the window, where I knew my stepfather was. He was in the madness I could clearly see, so without thinking I let out the loudest panther scream I had ever done, no more than two feet from where he stood. He almost fell down in shock, looking scared and glancing towards the window.

He was talking gently to my mother now. I could see it in my mother's eyes that she knew who had done this. Her eyes were smiling. I then opened my mind and reached into the pouch for the Scepter of Atlantis. Holding it in my hand I activated the key sending my thought to my step-dad. I sent sleeping, tired thoughts, with gentle images of soft wind blowing, the sounds of crickets singing, that he was getting so, so tired, that sleep was peace and full of good dreams. He started yawning and his eyes started dropping. I then sent him an image that he was ashamed for yelling at my mother, and he should love and cherish her, and he should tell her he was sorry and that he loved her.

My mother was startled by what he said. I quietly read my mother's mind. I did not know he did not talk this way to her. He never told her his feelings, so I quickly loosened my grip on his mind and instead sent the deep sleeping image. He hugged my mother and left the room. I released him totally then and ran back to my grandfather. He knew I was there again. Then he touched me and I led him back to our special place. I knew I would have to tell my grandfather what I had done. Even though I knew I had no right to do that, I had done what my heart told me to.

When he was seated, I waited for him to ask me, which was proper. When he did, I told him all I had done and why I did so. He sat there for a while and then said: "You know you had no right to use the gift against anyone without their permission, yet you did so out of love for me and your mother. Your heart is good but rules are rules.

"You put your personal feelings before the Law of Love, Freedom, and Choice. That was your mistake. You did it out of love, but I know you also had personal feelings involved. You left out about your feelings for the evil drink, and how it affected your young life. So you let that influence your decision also, since I know they were arguing about me. You also felt a personal motive to violate the Rule. Rules are placed for a reason, Eagle. They have a purpose. I cannot let my personal love for you excuse that fact. I do not know how the Spirits will deal with you on that, but they most definitely will one way or another. My personal punishment is that I will not help you tonight, because I know how important it is to you and how you looked forward to it. You may think that is a harsh punishment, but you must learn that you must never use the gifts on anyone without their permission, unless lives or life is in danger. We all have choices in life. You made a bad choice. Learn from it. Now leave and think about all I have said and what you did."

I hung my head in shame, for I had disgraced myself and my grandfather, and had violated a Sacred Trust. All that I had thought to do was help, but as I walked I replayed the whole event in my mind. How did I feel? What good would come from it? What bad would come of it? What would the Spirit do to me? What must I do to make amends? I began to have doubts about myself. If something as minor as this had caused me to violate a Sacred Trust, what would I do in more serious matters or events? How could I be trusted with responsibility? Would I not fail, or cause bad things to happen to others? Was I truly worthy enough to do these things?

As I walked I talked to both the crystals, especially the Scepter of Atlantis. I apologized to the Sacred Stone Person for using it the way I had, and that I had not meant to do any harm, and if the stones decided I was unworthy, to please let me know who I was to give them to. I took them back to my home in the trees and pulled out a plug I had made for my stash spot, which fit directly into a knot in the tree limb. I stashed them there and put the wooden plug in.

I stripped naked and climbed back down the tree, and

just started running, running to push my body to the limit, to purify myself. I ran all night long, and when the sun came up, still I ran. I prayed as I ran to the Spirits to take pity upon me, for I had broken the Rule. I did not want anything to happen to any member of my family. If punishment was to happen, let me be the one to suffer. I ran until my legs turned to jelly, so exhausted and dehydrated that my head was swimming. I found some black root and ate it raw, which made me throw up. Then I continued to run a little. I came to a beautiful stream and dove right in and went to the bottom. I never once checked to see if danger was near or not. If I were to live it would be the Spirit's decision. I let my air out, feeling my body go into shock. I lay there on the bottom feeling the heartbeat of Mother. I prayed to Mother that she would not let anything happen to my family or friends, that I should be the one punished. My muscles started cramping and I knew I must get out, so I surfaced and swam to the shore. Dusk was falling and I had things I needed to do.

I walked and searched for Sister as I walked. I wanted to put my body to test. Suffer I must, to make amends for what I had done. After a half an hour, I found Sister and got the root I would need. I jogged and walked for about another hour, until I came to the place I was looking for. I sniffed the air. Yes, they were here.

Snakes have a scent on them. A snake den or a snake nesting ground has a loud smell. I sat down and beat the root. I gathered the things I knew I would need, and began preparing Sister for what I was going to do. When I had it ready, I then went to the snake den. This was a place full of cottonmouth snakes. Hundreds of them were here. I made plenty of noise to let them know I was here. They were my relatives, but I needed their help as well. Several young ones were moving towards me and I sent them prayers and greetings and told them I needed their medicine. As they coiled up I moved to them and held my arms out to them. They did as I had asked and bit deep into my arms. Again and again I had them bite me.

I thanked them and moved away. I went back to where I had left Sister waiting. I then ate what was prepared. I sang my death song and then my personal power song. I sat down, and using a vine, I tied it to my leg and to a stake I pushed deep into the ground. I sang my prayer song as I pushed another stake into the ground and tied a vine to it and to my wrist opposite of my leg. I prayed to my spirit helpers to aid me in my quest to sacrifice myself to the Spirits so that my family, relatives, or friends would not be punished or suffer because of my actions. I felt my body go into shock, then I felt nothing. I let my spirit free to go back to Spirit. I looked back at my body to see myself as I had been, then my spirit left.

I was in another world now, the Spirit World, where I stood before a path. A large eagle sat there and asked me my true name. I told him my true name and he said "you now can go down this path."

In my personal experience, and what other elders as well as tradition tells us, no one can pass through the paths to the door unless you know your true name [Spirit name]. If you don't know, you do not enter and are sent back. I entered the door and walked down the path. I had not gone far when several of my ancestors were standing before me. I lowered my head, knelt on one knee and took my left hand and touched my heart and extended it to them. My great-grandmother took my hand and pulled me up and touched her heart with my hand.

She said: "My child, what are you doing? Why are you here?" I started to answer but she shook her head and continued. "Do you honestly think that what you are doing is going to correct what you did? Do you for one moment think you are the only one who has done something like that? You learn from your mistakes, child. You do not do what you are doing here for something like this. I understand you are feeling ashamed for what you did, but don't be so hard on yourself. You listened to your heart even though it was personal.

"You did it with good intentions. Spirit does not make mistakes. Only we make mistakes. Spirit chose you just as Spirit chooses all others, but even those chosen ones make mistakes. That is what you are learning, to experience and live, gain knowledge from it, and make your knowledge power.

You have a responsibility, and you are putting your personal disappointments ahead of your responsibility. You are too hard on yourself. This is what I say to you. Now listen to the others."

A very tall man came forth. He was very powerfully built. He said: "Blood of my blood, son of my great, great grandson, I am Hawk of the Wind Clan of the Cvsvtv, Muskogee. I have watched you and have seen your training, your growth, and the gifts you have been given in life. You are my blood, so I tell you this. This was a test; a test for you against yourself. There will be many tests in your life, but the greatest test always is against yourself.

"The inner battles you face will either make you or destroy you. Only you will decide that. For example, what you did to come here. You have tried to push yourself beyond even what your young body can take. Sister is a power all by itself. The power of cottonmouth is a power that is very powerful. We see your heart and your worry about what might happen to your family or friends. It is good that you try to protect them, but this is not the way. Who did you offend? Who did you do this to? That is the beginning of making amends. You must first apologize to that man, and speak from your heart. A true warrior stands before those who he has offended. He accepts that responsibility and whatever they demand as payment. This is what the Blood Law of the Muskogee demands."

He stepped back and a very old man stepped forth.

He said: "I am your blood. I am Big Beaver of the Bird Clan of the Ani-yun-wiya. I have watched my children and my children's children for sixteen generations. I have watched you battle yourself since you were born. Your inner struggles that you have fought are of your own making, because of your blood mixtures, the way you look, the way you think others look at you, the way you feel you must reclaim your father's honor for his banishment. These things you yourself have created in your own mind and heart. It was not your father's fault that you do these things. You are not your father. He walks his path and you must walk your own. He makes his own choices and so must you, just as you chose to do this now.

"What you did is not bad or good. It is what you make of it yourself. Have not the spirits already punished you, by you yourself creating your own doubts, fears and unworthiness? You will learn that we create our own fear, nightmares, and everything, as well as create our own problems. This is all designed for us to experience and learn from these battles within ourselves. You have just put your own body in terrible danger. Your flesh is Sacred, because it belongs to Spirit. It was created for you to use. Spirit created it that way for a specific reason. It is not a mistake, but only you can choose only you can fight this fight within you, and only you can decide whether to go back or to stay. You will make a choice now. That is what I say."

I listened to what had been said. I felt foolish for my actions. Their words cut straight to my heart. I stood before them now and told them. I have made my choice. I said: "Grandmother, grandfathers, I see now that your words are true. I have been selfish and made decisions that I must now make right. I will return to my body and I will make amends with the man I have wronged. I will accept his decisions. I also realize that I have created for myself all my own fears and doubts, since Spirit created me to look the way I do. Then, I will honor that as Spirit made me special, different than others, yet the same as well.

"Just as there are red birds, blue birds, brown birds, they are all birds. It is how they see themselves. I know you will be watching me so I say this to you: I will make each of you proud and honor our blood, our clans, and Spirit. I will do my best. I know I will make mistakes, bad choices, but I will continue to walk the path before me, and I will learn from my mistakes. I know I will see each of you again when my path and purpose is completed, and I pray you will open your arms to welcome me, and be proud of me."

I walked back down the path to the door and opened it.

The large eagle sat there and looked at me. Those wise eyes pierced into my soul.

He said: "You have my name, and my people's help. Honor us by being true to who you are, what you are, and what you are to become. We will always be with you. In time of need, call upon us for help. We have made a vow to you, and for you. You did not choose us. We chose you. Live your life in Honor, Loyalty, Justice, Love, Compassion, Beauty, and Harmony. To ride the winds of time and turbulence, even against the storms, you must be balanced and remain strong. I knew when you came that you should not be here, but you had to understand this yourself. Learn from this, young one, and let it make you stronger for it. Now go, so your body will have a chance."

I was thanking Grandfather Eagle when I painfully woke up in my own body. I was burning up with fever, and my arms were swollen as big as my young legs. Sister danced through my body, so I called upon her power to stop the pain. I forced myself to move. I tried to sit up but the stakes with the vines still held me. I forced myself to be patient, and slowly made my free arm move. I had to get myself free from the vines.

After several attempts, I finally succeeded. I called upon my spirit helper, Eagle, to help me. I made my way down to the riverbank and dug up some wet clay. I packed it on the bites, letting the mud draw the swelling down. I drank plenty of water to help my body fight the fever. I had to find some black root. I would purge my body. I couldn't find any. I looked but could see nothing. I heard an eagle scream and looked to where the sound came from. I watched him dive to the ground and I walked to where I saw him go down. He sat on the ground, and using his claws was digging in the ground. I knew this was my spirit helper coming to help me. I thanked him as I walked towards him. He leaped into the air as I knelt down to dig where he was digging. In a few seconds I had the black root. I looked up and he was circling me. I walked back to the river and washed the root. I ate it raw since I had no time to prepare it properly.

Then, I began throwing up. I puked until I thought my

guts were all gone. I crawled back to the river and drank some water, and rinsed my face. I had to go relieve myself badly. I crawled away from the bank and dug a hole and relieved myself. I thought I would die right there. I made it back to the river and crawled into the water. I prayed for help from the Spirit, Mother Earth, and all my ancestors to aid me. The fever was burning me up, so I just went to sleep in the water.

Remember to Walk in Beauty and Love Always!

Chapter Ten

The Ani-yun-wiya Part 3

I slept for a long, long time. My body was cold. My fever had broken. I was still lying in the cold water. The mud and clay had drawn the swelling out of my arms from the snake bites. I lay there a while longer just feeling the love of the water. I pushed myself around and went out into the deeper water where I bathed myself real good diving down and using the sand on the bottom to scrub my flesh. When I had finished I swam to shore. It was about 8:00 a.m. judging by the morning sun.

Then I said my prayers giving thanks to Spirit for giving me life, for helping me, and for the body Spirit had given me. I thanked my spirit helper, the bird people, and especially the Eagle people for coming to my aid. I thanked Sister Datura for her power that still flowed in my body and that would now help me to a speedy healing. I thanked the Earth Mother for her help in giving me life.

It felt so good to be alive. I was a long way from being all right but for now I was thankful just to be alive. (The mixture of these two deadly poisons would normally kill anyone. The venom of a young cottonmouth attacks a person quickly when it enters the blood stream. Being bitten simultaneously by different snakes is putting yourself to death. The poison of Sister is extremely deadly. There is no cure for her death. Mixing it together with the cottonmouth accelerates all your senses and organs, which means it even strengthens the venom of the snakes to be more deadly. It hits your heart like someone hitting you with a rock a big as a tire; with the force of a horse kicking you in the chest. Shock immediately sets in. Shock of this nature generally results in death by itself. This is something that is never to be tried by anyone, for it surely will cause you to die.)

I needed nourishment badly, so I searched the sands of the river looking for mussels to eat. They are a shellfish like an oyster. I found quite a few and ate them raw, washing them down with pure water. I came back to the bank and walked the shoreline until I found an inlet. I was looking for some cattails and I had found them. I gathered the stalks first and then dug up the roots. I washed the roots, which are tubers, and using a mussel shell, I peeled them. I then washed the "water potato" roots again and I saved the peelings. I went to a palmetto bush and gathered some leaves. I wet them down real good to make them soft, then placed the peelings on my wounds and wrapped them in the palmetto leaves. This would make a drawing poultice for now. My flesh was discolored, which is normal for the bites. It destroys the flesh like a spider's bite does.

I gathered my cattail tips, the brown tops, and my peeled roots. I then gathered hickory nuts, pine nuts, acorns, and some moss sponges. I went back to the shoreline and drank my fill of water. Then I dug a pit in the sand and made a fire. While my fire was burning, I cracked all the shells of the nuts and began beating them into a powder. I took the cattail tips, broke them up, and now I had my swamp flour. Using a couple of handfuls of water, I mixed the cattail flour to make dough. Then I mixed in all the nuts except the acorns. (I would have to dig another pit to soak them first.) I then went to look for the fungus plants that grow and mold on the tree bark. This makes excellent yeast. I used a rock and pounded it to a pulp and mixed it into my dough.

There was a good bed of coals burning now, and using a few palmetto leaves, I wrapped my swamp water potatoes in the leaves and placed them in the coals. I found a nice flat rock and built my fire up with the rock in it. As it was getting hot I dug my other pit, put water in it, and dropped the acorns in it. This would help remove the poisonous tannin that caused the bitter taste. When I had the acorns ready, I mixed them in the dough, and then pounded the dough out. I made the cakes flat and placed a few on the hot rock. They began to brown and rise.

I grabbed a big palmetto branch and then wet it. Then I laid it over the fire pit. This would help it cook fast and hold the heat even. In a couple of minutes they were done. Quickly I lifted them off the rock and placed them on another rock to cool. I added a few new ones to the hot rock. I picked up my nut cake, tossing it from hand to hand because it was still pretty warm. Ha! Ha! Then I tore off a piece and popped it into my mouth. It was delicious; plus very nutritional for my body. I laid the wide leaf back over the pit while I ate my nut cake. When those were ready, I removed them and finished by placing the rest of the dough in the pit.

Eating was a pleasure, and I was thankful to Mother Earth for all she had given me; most especially to all those who had taught me these things to survive. When my cakes were done, I used a stick and uncovered my swamp water potatoes. Now, this was a real treat. Plenty of nutrients are in them. I let them cool, because they were very, very hot. I broke one open to help it cool faster. I love these swamp water potatoes. They are very tasty and good for you as well. As much as I needed the food in me, they were especially good.

I had eaten my fill and drank lots of water. I cleaned up the area, removing all signs of my being there. I wrapped my remaining food up in palmetto leaves and carried them with me. I spent the remainder of the day just letting my body recuperate and gathering food.

I caught a large alligator turtle and decided it would make a good soup. I caught crawdads, bullfrogs, leopard frogs, some fat grub worms (wood maggots), and two fat largemouth bass. I gathered some wild onions, poke salad, thistle, wild rose petals, white willow bark, and wild orchid petals. I took all this back to my home in the trees.

I built my tripod, a mini stick tipi, and got out my big clay cooking pot. I fixed my fire to burn slow so I would have a hot fire. I cleaned and dressed all the meats, saving the turtle shell and its head. I would make a nice drum from the shell and a drumstick by using the whole head, dried out and smoked, for the handle. I got my pot full of fresh water and set it on the fire to boil. My neighbors were letting me know that they did not like the smell of fire, so I apologized to them and told them I would leave them some treats.

While my water was slowly heating, I went to a tree that I knew the bees had a nice hive inside. Slowly, using a stick, I got me some nice chunks of honeycomb. I then went and got some wild plums.

When the water began boiling I placed the turtle meat in it to cook. Turtle is real greasy. This would be the first time it was cooked.

While it cooked, I went down to the water and cleaned my arms. The swelling had gone down pretty much, but to make sure, I would clean and redress them. I went up to the tree house and got out my medicine supplies. What I looked for was the oil secretions from the alligator and his dried blood. The alligator, like the crocodile, has a very unique immune system. They do not get infected by any type of wound, so I used the medicine of the alligator on both my arms and redressed them securely. This would speed up my healing. I saved a little of the dried blood to put in my soup. This would get into my blood system faster.

While I was there, I got out my new friends. They were happy to see me. I carried them down to the water and left them bathing in the cool water.

My water in the pot was boiling, so I used a gourd dipper and dipped out the grease and left it in the gourd dipper to harden. I then dumped the water out and squeezed out all the turtle meat. (In properly preparing turtle such as this, it is necessary to do this.) Letting the blood and grease out as much as possible, I went and got fresh water, and set it on the fire to boil again. While it was boiling, I used a large leg bone of a deer and pounded the turtle meat. I then got my honey comb and squeezed the honey onto the meat, working the meat and honey together. When the water was boiling, I put the meat back into the pot. After about thirty minutes, I added the wild onions, poke salad, thistle, wild rose petals, the wild orchid petals, and the shredded willow bark.

I let this all cook for a while then I took the remainder

of the honey and mixed it with the hardened grease from the gourd. Then, using the frog legs, crawdads, grub worms, and the bass I had cleaned, I cut them all up into chunks and covered them with the mixture of grease and honey, and tossed them all into the pot, then added the dried alligator blood. Using a lid I had made from bamboo and had woven together, I placed it on the pot to cook real slowly. This would make a nice, tender, gravy soup of turtle. Then I went to get my new friends and to clean up again. When we were back at the fire, I went and got my makings. This was the dried cornhusks, wild river tobacco, corn pollen, dried hickory bark, dried cedar bark, dried ginseng root, dried holly, dried sweet gum bark, and dried dogwood. I would be making prayers and prayer smoke. This is my own special blend that I use to make prayer smoke. I talked to my friends while I prepared everything.

Now most of you in today's world probably never heard of using corn husks to roll tobacco in, but my people have done it since we were given the gift of tobacco and corn by Spirit. In the Ani-yun-wiya way, this was a gift from First Woman, as the story is told. When she was dragged to death and torn apart, corn and tobacco was planted with the beans. This is where corn and tobacco came to the people. In Muskogee tradition, this was when Grandmother Moon sent her daughters to us to teach us the way. It is where the Moon Dance Ceremony came for all the women. But those are the secrets of the women's societies, not for men to know these things.

See, Grandmother Moon loves Grandfather Sun, but Grandfather Sun loves Mother Earth. So Grandmother Moon, who has chased Grandfather Sun across the sky and is always slower than he is, decided to try and trick Grandfather Sun. Grandmother Moon sent her spirit-self to Mother Earth, looking like a young maiden, and beautiful in every way. When Grandfather Sun looked down to Mother Earth and was sending his warm love to her, he saw this beautiful maiden. Her hair was shimmering in his light of love. He came closer and closer. Mother Earth was getting real hot. Her desire for her love started making her shake and quiver. Her blood was hot with love. Her passion is very powerful. Whole mountains were shaking.

Grandfather Sun was looking at the young maiden, whose hair was now a golden yellow. Mother Earth saw what was happening, opened her belly up, and the young maiden was sinking in. Grandfather Sun was furious because he now knew who it was. It was Grandmother Moon, Grandmother Earth's sister. Grandfather Sun sent a piece of himself hurling down at the maiden, which turned her into a fireball. This burned her up. Mother Earth loved her sister, and knew that she loved Grandfather Sun as she did, so she used her gifts to heal her and make a symbol for all time; for all to see. She turned her into a gift for the People that they would always remember this love. Now Grandfather Sun felt ashamed for his actions, so it is until this very day we have lunar eclipses. Because he gives his love sometimes to Grandmother Moon, and why even today, we plant, harvest, and do certain things on certain moons, but all that is a different story.

I made my smoke and offerings to each of the directions, starting in the east, then to Spirit, then to Mother and then to Grandmother Moon, to all the elements, and all the four kingdoms (plant, animal, mineral, elemental), to all my Star relatives, and to all my spirit helpers, then to all my relations in the past, present, and future. I said my prayers and then smoked the tobacco mixture, letting the smoke carry my prayers to the Creator and all the directions. When I finished, I crumbled up the remains and scattered it in the winds.

Now it was time to eat. The sun was setting and it was beautiful here. Fireflies, or lightning bugs, were flying around. I was listening to my neighbors getting ready for bed, and to those who would come out at night. I knew the aroma of my cooking would draw the hunters out, but I was not worried because the smell of fire, smoke, and "man smell" would not agree with them.

I had a nice wooden bowl and I filled it to the top with soup. I got out one of my nut cakes and I ate with relish. My body craved food, so I ate until I was full. All the different flavors were wonderful and the meat was so tender and sweet. I took the pot off the fire and hung it up on a limb, hanging down where the smoke would hit it. That way the bugs and others would stay out of my pots.

Then I built up my fire and went to my shelter and got two water containers. One is a large gourd with a stopper. The other is a woven container that would hold water. I made my way down to the water to fill them up. I washed myself up and drank deeply. Then I filled both containers with the fresh water. Grandmother Moon was shining brightly, reflecting on the water, and showering her light on all the leaves and branches of all these people. I went back to my home and put the water containers up by hanging them on the limbs.

I went and got some clothes on then. Yeah, I had been naked the whole time but that wasn't unusual for me. I usually only dress with clothes when I will see people, or I am hunting; otherwise I usually don't wear much. Clothes are hard to make, and in the swamp with all the thorns, briers, and brush, they get torn pretty quick, or they make too much noise. Your skin gets tough like leather, just like your feet build calluses on them, so you don't wear shoes or moccasins. Besides, if you walk in the swamp, you will lose or destroy shoes or moccasins pretty fast. Moccasins are only worn on special occasions.

I spent many hours that night singing with my new friends, learning from them, and really getting to know them. I slept with them right next to the fire. During the night, I felt grandfather's energy speaking to me. I sent him a message that I needed rest and would see him the following night, and that I loved him.

I woke before dawn and checked my arms. All the swelling was gone down and the infection was only showing a little. I stripped naked and gathered my new friends and walked to my bathing area. I took them bathing with me then laid them in the sand to energize them with the sun. I did my morning prayers, so thankful for all that I had been given and especially thankful for my healing.

I dove down deep and swam under water like an otter.

I love swimming this way. It is very good exercise, but it is fun too. I had learned to mimic the swimming techniques of all my water neighbors. All of them are fun, and all are excellent ways to develop strength in your body. While swimming this way, I noticed some fresh water oysters, and in one of them was a beautiful black pearl. My mother would love this, so I made a prayer to the oyster, thanking it, and got the pearl, putting it in my mouth for safekeeping. Then I continued my swim.

When I returned to shore, the sun was up high. I felt good, and the warm sun quickly dried my body. I took the black pearl from my mouth. It was a beauty. It was about as big as my thumb. It would be a nice gift. I gathered up my friends and put the pearl with the scepter and put them in their pouches.

I had to do some things today, so I went back to my home and got the things I would need. By our Blood Laws, I had to make amends with my step-dad. First, I would make the gift before I stood before him. It would have to be a gift that I put a lot of effort and time in creating. I had to think about what this man would like. I could not make a gift that he would not use.

He was a white man, so most of the things I would make would be of no use to him. So I sat down and thought about what he would really use. White people were strange to me, since I did not go around them. It took me a long time to decide what to make. I decided to make him a hat, but it would be a good hat, one to keep Grandfather Sun off his head and to keep the rain out of his face. Surely a white man would like that.

I did not know how they made their hats, so I decided to make one using dried bamboo and palmetto. I went to work gathering the bamboo and palmetto leaves. I started a big fire and went to the water taking all I had gathered. I began stripping the palmetto leaves nice and thin and did the same with the bamboo by cutting them in ¼ inch slices nice and long.

When I was finished, I soaked them in the water. I then got some stakes and a leather thong. I measured my head. His would be bigger so I added some length. I then drew a circle using the thong as a measure, and put my stake in the ground. I then gathered some more of the palmetto leaves and took them to the water. While this was soaking, I got my fire going real hot and let it burn down to hot coals. Now it was time to work.

I first got all the things I had soaking in the water and brought them to the fire. I took the wide leaves of the palmetto and laid them over the fire pit, water still on top of them. Then I laid my strips of bamboo and palmetto strips on top and placed the other palmetto leaves on top of them. This would steam them and make them soft and real flexible. I had woven clothes, mats, chairs, baskets, and other items this way. Surely I could make the hat. All I had to do was try!

When they had steamed for a while, I got some of each out. Beginning at the center, I wove and coiled and wrapped the beginning. Each added wrapped coil was woven into the next. Now this is done different than a grass basket. See, I picked out seven long pieces of bamboo splits, putting two to run from front to back, two from side to side, and one to run diagonally from front to back on one side to crisscross at the top and center. Then, one ran front to back crisscrossing at the top, and one to run around the bottom to secure the bottom.

Now I would weave the palmetto in and out between them and pull them tight to the center, going around and around. To do a coil, you take a bamboo split and wrap the palmetto around the bamboo split. You add a piece by placing a new bamboo split and then wrapping it to the other split with the leaves. In weaving these coils between the splits, you have to take the coil then pull it to the top. Your work will get easier as you go. This is made easier by the fact that the bamboo and palmetto are wet and the steam allows them to bend like rubber. Once it is finished, you let the sun dry it and you will have a nice hat. The brim is done on the same principle.

I had learned this technique by weaving traps and snares to catch rabbits and fish, and by watching my grandmother weave baskets from grass, bamboo and other things. Interlocking the weave makes it water proof. It can hold water and you can even cook water in it.

It is almost like loom weaving, or using a beading loom, except you are weaving inside to outside. When I finished the hat, I placed it back on top of the wet palmetto over the fire to steam it softer so I could shape it better. As long as it was wet this way with the heat and steam, it could be easily shaped. When the hat was finished, I set it in the sun with a rock inside so it would maintain the shape and not shrink any more than the diameter of the rock.

While it was drying, I got a rattlesnake skin with the buttons still attached that I put up after eating the rattlesnake. This would make a nice headband to decorate the hat, with the rattlesnake buttons hanging free in the back. Normally, I would have dyed some of the palmetto leaves and bamboo to put designs in it, but I did not know if white people had clan colors or symbols. This way, if he did, my mother would do this properly for him. Using a bone needle and sinew, I sewed the rattlesnake band onto the hat, making it look nice. On the inside, I sewed a thin strip of brain-tanned deerskin. This would keep the sweat out of his face.

Since the hat was done, I figured I needed to eat and then go clean up. I ate some more of my soup and nut cakes. I wrapped some up in leaves and got a large gourd container to put some soup in for my grandfather. I then went to bathe again since it was getting close to dusk.

I put some clothing on so as not to offend my mother's husband and his children, gathered my new friends and the food, and made my way to my mother's home.

They were sitting in the house when I got there. I called out to my mother so she would come. She did, and I explained to her why I was there. I asked her to call her husband and my grandfather out. I would need my mother to help translate and explain what I was about to say. My mother went in and returned with her husband and my grandfather to stand before me. I lowered my head in proper respect to my grandfather and my mother. I waited to be acknowledged by my grandfather.

After a few moments, he said, "Eagle, is there something you wish to say?" I told him that I want to apologize to my mother's husband for what I did and that under the Blood Laws I would accept whatever punishment he demanded.

I then told him what I had done the night he was with the evil drink. I handed the black pearl to my grandfather and the hat, to give to my mother and her husband. These would not be for punishment. These are offered as a token to show sincerity in making amends for what I had done.

I waited while everything was being explained to my mother's husband, my stepfather. My grandfather then handed the black pearl to my mother and the hat to her husband. Both of them examined the items closely. They might not like them and they did not have to accept them. I knew my mother would explain all of this to her husband. I waited patiently for their decision.

After talking amongst themselves for a while, her husband went back inside. Mother addressed my grandfather and told him that her husband did not believe I could do anything like that and that he didn't believe in that type of thing. He would accept the hat anyway, and since our customs demanded something be done to me, I would have to clean up around the place. I would have to pick up all the dead branches and clear the brush back. I would have to clean the roof of any limbs, leaves, moss, etc. I would have to spade a garden where he marked the area he wanted spaded.

My grandfather listened to all of this and agreed, since he was my representative. My mother then came over and hugged me and thanked me for the black pearl and also for being a man and living by the code of the Blood Law. She explained that since her husband did not understand, that he required nothing, but to prove the point that punishment must be made, she came up with this and he agreed. I was to start tomorrow. She hugged me and kissed my cheek and then turned and went inside. My grandfather turned and began walking to our spot. When we got there he sat down and I waited to be acknowledged.

When he did, he said "Sit down." I did and then handed him the foods that I had brought for him. He took the stopper out of the gourd and smelled it. A smile crossed his face and he thanked me for the food I had brought.

He sat there for a moment and said, "How are you feeling?"

I told him I had gotten a lot better and that I would be fine soon. Then I told him all I had done. He listened and didn't say anything for a while after I had finished.

Then he said, "This was a hard lesson for you and doing what you did was very much going way beyond what I felt you would do. But, now you can see how something small can turn into something much worse just by the choices you make. I am glad that you are alive and not damaged by this forever.

"Now, you must also do what was decided. Start early and do as much as you can. You must get this done so you can continue with your journey. I do not want you taking any journey until you have completed this work. That is your punishment. You know you will be leaving here soon and return back to your home with your father's people. So work hard and get this done quickly, but be sure you do a good job as well. He is a very hard man, but inside I know he means well. He has never been taught compassion or affection of the heart, so put love in your heart when you do this work and remember it is your mother's garden you will be spading. He doesn't care about it but your mother sure will. I know you have brought your friends the crystals with you. I can feel them. Would you please introduce me to them?"

I took them out of their pouches and talked to them letting them know this was my grandfather Beaver, that he would be honored to meet them. I then handed them one at a time to grandfather. He greeted them in love and respect and thanked them for their help to me and the Circle. He said he had lived for a long time and had only seen or heard of them in his dreams, but that they were far more powerful and beautiful than he could ever have heard or dreamed. They were delighted with him and showed it very obviously, glowing and pouring out beautiful blue and purple light all around us. Their vibration of love turned to singing. We wanted to sing with them but did not want to disrespect my mother's husband by disturbing him. Our style of singing is not like he is accustomed to, and we knew he went to sleep early because he worked long hours. We sat there and just talked for a long time while he enjoyed his meal.

When he was finished he said "I will tell your mother to set the tools out that you will need. Now, go and get some rest grandson."

I gathered my things and then left. I got home pretty quick since I walked with a purpose in my step. As soon as I got home, I put everything up and went to sleep. I slept for about four hours, then woke up. I put together some things that would help me in doing my punishment, then stripped and went for my bath. I did my prayers and my bath and ate as much as I could. I also ate some "kirri-kirri", the root I would need to help me with strength.

Then I gathered my things and quietly walked back to my mother's. It was about a couple of hours away until sunrise, so I put my things up and climbed on their roof. I quietly walked around picking up the broken branches, twigs and such and put them all in a pile. I would drop them down later when everyone was up. I used my hands to scoop out the troughs where water ran off the roof. It was full of twigs, moss, leaves, sweet gum balls, acorns, and all kinds of many legged creatures. I carried this all back to the pile I had on the roof.

I then climbed down and began walking their yard area first, picking up limbs and such. I worked my way in ever widening circles around their home. I had quite a big pile of things piled up now. So I began picking up on their entire property. They had maybe fifteen acres for their yard. All the rest was woods, brush and such, about another twenty acres. I continued this even when the sun finally came up. I knew they would be getting up and have things to do. I did not want to be under foot, or even noticed so I continued until I had all of it picked up.

My mom and my two sisters were outside waiting when I walked up. My two sisters ran to me and hugged me. I loved my sisters and I always missed them, as they also missed me. My mom had a dipper of water for me. As she looked around, my half-brother was hanging from his basket from the clothesline pole. He was glad to see me even though he didn't know me yet! Ha! Ha!

He couldn't walk yet, so to keep him out of trouble and be outside, my mother had him hanging up in a woven basket-like chair that allowed her to let him swing in the air and see all the trees, bugs, animals, and birds. I told my mother to mark out the area she would want for her garden, but I did suggest the southeast section because of its location, plus the soil was good and rich with nutrients and minerals. But, also because there is a lot of warrior insect nests there. (The warrior insect, the praying mantis, protects your garden from insects and worms that would harm your garden crops.) There were also a lot less oak trees that have numerous big roots running everywhere.

She said she'd look. I got a straw broom she had set aside and threw it up on the roof, and then climbed up to get on the house. I threw off all the big piles of limbs and things I had dug out of the troughs, then, swept the roof good and then the troughs. It took me several trips but I got all the piles over to where they did their burning. Then I went around and picked up all the piles I had gathered on the property.

Then I got a brush axe and began cutting all the brush and little scrub oaks, and all the thorn bushes all over the property. I cut the stinging nettles and all the different weeds and grasses that would cut and tear their flesh. I pulled up poison oak and poison ivy so the children wouldn't get in it. I worked all day until late in the evening doing all of this. My mother's husband came home and just walked and looked around, then went into the house.

I went to get a spade, pick, and mattock and went to where my mother had stakes out for the garden. I first used the spade and began spading the ground. (Spading is done by taking the spade/shovel, digging into the ground and turning it upside down. This makes the grass, weeds, etc., die. Spading is done when you don't have a mule or horse to plow.) This is all done by hand.

I worked until about 9:00 pm, and then I went home. I then stripped and went to bathe. The water felt so good and refreshing. I scrubbed myself clean with the sand then just swam for a while, just enjoying the coldness of the water. I said my prayers, and then went to my tree. I ate what I had left over, and then went to sleep. I woke up about 4:00 am and went to bathe and do my prayers. When I got back, I dressed in clothes and ate the fruit I picked along the way, mostly eating the plums that I love so well. I went straight to work, spading the whole area, chopping roots, and digging up the stumps that were in the way. My mother came out later and brought me some water, salt pork, and biscuits. I thanked her as she looked around. It was taking shape. When I finished eating and drinking plenty of water, I went back to work. Using the mattock, I broke the ground up real good, then I used the pick to dig it deeper for later on. I worked until about 7:00 am, and then went home.

I went to bathe first, then to my fish traps. I had several good size fish. I took them out and then put the traps back and then cleaned my fish. I gathered wild onions, kudzu, clover, and wet clay. I built me a fire and put the onions, kudzu, and clover inside the fish and covered them in clay. Then I put them in the fire. While they cooked I went and got some willow bark.

This would help my blistered hands. Sweating comes easily in the swamps and the more you sweat while working, the easier it is to get blisters. I was no stranger to hard work. I enjoyed it and still do. But my hands were blistered, so I needed to help them. The willow bark would do that for me. When I finished, I ate my fish and what I had left I wrapped up in palmetto leaves and buried it under the coals. The scent of smoke and fire would keep all from getting at my food. I then said my prayers and fell fast asleep.

I awoke early and went to bathe and pray. Then I ate some more fish and saved the rest. I got back to my mother's early. It was about 3:30 am and I went straight to work. It took me three more days to get the work all done. I had completed my punishment and my mother had a very nice garden plot. I even helped her further by taking some of the warrior insect nests and moving them around so that all sides of her garden would be protected. When these fellows hatched out of their nests, there would be thousands of them. I then placed a lace weave of thorns interlocked around the plot. This would keep the rabbits, skunks, and others out. The rest, well, hawks and owls, and even eagles were plentiful here. Deer were plentiful as well. But by hanging their clothes, and putting tin cans that rattled around the plot, Mother could keep the deer nervous and this would deter them from the area.

When I finished, I went to my mother and asked her if this was good enough. She said that it was more than was required. She hugged me and told me that she loved me. My sisters hugged me too, and I held my little half-brother in my arms and hugged him.

Then I left and went home. I would see my grandfather tonight. I needed to finish my journey with him before I had to leave, for I was far from my main home, and I would need to be there soon. I went back to my tree home satisfied that I had done good work. Now I was free again to do whatever I needed to. I took a bath and said my prayers, telling the spirits that I had followed the Blood Laws of my people and met the requirements of those I did wrong. I asked the spirits to take pity on me and look into my heart.

When I finished, I went back to my fish traps and removed all that I had caught, and reset my traps. I gathered some herbs to season the fish and then cleaned the fish. I cooked my meal and then went directly to bed, so I would get up in a few hours and go see my grandfather. I slept real well. My body needed the rest. My training had always allowed me to awaken whenever I needed to, so after four hours of sleep I was up and ready. I took out the pouches with my new friends, and then proceeded down to bathe again. When I had finished, I gathered some of my fish and began my trip to my mother's.

My grandfather was waiting for me when I got there. I waited for him to acknowledge me and when he did, I sat down next to him. I handed him one of the fish I had caught and prepared for him. He accepted it and thanked me for thinking about him. He asked me how I felt and I told him I felt fine.

He said, "That is good, because you must take a journey again tonight. I will go with you to help you, but also to explain some things to you as well. These you must remember always, for the day will come in your lifetime that you will need to know these things, and you must give this knowledge to those that are to have it. For in doing this, you will start the new beginning. The Sisters who are to come will then begin remembering things; things they know but don't know. They will have flashes of insight; memories that will come to them. They will see things and think, 'I know this', because they will not have their full memories yet.

"You are not the only one who was chosen and accepted this task. Many were chosen; now there are only a few left. I was one, but my time here is almost over. You must honor your vow and continue the work. All of you who are left will have many difficulties. The world is changing and will continue to change, all for the worse. Because each of you will suffer, you must not lose hope. Never give up. Never forget your vow. Some of you will not make it. Some of you will, but will choose to forget because of all of the suffering you will endure in your lives. But there must be one of you left to start the new beginning; to help each of the chosen Sisters and bring back the Power.

"The place you now journey to was a place of power. The chosen ones gathered there. They did much good and taught many. People from Inca land came. Mayan People came. Aztec People came. Polynesians came. Ani-yun-wiya came. Even those from across the ocean came. But it was destroyed because Power was taken from the Sisters. Murder and assassinations were done to steal their power and their knowledge. The survivors scattered to the corners of the winds, being adopted in by other Nations. They knew why it all happened; why it had to happen. Every civilization that has come to power, that has tried to take power for themselves and to rule the lives of others, has been destroyed and vanished. You will see this in this lifetime yourself.

"You know who all think they have power now. But I tell you it will not last. Even this new Nation that is called America will be destroyed because of their greed for power and dominance of everything. You will see all the signs of the prophecies of what is written in stones. Learn all you can of your enemies. It will be like following a trail in the grass. Read them. Know them. And never underestimate them. They fear all who have knowledge and all who will not take on their ways. What they fear, they attack, so know your enemies well my child, for from this day on, your life will change dramatically.

"Your own family will never know you. Death will constantly be on your trail. There will be those who hate you and resent you even though they do not even know you. Bad things will be said about you. You will be accused of many things. Continue your work and journey on the path but let no one know what you do. As you grow, more and more will hate you, fear you, and attack you. Remember this: the more enemies you have, the more you are attacked, the more they accuse you of, the more you should know that you are doing something good. For only those that truly walk the path are hated, resented, and attacked for it.

"Now we must prepare for where we go is a place of power; a place where many that have true power will be. And, as always, there will be those who will try to interfere. There are many sacred objects there. Be extremely careful when you try to see them. They have been gathered there to try to unite all these different powers. But then you should remember all of this, for you once lived there and you were killed protecting one of the Beloved Ones. So look into your memories, for in your memories you will remember who your enemies were."

So I opened my mind up to my past. Memories began flooding in. I remembered being a guardian of the beautiful young priestess whose power all feared. I had to watch out for her constantly, for many had already tried to steal her power; her spirit. Yes, that was the key: the Spirit Bowls. I remember now: the evil ones, trying to take the spirits of each of the Beloved Ones, their Spirit Bowls, Spirit Pipes, Spirit Bundles, and yes, the Spirit Discs. These discs were beautiful. All were perfect in size, shape, and beauty. Each was made of pure copper, beaten, and designed with the Sun and Stars, and the Spirit name of the helper for the Beloved. All the great power stones were gathered and kept in a special chamber.

I remembered he who hated me most, the one that had ordered his men to destroy the one I was to protect. Eleven attempts had been made on her in the last six days. I had taken several serious wounds during that time. She was dancing with Sister at the time. Totally helpless only I was there to stop them from taking her. Her heart was beautiful. She glowed with love for all life. Even the other priestesses were envious of her beauty and mostly of her power.

Yes, now I was truly prepared for my journey. I told my grandfather that "I had remembered, so I will be prepared for what is to come. There is much power there. I will take the Scepter with me and I believe we should dance with Sister Datura, for these people dance with her plenty, and many will have her essence on them. This will hide us from those with power because we, too, will have her essence, and they will accept it easily as Spirit work, thinking our spirits are walking in the dance."

My grandfather thought about this for a while, and then agreed that it was a good idea. We prepared ourselves with Sister, and then made our prayers and offerings, and sang our spirit song. (A spirit song can be many things. The one referred to here is one that is used to let the spirit free, to ascend to the Holy Place within yourself, there to find your true spirit and release it from its physical shell.) Sister was dancing in our blood, and soon we were on our way.

Cahokia! People from many different Nations dwell here. This is a place of Power, a place where those who are gifted are all welcome to share their knowledge and their gifts with others like them. The place is of great mounds and the great wheel. Royalty dwells here. A strong warrior's guard is evident everywhere. Visitors of the Aztec, Maya, Inca, Polynesia, and the four corners of the Mother have come here to trade goods, ideas, beliefs, and teachings. Their relatives in these cultures cover vast stretches of this continent. Like a great wheel with its spokes going in all directions: to east, southeast, south, southwest, west, northwest, north, and northeast.

Mounds like a serpent are to the east, mounds like these here to the south, mounds like rectangles and pyramids to the southwest, mounds like towers to the west, mounds like plateaus to the northwest and crystal covered mounds to the north. The teachings are basically the same: the True Power, aided by the Crystal Skulls, crystals, the Great Medicine Wheels, the knowledge of the Stars, the knowledge of the Elements, and all things known as the Great Mysteries!

Agriculture is the primary food source. With the knowledge of the Mother and the elements, huge crops were planted and gathered. They used techniques that irrigate the fields, and the stars and moon for when to plant and harvest. Hunting and fishing were also big food sources. Buffalo, elk, deer, grouse, ducks, rabbits and all types of fish were part of the main staples. Herbs and spices from all directions were gathered and traded here. Craftsmen and artists were everywhere. Singers and storytellers worked their craft for all who would listen.

This was a vast civilization that gathered all to its heart. Ceremonies were plentiful and all must pay homage to the ruler.

Now at the time of this journey with my grandfather, a young man was the ruler. This young man was the offspring of several different genetic groups. His great-grandfather was Mayan royalty, married to a beautiful young maiden. His grandfather was the first-born from this marriage that bonded the families of the Maya and Cahokians. His other grandfather married into a visiting party of Aztecs, who was also part Toltec and Aztec. A very tall dark woman who was in line to royalty bonded the Aztec and Cahokians. This woman was very gifted and used her power to help her new family. She had many in her family use their influences to bring craftsmen, doctors, priests, and engineers to Cahokia.

The young boy ruler was the second child of this marriage, the first being a young beautiful girl who chose the path of the Beloved Woman. The boy had some gifts, but nothing like his sister or any of the gifted women. This envy is what ate at him inside as he grew up. He was cruel and malicious. His jealousy ate at him until his heart was turned to darkness. He was now at the young age of seventeen summers.

He had made a marriage arrangement with the Inca people. The marriage had produced two young beautiful girls, both who had gifts like their mother. Love was never part of the young ruler's decision in marriage. His thirst for power was the reason. His young wife, who was actually older than he, had been ordered by her family into this marriage. She was a true Dreamer, one who created her dream and brought it into this world as she walked in this world.

The young ruler feared her power and the love that the People of Cahokia had for his wife. She was a compassionate woman who was always there to help those who were in need. The young ruler had already ordered her from his home and she had gone to the Beloved Women's temple along with her two daughters. This is the time we arrived. The young ruler was on a rampage. He was trying to steal all the power from whoever had it, and from any of their Sacred Power helpers; medicine bundles, crystals, sacred pipes, sacred effigies, and even the very spirits of those who had power.

A thick tension covered the city. You could feel it in the air. The king's guards were posted everywhere. You could hear screams of pain and death.

I looked at my grandfather. He touched my shoulder and said, "Remember why you are here. You must not interfere no matter what."

We let our spirits guide us to where we needed to be. A young maiden was dancing with Sister. Her spirit bowl was in front of her as she sat inside the sweat lodge. We were in the sweat lodge with her. Outside we could hear and feel her personal guards moving around as she conducted her spirit work. We opened our minds to her, to follow her journey, looking into the spirit bowl, following the lines spiraling down to the center.

We connected with her as she stood before Mother Earth, who, in her true spirit, was radiating power in all directions. She looked directly at my grandfather and me. We immediately knelt to one knee with our heads lowered, left hand to our heart, and right hand extended palm up. She had eyes that blazed into us. I could feel the intensity of her eyes burning into me.

Then she said "Who is it that dares to journey here while this Beloved Daughter comes to me?"

My grandfather spoke gently and humbly, "Oh Grandmother, I am Big Beaver and this is my grandson. We mean not to disrespect or interrupt. We came to see this Beloved One here who came to see you. It is my grandson's journey and I am accompanying him. For it was shown to him by the Sister of the Stars, and the Sacred Crystal Skulls, that he must see here. He is a guardian, as I know you already know, as I was a guardian. My journey is almost over. He must continue the work and sacred vow he made. So I ask for your forgiveness, oh Great Mother."

Mother stood before me now and touched my shoulder. "Speak to me, young guardian," she said. I looked up at her; into her eyes. They were like the stars themselves, sparkling like diamonds in the dark of night.

I said, "Mother, Grandmother, I came to see this young maiden, for I was shown what I must do in my life. She was part of it, and she and I will meet again. She knows me already in this lifetime, for I am one of her personal guards. Just as I know her now, she must remember me now for the future. Here is the Scepter of Atlantis." I brought it out of its pouch bag and showed it to her. She looked, but did not touch.

She said, "I know you, young one, just as all my sisters and daughters know you. And yes, I know the Scepter. I gave birth to it in my womb, for we all know what was going to come to pass. I am glad it has been placed in your hands. But know this: in the times to come you will lose much; you will be looked down upon and be made fun of. People will think you are crazy or a liar. This must be, because otherwise the Scepter would not be safe. Some of your gifts you will lose for a time. This too must happen. Your enemies must not know you have the Scepter or who and what you are. Many times you may wish you had not taken this upon yourself. Many times you may even wish that you would die, for the path ahead of you will be filled with much pain and loss for you. You will be tortured, caged, abused, starved, and even experimented on, so you must lose parts of yourself. That way they will never know. But in many, many years in your future, memories and gifts will come back to you.

"People who thought they knew you will not know you now. Members of your own family will not understand you or how this knowledge or gifts came to you. You will learn pain so intense that you begin to welcome pain. All this you must endure. Your grandfather has suffered, but he has not forgotten his duty or the Sacred Truths. He has done well with you and I am pleased. For all that he suffered in his life will be rewarded to him when he is finished in this world. And always remember this: you have a deep connection with me.

"You will always be a part of me, and I will help you all that I can. Your heart and spirit are connected to all of my children, especially the star children. And my plant children will always help you when you need them. Your temper comes from me, because your heart is connected to my heart. Your compassion and love will also always be with me and with my children. You will love them as you love me, but it is a curse to you as well. Your spirit and ways will always attract the females of the world. They will want you. Some will even love you, but they will not understand the deepness of your love, or why you do the things you do. Therefore your heart will be broken many, many times. The wild free spirit of love will be like a flower to a bee.

"Females will want your love but they can't control your love, and since your heart is one with mine, you will always know the secret desires and passions of women. You will know where to touch, how to touch, how to take them to the heights of pleasure of their own bodies that they don't even know. You will do it out of love, pure love for them. They will not return the same to you. You will not be able to control this or even stop this. Since you are so sensitive, then this too will tear at your heart. There will be women who seek your knowledge, your gifts, your pleasure, and just try to be with you. Do not think this is for nothing.

"Everything has a purpose. For even in their own ignorance, they will learn their own hearts. They will learn true love, and this will help them heal themselves and their spirits. Many of them will come who have been abused, left for someone else, cheated, raped, and battered. Many will be neglected or have no confidence in themselves, or they will have low self-esteem. You will cure them of that. It is part of the healing they will need, and they will always be your friend afterwards, but it will teach you as well, for in your heart you will come to learn the meaning of free love, and more importantly, what is most important of all, total commitment to the highest calling: to serve Spirit for the benefit of all.

"This does not mean you will not have love in your life. It only means that love for Spirit, love for your duty and obligation, comes before all else. It would be up to you to find the woman who can understand this and accept this. You will have many, so you must not let yourself use any gift or influence on this decision. You will have many who will teach you many wonderful things, including how to truly pleasure the passion of a woman. Remember who you serve, young guardian.

"Remember the code you must always live by and honor the code of a guardian. Now, see this young Beloved Daughter of mine. I will help her once you have finished with her."

With that she vanished and I still knelt down before this young Beloved Woman. She had listened to all that was said. She looked me over very closely and said, "I know your spirit, but your image I do not recognize. I heard you say that in this time you are one of my guards who protect me. Which one are you?"

I told her that "I could not answer that. It is for a special reason that I cannot, but you will know me when the time comes for you to know this. You are to use your gifts and remember my spirit now, for you will return and meet me in the future. You are a true Dreamer. This I know about you already, and you are a special one that has touched the sacred crystals. Yes, Beloved Woman, I too am connected to them. You are the one that holds a key; a key in the future to what must be, for it is you who must be in the center with the Amethyst Crystal Skull when all the Beloved Women and all the Crystal Skulls come together.

"I know that you know what is happening, here in this time, must come to an end. Many dangers are everywhere. You are the keeper of the Amethyst Skull and the Wolf Medicine Bundle. These must be hidden from all. This is what is being sought now. You must warn all the Beloved Women to hide all the sacred stones, bundles, pipes, effigies, and their own spirit bowls, for there is a force here at work. It wants all these Sacred Power Gifts.

"After you have hidden everything, and you have helped your Beloved Sisters to escape, a great fury will attack, as now the Mother and the Star People are destroying this place. The crops will fail. Mother Earth will shake herself and floods will come. Lightning will come and strike down many, and winds will blow nightly destroying things in their path. The Star Power Wheel must be redone, so that others, later in time, will not know its use. Therefore, do not design it correctly. Many will come in the future seeking this Power, this knowledge. This knowledge must not fall into their possession.

"Remember the old story of young gopher, and apply that to all that must be hidden. With the Amethyst Skull, remember the story of the daughter of the Sun, for in the story will be your answer of what to do. All of this the Sacred Skulls have shown me. They must all be scattered and hidden until it is time for all to come together again. And know this, Beloved Woman, that in your time here in the time of your greatest need, a true guardian will never flee. Now there is another that I must see, so I will go and let you be with Grandmother who is waiting."

With that said I walked to her and looked into her eyes,

seeing the place where she would place the precious Sacred Amethyst Skull. With that done, I knelt and offered my respect as did my grandfather, and we traveled back to the lodge where the spirit bowl sat. We saw her deep in the dance and made our way outside. I saw myself standing outside on guard. I knew my own spirit, but I looked nothing like what I look like now. But I was proud of myself who stood outside for I knew that in the near future that I would battle all the king's assassins and guards that he sent to destroy her. I would be killed fulfilling the code, taking many with me before they got to her. She could have gotten away but refused to leave, saying that she would not run from this and would stay with me. They would cut her apart and take her head to the king, but that would mean his end, for in her would be the power that would destroy his mind. The people that survived would flee this place of so much blood and the spirits had spoken in many ways. I could not tell any of this to myself. That is one of the rules, never to interfere with what is to be, but inside my heart cried out to me!

My grandfather touched my shoulder and we let our spirit lead us to where it would need to go. When we got there, we were next to the river. An old woman sat there. Here sat one who was old and wise. This was my mother in this time. I wanted to see her one more time. My heart wanted to hold her but I could not, but I sent her love anyway just to let her know that her son loved her. Next to her were some of the belongings of myself who was living in this time. I went to a special bag, there to retrieve an item I would need in this time. It was a gift from one of my helpers, a true brother spirit the wolf. A wolf had come to me, here in the past, when I was on a journey. The wolf had dropped a tooth into my hand. It was a medicine gift; one that would help me in the world I now lived in, the one that had tried to destroy all the wolf people. Therefore, I wanted this medicine to help the wolf people come back strong. Now that I had it, I would use it in my time when I got back.

It was time to go and my grandfather nodded his head for us to return. So, side-by-side, we let our spirits free to come back to this time.

I did not see my grandfather again for a long time, and what he taught me then is a different story, but it is part of the circle, something maybe to be told another time.

I am old now, but still strong. All that I have been told in my youth by the Beloved Women and all my teachers has come to pass, except the ending, which will come soon. All that was forgotten, stolen, and destroyed shall return. The time is now coming for all of the Beloved Women to be called by the Sacred Skulls and Crystals. Mother Earth has called her relatives. Those who think they are in power will find out soon that they have no power. A cleansing will come! That is all that I can tell you at this time. Look into your heart and find the truth there. Hopefully, my words will spark memories in you.

Remember to Walk in Beauty and Love Always!

Chapter Eleven

Love Is The Answer

I've decided that I want to share with you a special story. I had to pray a lot about this, and I want you to share this so you will at least know the Truth about Life. This story is a fact and it is the key to life. All of the Ancient Worlds knew this knowledge. It was practiced by the Hofunv'lke and was passed through all the Children of the Stars. It is Creator's (Pucase Hesaketv) gift to us all. I've never shared this story or knowledge with anyone in the past due to the power that is involved, but Spirit said now is the time, so now I share it with you.

First we go back in time, back to when I was young and learning the Ancient Ways, back to when my Grandfather Beaver shared my life, and when I was receiving all my gifts. So please pay attention and let the love flow in your heart, for the Truth is the Key of Life.

Long, long ago when I was still young and learning, I was blessed with a journey, a journey that took me to the place of all Truth. I had recently become a full warrior, with many honors awarded to me. I already had two wives and was being honored by the Clan Mothers, who arrange all marriages, to be given another wife. I was a good provider, very responsible, and never had to be asked to do anything that needed to be done. I was also being guided and instructed by my extended adopted grandfathers who were all very Honored men, those who walk in-between worlds, those who worked with the Beloved Women.

I had already made my vows to accept my duty and responsibilities as a guardian since my childhood. I was now in Opelofv Uewv Lvste (The Black Water Swamp), a place of dangerous adventures and enchantment. It was a special place of untamed wilderness. This place was totally untouched by civilization, with the hvpv'tv rak'ke (great alligators), giants that were getting rarer with all the hunting to destroy them. Many ka'tcv opelo'fv (swamp tigers, what you call jungle cats or panthers) roamed this place. It was a place where the lo'ca hvlpv'tv rak'ke (giant alligator turtles) lived in peace from man. As I arrived, I could hear hakih'ketv el'kv (the death cry) of a suk'hvce honece (wild pig) echoing through the swamp. It was eerie but this was life and death - constant here in my world.

I was coming here to be alone. I was on a a'yetv (journey) for a nakhe ciho'cat (vision) for help for my people. We were being encroached upon more and more by white people and civilization. It was destroying the homes for all of our relatives, the four-leggeds, winged ones, those that crawled, burrowed into the ground and those that live in the water too. Sickness was attacking my people from the diseases being spread from these tvlepo'rv este lke (foreign peoples) who respected nothing.

Fevers were rampant, and rapidly striking our towns and villages, so I had come here after elauwe'cetv (fasting) to seek help from the Spirit World. My elders were knowledgeable in healing people, yet nothing we had tried had worked so far. I myself had been hit twice by two different sicknesses that had almost destroyed my flesh. Each time, though, my Spirit Helpers had come to me and helped me. I knew I would find an answer and help from the Hofunv'lke who would answer my cry for help.

So here I was, here in this Sacred Place of Ancient Times, where I would now release my body and live by spirit alone. I was exhausted from my travel and from the fasting, yet felt the strength of my spirit pulling me deeper and deeper into this jungle. Cetto mekko rak'ke (giant rattlesnakes) crawled, or lay sunning themselves, so I sent them my love and thanks (mvto) for guarding this place. This was my special place to come. As a boy I had found this spot when I was going through my training as a warrior. For my first vision, it seemed only right to be here. This was home, untouched by the outside world. A natural spring was there that had a pool of water that was ice cold always, no matter how hot or humid it was. It came from deep inside Ekv'nv Et'ske (Mother Earth).

I stripped naked and took out my offerings of hece

(tobacco), vce-enfulo'tkv (corn meal), vce'nv (cedar), es'sefv'ske (holly leaf), and all the items in my medicine bundle. My two friends, the Scepter of Atlantis and the Crossed Wands of Lemuria crystals, were laid out on the panther skin along with my wolf tooth and other items. I prayed to all of the directions and made my offerings of tobacco, corn meal, cedar, and holly leaf. I then rolled a smoke with a corn husk, using my special blend, and offered the smoke to all the directions, then smudged myself with the smoke. I then dove into the ice-cold water of the spring, letting this special water purify my body completely. I dove deeper and deeper into the womb of Mother Earth. The light was fading the deeper I went. The lime rock was no longer illuminated by the light. Still I dove deeper, the pressure squeezing my body like a giant vine.

When the pressure felt like it would crush me, I released my love. I poured out all the love in my heart. In my mind I visualized all the Beauty and Love I had experienced in my life. I began to feel the water responding. The energized water changed vibration and I felt the most love the mind could ever feel. My body turned warm, even though the water was ice cold. Electrical currents were now flowing up from Mother Earth's womb, totally penetrating my body. I felt every particle of my body come alive. I began singing a song of love from my heart, and the power increased and began lifting my body back towards the surface. It felt like every drop of water was touching me, passing me on to the next drop, until finally I was up to where the light of Grandfather Sun was now beginning to penetrate the darkness.

As the water continued to lift me up, I felt my body healing inside. All of the sickness I had suffered recently was leaving my body. Many old injuries no longer had pain. I knew I was being blessed and I sang prayers of thanks to Mother Earth and to the Water that is her blood, for this gift of healing.

Finally I surfaced and the power sparkled off the water and in the water as I floated there. The trees, plants, and birds were all singing and this place was transformed into the True Beauty of Life, as it was created by Spirit. I pulled my body from the water and lay on the moss and leaf covered ground, letting Grandfather Sun's power flow into me.

After giving my thanks and prayers, I reached over and picked up my two friends. The Scepter I placed in my left hand and the Crossed Wands I put in my right hand. I began my power songs of prayer and then the Ani-yun-wiya Breathing Way. Instantly I felt my spirit freeing itself from my body, as I spiraled down into the ice-cold deep spring in Mother Earth. Deeper and deeper I spiraled down, then the familiar sparking and popping, then flashes of light, and I was once again home - my true home - standing in front of Spider Woman, my Home Planet in the Stars.

She smiled and said, "Well Ahecicv Mvnet'te (Young Guardian), you have come again finally. I see you are developing very well. I feel the energy flowing from you. I know you have come for a purpose, so speak your heart."

I told her of the trouble of my People and all we had suffered, and that I was seeking help for my People.

She smiled and then laughed. She then looked deep into my eyes, and said, "You already have your answer, young guardian. What did you do before you came? Stop and think!"

I thought for a minute and failed to see what she was talking about. She then said, "The answer has always been inside of you, and every child that has ever been in your world. Why do you pray to the water?"

Instantly I knew and felt embarrassed because I had failed to see what we had all done since the beginning of time.

She said, "Come. Let's visit the Sacred Skull and see what has always been."

We walked over to the beautiful Skull and it began vibrating and humming, sending beautiful lights all over the chamber. I felt it pulling me.

Spider Woman said, "Go touch the Skull and see and remember all that is shown you."

So I walked over and set my two friends, The Scepter and the Crossed Wands, down beside the Great Skull. I took both hands and placed them on the Sacred Stone. Instantly my mind was filled with scenes flashing before my eyes. I saw every nation of every civilization, since the beginning, given the Sacred Knowledge of Spirit.

Spirit then spoke directly to me, saying: "I am in all of you. You are in me. You two-leggeds I have given extraordinary gifts. If you use your heart you can do anything. But your heart must be of Love. It is the Key to unlocking all mysteries to you. You can create anything you wish in using your heart, but it must be powered by Love. Love is a vibration power that, when activated, creates all energy around you to form and use all energy together. This Love is the Love that I created all with. It is centered in your heart. It is me. I am Love. Love is me. Your heart must control all of you, your thoughts, your actions, your words, what you see, and what you hear. If the thoughts of your heart are not True Love, then it will not work, nor will anything, for I am Love. When you think bad things, you create bad things. When you say bad things, you create them. You create all of your own problems. But this is my love for you that I give you freedom to choose; for you are eternal, as all are eternal. But only each of you can choose.

"Your body of flesh is made from the life blood of Mother Earth, as you call her. You are mostly water that is power and a conductor of power. As you have seen since the beginning, all have made prayers to the water, changing the water with the power to create or to destroy. Mother Earth herself has changed the water to destroy those that have gone too far wrong, or injured her or her children, so that they can come back again and try to do better. In your time now, not many pray anymore to the water or sing to the water. Not many send love to the water as they all did in the past. It is not only your people who are suffering. All the Children of the Stars will suffer from this, for they are all forgetting who they are, what they are, and who they are to become. And, as time goes on in your life, more and more will be forgotten. I will not interfere, for I already know what will come, as you do. More will forget the power they each have, that is inside of each of them. I listen to them now, always more interested in other things than what they already have, yet they don't even know it. Then, there are those who seek power and knowledge, yet they look in all of the wrong places, instead of looking inside of themselves, for each of you creates. What you create is up to you, for each of you is responsible for what you do, say, think, believe, choose, love, hate, etc.

"All that you create not only affects yourself but also all around you. You create your own little world in which you live. Now, young guardian, I know you, for I am in you. You have followed your heart but you have let the outside influences of others cloud you from the Truth; and you who know, have forgotten yourself. All you have to do is claim what is naturally yours, for I gave each of you that. You have suffered already, but you will suffer more and more. This is to be. You made your choice long ago. I accepted your choice. For others in the world will come to hate you, fear you, and do all kinds of things to you. That is their choice, and all that you know, all that you can do is live; live and experience it, learn from it, and keep your heart full of Love, for the time will come that you must bring back the Knowledge and Power to all that will listen.

"You are a guardian of the Beloved! You will help them remember who they are. Help them learn the Truth, and help them regain their Power that is inside of each of them. You will know when it is time, for in this, too, many will not believe, nor want this knowledge taught. The hearts of men have turned and created them to believe as they do, and your words will strike fear in them; fear of the Beloveds opening up their hearts to bring the Truth and Love to all of the children. Many will come into your life. Know them by their hearts. Now understand this: no one has to suffer, if you only live by the Power of Love and with Truth in your hearts; that is me. I will always be there in each of you. Now listen to the Sacred Stone and see how all can be healed and made new by using the water."

Instantly I was with the Skull again. And I was being shown the way of healing, using the Sacred Water of Mother Earth. After I was shown all that was to be known, Spider Woman touched my shoulder. I turned around and felt her love.

She wrapped her arms around me, hugging me close. I could feel her love pouring into me. When I looked into her eyes, a love poured inside of me from her that made tears come into my eyes. She too wept with joy.

She then pushed me back a little and said, "You have much to suffer, young guardian. I give you my love now because it will help you later in life when you need it most. Remember this love; that it carries you in beauty always, no matter what men say or do to you. When you go back, show only what you need to in helping your people, for there are those who are jealous in their hearts. Let others you show do these things for your people. Later, when it is time, tell and teach all who will listen, but be what you truly are, a Ghost in their own hearts, a Ghost that whispers to their hearts, telling them the truth. Later, the Beloveds will be reawakened and they will do their duties. Guard them well, young guardian. Now go. You must get back to your people, for many are giving up when they don't have to!"

I picked up my two friends, the Scepter and the Crossed Wands, touched them to the Sacred Skull, looked into the eyes of Spider Woman and let my spirit free. Instantly I was traveling in the energy that had me spiraling, then the popping sounds and the flashes of light, and I was back in my body once again.

I lay there listening all around. The jungle was alive with life. I heard a red-tailed hawk cry out and looked up at my friend, who was high in the branches above me. I sent him love, for I knew he was watching over me. He ruffled his feathers, spread his wings and looked directly into my eyes. We were brothers, he and I. He then leaped from the branch and flew down near me, circled once, and then began his flight through the trees. Later, I would set aside a gift for his help today.

I went to the pool and drank deeply, and thanked Mother Earth for her gift. Then, taking the Scepter and Crossed Wand, I sent my love into them, held them up to Grandfather Sun, and sang my prayer song and power song. I felt the crystals fill with power and vibrate with power. I then directed them to the water and plunged them into the water, sending my love into the crystals and the water. I felt the water respond, and energy pulsed from the water. The trees and plant people responded, all singing in the wind. The bird people began singing, and the bird people and the butterfly people began circling around me as I sang my thanks for all this love.

When I finished, I gathered up my things, got dressed and began my journey back, picking fruits and berries while I walked to strengthen my body. After a few hours of travel I found a good spot to camp for a while. I needed to rest and I needed to put food in me. I also needed to think about all of this; to understand all that I now knew.

See, it is one thing to be shown something. That in itself is not knowledge. Understanding the power, the truth, and how things work, that then becomes the knowledge. Many times in your life you have been shown something. You see it, know that it works, or whatever, but that doesn't mean you understand it. If you don't understand it, you will never have the knowledge until you do. So I needed time to understand all that the Skull and Spirit had shown me, and I was very aware of the warnings they had given me.

The place I had chosen to camp was a nice place. It was surrounded by giant water oak trees and had a small deep stream of fresh water. Eto-fv'ske (thorn trees), what the es'tehv'tke (white man) called devil trees, were everywhere. These trees were full of long sharp points that stuck out everywhere and would rip the skin or hide off of anything that brushed by it. They would help provide warning to me while I rested. I feared no man to be able to sneak up on me. It was the four-legged ones that hunt for food that I must be aware of. Any animal can sense a weakness in any prey. I was weak therefore I had to be aware of my situation. I was food for all that would not hesitate to kill me to eat.

First I made a shelter and gathered many of the old thorn tree branches, piling them up near the shelter where I would rest. My shelter was made by bending young saplings over and using vines to tie them together. Then, using palmetto leaves, I weaved these branches in and out together. Then I went to bathe and to drink.

The water tasted very good. Since my Mother gave me this life blood, I thanked her. I then dove down and searched the bottom for mussels. Mussels are a shellfish. Like oysters, they are very good to eat and good for you. Finding handfuls, I tossed them up on the bank and gave thanks for them. I spotted a large water moccasin, sent love to him, and said a prayer, for I must take his life for nourishment. He was my brother and I would always remember him. He moved towards me and I struck swiftly and took his life. I made tobacco offerings for him, and said a prayer of love for him and his people. Then I skinned him, cut his head off, removed the poison sacks, and saved them for the boys of my village to use on their blowgun darts.

Then I sat down next to the stream and laid out some of the water moccasin meat as an offering for my brother and friend, the red-tailed hawk. I began eating the snake meat and cracking open the mussel shells and eating them, occasionally washing them down with water. After fasting, one can never eat much, otherwise you will get sick, for your stomach has shrunken, plus your body is cleaned out from all the things that have corrupted it. Now, I lived wild and only ate what was natural, but even then your body has to adjust back to food.

It may seem strange to you that I ate meat raw but it was not strange to me. Yes, I enjoy roasted or cooked meat but there is nothing wrong with eating raw meat either. In fact, some meats taste better raw and are better for you.

While I ate, I sat and thought about all the things that I was shown, what I had done before, what I had seen my people do with the water, and our water ceremonies. Then I thought of the women's ceremonies and the women's bodies. Didn't they have a natural purification of their bodies through their moon times? And didn't they automatically have the power of water and the moon given to them? And did they not also have the true gift of Love, just as Mother Earth?

Now I was understanding more and more of this knowledge. I had even heard the stories of the es'te-hv'tke (white man) religion, about the man they called Ce'sus-Klis' (Jesus Christ), and about the part to paptisetv (baptize) people in water and his blood. I thought of all the things the to'htvlheecv (translator) had told us of their stories of their religion. Then I thought about all I had seen in my journeys to Egypt, Atlantis, Mayan, Inca, Aztec, Lemuria, to the Greek peoples, Romans, Celtic, Welsh, Cahokia, Serpent Mounds, Etowah, Jeru, Ais, and the Ani-yun-wiya. The more I thought, the more I could see all the connections. I even thought of the time that I journeyed to the Desert people, where they had built the place called Babylon and saw the tower and things there.

As I was sitting there thinking on all of these things, I caught the sudden flapping of wings from the corner of my eye. I turned and saw my brother red-tailed hawk flying over to me. When he landed, he looked at me then hopped over to the raw snake meat I had laid out there for him. I watched him with love in my heart as he relished this food that was his. He had been with me now for several years, since he was a young hawk on his own. We were brothers and we were friends. It is the way it should be.

Sometimes he left gifts for me, such as a rabbit, squirrel, or snake. We shared our life, our spirit, and our food. Mostly we shared our love and respect for each other. He was not a pet. He was free and so was I. After he had his fill, he came over a few feet and looked into my eyes. I felt his love and his thanks. I felt his message that he would roost above me tonight. I thanked him, and watched as he leaped up and flew to the tree over my shelter. I watched him clean himself up for a few minutes and then I went to drink some more water. I felt the power in the water as I drank my fill. Then I got up and went to my shelter. I got out my tobacco, cedar, corn meal, and holly leaf, made my prayers and offerings, and sang my special song.

Hey-ya-hey—hi-aei—hi—a—ei—ya—a—ee—i-ei—ii-hey
Hey-ya-hey—hi-aei—hi—a—ei—ya—a—ee—I-ei—ii-hey

Grandfather, look at me Grandfather, I know you

see—all the pain—— And suffering, that my people, have overcome————

Hey-ya-hey--hi-aei—hi—a—ei—ya—a——ee—i-ei—ii-hey
Hey-ya-hey— hi-aei—hi—a—ei—ya—a—ee—i-ei—ii-hey

Grandmother, so full of love, bringing forth life, for all of us, from her love—All life grows————can't you feel her—in your soul.

Spirits on the winds, talk to me. Spirits on the winds, touch all things. Spirits on the winds, listen, listen to them. Spirits on the winds, come to me. Spirits on the winds, set me free. Spirits on the winds——flow—through——me

Hey-ya-hey——hi—aei—hi—a—ei—ya—a—e—ii-ya-hey
Hey-ya-hey——hi—aei—hi—a—ei—ya—a—e—ii-ya-hey

All my brothers, sisters too. All living things are connected to you. You are part——, of the whole, as you live the circle grows. The circle will grow as long as love flows, So let your mind and heart be one. And in love————all things can be done—

Hey-ya-hey—hi—aei—hi—a—ei—ya—a—e—ii—ya—hey
Hey-ya-hey—hi—aei—hi—a—ei—ya—a—e—ii—ya—hey

Spirits on the winds, talk to me. Spirits on the winds, touch all things. Spirits on the winds, —listen, listen to them. Spirits on the winds, —come to me. Spirits on the winds—set me free— Spirits on the winds—fl—o—w through me——

Hey-ya-hey—hi-aei—hi—a—ei—ya—a—e—ii—ya—hey

This song is what is in my heart. I sing it with love, total and complete, for the words are true and attune all things to you. For there is power in words, power in sound, the vibration of my heart filled with love becomes a frequency of musical love throughout my entire being and all around me.

Then I lay down with my two friends, the Scepter and the

Crossed Wands, and let my spirit free to gather all it could while I rested my exhausted body. I awoke before sunrise, maybe about 45 minutes before Grandfather would look upon us with his love and send us his love and power. I went and made my offerings, and then said a prayer to the water and thanks to Mother. Then I went to bathe.

I was standing in the water when Grandfather came and showered all of Mother with his love. I thanked him for this love and all of the beauty that was created from this loving power. I then directed my love to the water in which I stood. I poured out my energy into the water and felt the change immediately. The water energy increased and flowed into me, filling my body with healing, love, strength, and power. I felt Grandfather smiling at me as he sent his love to the water standing on my flesh.

So much love, so much power flowed through me. Beauty was everywhere. I directed my love and energy at the Plant people, Tree people, Mother Earth, all the Winged ones, all that I could see around me, and watched them all absorbing this love, energy and power. I felt their gifts of love return to me. I thanked all of my relatives and knew that I must return to my People.

So I took apart my shelter, thanking the young saplings for their help, and looked up for my friend. He was looking off to the south. I knew instinctively that he was looking at his breakfast. I knew when he finished he would find me if he chose to. I sent him my love and gathered my things, got dressed, and continued my way back to my People.

As I jogged the warrior trot, I let my mind dwell on how I would pass this on. I tried to figure out who I could show this to so that it would help my People, yet not let it be known that I was involved. Finally I knew it had to be one of a good heart, one that was respected, and who would keep my name out of it. Her name was Tvffolupv (Butterfly). She was a Clan Mother and was known for her knowledge of plants to help people. She was also an elder and a member of the Mvliketv Lo'cu (Turtle Clan). Her grandson was a friend of mine, so it would seem normal for me to be around her. She was a grandmother of my extended family.

I increased my pace, running hour after hour, until it was almost dark. When I was near my village, I stopped to cool my body down and then went to the bathing area, stripped down, and dove in. When I had finished and made myself presentable, I went to the village. I made my way to my uncle's house, where I was expected.

All in the village knew where I had gone and for what purpose. None knew the location, just the direction I had gone. No one would be rude and stop me or talk to me until after I had spoken with my uncle. This is the proper conduct. None would even question later on what I had been shown or told, for that would be disrespectful.

Only on matters that Spirit instructs a person to tell his people or show his people would that ever be done. Messages, teaching, medicine, etc., were given to the individual from Spirit. It is a personal thing that is no one else's concern, unless Spirit directs the person to tell others. It is the same with dreams, etc. Those are not to be shared with others. It is a Spiritual Matter that comes from the Spirit World. Only if someone does not understand does it get spoken to a Holy Person (female or male), in private, so that person can help the one with the dream. It is never spoken about to any other, for those are personal matters between individuals and Spirit. It is Power.

I greeted my aunt and uncle the proper way, and then waited for my acknowledgement to be given to sit and talk. My uncle was a known Holy Man, a man gifted with many gifts. He was actually my grandfather's younger brother, so I guess in your terms he was my great uncle. I was apprenticed, as you would call it, to him. Amongst my people, I was being taught and instructed by him. He was a good man. He knew from the start what I was, and he knew that I had found my answer, and more.

He offered me to join him in his smoke he rolled for us. He made all the prayers to all the directions, and we should breathe with Spirit. When he was finished, he asked my aunt could she spare some food for us. My aunt was a good woman and she could cook very, very well. She brought in two gourds of water, then a plate full of nuts, berries and fruits, and then a bark dish full of acorn bread with chunks of alligator tails.

It is always proper to not talk while eating. Eating time means just that, eating! And it is always proper to eat all that is put before you. So my uncle and I ate, and ate even though we were past full, until all that was before us was gone. My aunt came and asked if we would like some more, and we both thanked her for the delicious food and said that we were full, patting our bellies as we leaned back and showed her our bulging swollen stomachs. This was also proper behavior, for it is an honor to her for us to enjoy her cooking. With love in our hearts, we thanked her again and we meant every word we said!

While we leaned back and relaxed for a while, we gathered our thoughts of what we would say. This too has a purpose. One never speaks without thinking just what one is going to say, for words are very powerful. I must wait until my uncle decides it is time to talk. This is proper also. This may seem strange to you, but these are the old customs of all people. It is done for a reason, not like today when there is no respect, no thinking, and no discipline of the mind or body, especially the mouth any more.

Finally my uncle said, "I see your journey was successful. Is there anything you can tell me?"

I told him, "yes, I found what I had sought" and then went on to tell him what Spirit said about being careful of who I showed this to because of those with jealousy in their hearts. My uncle nodded, so I continued on explaining what I was shown, and then how I would pass this on to Tuffolupv. My uncle sat there for a while chewing on my words, to digest all that I had said.

Finally he said, "I see and understand what Spirit has shown you, for when I was a young boy I remember the old ones doing things like that. I see we must have forgotten the reason and purpose of this way. It is true that many of the Tribe fear you and are jealous of you because of you being a este ha'tv-ha'yv (half-breed) with tur'wv hola'tte (blue eyes), and that you have spent your whole life learning from the old ones. It is also because you are a young guardian of the Hvm'ken Vnokec'ke (Beloved Ones).

"Many half-breeds are in the Nation. Few are paler than you. Most are darker than you. Many have a different color of eyes, but none of them are a young guardian. Few full-bloods are guardians, and fewer yet have your gifts. You have learned through your childhood that things would always be different for you, so at least you understand why. It is good that you chose Tuffolupv. She will do this and keep your name hidden from others. In the morning I will ask your aunt to speak with Tvffolupv and see if she will arrange a meeting with you that is not for others' eyes."

He stood, and I stood up. He embraced me in a hug, proud of me. He got up and left because he had to go to the lodge, as was expected for him to do. My aunt came in then and hugged me. She said that it was good that I was home, for she had missed my smile every morning. I kissed her cheek and told her "it was good to be back home". I asked "how were the people with the sickness?" She looked sad and said many more were sick, and word had come from the other towns and villages that many were sick. I, too, was sad. She lifted my chin up and said, "I know in my heart you can help them. I also know that you will let others do this. You are like my own flesh, my own heart, and I am proud of you. I will help any way I can. You know that."

I thanked her and told her that I loved her, too. Then I went to do my evening prayers. I returned later and went to bed.

The next morning when I got up, everyone was already up and gone, even though it was still dark. I went and gathered my things, and then went to do my prayers and offerings. When Grandfather Sun came up I was already in the water and did my prayers of thanks to him. When I was finished I made my way back to my uncle's home. My aunt was there getting ready to go into the fields. I set my things down and got my digging stick and water gourd. My uncle joined us. All members of the village or town were expected to help in the fields. No matter what position you may be honored by, the people were one of the same fire.

As we followed my aunt, other families were also making their way to the fields. My uncle touched my shoulder and whispered, "Your aunt has made the arrangement. While in the field, work the southeast side. Tuffolupv will meet you there later, so you can talk in private."

We continued on until we parted. I turned to go to the southeast section when I looked up and saw my aunt smile her beautiful smile at me. I picked my pace up. Much work needed doing in the fields, for many were sick with the fevers. So I worked hard until my body was soaked in sweat. I worked until around mid-day when I noticed Tuffolupv standing near the tree line. I went on working for a few more minutes, then casually walked towards the woods.

Once I entered the woods, I made quick time getting to her. I lowered my head and waited for her to acknowledge me. When she touched my shoulder I looked up into her eyes. She was smiling. She said, "Grandson, it is good that you have returned. I welcome you with my heart. I ask from my heart that you show me the old way to heal so that I can help the people. I will do as you request and keep your name out of it. I will take care of this now, so please sit down and explain this to me, for our People need this now. We will send runners to the other towns and villages of this news."

So I sat down with her and told her all I knew and understood. I had her try it with a gourd of water. She was amazed and full of love. I helped her to her feet and she thanked me and hugged me. I quickly left, taking a different route back to the fields, and went back to work.

The next day an es-hu'ehkv (crier) ran, announcing that a healing of the sickness was found. Butterfly was teaching the old way to the healers so all could be healed. I smiled, for now my People would know the way again. I made my way back to the fields, for the crops needed to be tended. Later, all would be in good health and the fields of crops would have many taking care of them, but for now I would continue to take care of them and give them my love.

Six moons had passed and I was on my way to see my grandfather Beaver, my mother's father. It had been a long time since I had seen him, and I knew this might be the last time I would. I felt him calling to me strongly, when I decided that I must come. When I got there he looked already gone. I approached and waited and waited. I thought he was asleep, and then I felt him. He motioned weakly for me to sit. I sat next to him and waited. He lifted his hands to my face, fingers touching my face all over. He always could see with his fingers. His hands next went to my shoulders and chest, then to my arms. I knew he was seeing how much I had grown since he last saw me.

When he finished, he smiled and said, "It has been a long time since I have been with you, yet I see you are doing well, and I can feel your energy, so I know you have grown in your gifts as well. You make me very proud of you. I can feel that you have something you want to share with me. It is pouring out of you like a stream of water from a bag with a hole in the bottom. So tell me, grandson, what it is that you want to share with me."

I waited and gathered my thoughts. When I was ready, I told him all that I had experienced since we were together last, and recently, the journey to help my People. He listened as I described what Spider Woman and Spirit had said to me, and he listened carefully as I described to him what the Sacred Skull had shown me. I then went on to explain all that I had thought about, including all the things I knew from my other journeys to all of the Ancient Places, and the stories that I heard told of the different religions of the foreigners who had come to this land. I told how all these religions had initially used the water, yet now had forgotten the old way to use the water. Now it was being done only as a routine gesture, with no thought or understanding of the real reason and purpose.

Then I told him how I had done these things myself and how I had shown Tuffolupv how and why to do this; and why I had her do this. When I was finished, he sat back for a while and thought this through.

When he finally had his thoughts together he said, "What you say is very powerful. I remember too, when I was a small one, of these things being done. The ones that did these things were called Heals With Water. Many people I remember being healed totally. They were like new: stronger, more beautiful, like they were better than they were ever before. I remember when the spotted disease struck us hard. One of the Heals With Waters came and healed the entire town. I can't remember any others doing this later in life. It is like the gift of this knowledge disappeared.

"You must do as Spirit instructed you, though, and be careful with this knowledge. Many would now hate this coming back to the People. The government officials, the foreigners, and especially all of the other religions would hate it. They would hunt you down and destroy you, so keep up your learning but always be cautious. Your uncle is a very wise and good man. He knows, as I have always known, that you will always suffer because of your blood being mixed and this knowledge and power that you are developing. Plus many of the Nations of People are taking on the white peoples' beliefs about women. Now many treat the women like slaves and animals. My time is near now, grandson.

"You, of all my blood, have grown to be the joy of my heart. And you have honored me by becoming all that you are and more. You have learned more than I did in my life, yet you still hold it in your heart about your heritage. To you I say this: clean your heart of pity and pride. You are what you are. If you let the words and feelings of others hurt your heart, they will win and take away from you the beauty of love in your heart. I know it hurts you what people say about you because of your skin tone and eyes, plus your father's shame is still thrown at you. Let it all go, my grandson, or it will destroy you from your own heart. Your heart is of Spirit, and I know that you know this, so I ask you to please let this out of your heart and mind. In time people will see the real you. Even if you were a full-blood or even looked like a full-blood, there would be those that are jealous or ignorant, or their egos and pride would make them attack you. Knowledge is Power; not foolish power, but the True Power.

"I will leave this world soon. I called you here because I wanted you to hear me say this one more time. Your life was meant to be this way. You can only make it harder by listening to what people say. All the true ones see the love in you. Those are the ones that matter. In your future you will make difficult decisions that will affect you. Just listen to your heart though. It matters not what people say is right or wrong. Only Spirit knows the Truth in you. Do your duty with honor. Protect the Beloved Women. Awaken them all when it is time. Give them back their True Power of Love. This is your duty, your purpose in this life. I give this to you to do. Do not fail. Let nothing, I mean nothing, stop you from doing this. Your life belongs to Spirit. Your purpose is to the Beloved Women. Your heart, your love your gifts, serve Spirit and the Beloved Ones."

I felt the tears come down my cheek, for his words struck true in my heart. Sometimes the truth is painful. I know what people called me or said about me hurt, but I tried to ignore it. I tried so hard to prove myself to all that I was true, but it seemed the more I did, the more the attack of words came. I no longer did much with anyone except with my family and my wives, who I always took care of. My duties were also to my uncle, who was instructing me, or the Clan Mothers who decided what should be done. My two sons were accepted as full-bloods. My daughter was too. They all looked full-blooded which I was thankful for. But hearing his words also struck home another truth to me. The children were my blood, but they belonged to their mother's clans. I loved them and they loved me, but I knew with my future that my life would not be with them. My heart cried, but I knew that my duty was to serve Spirit. I had chosen this above all else. Spirit had accepted me to be the guardian of the Beloveds, and to them I would serve my life as well.

I left my grandfather Beaver that night. It was the last time I got to be with him in the flesh. He crossed over and went to the Spirit World as his true self. He lived through many, many changes in this world. He was born in the late 1800's probably. I can guess around 1879 or so. Much had changed in his world. He taught me many things and was a true guardian of the Beloved Women. He inspired me to keep my vow to him and to let nothing stop me from my duty.

I come to you now, to let you know the Truth of the Healing Water. So please listen to my words carefully. Over the years of my life, I have worked and worked on these things. I know the Power is Real! You will too, if you only try this with Love in your Heart; Pure True Love.

Now the waters of the world are mostly polluted. Your bodies are polluted by sugars, acids, drugs, caffeine, alcohol, pharmaceutical drugs, and snack foods. For those of you who want a new life, a cure for all of your pain, disease, or sickness, if you want your body full of energy, stronger than you have ever been, if you want to have increased memory, and to enjoy life like you never have before, then listen. This you must truly want. You will have to give up many things that are destroying your body. If you don't want this, then you will not go through what is required. Love! Love Yourself! Your Spirit is in your own heart. Love yourself by giving up the alcohol, drugs, and many of your bad habits.

But first, let's give you a taste of what is there for you. I want you to fast. Yes, you must fast to rid your body of all the bad things in you. Fasting is only as hard as you make it. Either do it right or don't even try. Fasting means no food, none whatsoever. (If you have never fasted before, start at one day, then two, etc., until you can work up to the total eight days.)

I want you to drink only fresh spring water that you pray with first; sending love, your love to the water. If you have crystals use them correctly (be sure your crystal is attuned to you). There are many books that talk about how this is done, as well as clearing them, etc. Put the crystal in your left hand to receive all of the love, and then put it in your right hand to touch the water.) Send your love into them, and then send the love into the water. Send Pure Love; love that is deep in your heart. Drink the water as much as you like for four days.

After the fourth day, drink nothing at all. Pray every day, eight times a day or every moment if you will. Keep only love in your heart. On the fourth day of no food, no water, which is a total of eight days pray over your fresh spring water. Send your love into the water. Pray with Pure Love from your heart. Now sprinkle the water on your entire body, sending this love to the water. Feel the power of the water that vibrates. It has changed as it touches your flesh. Then drink the water not much at first. Let your body adapt to this life-blood of Mother and of Spirit.

Feel the difference in yourself. Now that you have started this, change your eating habits. Leave alone all those things that have any type of acids in them, caffeine in them, and sugars in them. Leave all alcohol and drugs alone. Eat fresh fruit or vegetables grown what you call organic now. All others have genetic mix-ups and pesticides and other things in them. Leave alone lots of red meat. I eat meat but I do so in small portions compared to my plants, herbs, and such.

This I tell you: if you truly want life, love, beauty, knowledge, and seek the Beauty of the World, you will find it this way, for the water, for the water that is in your body is polluted. Spirit is in you. You are in Spirit. You can do this. It is your choice now! All of the Beloved Women, this is your key! I have waited a lifetime for your awakening! It is time for you to claim your rightful place in this world.

I am Ghost, the Guardian of the Beloveds, and the Keeper of the Ancient Ways for you. You are all True Love. Feel my words in your hearts. Let the vibration of love from the water open you up to your True Power, and heal you and return you to your gifts.

Spirit calls to you. Mother Earth calls to you. All of the Star People call to you. And the Children of the Stars await you! Come Dance in your True Love, True Power. Come be what you truly are! I await you. When you have all come forth, you will hear me, and feel me in your hearts and dreams. You will then know where to come, for I will show you in your dreams. Heal those around you. All who hear these words wake up to the Truth. The Truth truly will set you free from the poisons of your own minds and heart.

I await you all. Muto esyo'men omvlv eto'h. Thanks to all of you! Men can also do this to heal themselves, and become better men in their rightful place.

Remember to Walk in Beauty and Love Always!

Chapter Twelve

Always a Warrior!

It was 1958 when we heard that people had come and were asking the Clan Mothers and elders for the young warriors to come and join the services of the military. Many of us didn't think this was going to ever happen, especially knowing how many of our elders had been treated in the previous wars. The Korean War was over. Many of our uncles and fathers had been there. Grandfathers and uncles had also been in the Great War (WW I). War was something my people knew very well.

All of us waited while the elders discussed these things. I thought back to my younger years, all the training by my people, and being trained by other tribes as well. Then I thought back to my grandfather deciding to have me train in martial arts. The people he and my uncles knew always amazed me. I was so eager to learn.

I was trained by two of the great masters of martial arts, and what was funny is that we couldn't talk to each other because of our different languages. But we managed to understand each other very well. If I made a mistake, a whack on the head, or back would quickly get my attention back on focus. I was taught Aikido and Tai kwon do, and Jujitsu. These old men made me respect them very fast. I was truly amazed at all they could do and I wanted to be even better. I was young and strong, so naturally I thought I could take on the world. I always got my ego knocked into place by these two masters, for no matter how hard I worked to learn a particular move, stance, or strike they always had an answer for my move.

It amazed me that they could so easily defeat any attempt that I made. This inspired me to learn from these great warriors, how to be one with myself, and fight a fight before it ever happened. To see the moves in time and space before they actually were energy was the key. I learned to think as my uncles said I would. They had learned this when they were in service. My hands, my feet, my entire body ached many, many moons trying to accustom my body to the techniques, the moves, and the protection of myself. Hardening my body and toning it to be one complete weapon or a design of healing.

These teachers were very different than any I had met in my young life. They love beauty and taught life was beauty as well, very similar thinking to my people. That even a warrior is an artist of beauty, for in acts of war there is a passion of life and death. For death is just another form of life. All is beauty. The act of fighting was a dance of life and death.

Participants all viewed their own selves as their main event, but we all are participating in the dance of life, for there is a struggle in our own selves to fight a fight with our own self. For the self is our greatest enemy. Our ego, our pride, our own issues we face each day is a worthy fight. To war with ourselves is to be better than we began, to learn from our own experiences and those of life all around us.

My memories made me think again about this. All my life I had been trained as a warrior, the lessons and instructions of my uncles and others of my people, made me fully aware of what was to come. My body had been conditioned to handle anything and everything. I had worked my body using the old wooden clubs. These were used by warriors to loosen up and strengthen their bodies, by twirling them in one hand or both hands, swinging them, throwing them. Hour after hour we worked our bodies, building muscle, and stamina, running in sand, water, and swimming, all helped condition us. Practice fighting with the war clubs, sparring with your brothers and uncles, built your reflexes to respond instantly or you were seriously injured. Throwing our cast nets and wrestling the alligators and crocodiles, made you learn how to use techniques and balance to defeat a larger and more powerful opponent.

I heard a shout and we all looked up to see what was happening. One of my uncles came to announce to all of us that a selection will be made by the elders who would go. I prayed I'd be selected. My whole clan had always been in wars. I knew that I and many of the relatives next to me all wanted to be selected. But all would not be chosen, for the tribe had to have some here for the protection of our people, our lands, our very survival. But inside I was bursting with excitement. We all waited to see if we would be pointed at. If so we bowed our heads in acknowledgement and went over to our Clan Mothers and elders. After watching one, then another be chosen, I was beginning to think that I wouldn't be chosen.

After what seemed like forever I was nudged by a cousin, and looked up and saw I was being pointed at. I bowed my head and jumped up, hurried to my uncles and Clan Mother. I felt the heaviness in my heart that I would be leaving my world again. This place I had come to love so much for its savage beauty so untouched by the outside world was so pure and wild as it was intended to be. Where was I going? What would it be like there? How were we supposed to act? All this was going through my mind, as my relatives were all hugging and praising us.

We all got caught up in the excitement. And it would last for a few more days. Feasting and ceremonies must be done. Then we would leave, some never to come home, some coming home but never the same. We weren't prepared for what we were getting into. But we would adapt for that is our way. So for now I would just think of my family and the ceremonies, I would let the future be what it would be.

I remember the long train ride. All of us grouped together, in the rail car. We stopped several times and more got on and joined us. We could feel these others looking at us like we were dogs or something unwanted. We stayed to ourselves, and only spoke to each other. Four of our elder uncles who could talk good enough in their language (English), talked for us to any who spoke to any of us. We could all speak some words but not really much at all.

The talk they talked was hard to follow. Once you learned a word and its meaning, they would laugh and say it meant something new now. How did they think we could learn to speak if they kept changing the meaning of the words? Like the word we all grew up hearing: "bad" now it means "cool" and "cool" means something different like "groovy". Is that like the word gravy, are they alike? Why do they change meanings? I never knew and still don't know why they keep changing the meaning of their words.

We rode for a long time. We were then told the train would be stopped here for a while. We could get off and stretch if we wanted to. So we all got off and were standing over by a tree under the shade and rolling up "hece" (tobacco) in our corn husk. Some were smoking pipes (made from corn cob or clays and some were of green soap stone.) Anyway we were making prayers and offerings, and people were walking by looking at us like we were on display or something.

A couple of the older brothers decided to scare these people, so they drew their war clubs and screamed their war cries and charged at them. Boy you never saw people yell and run so fast! We all roared with laughter, and figured that would teach them not to stare at us. (It is considered a challenge for someone to stare at us. Also it is very disrespectful.) A little later we got back on the train and continued to ride.

We got to wherever it was they took us. Many of us were a little dizzy from riding the train. I kept falling down, because I had learned to rock with the movement of the train, to walk or move while it was moving. To ride the train was to walk like a man drunk on crazy water, madness water, spirit water (alcohol). Now we saw that we were in a large place filled with people. And one of our uncles was talking to some men with markings on their clothes.

Our uncles motioned for us to follow them and we boarded a big bus and rode for a while until we came to a huge place with a fence. (Later I came to know this was our training base.) Our uncles got us off after some men came and began hollering at us like we had done something wrong. Our uncles told us that these ones always hollered and screamed at everyone, that their feet must have hurt or their pants rubbed them the wrong way. Anyway we were now where we would be for a while. Our uncles told us that they would stay with us and help us get to learn this way. This began our training.

The others who were there were of all nations and races as well. We watched them they watched us. I guess none really knew anything about each other. Whites all had several buildings to themselves, while blacks had their own, and all others were housed together. We could and did train together, on many things and it was very competitive.

I had never seen a swimming pool, but this one was big, and they had high platforms way up in the air for us to jump or dive off. If they couldn't swim, or tried to refuse, those men who holler and scream all the time, yelled even louder at them, hit them with long poles knocking them off the platform and into the water. If they were splashing around screaming for help, men with long poles pushed them even more, making them try to swim, acting out how the person was supposed to move arms and legs. We couldn't believe how many people couldn't swim. Later we learned those who couldn't swim were called "rocks" because they sank to the bottom like a rock. Ha! Ha! And they would stay in rock school until they learned how to swim.

They tried to cut our hair and boy did that almost start a big war. Many, like me, believed that if you cut my hair I lose my spirit. For our hair is a reflection of our spiritual growth and is a very big part of our own spirit. Anyway our uncles explained that the way these people did things we would have to cut our hair at this time, to make sure we have no diseases, no bugs such as lice, crabs, etc. We knew we didn't have these things, but our uncles said they were told the same thing many years ago too.

As their elders told them, we were told that we could save our hair if we wanted to. I wanted to save mine. Another word I had to learn the meaning of again. I thought save my hair meant I would keep my hair safe from them. I did not know it meant I could pick it up off the floor mixed with others' hair. It was all my uncles could do to stop me from killing the man who took my hair.

His eyes got opened that day to how fast we could really move. My knife was going for his throat when my uncle caught my arm saying no! No! You must stop! That was a day I never forgot, for it was a change from war braids and manhood to a man of mourning and child. I guess you could say both. I mourned the day for my spirit and my hair. Also I was a child to this world which I knew nothing of. I began to question my own self. Was I really ready for this? Did I truly want to do this?

These people were always hollering and screaming at you like they hate you or you do something wrong, now they take my hair robbing me of my spirit and disrespecting me. I was and am Muskogee, a people who have never been defeated in war and never will be. Who are these people asking for us and then acting this way towards us?

My uncles talked to us all that night, explaining that this was like an initiation to a clan or war society, that we all had to go through this to prove to them that we were willing to do whatever it took to join the fight. They did a good job explaining otherwise we would have left then and there. Anyway we were now in the Navy, and only beginning to learn of the true challenges that would face us.

This was a new world for all of us native people. Yeah there were brothers from all across the country. Many of us made lots of new friends while others were more standoffish, and kept to themselves. I could understand their feelings. Many of us were traditional enemies, yet now we were asked to be together as one.

I really didn't even want to help these people who had fought against all Native nations. It was like we were supposed to forget all the mass murders and atrocities they had committed to all our peoples. Raping, stealing, robbing, even using poisons to kill our babies in the foods they offered as gifts when they came to talk. Always the same with everybody they dealt with. Lies and treachery were all these Americans had ever done and shown to all peoples of north, central and south America. They had no honor, no truth, and would always believe they were better than everyone.

I had asked my uncles and grandfathers about these things many times. Why do you help the enemy of all life? They always said that it is war, these people are our enemy. Never doubt that, but even then you must use your head, know your enemy. You can learn a lot and then you will know their weaknesses always. Plus we do it for honor. It isn't like the times of old when we can go raiding, or to war to gain honor, and to test ourselves. This way we can do this and learn all about them, and see the world we don't know and gain honor for our people! One day you will be glad you learned and experienced this and from that you will be able to help our people more.

Now here I was with all these others, all of us thinking about the same thing. Do I really want this? Do I want to be hollered at by these foolish men? Do they realize I could take them any time? What have we done now? Oh boy I really think I made a mistake in wanting to come here! You could see it in everyone's faces. None of us were used to being treated this way. Our people didn't act this way. Oh well, our elders had spoken and we had stepped forth to be chosen. We could not quit or leave now, that would dishonor our families, our clan, and our nation. Each of us knew that we would go on, even if we had to put up with these stupid acts.

Week after week we trained. Sometimes it was fun, all the exercising was fun to us, it was the working on the other things that sometimes was aggravating, and frustrating. All of us were divided into groups, and trained together. Guns, we knew, but these big guns were something new to us. Machines were learned, fires we learned, (fuel, jet fuel, oil, all kinds). It was training that kept us busy and our minds off of other things.

After boot camp, most of us were sent to different places to learn more. About 80 of us natives were sent to learn bombs and explosive demolition, and dismantling. We learned so much my head hurt. Time after time, again faster, faster, till you could do it blindfolded. Week after week, we were in the water, and out of the water. We worked. I know we enjoyed the water. We were all otters and dolphins and gators all our lives, so the swimming and all was the best times we were having. The hand to hand fighting was natural for us.

It was really easy for my all my Muskogee brothers and me. We had all been taught martial arts since we were real young. This really impressed the people there training us and those who watched us all the time. Everyone saluted them. At the time we really didn't pay them much attention. We should have I guess? It might have taught us to respect them a little more. Later on I would constantly be in trouble for not paying them attention or saluting them.

Finally we were sent on a mission test. At the time they didn't tell any of us it was test. We thought it was real and we acted that way too. There was no panic; just men doing what we were trained to do. Many times they took us on long flights, then on to a ship, and then into the water we went, like sharks hunting, like real water wolves. Each time we were gone longer and longer doing more difficult and more dangerous things. This was beginning to be fun.

We worked with people of all races now. Our groups were split up and mixed up. No more than two or three natives per group with others that were of other peoples, and whites, and I learned even amongst them they were split. Irish hated Italian. North hated the South, or they acted like they did anyway. We were grouped up to where we were so mixed we had to get along or we'd fail. We were on the go all the time, either on missions or constantly training. While others got leave to go home we never did. We didn't feel we earned that yet-to go home. We would go when we were done.

Weeks had turned to months. Months turned to years, and everything changed again. War was now here and we were asked to join the SEALs. Just what we were told made all of us say "Yes". Now more training, more fun, more blood, sweat, yelling and hollering at us. I came to realize if they didn't yell at us they didn't like us. We were in training most of the time, and it was constant day and night, together, more as one unit, know what each is best at, and use that skill to the best advantage for the group.

We trained so much, that even in my sleep I trained, different weapons, new techniques. New instructors were all giving us useful tools for what we were, Warriors, plain and simple, shaped, molded and honed so everything we did was automatic reflex, no thought, no hesitation, just instantaneous action.

They brought in a man one day that changed my mind about bombs and explosives. This man was a master! He showed and taught us how to take ordinary household items and make a highly explosive bomb. Then he taught much, much more, always taking time to answer any questions we might have; or going over things again and again. We learned how to design just about any type of nasty surprise that would inflict terrible damage.

We had men come and teach us about different countries, their religions, their customs, their everyday clothing, weapons, and terrain. We had to know about these places, normal and not so normal climate, what type of animals, reptiles, birds, that lived there. We were told we could choose any weapons of our choice, that we would not be under any regular branch of service but be under one CO (commanding officer); that we never would be allowed to discuss anything about what we did, or where we went; that we were always the first in to gather intelligence, create chaos, or disrupt any movements of supplies or troops; that we would be expected to do the impossible; that yes we would suffer higher rates of casualties, but also that we at no time will ever leave any one behind, never would we surrender, or be captured. Most of us made pledges to each and all in our groups that if we were sure we couldn't get away then we would fight to the death.

Many days, weeks, months of preparing, some came, some went, many to become advisors, recruiters of the mountain peoples of Vietnam. While most like me, continued to train to be sent as a group to certain areas to do what we were asked to do. Yes we lost people, they had to be replaced; we trained with the new ones as a unit, as one, until we were comfortable with them.

Any one new had it rough though. It is hard to replace someone you grew to trust, need, depend on, and yes to even become a friend. I never thought I would have friends that weren't of my people. But yes I came to understand there are good and bad in all peoples. And even though we were told never get to be friends with anyone by our instructors, still we did. And to lose any one of us, was a blow to us, because we felt that we must have messed up otherwise he would be alive.

We all felt we could take on anything and win! We had to believe in ourselves otherwise we could not function as we did. We were the best of the best. We were warriors, gladiators of the old stories the instructors told us about. We saw ourselves as invincible, unstoppable, and nothing could stop us from our objective. This was what they created in us.

Now we would put this to the test. Mission after mission my unit was called on-all successful! Finally the day came and we got orders to go report to Vietnam. Our war had begun for us. Now we would do what each of us had been training and waiting for. War!

Being in the country behind the DMZ (demilitarized zone), far into the mountains, our unit was operating at a small village where we trained and recruited the mountain peoples to work with us. Their "maja" and "majo", (holy man & holy woman) taught us their ways, beliefs, their way of life. We were teaching them how to use different weapons, set booby traps, gather Intel (intelligence), and work as teams!

We were on the trail of a large group of VC (Viet Cong). These people had been raiding, raping, and robbing the villages in the area. This was our game time. I led as point. I set the pace at the warrior trot of old time, mile after mile, keeping the pace, yet fully aware of my surroundings. One of my brothers followed my trail and led the others about a klick (about a mile) behind me into the mountains. It is hard to gauge distance as in a straight line, because of the terrain, up and down, and around!

Anyway I picked up a flanker and quickly took him out with my blow gun, using poison darts. I like to mix different poisons together, for a better result and faster delivery. This takes time and skill. So don't try these things. They are deadly! When I found other sentries I took them out one by one. I mimicked one of the native birds, knowing my brother would understand. Moments later I heard his answering call. Now he would relay that they had been found and they would come on the run, and be cautious as well! In minutes the whole group was there! Now it was time to give them the "what for"!

The mask is called a booger mask. They are designed and made to frighten away evil spirits, for use during ceremonies, and for war to frighten the enemy. This one is made from oak tree bark, with attached branches and moss with poison berries hanging from the branches.

All of us checked each other to make sure all was ready again. This would be fast and chaotic to them. We spread out and circled. On a prearranged signal we attacked from all sides at once, aiming for legs, faces, killing, maiming, screaming in our war cries, panther screams, our faces all painted or disguised, flashing in and out of their view, never allowing them to get us pinned down or guessing where we were, or where we were coming from.

Then quiet again. We were gone, while they were panicking, trying to figure out what had hit them! We pulled back and just watched. My brother to point and I rested. A Kiowa brother watched our rear, and the rest reloaded, regrouped and rested while we let the effects have time to sink in with our enemy, let them think we were gone. And then we hit them again.

All day and all night we stayed on them, never letting them sleep, have time to rest or eat. Constant attack after attack, hit and run, hit and run. They had so many injured and wounded that half of them left were helping each other move. Still we kept the pressure on. Poison darts, bows and arrows, always striking silently taking out their sentries, and leaders. Grenades were thrown amongst them sleeping or eating. They were so scared that they couldn't take a dump or a piss without fear either. Man doesn't like to die exposed! Ha! Ha! After three days they were dismantled, mentally, and physically.

Being a member of a unit like this was far safer to me and others than being in the regular service. Here we knew if we weren't there for each other we all would die. In other units and services they still hated and they definitely were still divided and separated by race, region, and religions, and that could get all of them killed. They were a danger to be around. If and when we were amongst these other regular military, army, marines, air force, navy, we stuck together. No matter if you attacked one you were attacking all.

No one wanted any part of us. But they all wanted us around especially when there was a fight in the making, so to most that we had to be with for a period of time, or on some kind of routine activity, jointly we felt that they didn't want to be fighting there. That most were forced into joining because they had been drafted. And all they were concerned with was finishing the tour and going home.

With us, we had all joined by choice and we were what we were-Warriors. We fight because that is what we do. We either fight for something or die for nothing! It was that simple to us, and here was as good as anywhere to us. It made no difference, what terrain, what geographic location, or what the politics were; that was not our concern or job. Our business was fighting. That and only that, and to win, either succeed or die trying to win! There is no second place, third place. You either win or you lose. It was as simple as that.

Most of the fighting we did was sudden, no second to think, but only to react. Since we had our own choice of weapons each of us had different styles, but it sure caused havoc amongst those we attacked. I loved my big heavy machete. It weighed about 12 pounds, but it caused so much damage up close and personal, that those who survived couldn't believe what they saw when they looked at those that were hit and struck by it. It could take a limb completely off easily, or your whole torso, split you right down the middle, or behead you faster than you could blink. And it was balanced perfectly for throwing as well. Anyone hit by it, after it was thrown, was immediately knocked flying and dead as well.

Imagine walking or marching with a whole platoon of your friends, thinking you are safe with all your numbers. You see nothing that even remotely looks like any trouble. Then all of a sudden, death has just raced right into and amongst you while you were talking. The guy in front of you, his head has flown off his shoulders, blood splattering all over you, then you feel the brush of death as your body is flung backward by the force that struck you and cut into you. Your mind doesn't even have time to register that you are dead and falling. As the next falls around you, screams fill the air. As men or beast attack, faces that are a nightmare in your eyes as those all around you, cry out their death screams, then they vanish. Gone!

Out of nowhere they came, into nowhere they suddenly disappear. All that remains is the dead and the mangled. Screams of pain and fear! Urine and feces; smells reek in the air. Gunfire blasts everywhere but hitting nothing, only a release from those who still shake from trying to understand what just happened. Men staggering in shock their minds not ready or equipped to deal with the sight before their eyes, or what they just experienced. Questions they ask in their own minds. Is this real? Is this a dream or nightmare? Someone wake me up! Is anybody home in there?

The aftermath has you on edge until your nerves are worn so tight that anything will cause you to snap. You fear sleep. You fear moving, leaving the safety of your group. Suddenly it starts all over again, grenades falling in all around you, bodies blown, flying apart in all directions and still you can't move. You look for a target but see nothing. Suddenly you see right before you a painted face grinning, as your body is falling, falling down, then you feel the blade as it turns in your guts, and you know, you are dead.

This is what everyone who faces the SEALs feels: There is no defense, there is no warning. There is none better or better trained. We are what we are: Warriors. It is what we do! We chose this. We are born for it! Of all that served in Nam, we never had any captured. We don't quit.

We were asked to stop the supply routes, troop support, and troop movements, and that is what we did. Supplies were shipped from numerous different countries. Our Intel (intelligence) was always pretty much on target. Sometimes we just gathered our own. We used the same hit and run tactics in the boats as we did in the jungles, always striking, never giving them any time to move or protect their cargo whether it was supplies or troops. We also had to stop the black marketeers who profit by smuggling stolen medical supplies, (a lot were from our forward bases) drugs, and weapons. You have to remember, wherever there is war there are those who will always try to profit from it. Yes even companies, politicians, individuals, or groups of people. War is an ugly business.

There are no winners or losers, because everyone loses in a war, one way or another. And just when you think "No it don't mean shit to you, can't touch you", BAM, it smacks you right in the face and it isn't just those that are there, but your families, girlfriends, kids, friends, your community.

War affects everyone in one way or another, wife sitting at home or on the base, waiting, worrying, if she will get the news today, the stress aging her, wearing her down trying to take care of everything by herself. Every time the phone rings, every knock on the door, her heart stops and begins pounding. Your mother goes through the same thing. Your kids feel the stress of your wife, she cries they cry. They don't understand. Your sisters, miss you, they too don't know why you went. Then there are those who protest, start riots, and when some come back they are spit on, or have trash thrown on them.

People are calling you a murderer, baby killer, pig, and some really bad words. One thing about the military you can really learn some words! Words sometimes that can't even be found in a dictionary! I had to learn these words. I got called them many times so it was important that I learn what they mean. And as I learned I got mad.

In Native languages there are no curse words, and we sure don't curse the Creator, or put bad words on Him or Her, depending on the beliefs of each tribe! Even in Nam we were cursed by all our enemies, but some of those in the other militaries, bases, contractors, (never did understand contractors) we were not like them, didn't act like them either. Our enemies put out rewards for our capture, our identities. We knew this. We also knew there was a war going on even between our own military.

Race issues were still very obvious to all. And even those who tried their best not to be that way, it still was pushed upon them. It was "never safe anywhere" was how my brothers and I felt. The only ones we could trust were our SEAL brothers. It was bad that you come from being in the country, (behind enemy lines) thinking you could get some rest, report, get re-supplied, and gather things to take back for the local villagers.

But instead behind the DMZ (demilitarized zone) a grenade could land in your lap. Someone would scream "sniper" and firing begins everywhere and you get hit because one of those hating you just took a cheap shot to take you out.

Not all people were racial, many good men and women served in all the branches, but it didn't take many to ruin it for everyone. One bad apple spoils the whole barrel.

Then there were all the mistakes of war. Being in an area waiting to ambush a platoon, then artillery opens up and they are dropping rounds in your lap. Or pilots begin dropping napalm on you instead of the enemy. Choppers come in guns a blazing but they are opening up on you. Mistakes are made in war. Always have and always will! The pressure of accepting your mistake and going on is also there. Some can't deal with it, and crack, either turning to alcohol or drugs to drive the demons that haunt them from their minds. Some turn inward and are a complete vegetable. Others turn outward and blame everyone else for their mistakes and take it out on everyone! Every person handles their mistakes differently.

If you cause one or more to die, that is something very hard to deal with unless you have no soul, no conscience, or you're just a sick individual. And being a SEAL is no exception. Most times though it isn't a mistake that haunts you, it is all those faces, their eyes looking into yours that you have killed that haunts you. Because being a SEAL, most of your kills will be up close and personal, not from long range, right there in your face, your hands on him, you feel his heartbeat, smell his breath, and see the fear in his eyes. You block it out. You go on and do what you are trained to do. Your mind and body is a machine that has one purpose and that is to complete your mission. It is only after everything is over and you're sitting around relaxing that it hits you like a sledge hammer, or in your sleep as your mind plays the scenes back to you.

The images: bodies burning from napalm, screaming, bodies blown apart, holding a friend or a stranger in your arms as he fights to live yet nothing you can do will save him. Or a man begging you to stop his pain, finish him, stays in your head.

Yes war is ugly and anyone stupid enough to say it isn't hasn't ever "been there, nor done that"!

I grew up preparing for war, trained all my life, had the best teachers ever of guerrilla warfare, pain, torture, conquering our fears, martial arts, judo, and every conceivable method: weapons, poisons, anything you could possibly imagine. I had already killed before I was even a teenager (when I was around 8 years old). I'd been told and warned by my elders and other vets, and instructors, but nothing can prepare you for what it is actually like or how you will deal with it, because everyone will deal with it differently! I buried mine in my head, kept pushing it back further and further, to just try to forget it. I would do a cleanup ceremony once I was home and everything would be okay!

This is what I thought and did. But later in my life it surfaced and I hated myself, hated what I had done to so many, hated that I thought it was over it but I was just beginning to realize that I had been a monster, something created by war, that thrived and excelled with all the things that I had done, even though it was needed, endorsed and sanctioned. I had taken it to a whole new level.

I had taken my warrior training by my people, and the art of using poisons and blow guns to another level attacking my enemies through their own fears (poisons that are used to induce your greatest fears and bring them right before your eyes and in your mind), gathering Intel about shipments of men and supplies, to create chaos and fear amongst our enemies, to such an extent, that my own people and my brothers of the SEALs looked at me as if I was a monster. I used my knowledge of these peoples' beliefs and customs to attack them psychologically which increased their fears. I could make them feel pain that was never even from touching them. I attacked their minds, using the poisons, where every word I speak or had someone else speak, becomes their vision, what they see and feel in their minds. This is the most mind controlling drug in the world. None were safe from this. None could hold back anything.

The CIA and other Intel agencies used me to do this. They patted me on the back and said "good job, or well done, you need to teach others this or at least show us what it is to make this stuff. Your country needs this to save lives and you would be doing a great service to your country".

I always told them I didn't know all the ways of my people, but I would have to get their permission. Yes I lied. I did not trust these people in suits or nice clothes. They were never dirty, never ever told "no" by any commander, even those with all kinds of things on their chest, caps, hats. I know it was ranks, or medals, but they didn't mean anything when these men could just come in and tell them what was what. I have always withheld my people's secrets of the poisons and I always will. This is for our warriors only.

Anyway the things I did, even though they did give me medals and all kinds of papers with president's name and seal on them, they were nothing to me, and still are nothing. My mother burned all of those things when I came back because I had become a monster! I was different. I had changed so much my own mother didn't want me around. My elders did all kinds of ceremonies on me trying to drive the evil spirits away from me, trying to clean up my own spirit.

And even though I thought I had gotten myself well, I was wrong, seriously wrong. The monster was just hiding deep inside where I had pushed it away all those years. And when he came out again, I was in serious trouble. I came home from war, only to have to experience another war, one within my own self, and one with the government who was once again killing and murdering native peoples, and even some of my own family.

Now I would take my skills back and use them against those who once I did things for. They too would find out what it is to face a man, not a woman and little kids who they murdered that were unarmed. Now they would know me as their enemy, and I was enraged and willing to do anything. I was a perfect tool again for others to use as they needed. But that is another story, maybe to tell you one day. But not right now, for now I will just talk to you as you need to hear about Nam.

Very few talk of why we got involved in Vietnam. Very few of the public even know the truth, because it was another one of the things the government didn't want anyone to know. But you have to study their history. You have to know when they won their independence, and how they tried to become like the US and begged the United Nations for acceptance with their democratic government they were putting into place. See what happened after they elected their president, vice president, members of their own congress and senate.

I cannot tell you these things because I'd be violating laws which are in place but you can do the research and learn the truth as I did! And to the Vietnamese that I have apologized to and asked for forgiveness from over the years, and to all those I have not seen, or their families, and to all the other peoples I met and had contact with one way or another. I APOLOGIZE FOR ALL MY ACTIONS AND I BEG YOUR FORGIVENESS FOR ALL THAT I DID!

I know it is not enough, and for that I will face the Creator one day and be judged for it and I will accept that.

Many people think "Oh I could do that, or anyone could do it". Many people watch too much television, and think they can and honestly believe it. But there is a very big difference between television, and the real thing. I cannot speak of many or any of our missions, or what happened, or who was there. I don't have the clearance or permission from those who were there. What I will do is give you a hypothetical incident, so all those who think they could, might just get a small taste........

IT WAS DARK, and rain was falling heavily. All day long the rain had fallen. Up and down the mountains, through the swollen rivers and creeks, we moved, all the time watching and ready for the attacks to come. We had jumped from the plane in the middle of the night. Radar must have picked up the plane because artillery had opened up.

We had to jump 30 minutes too soon. We were about 200 miles behind the DMZ, (demilitarized zone) and were in the heart of our enemies' stronghold forward bases. We had our orders and every man present knew what it meant. We were on our own. If we survived it was up to us to get our own selves out. No help would be coming. We were alone, except for all our enemies in every direction.

And it would be with total joy and rewards if they captured or killed any of us. They would want us bad and to be captured would mean endless torture for information, and their pleasure for all we had done to them. No illusions on our part. Each of us knew full well what was at risk, but this was our job, our duty, and we would complete it even if it meant we all died. And we would leave no man behind!

I was on point. My job was to get us there to our objective, silently, and with no one knowing we were there until it was time. Intel said there would be major players here at the meeting tonight. Our job was to get information, papers and any one we could take alive, and bring back. Getting this would not be easy, but not near as hard as snatching people and getting out without anyone the wiser, and it was a long way back. We could possibly call in for an airlift for the targets we snatched, after we got real close back towards the DMZ, but not before. Once they became aware of those missing, a massive search and hunt would be under way.

My mind had these thoughts going through it when something didn't feel right. Instantly I froze, and moved nothing but my eyes. My senses picked up something, therefore danger was near. I just had to find it. My brothers were behind me, flankers and one trailing watching our backsides. I took care of the front. I made the sound of the peafowl, my call mimicking the bird perfectly. My brothers returned their calls, and were ready. All now knew to be on edge for the enemy was real close. It was my job now to find him and take him out. Slowly ever so slowly, inch by inch I lowered myself to the ground without a sound. No sudden movements, only the breeze moving the branches and leaves as the rain poured down. Minute after minute I used nothing but my eyes and senses, trying to locate what was wrong. Suddenly I noticed a shape that was unnatural to the contours of the tree and the ground around it. I never moved. Thirty minutes passed by, still I waited.

Then ever so slightly I saw him. Oh he was good, but his lack of patience would cost him tonight. Maybe in his next life he would learn better. I waited until he was blind to me and I moved like the panther of my home, silently, barefoot, my equipment all left on the ground, my breechcloth, and knife was all I needed.

Using one arm I pulled myself up from the ground, my hand gripping the limb. Once I was up I went up the tree like a snake, silently moving using every bit of cover I could. He was looking, but could not find what he thought he saw, and when he got beneath me, he never had a chance to even fire a single shot. My knife had gone straight in to the hilt. My free hand pulling his head back so fast that it snapped before it even registered to him that he was dying. My fingers blocked his finger from depressing the trigger as he died.

Gently, I laid his body down and my eyes scanned the area looking to see if he was alone or if he had friends. A peafowl called again, with a slight echo and a smaller call. All was clear. My brothers had taken out the other enemy. We would be getting close now. These forward lookouts were just the beginning. We had to move in to get what we came for.

We were now there, sitting in the cold rain watching and waiting for our chance to move. We had successfully made it inside their perimeters, and now were amongst them and they didn't know it. We had watched and seen who was doing most of the talking, and we had seen some of those that were in the Intel photos we were shown. We watched now as they all settled in for the night. We watched and waited feeling the rhythm of the patrols, and the camp.

Everything has a rhythm. You must find that to be invisible. Finally the signal was given and each of us was paired up. Each pair had a target to acquire and to get back to our planned route. If things went wrong, oh well it would be the end for many that night then, because we don't quit, we don't lose, we don't leave anyone behind. It's as simple as that. If we had to die, well that was that, oh well!

We had our targets each selected. A young man from Tennessee was paired with me. We would get the big guy from Russia, since we were the largest two and he would have to be carried. We all moved in to where we were in position, each mentally counting so that each of us would strike at the same time.

The guards that were stationed outside each hut we took out silently, all with their necks broken, and their larynx crushed. We moved in, in less than one minute. All those targeted were in our hands and fast asleep! The cobra strike is a martial arts move and strike that takes down and out the largest and baddest of men! It can be used to kill, paralyze, or used to put someone to sleep. Since we needed these people alive, they were just sleeping and would have no memory of what happened.

I tossed the big guy on my shoulder and my brother led the way. We would all meet at our planned point. Silently we vanished into the night, our prisoners, carried like rag dolls, as we ran! For one hour straight we ran, my brother leading the way taking out any enemy that happened to be where we were going, and we knew the others would be doing the same thing. After an hour my brother and I traded positions. We had a long way to go and must be prepared for anything! As I laid the prisoner down my brother secured his hands and feet, binding him, and gagging him with a rag stuck in his mouth.

Just before I placed him up on my brother's shoulder I struck the prisoner again with the cobra just to keep him out longer. This made it easier for us to handle him, and he couldn't slow us down. Right now we needed as much distance from here as possible. Off we went our pace set this time by me, with me leading the way out front a good hundred yards in the lead.

In a few hours it would be daylight, and we would run all night until then, only stopping every hour to switch positions. Daylight came and we all met up at the rendezvous point! All were present, which was a relief for us! If not, we would be going back in for whoever was missing, screw the orders, brothers before orders! We all would die for each other if need be and all knew this. It was just our way, right or wrong. We stood as one on everything. That's another reason we have an edge! We are a unit of one!

We ate a power meal, drank as much water as possible, and made sure our prisoners were all awake. We never gave them a break. All were checked to make sure they were secure and all were ready. We moved out as a unit. I took point, my brothers trusting me to lead the way and get us out. Others all took up positions. The prisoners had no choice, either they run with us, or they will choke on their restraints. All took up the trot or jog as it was; any slowing down on their part cost them a good reminder at the point of a sharp knife.

An hour after the group took off we knew the alarm was given. The jungle has its own rhythm and it was now out of motion. The forest was coming to life. All the animals went silent. We were in for a fight, and I signaled my brothers with our signal. Each prepared their own way. My duty was to cut a path through whomever or whatever tried to stop us. My brothers on the flanks would do the same thing, and our brother guarding our backside would do the same. There was no reason to talk. Each knew what had to be done. Each knew their jobs, and all knew we counted on each other.

"Let's move" I signaled. One hand gripped my machete, (one that I chose not the normal kind). The other, my weapon of choice, was a pump action 12 gauge, shooting ball bearings that were cross cut. This would stop any man or men. The barrel was cut off and had an extension magazine for it. In close quarters this was my way of cutting a path. If we met a group I'd take them down. The sound alone would panic brave men. I ran full speed now and when I saw movement I screamed my war cry, and attacked, shotgun blazing, swinging left to right as I fired. Those that remained standing, I went after with the machete, steadily going forward, tossing a couple of grenades. I heard firing all behind and to my left and right, reloaded my pump and off I went again, anything and everything that was in my way, died.

In moments it was over, my brothers all checking each other, all reloading, and checking on the prisoners. Seems some had tried to kill them. It's a rude awakening to know your own comrades want you dead now. This would help also later on during their questioning. The Lt gave the signal and I led us out. Day after day we were hunted, but finally we made it back to the DMZ with no sleep, no rest. We made good time. Now we hand over our cargo and go get some chow and shut eye because we don't know when or if we'll get the chance again.

I want to say thank you to all SEALs, members from the past to the present. The public owes you more than they will ever even know. Your honor and duty requires you to remain invisible. But we thank you! I personally am honored and thankful for each of you. I don't need to name any of you. You all are my brothers and what we share none can ever break or understand. I thank you, each and every one who I served with, trained with, lived with, and fought beside. You each are remembered every moment of my life! And I can hold my eyes up to the heavens and know!

In closing, this part of my life is a constant struggle to heal and help those others heal who suffer as well. War is never over. We battle each of us a monster that is in us. We all have it inside of us, one part good; one part bad. The battle rages each day, each moment within each of us. Which one will win? Which one shall rule now? It is always the one you feed the most. I live in the moment each and every moment, to enjoy it for what it is, but the battle remains, memories, injustice, prejudice, racial or otherwise. Each of us faces this. How will you deal with it?

War is never somewhere else, it always starts within us, and no one wins in a war; even the war within yourself. It isn't over. Neither side wins, because each moment is a different issue. Just as in school, you have the choice, put yourself into it to really learn and gain from it, or sit there, do as little as possible just to get through it, and use none of it. It is the same in any job, any religious belief, and any relationship you ever have. You only get out what you put in. You put in a little, well you get very little. If you put in a lot, well you get a lot!

As in life, as in a relationship, we all have different things we like or dislike, so we must try to find the little things that help us through each day; to tell the one you love how much you truly do love them; to tell the Creator thank you for the air you breathe or the water you have to drink; or to look the one you love in the eyes and ask them what can I do for you right now because I love you so much. There is nothing I would not do for them!

Or pick up your child which is a gift to you of love, and tell this child just how much you love this child, and if you have more than one, do so for each one and make sure to let them know you love them all equally. This is another war we each face every day, making sure we take the time to give thanks, and love to all those around us, listen to them, not just hear them, but listen. Each of you have within you a warrior spirit, one that makes you fight for what you believe, love, need, or want! Fight the enemy of yourself, the one always never opening up to experience true love, never saying you are sorry, or excuse me, or even please. Fight the side of you that never gives respect but then wants it. One of the hardest things to do is be honest with your own self!

Each of us knows right from wrong. How many of you could tell someone you truly love, that they are bad, you hate them, anything to drive them away from you because you love them, and don't want to see them hurt. Because if you can't set them free from you, how can you truly love them if you are not good for them? Is it better to hurt them, ruin their life, or to tell them to get out of yours, because you can't give them the love you need to give them? Think before you decide which is better. This is a war within you! This is life! A second can change everything around you. It is a constant war! You fight it every day.

Now look on a bigger scale. Wars aren't started by one person. War is started by those in a position to do the right thing. But sometimes those in power make terrible decisions and we all pay for it. Make better choices in your life, and always make sure your fights are just within your own self. Vietnam was another war that should have never taken place, but it did, and for all the wrong reasons. And because of that we all suffered. Just as today in Iraq and Afghanistan, what were they honestly for? We found out about the lies! Just so you think! Remember the war in yourself!

Remember to Walk in Love and Beauty Always!

Chapter Thirteen

The American Indian Movement

I was born a Red Stick Seminole, trained and conditioned for war, and to walk the Sacred Red Road! I was brought up to follow in my grandfather's footsteps, to learn, and practice the old time ways, beliefs, customs, ceremonies, and rituals of our peoples. I also was taught the old time ways of my mother's people the "Ani-yun-wiya", what you call Cherokee! I was also born as a breed, half breed that is, but only by blood quantum.

Because I look different than my full blood brothers and sisters, this caused me to train harder, learn more, and try harder than they ever even tried to. This was not necessary in anyone else's mind or heart, but only in my own, before I learned better. This now helps me, for it conditioned me, taught me what I might not ever had taken the time to learn. It made me, so even now I'm thankful because it helped far more than I ever thought possible.

I was very fortunate to have the grandfathers that I did. They, on both sides of my family, made sure that I learned not only the old time ways of our ancestors, they took me to friends they had met in the Great War. They took me to South Dakota to learn the Lakota ways from those that lived and practiced the old time ways, all the ceremonies, songs, beliefs and stories, along with the history. I was adopted by a couple of the old Lakota families, which was an honor as well.

They took me to their Apache friend who taught me the ways of his people, and trained me in the desert peoples' ways of survival. He taught me old time songs, and the old ceremonies. They took me to the Grandmother Land (Canada) to learn from an old time medicine elder of the Sacred Prophesy teachings of his people. He taught me the old songs and ceremonies, and the Sacred Way of the Fire that was his medicine. These teachings were part of The Prophesies as well.

They sent me to Central America to learn the old time

way of the Mayan peoples and their knowledge of the stars, and the Mayan Prophesies, the Sacred Star Dance Ceremony, the Serpent Dance, and the Jaguar Dance as well. They sent me to the old ones of the Azteca and Toltec peoples to learn, and to their friends of the jungles in South America, who kind of had me worried since they told me they were cannibal peoples.

I sure was worried about if they might decide to eat me since I was good and healthy. I made sure I didn't eat anything on my way there, that way by the time I got there I'd be skinny and they might not want to eat me. It worked because I'm here and they didn't cut me up and eat me. Whew I was relieved. No, I was scared; just a little nervous is all. I mean I'm Seminole, I don't get scared, just a little worried at times!

It's one thing to die in battle or whatever, but to get eaten alive, well, it kind of made me keep my hands ready at all times, even after they were assuring me that everything is alright. Several old men, sure were looking at me like a gator looks at a dumb duck not paying attention to him. Well I wasn't going to be no dumb duck that was for sure, and when a couple old women came up to me and started squeezing my arms and patted my chest, yeah I would be going without sleep for a while, and with my machete, and club in each hand.

Now these weren't like most different tribal peoples I had met. These were very short people, at least short to me. I was a good sized kid, a warrior already, I might add, but these people were smaller than me, even though I was tall for my age, and had more growing to do. These were grown already. But I survived and they taught me quite a bit and they made me feel safe as well. They also taught me the arts of shrinking skulls, and believe me it is amazing. I know I have shrunk a few in my time. They also had me eat with them, something I dreaded, but my grandfathers had told me to respect their ways and honor them always.

Anyway all this traveling and training would lead me to another world and another culture. As I grew, my training in many ways continued. Then one day men in suits came to meet the elders in the main clearing, elders from the various different camps and villages were present, and many young men my age and a little older were recruited to the US militaries. I was in the navy and became an underwater demolition technician, and later was asked to join the SEALs. After coming back from Vietnam, I was recruited this time to a different war, and here is a small part of my life that maybe you can learn something from.

When I came home after debriefing and quarantine, I came back to a whole new world. Things had changed from 1958 to 1972. People were dressed in different clothes, hair styles, shoes, cars, trucks, everything, and the language was changed again. These people drive me nuts, constantly changing the way they talk. Of course what words and talk we had learned in military service was different than this too. So once again I was lost.

I had changed too. I had grown larger in the chest, arms, and legs from all the training we did for everything. I came home a wreck. Every sound had me ready for action. My elders had already completed my cleanup ceremonies, making me ready to come back to the people. I tried real hard to fit back in. Now I really understood all our uncles and grandfathers about their words of what happened to them; how they had to battle themselves every moment of every day just to get through it. I met with family and relatives, and went to our welcome feasts, met Clan Mothers and clan members, new children and young men and women. I had been gone for fourteen years. It didn't seem that long since I had been here.

Day after day, I stayed busy trying to fit back in! Things were some different, but I wanted to get back my peace, my balance here, and it wasn't working. I decided I would go see others of my families, wives, kids, mother, sisters, aunts, uncles etc. So I said my goodbyes and left the next morning. Seeing my children, who now were grown shocked me, but I dealt with it. Seeing how the world was changing wasn't helping me.

My sons and daughters kept telling me of a new movement. I didn't know what a movement was, and finally my oldest told me. And I was glad that finally native peoples were standing back up again! It made me feel good, but that was short lived. I went to see my mother, and the family. Her husband Roger even greeted me like he was glad to see me. He had been in the Great War too. He also was navy. He said we had common things now.

My mom had all my papers that the government sent her, medals, etc. I didn't want them. She tried to give some to me. She said I would have to have an ID which didn't make sense to me. I know who I am. She said it would be hard for me because I didn't have a birth certificate. She got an ID because of a Bible. Something about her name in Bible and date written by her mother got her hers. I went to sleep in the chair. I woke suddenly and had pulled my gun and was firing. I shot my mother's television and scared her family to death. I had grabbed her by the throat and was fixing to crush her larynx before I caught who it was. They were all scared of me. My mother told me to leave and don't come back till I was right in the head. She went out and took all my papers and medals and burned them, saying these caused me to be this way, they are no good.

I left and went to a gathering where my oldest had told me about. This was an AIM gathering (American Indian Movement). I couldn't understand what was being said, so I just sat there in my jungle fatigues with my rucksack by my side. After the meeting was over a couple of brothers I had noticed eyeballing me earlier walked over. They introduced themselves and I told them who I was. They asked me when I got back. I told them just a few weeks ago. I told them how long I was gone. They looked at each other and ask what I did. I told them UDT Navy SEAL.

They looked wide eyed and said welcome home brother, and gave me a true brother embrace. We talked long that night and they wanted me to join. I said no I was just passing through. We shook hands and I left. I was on my way to Pine Ridge Indian Reservation in South Dakota, to see another one of my wives and kids and my adopted family, an event that would change my life again.

I got to Pine Ridge in a few days. It was as cold as ever, snow blowing in off the badlands! It had been over fifteen years since I was here last. I just hoped I was welcome. People were staring at me like I was a monster coming out of the cold. I saw armed men ahead, and I decided I might want to stay away from going up there. I took one of the many trails that I remembered from before.

My mind was on my wife, had she taken another husband in my absence? These things will run through your mind if you had been gone like me. I wondered still what of my son, would he even know me, or did he have a new daddy; that he knew only as his dad. It would be alright as long as he was good to him and his mom. I wouldn't even cause a scene; I would leave no one the wiser.

I decided that my best deal was to just check around first, find someone to strike up a conversation with and see what I can learn. I had plenty of smokes with me, since that is the universal opening amongst all native people and especially getting any help from any elder. Even if I didn't need help from an elder I always offered them smokes out of respect. I didn't smoke, but I would not offend anyone by not smoking. I just would never inhale. I would just puff and blow it out.

Many people believed if you wouldn't smoke with them, you had something to hide, especially the old ones. And you never went to any elder for help without bringing a gift of respectful offering. An elder could be anyone who knew something that you didn't, and you wanted to know. Being an elder did not have to be by age. If you had been doing a particular thing for say five years, and I had just to start to do this, yet you were younger than me by age, you would still be an elder of that particular thing. No, I would not address you as an elder but I would still offer the gift for your help.

This is all about respect. And when you show respect you will get respect. Or you should, if not, then the one or more who did not give you respect is in the wrong. My rucksack had eight cartons of smokes in it.

I still had my dog tags on, and I still could get on any

base and go to a PX! But most tribes have a smoke shop, and we don't pay all those taxes, but when I left home to start this journey I made sure I had plenty of smokes.

I walked up the hill behind my wife's family's house. I could see that there was light coming from the covered window. I figured I'd just wait and watch for a while. After sitting for an hour or more I was just fixing to get up when gunfire ripped through the night. Instinctively I stayed down and rolled away. I let everything sink in.

The gunfire was at a little distance to my left maybe a half mile away? (Sound carries farther in the cold dead of night.) I raised my head and began studying the area, as I did I saw several trucks and men with weapons. What surprised me was that these were military weapons. I had heard that gunfire for many years. It would remain with me forever.

Every gun has an individual sound. And what I was hearing was M-16's firing. Now what were M-16's doing on a reservation? That didn't make sense unless some of these brothers had managed to smuggle some back from Nam, or they stole or bought them. But that was highly unlikely. M-16's would cost more than anyone here could pay on the black market. They must have stolen some or a few brothers from Nam had smuggled some home I figured.

Boy was I wrong on all accounts. Suddenly the ones firing the M-16's threw some Molotov cocktails. These are bottles or containers containing gasoline, with oils mixed or just gasoline, with a rag stuck into it and lit with fire. When you throw it and it hits anything, it blows up and catches everything that the fuel touches on fire.

These hit the house they threw them at and it was now burning. They fired a few more bursts and drove away, whooping, and hollering. As they drove away I heard screams and crying coming from the burning house. I ran as fast as I could through the snow. I had left my rucksack lying where I dropped it. It wasn't as important as giving help to those inside the house. I didn't know what was going on here, but I would find out!

I saw a window and went up to it, felt it to see if it was hot to my touch. If it was it would mean fire was in the room and any air that came from opening or knocking out the window would cause it to feed the flames that much more, and would cause the flames to come straight at the window as well. I thanked the Navy for the fire school training and went to work.

The glass was still cool to my touch, so I tried to open the window. It wouldn't budge, either frozen shut or locked from inside. I didn't waste time. I busted the glass out with my elbow and knocked glass to the side and climbed in.

Once inside I could really smell the smoke. I called out in Lakota that I was a friend and checked the open door to see if I could locate anyone. I heard scuffling of feet and turned to see a grandmother staggering towards me. I motioned toward the inside of the room and asked her who else was in the house. I had forgotten much of the language, so I led her to the window to get some air and I went back to the doorway.

I called out again and tried to hear anything. I could hear crying and I finally saw a middle aged woman, dragging a young boy on the floor. I ran and grabbed him and she shook her head no, and was coughing and pointed to another room. It wasn't hard to figure that is where help was needed so I ran into the room as low as possible, and started looking around. I could hear others hollering from outside. More help was now here.

I found an old man face down on the floor. He was breathing as I checked him and just grabbed him up in my arms and carried him back the way I came. The old woman and the young boy were gone. The middle aged woman had her head hanging out the window. As she saw me I could see tears in her eyes. I gave her a "thumbs up", and asked her was there any more in the house. She said one more but she thought he was dead.

It was her brother that was shot. I ran back into the room where the old man was as I saw some others climbing through the window. They looked at me and I said there is one more in here that is shot. The room wasn't big, there was just so much smoke that we had to crawl to see, and breathe.

We found the brother at the same time and took him to the window the other guy came through since it was closer, and we were coughing our heads off. We got the man outside and he was hit hard. He was alive but barely. His pulse was very weak. I checked as best I could with the others letting me since I guess they saw I knew what I was doing.

I found the entrance wound and ripped up my shirt and made a compress, covered it over the wound, and told one of them standing there to hold it down tight. I turned the man over and looked for the exit wound, found it, and tore up some more of my shirt, made another compress, covered the wound, and asked the nearest one to hold it. They did. He was bleeding bad and already lost a lot of blood. This area didn't use to have much of a clinic and I didn't think he would make it that far without me getting the blood stopped.

I pulled out my knife and ran to the fire burning on the house. I asked a young boy to please hold it in the fire till it glowed red to white. When it did, to bring it to me fast! A lady arrived and others gave her room. It was the same middle aged woman from the house. She looked at what I was doing and told someone to bring some water and find some more cloth for bandages. I looked at her and she mouthed thank you. I just nodded. Some others arrived and they were all talking. I heard some words I recognized as cuss words so I figured some of these others were really pissed.

The boy came running with the knife and I had the cloth compress off in a second and I burned the wound. I let it burn till I figured it had been cauterized and flipped the man over and did the other side. The smell of burned flesh brought back memories. I shook them off and asked the woman if there was a clinic still about fifteen miles away. She said "yes". I told her you need to get him there and quick, and to keep him covered in blankets to keep shock from getting him. I didn't know if he would make it or not. But the woman squeezed my arm and said "thank you" as others picked him up and loaded him in a truck.

I noticed the old man and the old woman were being put in an old station wagon, and I saw a young man carrying the little boy in his arms and the boy was in tears. As the vehicles were leaving, and the house continued to burn, we watched to see if a fire truck would come. Probably not! This was Pine Ridge, one of the poorest reservations in North America, and it could compare to the poverty of third world countries when I had last been here.

As I stood there several of the young men and older ones all started looking at me. Then a couple of them came over and shook my hand, and introduced themselves. I told them my name and why I was there and could they tell me if they knew my wife and son, her family, that if she had gotten another man, it would be alright. I wasn't here to cause problems. When I mentioned her name, they looked at each other and I wasn't sure if this was going to be a problem or not.

My speaking in broken English mixed with Lakota that I remembered was making me wonder if they understood what all I meant to say. I pulled out a pack of smokes from my coat pocket, and offered each of them a smoke, and grabbed one myself, then passed the pack to those that were standing there.

As they lit up the smaller one spoke and told me "brother we have some bad news, those that did this tonight have been doing this for a while now and many families are getting killed and burned out. I'm sorry brother but those you ask about are dead. They were killed a few weeks ago by these same ones brother. They are all dead!" I fell to my knees. No! No, this can't be!

I was on the ground crying. Why? Why did this happen? I felt the brothers' hands on me, as I cried. They never deserved this. I don't know how long I stayed like this but those brothers stayed right there with me. No fire truck ever showed up! Eventually I got up with the brothers who all came and embraced me in a warrior's embrace. I asked them to tell me.

I want to know what is going on here. Why were they killed? I was not allowed to mention their names now that I knew they were dead. Or as we natives say "took the journey", or "crossed over".

These brothers said that the tribal chairman was working with the FBI and some politicians and getting weapons from the feds to issue to the gang that the chairman had put together! They hired thugs and foreigners even and gave them a license to kill, burn, rape or whatever to any of those that were traditionalists, their families, and anybody who opposed him on anything.

I asked who murdered my family and my adopted family. They told me. I pulled out my knife and I began cutting off my hair, all of it, then I began singing a Lakota prayer song from the Sundance, as I cut myself offering my flesh in the traditional ways of the Lakota.

My memory was coming back to the ones who had taught me here on this reservation. When I was finished these brothers offered me a place to stay, and asked if I would talk with them. I agreed. Later that night, after talking with these brothers, I made a pact with them, and the couple of men who came over later. All of them paid attention to these two and the young man following behind them.

Once every one was there, the young man who was following behind the other two got up and made a smudge and we began smudging ourselves, (smudging is a form of ritual purification with smoke/incense) and he brought out a cannupa (Pipe) and began loading (filling) it. He was surprised when I started singing the traditional cannupa songs. He allowed me to continue as he loaded the cannupa. When it was loaded he finished his prayers and a couple of brothers opened up with a prayer song and I joined in with them. We smoked the cannupa, and then we talked some more. We shook hands afterwards and I left. I was now a member of AIM but others were not to know because I would be using my skills now for another cause.

Now the US, and especially the FBI, would learn soon

enough that they made a very big mistake. I realized I had left Nam, leaving a war behind and now I was beginning a new one. My days of peace were over, now I walked the war walk. And this was a just cause, and whoever got in my path better realize "it was a good day to die".

Throughout 1972, I was everywhere and into everything that needed to be done. 1973 brought more atrocities by the government. They didn't know the name of the person they sought, all they knew were names that were used in contacts.

I only met with the original ones I met on that night of the fire. It was better this way. I could move around with no attention to me. I could walk in two worlds.

AIM was founded on the needs of the people. It was done as a reviving of the old times way of religion. It was guided by that very principal fact that everything would be directed through traditional beliefs and always following the cannupa. No act was done without first the asking of AIM to come, and that we did so peacefully and under the guidance with the cannupa present.

And even though AIM was labeled by the feds as violent terrorists and thugs, it actually was a religious movement that was non-violent, and AIM only acted in self-defense. It was the action of the US Government, US Army, and the hired guns supplied by the FBI that brought the violence each time.

It is a wonder that any are left alive, because hundreds were murdered and there is still no investigation into those murders. It is strange how a person can be in custody and in handcuffs behind their backs, and later found shot and dead, laying in a ditch, gulch, or elsewhere and then suddenly members of AIM are accused of the murders. Strange things happen in this country, don't they?

This is all I'll say about AIM other than this in closing. AIM was a vital force that brought much needed change to Native American issues, and laws that were made to help protect those rights of Native Americans. It was these acts of defiance to a Super Power that brought recognition to the world, of the plight of all Native Nations. It came at a great cost and injustice to those who stood proud, who were there and faced all that came with it.

To all of AIM from those days, we all owe a great gratitude, whether you were for AIM or against it, all Native people owe what they have now, and have enjoyed, and what they will enjoy to AIM!

Remember to Walk in Love and Beauty Always!

Chapter Fourteen

What Is the Near Future

For thousands of years, upon millions of years, the Children of the Stars have asked what is ahead in the future. Through each generation this has been the big question for all peoples. Yet none have ever given a true answer. Why, because we are each given choices to make, each and every moment of each and every day. People change then change again. Some make changes for the better some make changes for the worse.

Through each period of civilizations, some rise to power to dominate most of the world, only to fall and disappear. Why does this happen? Many scientists, archaeologists, geologists, and scholars will all give you reasons. But not the truth! Why, because they don't know the truth. Everything that happens does so for a reason. You can't have a lie without truth, and you can't have truth without lies. Positive must have negative. Good must have evil. Men must have women. Nothing can exist without its opposite. It is called Balance, Harmony, Yin and Yang, and many different names. What purpose does it serve? Well, how else will you experience all the different experiences without this? How will you mature and develop your highest potential without this?

Each of these experiences is for you, to help you, to teach you about you! For whatever is bad in the world, it is you! Whatever is good in the world, it is you! If you hate someone, then you hate yourself; for you are part of every single thing in the universe.

Hate is a disease that eats at you, until it either destroys you and all you love or it changes you to see how ugly you have become. For in this hate, you are no longer alive. You are just a shell. To hate someone or thing, shows that you are not as mature or developed mentally, emotionally, physically, or spiritually as you thought you were. For what can another person do to you that would make you hate? Is it your pride, ego, feelings, physical hurt, insecurity, lack of beliefs? What is it? There is a difference in not liking someone, because of their actions, inactions, or character flaws, than hate. Hate is the opposite of Love. Love is good. Hate is bad.

Now, I know you may say, bull crap, but I ask you to please stop and think a little bit. What really made you hate someone or something? If someone hurt you real bad physically, emotionally or even mentally, what did they really do that made you hate? Because you feel pain, you think this is enough reason to hate? Ask any woman who has given birth to a child about pain. Then ask her, does she love that child? Childbirth is the worst pain a human can possibly suffer.

I would like to share a personal experience. This is a true story but I warn you it could, and probably will, upset you and shock you. I am from the Deep South where racial and religious prejudice is still very much evident. But at the time this took place, it was not only allowed but protected under the law by the southern courts and law offices.

I was pushing a case in Federal Court for Native American Religious Freedom. I had filed the case myself, and was warned by law officers and officials that they would not stand by and do nothing. True to their words they were. They took me and beat me day after day, breaking every bone in my body.

Not once did they even blink an eye. In fact, they made fun of my Native Race and Native Religion. They hung me upside down and beat me more and more. They used their pocketknives to cut my hair, taking chunks of my skin, screaming they were taking an Injun scalp. Hanging upside down, broken, battered, and naked, they burnt my genitals then beat them with a nightstick. They destroyed all the legal papers I was preparing. Townspeople stood around while this was going on, all laughing and encouraging these acts.

I was kept this way day after day, week after week, month after month. For ninety days they fed me nothing. I had to swallow spiders, roaches, grasshoppers, etc., sucking the juices and nutrients from their bodies, thanking them for helping me by offering themselves to me so I would live. I am over 6' 4" tall. I had weighed 235 pounds of lean muscle. Now I was down to 115 pounds.

The governor, state's attorney general, and the public all supported these acts against me. Many times I sang my death song. Many times I knew I was and should be dead, until I got so mad that I hated them. I decided I would not die. I refused to let them see my pain. I made no sound as they continued to beat and torture me. I let the pain strengthen my hate and will to survive to make them pay. I lived on hate.

No matter what they did, I could feel nothing but power now. I was never given any medical treatment. I only prayed and called my spirit helpers to help heal my body; give me strength. I would pray until every time they beat me I would severely injure at least two or three of them, which would cause them to beat me unconscious. This repeated itself over and over. I had been consumed by hate. My thoughts were of all the atrocities I would inflict on them all, until they begged me for their deaths. It consumed me day and night.

Then during one beating, they were so angry for me crippling two of the officers so bad that it would be for life that one used his knife and stabbed me in the side while the others battered me with nightsticks until I was a bloody pulp and unconscious. When this happened, I went to the spirit world. There I met with Spirit, and was shown what I had become. I was empty, dead, just a walking shell of evilness and ugliness. I had lost my true spirit and had become exactly like them. I was ashamed of this and knew that I had to let this hate go; let love fill my heart and heal my spirit and body.

Spirit showed me that by allowing hate to enter my heart and consume me, that my spirit was dead, that I had failed to live what I had been taught and shown. I cried, for this was my fear. I had a purpose; a duty that I had chosen and vowed to do. I cried out to Spirit to touch my heart, my spirit, and to give me life. Let me start again and I would never fail again.

I came to with a new understanding and purpose. I felt only love when they beat me now, for I was being tested for my worthiness for my duty. I would not fail the Beloved Women or Spirit ever again. I was honored that I was chosen. While they hurt my body, my heart rejoiced. The love of all of the Beloved Women poured into me. All the love of the Ancient Ones smiled into my heart. The officers saw me smiling and it infuriated them to beat me more, until they were exhausted. And, even though I was never given any medical treatment, my body healed itself. Broken bones mended themselves. Torn bloody wounds closed and healed.

And, as time went on, the officers began apologizing to me. Many cried tears of shame. Respect began filling their hearts, and Spirit showed me what the true power of love can do. They showed me that people hold the key to the future. The more people who fill their hearts with love, the more the power of love is spread and heals. We, as a people, hold the future in our own hearts. If hate is more dominant, then we know what will happen. But if we spread love and love gains more power, we know that life will continue and become so much better.

So, what does the future hold? That depends on each and every one of you. You can make a difference. Every single person makes a difference. I told you these things so you can see yourself, what is truly in your heart. And maybe through understanding my personal experiences, you can see the truth. What is the future? Only you know that!

Remember to Walk in Beauty and Love Always!

Chapter Fifteen

Life with the Wolves

I've been asked to write about my life with the wolves. First, let me say that it is not a life for everybody. Wolves are not dogs and cannot be expected to act like a dog nor be treated as a dog. Wolves are to be respected at all times. Never have I ever even thought of myself as being better or even smarter than a wolf, for wolves are highly intelligent and they all watch and remember what they see. Wolves are totally loyal to the pack, and they are the most loving, caring, supportive people that I have ever known.

The wolves I lived and shared my life with, and shared their lives, were truly beautiful people. We traveled together, slept together, shared food together, fought for each other, cried, laughed, and learned from each other. We went to nursing homes, handicap schools, autistic schools, grade schools, malls, powwows, art and craft shows, the beach, into casinos (that's right, in Las Vegas), motels, restaurants, fairs, mountains, deserts, swamps, fishing, hunting, and even mining together. We truly were family, and still are. People all over this continent had the chance to see and experience these lovely people in my life, from Florida to the North Pole, from the east coast to the west coast. People came to love them as much as I did (hopefully).

Wolves are very emotional people. They cry, pout, throw temper tantrums, get jealous, crave attention, love to play, love to play tricks on you and laugh, love to travel and learn new things, get lonely, have bad days, sometimes don't feel good, and just want to be by themselves, alone, for quiet time. They love to dance, sing, wrestle, eat, watch movies or outdoor programs, get dirty, love to groom themselves, and even pick out their own dance outfits.

I don't know how to start in telling this, for it involves every moment of my life with them. It is hard to tell because it is painful and sad and has a terrible ending in tragedy and injustice.

But I will tell you some events that you might find enlightening. This is the story of Shungamanitou and Montaseetha and their children. It is with honor, love and respect that I say these words for my friends, my brother and sister, my family of these lovely people. It is them I truly loved, and always will.

Shungamanitou came into my life by a miracle and by destiny from the Spirits. He had been captured in Colorado as a young pup. He was trained by the military as a weapons and drug finder. But his handler got him addicted to drugs and alcohol, and mistreated him. I got him from a friend who let me know he was going to be destroyed. Boy, I had my hands full. But what is amazing is that he was considered mad, attacking everyone. But when I showed up, he ran up to me and jumped up to my arms. I calmed him down then had to leave him to go through the legal paper work. He went off again thinking I was leaving him. I came back, released him, and he followed me to my truck. I opened the door, and he jumped in and made his new acquaintance to the truck.

Before I got home, he had gone into withdrawals and was in terrible pain. I talked to him, and pulled over and got out with him. I gave him an herb mix that I have used on people who had the same problems. It settles the stomach and relaxes the muscles. It is also a mild sedative. I won't mention the herbs because people have a tendency to try things they are not trained for, and that can lead to problems.

Anyway, when I finally got him home he was still sleeping, so I picked him up and took him to a fresh, clear river that was spring fed to clean him up. He woke up and boy did that cost me some hide and blood. After he realized that I was helping him, he calmed down. My body was covered in scratches and bite marks, so I had to clean myself up as well.

Once I got him to the house I fed him a good fat rabbit that I had gotten that morning. He devoured it. Then he inspected my home and began marking his territory. Cat Dancing was my woman, and she was having a fit. This wolf was destroying her well-kept house. I told her to calm down, and let him get used to the place in his own way. I would clean up all his messes when he was done. I then took him back outside and had a long talk with him. I smelled him, looked into his eyes and into his soul. I saw all his pain and his confusion, so I began to understand him. We communicated this way for hours. I lay down with him in the grass and slept right there with him.

To understand a wolf, you must become a wolf. You must understand their laws, customs and beliefs. This applies to every living thing. I knew I would have to challenge him to be the alpha wolf, but I must do it the wolf way.

So I went back to the river, got totally naked and washed myself, using the sand to scrub my body clean. My friend joined me and he too, bathed.

Now I led him on a hunt for a kill. I spotted some fresh rabbit tracks and began my stalk. My friend watched, curious and fascinated. I motioned him to come and smell the ground with me. He did, and he knew what I was doing. I stalked on all fours just as a wolf would, until I spotted the rabbit. I lay down and so did the wolf, looking at me, wondering what I was about. I began to crawl and he started too, but I put my hand out to hold him back. He stayed. He stalked the rabbit making no sound, and I was down wind. I said a prayer for my rabbit friend, and told him I needed his life to support my life and that of my friend. I sent my energy out to the rabbit. He never moved, not till I grasped his ears. I held him up, said another prayer of thanks, and broke his neck swiftly.

The wolf ran up fast. But I growled and arched my shoulders, rumbling in my chest as a warning. He looked confused again. I ripped the rabbit apart with my teeth, drank of the blood, took a bite of the raw flesh, and ate it. Then with my mouth, I picked the rabbit up and dropped it at my friend's feet. He looked at me and then immediately tore into the rabbit.

Now I know you're all thinking I'm crazy. Maybe I am. But I am a wolf. I must be a wolf so my friend respects and understands. Any wolf pack knows the Alpha wolf eats first. This is the Wolf Law. I did this so my friend would understand that I would challenge him to be the Alpha wolf of our pack.

After he had eaten, I knew it was time, so I got on my

hands and knees and began growling, rushing up at him. He also had begun raising his shoulders and growling. I knew I had to do this quick, so I rushed him and hit his shoulder with my shoulder, and bit his throat with my mouth. I did not bite hard, just held and growled as a wolf would do, until he submitted by rolling over on his back, exposing his whole neck to me. I released his neck and sat back. My brother now came up and started licking me, rolling over and over, and rubbing his face up to mine. I took his jaws in my mouth lightly, and let him know I loved him. This began our life together, and a wonderful life it was.

Cat Dancing had a hard time at first adjusting to the wolf, but I taught her the way of the wolf, and she came to love the wolves as much as I did.

A couple of months later, I heard that someone had captured a young female and was abusing her. A friend told me that someone had been up to Minnesota and captured a young wolf. They had sold it to a couple and the couple could not handle this young female.

They had beaten and beaten her to try to control the wolf. They had starved it and refused to give it water. When I heard that I got mad. I told Cat, "I'm going to get her, one way or another." Cat was upset as well, and said she'd better come to keep me from doing something crazy.

I found out where this couple lived. I arrived and asked about the young wolf. They said they would sell her. This made me mad, because they didn't create the wolf. The wolf is a free person. But I reasoned it would be less trouble if I bought her.

The couple told me the price but I didn't have that kind of money on me. They told me they would give me an hour. After that, they would find another buyer. Cat and I drove to a friend's house and my friend loaned me the money to buy the wolf. Shungamanitou was with us and he was upset because he had heard the pain of the young female. We went back and bought her.

After I got the bill of sale and had put her in the truck with Shungamanitou, who was calming her down, I told the couple what I thought of their treatment of the wolf and told them they were very, very lucky that Cat Dancing was with me. My anger was very bad. I ought to do to them the way they treated the wolf.

Fear was in their eyes and I could smell the fear pouring out of them. I told them to be very, very careful, that if I heard ever again of their mistreating any of my relatives, whether it be wolf or any other, I would come back and give them a pain that would last forever.

I am sorry if I shock any of you, but I am what I am. I am a gentle-hearted person, but when I am angry I can become a real nightmare to any that has riled me. I do not like violence, but it has been in my life. It is the law of survival, and survive I will always do.

Anyway, the young female became Montaseetha. This was because of the beautiful morning star that was designed naturally in her forehead, and because of her beautiful personality. She was very, very sick when we got her. She had been abused real badly. Her injuries not only were physical, but mental as well because of what people had done to her.

It took a lot of time, love, respect, and caring by Cat Dancing, Shungamanitou, and me to win her over. Running Heart, a young Potowatami lady who was Cat Dancing's best friend, and a friend of mine as well (we used to all live together), also helped. Vickie and her two sons, Kenny and little Joe, also used to come and learn the ways of the wolf. Vickie was the one who told me about Shungamanitou. Jason, Bobby and Faith, Dan, their two children, and members of the tribe, also took interest in the wolves.

Anyway, Monaseetha became a member of the pack. People in the surrounding counties and all the communities got used to seeing the wolves with us, watching us run in the evenings and at night. Children in the community got to meet the wolves up close and came to love them. Business owners opened their doors to us and came to love the wolves.

The wolves were like celebrities. Children, young teens, adults, and even elders, all came to know the wolves, and love spread everywhere for them. Montaseetha and Shungamanitou were great with children, entertaining them and working a healing on them.

We took them to the Morning Star School, a Catholic School, for handicapped and special children. The wolves had a ball and the children there had improvement in their attitudes and reactions to others, while Cat and I taught them to do some arts and crafts. The school administrator then asked us to do this for the entire school. Boy was this exciting for the wolves. Later we were invited to go to a nursing home for elderly citizens. This brought joy to these elders' hearts for us to visit with them. We could teach some things, sing, dance, and get them involved with the wolves.

Then we were invited for Springfest in Seville Square in Pensacola, Florida. This was a real test for the wolf pack, because millions would be there, along with TV and radio coverage, newspapers, reporters, people from all over the world, and big name bands of country stars and rock stars.

I set up our spot with the help of Cat, Running Heart, Melody, Michelle, Evan, Darla, Angela, Shauna, and Vickie. My art was featured. Yeah, I'm pretty good in art. My actual portrait of Osceola, Red Cloud, Powwow princesses, and other paintings brought a lot of attention. Even today they advertise this event with my paintings. Along with the wolves, we also had our arts and crafts, jewelry and I did readings for people.

I know most of you don't believe in these things. I'll just say that I've never been wrong and many, many have tried to prove me wrong and failed. Yes, I was pretty well-known, working also for Psychic Friends Network, and doing Psychic shows all across this country.

In fact, in 1994, I did two big shows in St. Louis and was featured as one of the top ones in the Gathering of the Psychics, specializing in crystal works, crystal healing, crystal power, palmistry, and third-eye development. While doing a healing and reading for two ladies at the same time (which I don't like doing that way), the girls were supposed to be watching the wolves.

Joan Baez and her band were jamming in the background when there was a big commotion. I got up and asked Melody what was going on. The music had stopped. She said that Darla had taken Shungamanitou and Montaseetha over to watch Joan Baez play. I left immediately and heard Joan on her microphone asking who was stealing her show. Shungamanitou and Montaseetha had been dancing with people in the audience.

Joan was laughing and started playing again. I stood back and let the wolves dance with the people, who were truly enjoying it. After the song was over, I howled, calling the wolves to me. People didn't want them to leave. But I felt it would be better and safer for them if they came back. For three days and nights we were swamped with people coming to see the wolves, view my art, and get readings.

News reporters were there getting their stories, and advertising agents wanted to buy my friends. I told them my friends are my family and they are free people and could never be for sale. We did have a great time though.

Osceola's great granddaughter came and got the only actual portrait of him ever done in color; with prayers, colors and designs of him; using his beliefs, customs, and ranks. A Lakota woman got Red Cloud's actual portrait and said she was getting it for the Red Cloud School in South Dakota. All in all, it was fun for everyone.

Now I'll skip some things and tell you of the first encounter with bears. This will make you fall over laughing, but it is a story told by my friends and members of my tribe; who heard it first as told to them by Cat Dancing after we got back.

Cat Dancing, Shungamanitou, Montaseetha and I were all going on a mining trip to Mt. Ida, Arkansas, then on to the Cherokee Reservation and then to the Creek Reservation, both in Oklahoma. We left Florida early one morning in my old antique Chevy truck. It was green and looked rough. It was a work truck, reliable and mechanically perfect.

We arrived at my mother's home in north Alabama that afternoon and visited with my mom and step-dad. Let me say this: my mom and step-dad grew very much in love with the wolves, and the wolves loved them as well. But that is another story.

Anyway, we left my mom's at 10:00 pm driving to Arkansas. I drove all night, but on the way, the wolves were getting hungry, I didn't want to turn them loose to hunt, because a wolf lives on its own time, and I needed to get to Arkansas at the mine before 6:30 am. Nothing was open for miles and miles until we found a place, Kentucky Fried Chicken, open at a drive-through window.

They were in the process of closing. I drove up to the window, till they finally came and I told them, "I need food for my family." They looked in the truck and only saw Cat and me and said, "What family?" I said, "Listen, I will buy all your leftover chicken, cooked or even uncooked."

Now the manager came up to the window, thinking I was one strange guy. I could see it in his eyes, the fear and the mentality, as he looked at me like I was a nut case. I told him, "Look in the back of my truck. My family needs food. I'm willing to pay for it."

When he looked and saw the wolves, he hollered for the other workers to all come look. Shungamanitou and Montaseetha did their part, looking so pitiful, and begging to these people.

The manager had a good heart. He said, "You don't have to pay. We always have lots to throw away every night. You can have it all free."

I told him, "I thank you and my family thanks you." He ordered his people to bring all the throw-away chicken to the window. I got out and started throwing the chicken over into the back of the pickup. Now my pickup has side-boards that went up over the cab to about two feet higher than the cab. It was designed by myself and made of treated hard oak.

I threw all the chicken over into the bed so my family could eat and be content. I got back in the truck and drove on. It was now early in the morning, around 4:00 am. It was drizzling rain and I was exhausted. I had not slept for the last 48 hours. We were getting near to where we were going, so I finally stopped at the National Park in the Ouichita Mountains and decided to sleep for two hours.

Yeah, I can wake up whenever I want. I was trained to do this as a child as part of my warrior training. Anyway, I got out, let down the back of the truck, hooked the forty feet of chain to the wolves, laid on a tarp on the ground under the truck to sleep, and let Cat have the cab to get some sleep. The wolves naturally were stretching their legs and relieving themselves. I immediately went to sleep.

Suddenly I was awake. My senses were on alert. I noticed immediately that the wolves were on both sides of me, rumbling in their chests quietly and that their hair was standing up, bristling, and that their fangs were bared. Both were moving all around in every direction under the truck with me. Then I heard what it was.

Lots, I mean lots of bears. Now I knew I was exhausted. I had not been thinking. All of that chicken was in the back of the pickup. Those bears had all smelled this food. Now I had a big problem on my hands.

The wolves would fight to protect, but there were bears all around us. I crawled out and started hollering at the bears. They just came closer and closer. I reached through the side-boards and grabbed a sledge hammer and pry bar from my tool box. I then banged them together. Still the bears came closer. I started hitting the side of the truck telling Cat to open the door.

Now Cat is a really heavy sleeper, not one to wake easily, and she was sleeping real hard. I kept hitting the door telling her to unlock the door. She woke up barely and said, "There's no room in here to sleep. Leave me alone."

I told her: "Listen woman, there are lots and lots of bears out here surrounding us, so open the door and let us all in."

Cat being groggy from sleep said, "You're all wet and cold and you're an Indian, so handle your bears and let me sleep."

By this time a huge male bear had come to the back of the pickup and was in the act of climbing up on the tailgate.

Shungamanitou was enraged and started to go for him. I ordered him to stay and come around the truck. I hit the tailgate hard with the sledge hammer.

The bear dropped down and moved off about ten yards. I guess he was figuring out what to do and waiting for his army of bears to rush us. Now you probably think I'm nuts and maybe I am, but I had to do something, so I started singing and drumming my song on the truck with the sledge hammer. Montaseetha and Shungamanitou started howling and growling, adding their voices to mine. The bears must have thought we were idiots and therefore not to be bothered because we were mindless creatures.

All the noise finally woke Cat up and she was upset. "All right, all right, I'm up now." Then she saw all the bears. And boy did she yell then. "You didn't say you had all the bears in the woods after you. Get in the truck. All of you."

So I unhooked the chains from the wolves' necks, threw the chains in the back of the truck and got inside. We were soaked. Then I remembered the tarp.

Cat said, "Let the bears have it and just get us all out of here." That is the bear story that had people all over laughing about it.

Later on in life, the Canadian Rockies would hold another bear encounter, one that almost cost me my life. But the wolf pack saved my life from the grizzly then I had to save theirs. That's another story though. Every day was a story, a moment to remember.

For instance, the wolves were dancing at a powwow and startled everyone. They had watched and watched the dances and were just dying to get into the arena area to dance. They loved the music, the drum, and to dance. But to everyone's amazement, they danced and mimicked the moves of the dancers. This tickled the dancers, so they really got into it and tried all kinds of moves to watch and see if the wolves could do them. To everyone's amazement, they not only did the moves, they were in time with the drum.

Yeah, my life was blessed with these beautiful friends.

They did have children, and these in turn had children, etc. I will close now because I miss my family.

Remember to Walk in Beauty and Love Always!

(Photo of Ghost and Shungamanitou
on inside front title page)

Section 3

Ceremonies

Chapter Sixteen

Morning Bathing And Sunrise Ceremonies

In the old days and when I was growing up, the Sunrise Ceremony was and is a very important ritual that was performed even if it was raining, cloudy, dark, or cold, no matter what, it was to be done by everyone. For it was our way of beginning each day clean, pure, and with a sacred love and heart.

The Sunrise Ceremony begins actually before the sun comes up, as you begin to start your day. I will tell you how I lived it, how I experienced this as a child, and as a man.

I wake up and it is still dark. All the night time creatures are still moving and making their preparations to go to their places to sleep. There is a chill in the air, as the dew moisture still lingers strong, and the light breeze moves the moisture to settle on my skin. I get up and pick up my smudge bowl, and gather up my cedar, holly, corn pollen, cornmeal and tobacco bags.

Naked as the day I was born, I prepare to begin my day with my traditional prayers. This was done for me when I was a baby, up until I could just begin to walk with someone to hold my little hand, and lead me to the river, creek, or stream. Since the time I could walk on my own two legs I have I done the ceremony by myself. Now as a man I still perform it the old way.

I gather my things, along with my clothes that I'll put on later, wrap a blanket around my waist and begin my walk to the water. Stopping by my fire I get a hot coal ember and place it in my smudge bowl (used to make purifying smoke to bless and purify oneself) and add some cedar shaved bark that is dried and kept on the wooden bowl next to my fire, along with my kindling next to that. The dried bark will burn slow and keep my ember burning while I make my way to the water. I will walk to the men's section of the creek, taking the path to the left. The women and small ones will take their bath to the right. Others walk as I do, each nodding their heads in acknowledgment to each other.

Once I arrive at the water's edge, I lay my clothes down separately and put all my smudge things together. I get my cornmeal and tobacco bags out and grab a handful of cornmeal and offer it to the Creator, then to the four directions, East, South, West, and North, then to Earth Mother, then to the Sky people, and those of the universe (Star People). I do the same with the tobacco, cedar, holly, and corn pollen. I place a pinch of each, one at a time to the hot ember and smudge myself with the smoke of each, one at a time. Once I have smudged my entire body, I place a larger portion of each on the hot ember. This will allow it to stay burning while I greet Grandmother Sun as she rises in the east.

I walk down into the water singing my prayer chant of blessing as others all around me are doing the same. The women are doing exactly the same things at their area. The only difference is that they are also performing it for their babies if they have them at this time. They are also doing this for the small ones who are just trying to learn to walk, and helping the young girls who can now walk on their own two legs but still need guidance in doing the ceremony. They have different songs they sing, and they perform their own rituals that connect them all as women to their Mother and Grandmother.

I begin to sing the song of "She is Coming, She is Coming", as Grandmother Sun begins to open her eyes and bright rays of light begin to burst across the sky.

As she rises more, I sing the song, "She Is Here Looking At Me, She Is Here Looking At Me".

Next the song is, "She Blesses Me With Her Love, She Blesses Me With Her Love".

And then I sing the song, "With Her Love All Life Grows, With Her Love All Life Grows".

Then after this final song, I look directly into her heart and speak my prayers to her for this day, for I thank Her for all She gives to me, and I let Her see my face and my love for Her.

Now that the Sunrise Ceremony is finished I begin my morning Bathing Ceremony. I look into the water that is the life blood of my Mother and I sing my love to her. I am within her singing as she used to sing to me when I was in the womb of my mother. I am standing in the water singing my thanks for her love now! Because the first song let her know how much I love her, and now my song of thanks lets her know that I thank her for her love and her gift of life.

She provides for me to drink to continue my life. I sing now of my being blessed with her cooling healing water that heals my body soothes my aches and pains. I sing of feeling her heart beat as one with me, and after the traditional four times, I let all my air out and submerge my body completely under her and allow myself to sink to the bottom and lay there in her womb and feel her heart pounding throughout me. I can feel her healing me totally and completely, every single part of me is being loved by my Mother and she makes me new.

As I come back up above the surface I sing my love for her, as I walk back to the shore. Once this is done, I will go to my clothes pick up my soap root, honeysuckle, and morning glory petals and return to my Mother. Putting some soap root into my long hair I work it into lather and then wash the rest of my body. Once I rinse off I add the honeysuckle (a yellow flower that smells good) and the morning glory petals (a flower that has blossoms of different colors and it depends on my mood which color I use) and rub them into my body, and hair.

I stand naked before my Mother and Grandmother and thank them for their gift of love to me, and for the gift of this day, for I am new. I start each day a new born ready to learn and to enjoy life and experience the wonder and beauty that is everywhere. I walk back to my clothes, put them on, and head back to the village.

This is a short way of explaining to you these ceremonies. The true deeper understandings and meanings would have to just be experienced. But to try to explain it would be to say that each day should be taken and enjoyed as a new day of life, to fully love and be loved, to enjoy and experience all that is given to you to enjoy.

What happened yesterday is gone. You are now a new child waiting to see everything, touch everything and love everything that is here.

Now other tribes see the Sun as Grandfather, but I only speak to you of my way. All is to be respected even if it isn't your way. We are all different just as our bodies are; our hearts, our minds, and our spirits. But we must respect the life we have been given and that starts with respecting yourself.

Once you truly respect yourself, you will understand how to always respect others as you want them to respect you. And always remember to respect all that gives life to you. And most of all respect Creator, no matter what name or title you put to that, it is the same. And always respect another's way of believing. Even if you don't agree with it, still respect the person and then you'll respect that person's belief. Oleha mvto vnhesse! (At Last, thank you, my friend)

Remember to Walk in Love and Beauty Always!

Chapter Seventeen

Sunset Ceremony

In the old days and all my life I have practiced the Sunset Ceremony and the welcoming of Grandfather Moon. I realize that most people today are too busy or just don't know or think about these things. But just as there is a Sunrise Ceremony there is the balancing Sunset Ceremony and the welcoming of Grandfather Moon. I will do my best to explain and describe this to you.

I was a little person (a child) when I first remember participating in this ceremony. My grandmother took my hand and helped hold me up while my stubby little legs tried their best to walk upright on two legs as the big people did. My grandmother was tall even for a big person because I could see she was taller than most of the other women around her. But she carried other things in her blanket that she just wrapped herself in and tied.

It looked like my swing hammock that hung between the trees was in there. I loved swinging while I slept. I could see myself floating and riding the wind like the cloud people. At times I wanted to be a cloud, but my grandmother said cloud people had bad tempers and when they got mad they called their friends the thunder people and they threw things everywhere, and poured water on everyone. And sometimes they wrapped themselves together and made themselves twist and turn and tore everything up, even the tall people (trees). They just pulled them up roots and all, and threw them a long, long ways! But mostly I just wanted to be like my spirit helper, Eagle, so I could fly like he does and see everywhere at once and go real fast too.

Anyway she was walking and half the time dragging me along, trying to help me keep up. She told me we were going to sing to Grandmother Sun so she could go to sleep and rest because she worked hard all day for all of us, so we could grow and live.

She made everything grow. "Even the stone people?" I asked my grandmother, and she said yes. Stone people are Mother's first children and they are the oldest of us all. Anyway Grandmother Sun needed her rest, and she only could get it if we sang real good and helped her fall asleep.

Now you ought to know that I really was going to sing as best I could because I loved Grandmother Sun. She made me feel warm all the time. When she was gone to bed sometimes I was cold. And she was helping all of us. So yeah, I was going to sing like a bird for her.

Anyway grandmother led me down to where everyone else was, and we all waited patiently as we could see Grandmother starting to get tired because she was dropping out of the sky and getting closer to her home. Many of the big people started lighting their smudge bowls and burning the different plant peoples in them. Later I learned it was cedar, holly, cornmeal, tobacco, and corn pollen. Sometimes they used the bark of the cedar instead of the dried leaves. Anyway they were all smudging and my grandmother smudged me and then herself.

Then our Clan Mother began to sing and everybody started singing with her. I tried to pay attention and remember the words because I know they would sing it four times and I wanted to sing too. So I listened to my grandmother and tried the words slowly, first just getting the rhythm of the song so I would fall right in and not mess up.

As a small person I was always to be quiet and listen to learn. I am expected to pay attention, because my grandmother would question me later to see if I did. She didn't miss anything. She like always knew even if my eyes wandered. Then a whack on my head with her cane came from nowhere.

After the first song which was simple, a song of love and thanks for loving us and giving us her love, we sing a second song about beauty that awaits us in our dreams where all things are in perfect balance and harmony. The third song is of dancing in the stars as she lights up the universe. And the last song is for her to sleep and come back to us when she wakes up, for we will be waiting. When we finish my grandmother says "we will now welcome Grandfather Moon".

Grandfather Moon is a very love sick man. He loves Grandmother Sun and is always chasing her and he loves our Mother also. He shines his love down upon her at night and lights up the sky for all the star people too. He gets Mother so in love that her waters comes in waves, and causes the plant people to either rise up or go hide. And his power is so strong it affects all of life too. So grandmother waited until our Clan Mother began to sing then she and the others all started singing.

"Come, come Grandfather we welcome you. Shine your beauty for us all to see, light up the sky so the star people can see us". The song goes four times.

Then the song of "Mother loves you, we love you, all life loves you, give us your love". Four times this is sung.

Then the song of power is sung: "So all will grow and all will help each other with life" and four times we sing this.

Then we sing this. "Thank you Grandfather for your love and the gifts you give us". Four times this is sung.

As Grandfather now shines in the night, my grandmother tells me this is what you must do every day at this time as you are able. If you cannot come out because you are ill or hurt or for what other reason, you still do this in your heart and mind. This is our way. It has been our way since the beginning, and it will be our way for all time.

Remember To Walk in Love And Beauty Always!

Chapter Eighteen

The Corn Planting Ceremony

In the old times, the corn was a main part of our diet, and the corn was very special to us religiously. I was a small boy when I first was present for the ceremony. But before the actual ceremony there was much more that had been done in preparation for the actual ceremony.

I had watched as the Clan Mothers had gathered and walked around area scrub brush, palmetto brushes, and saw grasses. They took sticks and walked and marked out the field, by sticking the sticks in the ground.

Then they gathered and called for some young maidens (those girls who had not yet had a moon time). And they all prayed together and tossed some corn pollen in the four directions.

And then the young maidens began singing one of the women's songs. It was a song asking the Earth Mother to hear their prayers and bless these grounds, to be plentiful.

When they were singing you could feel in the air the power that was flowing through them all. I watched in wonder as to what they were doing. I was a small person so I kept quiet and just watched for now.

They began walking and touching the ground periodically with their hands, all around the marked area they walked and sang this beautiful song, their voices vibrating with power. (Young maidens have more natural power than an adult, because their life force energy is so new and full of power. A young female child is very powerful and sometimes was asked to be present for a special healing or ceremony.) The maidens were shaking Gourd and Turtle rattles and even the wind swayed and blew gently in harmony with them.

After they had finished their singing, the Clan Mother, the head one of all, called out and some young warriors came with burning torches, the Clan Mother nodded her head and the warriors split up and each began lighting the bushes and grass around them. They went to each corner, and each side, and flames began bursting up in all directions. The Clan Mothers and young maidens began singing a thank you song for all the Plant people who gave their lives to help fertilize the ground beneath them. When the flames tried to go outside the marked areas, warriors and young ones like me rushed to put it out.

The whole band was present naturally for this important event, and we all would work together to take care of all the Plant people who would grow here. After all the area was burned off and all the hot coals and embers were put out, the Clan Mothers made offerings of corn meal and holly leaves crushed up.

All of us prayed then and asked that our Mother Earth hear our prayer and bless these grounds, and we would honor these Plant people each day with songs and prayers for them and to her and to Grandmother Sun as well. We would be thankful of their gifts of life for us.

We then prayed and asked Mother to forgive us and allow us to dig into her and chop up the roots and make the ground ready for planting. After we finished, warriors picked up their hoes and stick poles and began digging into Mother, and turning the ground up, so that Grandmother Sun could bless the grounds for us as well.

The next day we all worked on the grounds adding any of the left over remains from the hunts, or fishing that was brought in, and had been saved for this purpose to enrich the ground with food for the Plant peoples that we would put there. The whole time we all worked, the women only sang songs for the Plant people, Mother Earth, Grandmother Sun, and to the Cloud people to bring the gentle female rains to us. (Yes rain is sometimes male rain and sometimes female rain. Male rain is hard and stormy. Female rain is soft and gentle.)

After a few weeks, the ground was ready. The Clan Mothers all were gathered and the young maidens all came in singing and shaking their rattles, everyone joined in with the songs, as the Clan Mothers offered up the Seed people to Grandmother Sun asking for her blessings. Then to our Mother, the Earth, they asked for her blessings. Then they took their sticks and began making long lines in the ground.

When they had finished they called all the young girls and maidens to come to them. They passed out the Seed people to them. The young maidens would put the seeds in the ground and the young girls (children) would cover them up. The young maidens sang their power songs and the young girls (children) were singing now with them, and covered the seeds up.

The whole time all the married women were singing all around the area, the power was enormous, as all men, young warriors, and boys such as me danced, our feet in time with the singing, and the rattles were joined with the drumming of a couple old men using their hand drums.

This same dance would be used by us at our Green Corn Ceremony that lasts for seven days. Anyway once all the seeds were planted, and everyone was gathered, the Clan Mothers led us in our prayers to Grandmother Sun, Mother Earth, and Grandfather Moon, to bless these grounds and these Plant people with an abundance of life. Let them know how much we love them and thank them for all they do for us, and that we would care for these Plant people each and every day.

Remember to Walk in Love and Beauty Always!

Chapter Nineteen

Building the Purification Lodge

Remember that as you build this lodge, your hearts must be full of love and you are giving your love as you build the lodge, to the lodge itself. The more people involved and building it with love in their hearts, the more powerful the lodge becomes. The more you pray and use the lodge and grounds, the more powerful it becomes. This description was used by both of my grandfathers, the Ani-yun-wiya and Muskogee, as a gift brought from the Stars when we came here. All of the Children of the Stars brought this with them.

In designing the Purification (sweat) Lodge, the diagrams that are also included should help you better understand the completeness of the Oneness with everything. This should also help you learn how the positive and negative forces affect you and everything around you. It will show you what spirit to call to ask for help when you are sitting in the lodge. Match your position to the animal, element, kingdom, and forces that are there. Use these diagrams with the ones on the Medicine Wheel to understand yourself even further. This is the Ancient Way. This is not what is taught today. Very, very little is taught in truth any more. So much has been lost that now falseness is taught to many as truth.

The Sweat Lodge has many purposes and it is used for Purification, but many more purposes and ceremonies are done inside of a Lodge.

I will explain how to build this the proper Traditional Way, as I have been taught, and how I have built them myself all of these years.

First, you must only cut the willow poles after you have prayed and made offerings to the willow tree people. Ask them for their help and for their forgiveness. Now you must cut them on a Full Moon only. A few days before or after is OK too. Why? During a Full Moon, the moon draws all the minerals, nutrients, sap, water, and medicine up from Mother Earth, up from the roots, up to the trunk, branches, leaves, and fruit or flowers of the plant people.

Now it is very important that you understand that you want these in the poles that you are cutting. This brings the power to the foundation of the lodge and since the sap and water is filling up the trunk and limbs, this makes the poles very flexible and easy to strip the bark from. This also provides the medicine that is gathered for the Pipe. Also the medicine is used to make the medicine teas that are used to pour on the rocks (grandfathers and grandmothers) and also for those in the lodge to drink to help them as well.

This is the old way that I was taught by my grandfathers, and they were taught by their grandfathers, since as long as can be remembered. I personally have talked to Spirit and fasted numerous times to seek guidance on these matters. Spirit has always answered me and shown me that what I do is correct as to the reasons and purposes of these specifics.

Once you have the poles cut, soak them real good in water. I like to tie them in a bundle and place them in a spring-fed stream or creek while I prepare the ground itself. Once the site is chosen, it must be purified and blessed. This is done by using corn meal, tobacco, cedar, sweet grass, sage, and holly leaf, etc. Smudge the whole entire area with sage and sweet grass. Sprinkle the offerings of cedar, sage, and cornmeal all over. Once you have done this and prayed to the Spirits of all of the directions, it is time to mark the area out so you have it correct. You begin in the East.

Mathematics is very important in numerology. And numerology is Sacred in design and purpose to all Native Peoples. Therefore the lodge will be built using this Sacred Numerology.

First select where you want the Sacred Fire Pit built. This can be done any time. Make sure you know exactly where the East is located because you are lining up the rising sun due

East to the center of the Sacred Fire, and the Altar, and the Rock Pit center with the exact alignment to the West. If you are not sure, use a compass!

Once you have the Center of the Fire Pit and your alignments, place wooden stakes to mark your spots. Place one stake for the center of your Sacred Fire. Now take seven strides (the normal steps you would use in walking). Make sure you are aligned directly in the path from East to West. Place another stake here for your Sacred Altar. Now take another seven strides, making sure you are exactly lined up with East and West and exactly with the stakes you have placed for the Fire Pit and the Altar, place another stake for your Rock Pit. This will be the center of the Rock Pit, where you place the rocks brought in to your Lodge.

Using a string tie one end to the stake in the Fire Pit and the other end to the stake in the Rock Pit. Now squat down and look down the string, making sure each of the stakes is lined up in a straight line from East to West.

Depending on how many participants will be using the lodge, determine the circumference. If the lodge is for your personal use or a small family's personal use, use the measurement of 48 inches or four feet. If it is for a group of 5-9 participants, use 60 inches or five feet. If you are using the lodge for a large group, say 11-18 people, then use 72 inches or six feet. When I say use this measurement, I mean exactly that. Cut a string. Tie one end to the stake in the Rock Pit. Now measure off the exact measurement you have decided upon and cut the string. This will be your free end to move around like a compass to mark your holes for the poles and completing your circle.

Now please examine the diagram to see how you are to mark your holes by their number, starting at the East, your door, with the string from the Fire Pit to the Rock Pit, lined up dead center exactly, acting now as the center for your door.

Measure 18 inches to your left and make a mark. Now measure 18 inches to your right and make a mark.

Then, using your measuring string from the Rock Pit with the desired length, line up the string to your mark on the left mark, and drive a stake when you have found the exact alignment and measurement. Repeat this for the mark on the right side of the string. This is your door you are marking. It will be a total of 36 inches. This allows the older or bigger bodied participants easier access. Also, this stays with the Sacred Numerology that must always be used. This is for poles 1 and 3.

Now walk directly to the West, and in exact alignment with the poles 1 and 3, repeat the process that was used and measure and place your stakes for poles 2 and 4. Then using the same process, and the string compass from the stake in the Rock Pit, mark poles 5 and 6, and then 7 and 8. Use your compass to check your accuracy of North to South. Using this same process continue marking and staking out your pole holes by using this technique and using the diagrams provided, showing the exact pole numbers and sequence of each one, until you have all 16 holes for the poles marked and staked.

Now go back to your Fire Pit (to the center) where your stake is placed and tie a string. Measure a length of 7 feet or 84 inches and cut the string. Then, using the string as your compass, since the one end is tied to the stake in the center of your Fire Pit, hold the loose end of the string and walk due west until your string is at its end and is lined up directly with the string running from the Fire Pit, to the Altar, to the Rock Pit.

Then take two strides (your normal walking step) to your left and holding the string in your hand from the Fire Pit (7 feet long), mark the spot. Keeping the string tight, take another step and mark the spot.

Repeat this process marking your spot every step until you have completed your path all the way around until you are back to your right side of the string running from the center of the Fire Pit to the Rock Pit (East to West).

Now measure two strides to your right and mark the spot. This will be the opening of your Fire Pit. You will have marked out a crescent shape or a little more than half a circle. There are about 4 strides marked for the opening, two to the left and two to the right.

Now you have your Fire Pit, your Lodge, and your Altar marked out. Next go to your Altar stake and tie on one end of a string. Measure off 40 feet of string. With one end tied to the Altar stake, walk due East through your Fire Pit and continue until you are out of string. Use your compass and make sure you are lined up directly to the East, and mark the spot with a stake. This is for your directional poles (Flag Poles or Spirit Poles).

Now, still holding onto the end of your 40 foot string, walk to the South and make sure, using your compass, that you are directly South from the center of your Altar and place your stake for that pole. Then on to the West and making sure you are lined up with the East pole stake, Fire Pit stake, Altar stake and Rock Pit stake, directly to the West, place your stake for the West pole. Then continue for the North, making sure you are aligned up to the North, and place your stake.

Then walk back to the Altar and tie another string to the Altar stake measuring 10 feet of string. Holding the loose end, walk directly towards the Fire Pit center. When you reach the end of your 10 feet of string, walk due South, until you are half way between your Fire Pit and the South pole. Place a marker stake.

Then walk back to the Altar and walk East towards the center of the Fire Pit and reaching the end of your 10 feet of string, walk toward the North pole until you are half way between the Fire Pit and the North pole, and place a marker stake. These two marker stakes are for the Earth Mother in the

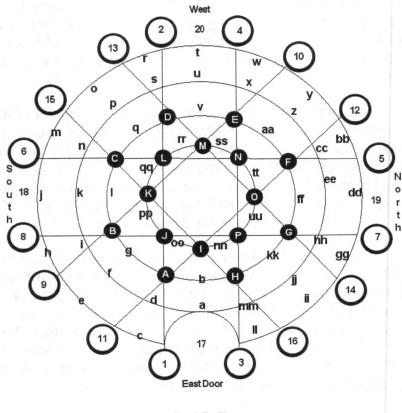

Altar & Fire Pit

Diagram One

This is an overall diagram that shows all of the important knowledge of the lodge. See the legends in the following diagrams to find the descriptions of each marked place. The following diagrams break this down into smaller views that are easier to grasp.

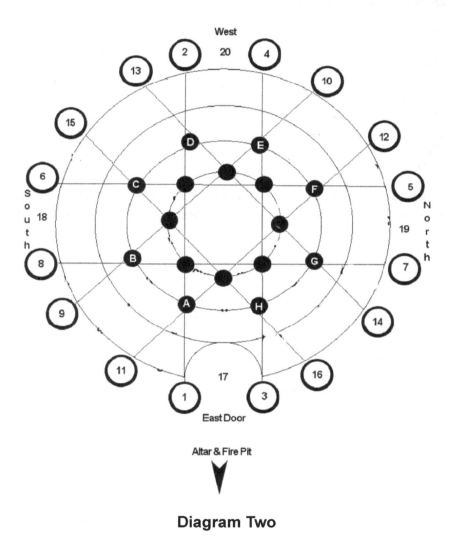

Diagram Two

This diagram shows the poles and some of the key intersections that have meaning in the lodge. See legend at right.

Four Directions –Four Elements Four Sacred Herbs – Four Colors Four Seasons – Four Kingdoms Four Heavenly Bodies – Sacred Numbers

#17	#18	#19	#20
East	South	North	West
Fire	Water	Air	Earth
Tobacco	Cedar	Sage	Sweetgrass
Yellow	Red	White	Black
Spring	Summer	Winter	Fall
Human	Plant	Animal	Mineral
Sun	Moon	Stars	Earth
One	Three	Four	Two

Planets, animals, and directional understanding of the Lodge, pinpointing for you the exact positioning and your power pole according to your power number by your date of birth.

1 Sun	A Mercury
11 Infant Humans	9 Deer
B Neptune	8 Spirit Ancestors
6 Moon	C Venus
15 Southern Lights	13 Plants
D Saturn	2 Earth
4 Spiders	E Mars
10 Bear	12 Minerals
F Uranus	5 Whirlwind & Blizzard
7 Rock	G Pluto
14 Animals	16 Stars
H Jupiter	3 Winged Ones
17 East Door	a Eagles

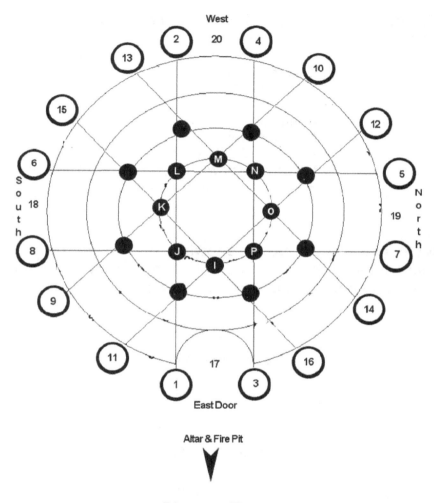

Diagram Three

This diagram shows some of the key intersections that have meaning in the lodge. See legend at right.

Spiritual, Emotional, and Physical manifestations of the Lodge and where they are at:

        I Enlightenment
        J Spiritual Emotions
        K Love
        L Songs and Dance
        M Magic Powers
        N Wisdom, Spiritual Knowledge
        O Universal Knowledge
        P Philosophy, Quality Listeners

Male and female poles showing the power of each manifestation inside of each of us, and what we should know and understand about ourselves.

1 and 3 Male

2 and 4 Female

9 and 11 Male

10 and 12 Female

5 and 7 Male

6 and 8 Female

13 and 15 Male

14 and 16 Female

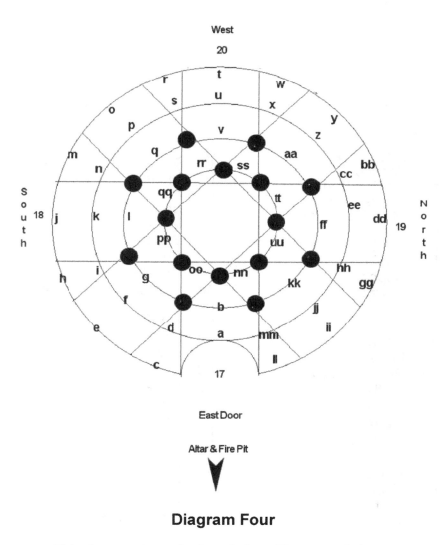

Diagram Four

This diagram shows the knowledge of the support pieces and the four directions and herbs.

The herbs, animal, winged, fish, and reptile diagram showing you all the poles and directions, where these are represented in the Lodge, and where you can sit to learn from and get help in understanding from them.

17	East Door	20	Sweet grass
17	Tobacco	t	Spider
a	Golden Eagle	u	Frog
b	Red squirrel	v	Bear
c	Meadow Lark	w	Horse
d	Deer	x	Badger
e	Hummingbird	y	Bat
f	Robin	z	Coyote
g	Bobcat	aa	Grasshopper, locust
h	Buzzard	bb	Owl
i	Canary	cc	Mink
18	South	19	North
18	Cedar	19	Sage
j	Mouse	dd	Beaver
k	Red Tail Hawk	ee	Buffalo
l	Turtle	ff	Wolf
m	Rabbit	gg	Wolverine
n	Manatee	hh	Loon
o	White Crane	ii	Raven
p	Snake	jj	Cougar
q	Alligator	kk	Caribou
r	Lizard	ll	Whale
s	Catfish	mm	Reindeer, moose
20	West		

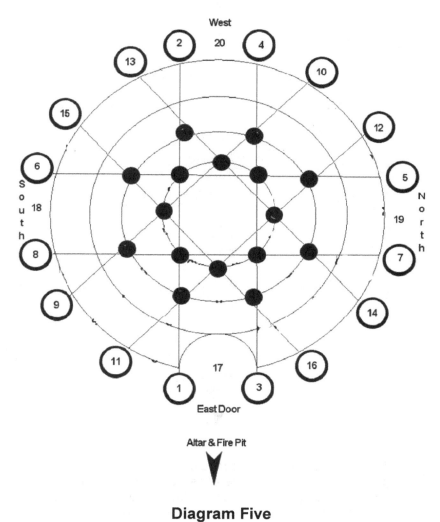

Diagram Five

This diagram shows the gender of the poles. See page 274.

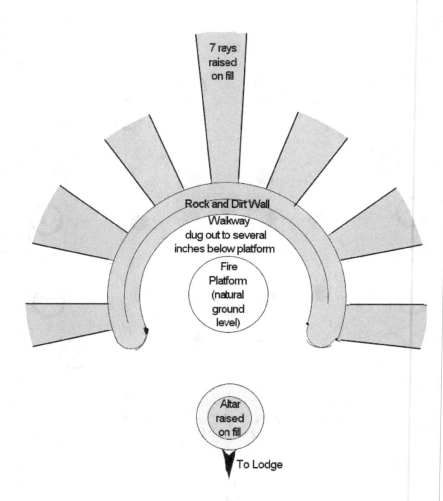

This should look like sun rays from above, with the one going straight east being the longest one. Also leave room for the fire keeper to walk around the fire inside the wall. This also allows the participants to walk around the fire before entering the lodge. The altar should be constructed from the dirt that comes out of the pit inside the lodge, thus they are spiritually intertwined. Also, the area dug out around the fire platform should have a way to drain any heavy rainwater.

South, and the Winged Ones, Cloud People, and Sky People in the North. The Altar will have a Pole for Grandfather Spirit - at the eastern part of the Altar. These are your seven directional poles.

The willow poles have been soaking in the water. This keeps the water drawing up inside of them. Now is the time to gather the offerings that you will place inside the holes for the poles. Look at diagram 4 with the animals on it. Not only are you making offerings of tobacco, cedar, sage, and sweet grass but also you will want to offer special offerings for the bird, animal, spirits, you are calling to come to the lodge poles and lodge but the directional poles as well. Use common sense in doing this. Bears love honey, berries and fish. Eagles love meat and fish. Horses and buffalo love grasses, while deer love clover and acorns, etc. You are doing this in honor, respect and humbleness and most of all LOVE!

Once you have your offerings ready you must prepare your holes. Everywhere you have placed a stake, except the Rock Pit, Altar, and Fire Pit, you will now drive stakes into the Mother and offer prayers of love as you do so. Your lodge poles need to be driven in at an angle, which helps in the bending of the poles and strengthens the support of your lodge. Try to drive the holes for the poles no less than two feet deep; and deeper if the ground will allow it. Wallow out the holes, with a steel rod or crow bar, so the poles will slide down easier. Also, sharpen points on the bottom of the poles which allows you to drive the poles point first into the holes, and with the help of the others pulling, you can drive the pole deeper.

When you have all of the holes made and wallowed out for the lodge, place your offerings in the holes and offer your prayers for the help of all of the spirits. All holes must have offerings placed in them and all present must participate in this. The prayers and love must flow from the builders into the lodge.

Begin by selecting your door poles first. Once you have the 4 poles selected, begin stripping them of their bark, trying your best to keep the strips in long pieces. Place the strips of bark in a large container of water to keep them soft and pliable. Once you have the 4 poles trimmed and stripped of their bark, sharpen points on their bases. Starting with poles 1 and 2, place them deeply in their proper holes, driving them in as deep as you can.

All of the poles may be stripped at once and the bark soaked. Be sure to make the strips as long as possible.

In bending the poles, you must take your time and be gentle in your bending. Have someone squat down in front of the poles 1 and 2 (inside the lodge). Have others stand outside (holding their feet and knees on the poles as they push them) and push the poles gently over the backs and shoulders of the ones squatting inside. With others standing inside the lodge they help by pulling the poles down slowly towards the Rock Pit stake. As you pull down on each pole, you push it towards the other pole across the lodge until they are bent down to about chest high.

This allows for the taller ones to sit up tall inside the lodge. It is most difficult when a large, tall person has to stay bent over in an awkward position because a lodge is built too small. I am a very tall man therefore I truly understand when a person is in total pain because he is in an awkward position, causing cramps and muscle spasms.

Always be thoughtful for the large people who come to participate and pray. Many may tell you that you didn't come to be comfortable. They are right in that, but it is in how it is applied. I come to sacrifice myself, to give up the flesh, to let my spirit take control, to let my spirit free, to pray for all of my relatives, and to help and to heal others. Yes, I will suffer but not because a lodge is built too short or too small. Many times those who say those things are smaller ones, and I invite them to come up top with me in the old warrior way, to where the Eagles are! That's right. Stand up. Grab the poles with your hands standing directly above the rocks as the water is poured, and the fans are fanning the breath of Spirit directly into you. Sing now. Remember the lodge is teaching you humbleness, and you must humble yourself!

Once you have the poles bent to the correct level, chest high, take strips of the wet bark and wrap the two poles together tightly. Wrap them good and tight and in several different locations. This strengthens each pole. Once you have the two poles tied together, now pack the poles in hard at the holes. This is done with a tamper stake. (This is a stake that is round and flat and is pounded on the ground around the hole.) This helps secure the pole firmly in the ground.

Now that poles 1 and 2 are finished, do poles 3 and 4, exactly the same way. Then repeat the process with 5 and 6, as well as 7 and 8. This will make your four directions pathways. As you finish each combination, tie them together as they cross other poles.

Look closely at the drawings and see exactly how the next poles are sequenced. Do poles 9 and 10, then 11 and 12, then 13 and 14, and 15 and 16. Now when you have all these poles finished, check and make sure you have them all good and tied down. And where the poles cross over the center, make sure you tie these areas as well.

Next take one of the limbs that is pretty solid, and bend it to help make your door and tie it down to both sides of the poles 1 and 3. Then take a long pole that is not too thick. Strip it of all limbs, branches, and bark too. Starting at pole 1, run it inside at pole 11 and outside at pole 9 and inside of pole 8. This is a weave pattern. This not only strengthens the poles and the entire structure, but it is done as Spider Woman does in Creating. We are creating something Sacred, inside the lodge and outside the lodge, in this world and in the universe, from this world to the Spirit world. Then strip another pole like before. Starting at pole 8 on the inside, run this pole to your left outside of pole 6, then inside of pole 15, outside at pole 13 and inside at pole 2.

Now I want you to go back to pole 1 and slide down the pole you ran from the left, all the way to pole 8. Slide it down until it is only 12 inches (one foot) off the ground. Using bark, tie this pole in place by using a X wrap that locks the pole in place. You do this by wrapping the pole from both sides and crossing them over each other and reversing their positions with each wrap, one time over, then one time under the cross pole. Do this at all of the poles.

Now at pole 8, where the ends of both of these poles come together, tie down the end of the first pole, then lay the other pole end above or below the other pole making sure to overlap the poles of each other. This gives strength and added support to the poles and lodge. Then slide down all of these poles, 12 inches, one foot, off the ground all the way to pole 2 and repeat this process of tying this pole with the stripped bark to all of the poles. Now strip another pole and start it at pole 2 on the inside of pole 2 and run it outside of pole 4, inside of pole 10, outside of pole 12, and inside of pole 5. Now strip another pole and weave it inside starting at pole 5, then outside pole 7, then inside pole 14, outside pole 16, and inside pole 3.

Starting at pole 2, slide the pole down until it is 12 inches (one foot) off the ground, all the way to pole 5. Then tie this pole down, making sure that you overlap the two poles at pole 2 so they help support each other. Then continue to tie this pole to all the poles using the bark.

At pole 5, making sure that you overlap the two poles, tie this down and continue this to pole 3. Now take another pole and strip it, and starting once again at pole 1, but this time starting on the inside of pole 1, run this pole outside pole 11, weaving it inside of pole 9, and outside of pole 8, and inside of pole 6. Now slide this down until it is 16 inches above the last pole (the bottom row of poles) you just ran around the lodge.

Insert another stripped pole at the 6 pole and weave it outside of pole 15, inside of pole 13, outside of pole 2, and inside of pole 4. Then slide this down until it is 16 inches above the last pole you ran around the lodge previously. Then go back to pole 1 and tie this pole in place with the stripped bark, and tie it to every pole it touches using the X weave pattern always. Remember to overlay the end poles at 6 and secure them down. Tie all the way to pole 4.

Now weave another stripped pole starting at pole 4 on the inside and weave this pole outside of pole 10, then inside of pole 12, outside of pole 5, and inside of pole 7. Take another stripped pole and starting inside pole 7, weave this pole outside of pole 3, and inside of pole 1. Now slide this pole and the one previous to this that you just added down until you have them 16 inches above the lower side poles that you did before. Now go back to pole 4 and overlay the two pole ends. Tie them down and in place, and then tie this pole to all the poles it touches, remember to overlap the poles at 7, and continue to tie this pole down all the way to pole 1 and overlapping those two poles as well. Now also tie your top part of your door pole to this pole. Look at diagram 1.

Look at your door. You will see all of the wrapped bark securing the door for you. This will secure this most used area and provide strength for when you raise the door flap and toss it on top to enter or exit the lodge, or for when the door is opened.

Once you have all of this done, strip another long pole and starting at pole 11 on the outside, weave in this pole to the inside at poles 9 and 8, then to the outside of poles 6 and 15, then to the inside of poles 2 and 13 and outside to poles 4 and 10. Slide this pole down until it is 16 inches above the last side poles that you placed. Using the wet bark, tie this pole in place.

Overlapping the poles at 4 and 10, start another stripped pole on the outside and weave it inside of pole 12 and 5, outside at poles 7 and 14, inside at poles 16 and 3, and outside at poles 1 and 11, making sure to overlap the ends at both of these places. Then slide these poles down until they are 16 inches above the last side poles around the lodge. Tie these poles in place using the bark at each pole.

Now strip two shorter thinner poles (or thick limbs) and starting at the crossing of poles 11 and 16, on the inside weave in the first limb/pole going outside at the crossing of poles 1 and 8 and inside of 13 and 10 and overlapping the last pole. Weave this one outside of poles 4 and 5, inside of poles 12 and 14, outside of poles 7 and 3, and inside of poles 11 and 16. Make sure you overlap the end of the poles. Now slide these two poles down to where they are 12 inches, one foot, above the last side poles. This will complete the amount of poles and the Sacred Numerology. Now tie these all in place.

Look at Diagram 1 and make sure that you have them all lined up accordingly. You must also check and **make sure that you have 28 poles used in constructing this Sacred Lodge**. Twenty eight is a Sacred Number which is important in the Native astrology of the stars, planets, moons, and our calendar! You will hopefully have noticed that your first side pole was 12 inches off the ground and the next round was 16 inches from that which made 28 as well. Which when doubled for the next two rounds combines to 56 which is the Sacred Number of positive - negative, and male - female.

Also notice in Diagram 1, at the top of the lodge, is formed the Diamond Star, known as the Morning Star. Hopefully you will have built this lodge with total love in your heart and sent love to the poles, holes, Mother, and all of the spirits.

Now divide yourselves into work groups to work more

efficiently. Two people need to make and put up the Directional Poles. This is done by making Prayer Flags with offerings for the spirits at each of the directions. Also making the holes for the flags and placing the offerings in the holes. Then tie the Prayer Flags to the poles, and place the poles in their proper hole and tamping it down real good. Sometimes it is good to add support for the poles by driving in wedge stakes (short stakes) next to the pole. Drive them in deep and tie them together to the pole. This adds more strength to the pole for when strong winds or storms come.

Two people also need to work together to make the Rock Pit inside the lodge, while someone else makes the Sacred Hoop for inside the lodge. Then others should be making the Fire Pit, and others are preparing the Altar.

The Rock Pit inside must be dug 12 inches to the east of the stake and 12 inches to the west of the stake, 16 inches to the north of the stake and 16 inches to the south of the stake, and it needs to be 12 inches deep. The dirt removed from this pit must be used in making the Altar.

The Sacred Hoop is made by using two limbs, stripping them of their bark, and tying them together to form a circle. Then using red felt, cut it in long strips and wrap the hoop with the felt completely; all the way around. This hoop is then tied up underneath the Morning Star center in the lodge. Tie it up at the cross meetings of the poles. This Sacred Hoop is used to hang prayer flags, and prayer ties and Eagle feathers from for the ceremonies. It is also used when you are sweating the Pipe by placing it up in the Hoop and tying it in place. It should be of a size comparable to the lodge itself circling the Morning Star of the lodge.

In making the Fire Pit, it is important that you build up the mound for the fire to sit up on. This is for when it rains so your pit won't be under water. You slope your sides off so the water will drain off, helping you to always have a fireplace even in wet weather. It is also important that you build a mound wall around your pit. Your mound should look like the drawing shown on a previous page. The rays are made of the removed earth from around the pit and river rock, and rock debris as the pit is used.

This is done so that you make it look like a sun with beaming rays. I usually only make seven rays with the longest being in the center of the wall going to the East. I also leave room for the Fire Keepers to work around the fire and also for those participants to walk around inside the fire pit as they enter or exit the lodge; completing the circle and figure eight pattern.

After all of the poles are up, the Lodge is built, and the Altar and the Fire Pit are finished, make sure you put the staff on the Altar. Make sure that you sprinkle everything in sage, cedar, and tobacco; also that you sing and pray for all of the Spirits to come and help you. I call the Spirits to the Fire, to the Poles, to the Altar, and to the Lodge. I invite them to come to this place and stay with us. For this will be a Holy Place, a place of Love, Truth, Honor, Respect, Humbleness, Generosity, and Courage. All that come here will be seeking the spirits' help, and will always be thankful.

With all of the limbs and green parts left over, make medicine. Strip the bark off the limbs using a knife, or even a rock. Scrape the top part of the wood. This thin layer that comes off is the medicine. It is used in loading the Pipe, in making ceremonial tea to drink as a Healer, and in making ceremonial water for the lodge to pour on the rocks. This medicine is what is used in making aspirin! It is a mild sedative. It is a good antibiotic, and is very good for pain.

Please figure out where you should sit in the lodge to be in your power spots. This is done by first starting with your date of birth.

For example: 1-16-1941 Add it this way 1 + 1 = 2 + 6 =8 + 1 =9 + 9 =18 + 4=22 +1=23 Then 2 +3 =5. So your power days would be any day with a 5 in it 5, 15, 25. Days not quite as powerful would be 10, 20, 30.

Look at the diagram of the lodge and find pole 5. This is where you should sit in the lodge to get the power you need during the ceremony, for the spirits, plants, and all apply to you.

Let's do it again so you'll understand. Let's say your birthday is 5-11-1964.

Take 5 + 1 = 6 +1 = 7 + 1 = 8 + 9 =17 + 6 = 23 + 4 = 27 and 2+7=9.

So your power number would be 9. Look at the diagram of the lodge and find this pole. This is where you should sit, and your power days would be 9, 19, 29. Also you should make any good decision, important decision, or any commitment on those days.

It is important that you invite the elements into the Lodge, the Fire Pit, and the Directional Poles. You do this by getting Fire, Water, and Earth and using a feather fan or wing fan to fan their spirits together in the lodge at their proper locations, and calling the spirits to join in. Look at your Medicine Wheel and the Lodge Diagram 1.

It is important to keep your Sacred Area clean, beautiful, and full of Love.

Remember to Walk in Beauty and Love Always!

Chapter Twenty

The Sacred Fire

First I wish to say thank you to all of the ancestors who passed this knowledge down from generation to generation. I thank the spirits and most, the Great Spirit, for blessing me with all who have passed the ancient knowledge down to me. I, in turn, now pass this on to my children and grandchildren.

Mvto, Mvto, Pucase Hesaketv
(Thank you, Thank you, Master of Breath, or Master of Life)

The Sacred Fire is a living, powerful spirit, for it is created with love and power, in humbleness, respect, honor, truth, and generosity. It consists of all four elements: earth, water, air, and fire. It is a powerful gift that was given in love to the ancient ones to always remind them of the pure love and sacredness of all life.

To begin you must have a fire pit, which I have already described to you. (See Previous Chapter) This fire pit must be purified and blessed with sacred offerings of tobacco, sage, holly leaf, corn meal, cedar, water, and naturally it must be smudged. (Smudging is the purification with smoke, with sage, cedar or sweetgrass usually, made by lighting the herb, blowing out the flame, and letting it smolder, and fanning this smoke all over and around yourself, another person, or an area.)

Once you have the fire pit ready, now attention must be paid to the wood and rocks. I always make tobacco offerings to wood and rocks and I always pray with them and for them. I also make sure to always ask the wood and the rocks for their help. I do this several days before ceremony, usually 4-7 days before I do a ceremony. Sometimes I even sleep with the grandfathers (stones) to attune my spirit and heart to them. I tell them that I am asking for their help, for my relatives, or for a specific purpose explaining what help is needed. I also pray for the Mother Earth and all of my relatives to please help me.

On the day I am to build the fire, I make sure that I have nothing but good thoughts, and my heart is full of love. I have prayed and asked permission from all of the tree people, stone people, water people, air people, star people, spirit people, and most of all from Creator. I ask to please allow me to create this Sacred Fire and bring it to life, full of power, love, healing, purifying, and blessings.

I then face the Morning Sun and sing a prayer to the East spirits, Sun etc. (See Med Wheel Chapter) asking for them to accept my offerings which I have in my hand and come to this Sacred Fire and add their power, medicine, and love to this fire. I then release my offerings in my hand from the east trailing a line to the center of the Fire Pit.

I then do this to the South spirits, repeating my prayer song as before, just changed to call the spirits from the South. Then make my offering in a line back to the center of the Fire Pit.

Then, I do this for the West spirits, repeating my prayer song as before just changing it to call the spirits of the West. Next I add my prayer offerings in a line from the West back to the center of the Fire Pit.

Then I repeat this process for the North, for the spirits of the North, repeating my prayer song as before, just changed to call the spirits of the North. Then I offer my prayer offerings in a line to the center of the Fire Pit.

Between the East and South I call and sing my prayer song for Mother Earth, Grandmother, and Mother, and offer my prayer offerings in a line to the center of the Fire Pit.

Then between the South and West I call the spirits of the Sky, Wind, and Clouds, and sing my prayer song as before calling the spirits and offer my prayer offerings in a line to the center of the Fire Pit.

And between the West and North, I call the spirits of the Universe, the Star Peoples, and sing my prayer song as before just changing the spirits, and offer the prayer offerings in a line to the center of the Fire Pit.

Between the North and East I call the spirits of the Winged Ones and sing my prayer song and then offer my prayer offerings in a line to the center of the Fire Pit.

Then, stepping into the center, I pray to the Creator and ask for help. I sing my prayer song and offer my prayer offerings in the circle in the center to the Creator.

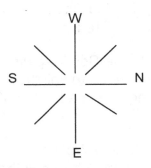

Now I repeat this whole process with the pieces of wood. Starting in the East and holding the log up and facing the East, I sing my prayer song to the spirits of the East and ask them to please help me and to come to this tree person who has offered to sacrifice its life to help us; and that the tree person will honor and sing our love for its sacrifice; to please add their power, medicines and prayers with the tree person and our prayers. I then lay the log on the prayer offerings that I had laid in a line from the East to the center of the Fire Pit. (See Diagram)

Next I take a tree person (log) and facing the South, hold it up and sing my prayer song for the spirits of the South to help us. I repeat the process I did with the East, just changing the prayer song to direct the song to the spirits of the South. Then I lay the tree person on the offerings that are lined from the South to the center of the Fire Pit.

Then I do this for the West. Holding up a tree person to the West I sing my prayer song to the spirits of the West, and then lay the log down on the line of offerings from the West to the center of the Fire Pit. This whole process is repeated for each of the directions laying a log on each line of offerings in the same order as before.

After the eight logs are laid on the offerings, I then place kindling between the logs (tree people) and add used paper so it will light quickly and easily. I then fill in the gaps with smaller logs (tree people).

Once this is done, I now take the first stone person and starting in the East, sing my prayer song while I hold the stone person up towards the East. Then I place it on the tree person on the line from East to the center. I place the stone person on the end farthest from the center of the Fire Pit. I then repeat this process for each of the eight directions using one stone person at a time in the same order as the original offerings.

When this is done, I then begin to build the medicine stone wheel. This is done by placing the stones in the gaps of the wheel starting on the end and gradually working the pile of stone people towards the center. The higher the stack of stone people, the taller this will be. You will stack them until it is like a tipi with a hole in the top that you can see all the way to the bottom.

At this time I make more prayer offerings and sprinkle tobacco, cedar, holly leaf, sage, and corn meal on all of the stone people. Then I gather large tree people and stack these around the stone people, filling in the gaps with smaller tree people and kindling. Then I stuff old papers, cardboard etc. in between these.

Once this is done, now the prayers are said again asking for the spirits to help. And I thank all of the tree people and stone people for their sacrifices and for helping us.

I now have my fire keeper light the fire starting at the East, while I sing my fire song. The song is telling the Spirits that I am beginning to pray and I am suffering, so please help me; for I do this for all of my relatives; that all who are participating need their help. I sing to the spirits of the Sun, tree people, fire, stone people, water people, Mother Earth, winged ones, 4-leggeds, ancient ones, star peoples. I ask them for their help to bless this fire, and add their power, medicine, and their love to this fire; to purify and heal all of those who are about to pray; to send their power and medicine to those we direct them to; and thank them for all they have given to us.

Once I have done this, I smudge myself using the flame and heat, to touch my body and then offer cedar and sage to cover me as well. I then use my eagle feather and while I pray I direct this purity and power to the Sacred Altar, and to the lodge.

After the lodge is set up, I will have the fire keeper(s) bring me a smudge bowl and smudge the outside of the lodge, the inside of the lodge, and then the entire area, including all who are present.

Now that all of this is finished, I will go inside the lodge and pray alone, and design the medicine wheel in the rock pit with cedar, sage, tobacco, holly leaf, and corn meal; for as the fire was created, it will be recreated again inside of the lodge as well. Once this is done it is time for me to call the spirits to help me on this day. I will call them to show me what they wish to be done.

(Before I conduct a ceremony, I always prepare myself physically, mentally, and spiritually, usually at least seven days in advance, but no less than four days in advance.) I conduct ceremonies as they are needed, and each time it is different. I've been to lodges that others have conducted. I really enjoyed the lodges of my youth, all being conducted by all of the truly old ones.

Today, most of them are all gone and most that do these things today don't have a clue about the old ways or why things are done. Today it seems to be all about short cuts, comfort, or just plain forgotten. Almost none of them instruct newcomers on where to sit for their own power when they need it. It is important that lodge participants sit in their power place, and it is also important that they experience every single place in the lodge. Things such as these are not taught any more.

Many think they have to sing every single moment while they are in the lodge. Oh, how wrong they are. How can you hear the spirits if your mouth is constantly going? You must sit in silence and listen to the spirits. The lodge is not to be used to hurt or punish anyone. How hot a lodge gets is the response of Spirit. It is not used to see how hot you can get someone, or show everyone how tough or strong you are. Remember, you must humble yourself! You are there in humility, love, respect, honor, truth, generosity, and courage. You are there to pray!

Hopefully, this will help each of you in your lodge.

Remember to Walk in Love and Beauty Always!

Chapter Twenty-one

Dancing With Fire

When the people first came to this world, they came from the Stars. Grandfather Sun gave his love to this world, to Mother Earth and to all his children. Fire was here, coming up from Mother's womb, what we call volcanoes, but also from the sky in lightning and meteors. All the different children of this world had crystals and knew how to use them, but fire was sacred to all the children. It belonged to Grandfather Sun, so only certain people were chosen to keep this Sacredness that was a gift.

Today many people think that the Sacred Fire was lit by rubbing two sticks together, or by a burning ember from a lightning strike, or something else. But the truth is that in the Ancient Times fire was Sacred and it was a Sacred Ceremony to light the fire.

The Sacred Fire for a town, village, etc., was kept and taken care of by a Fire Keeper, who had others he taught and trained his whole life. It would be lit during the ceremony of the Spring Equinox as it is now called. But, in the old days it was done during the Green Corn Ceremony. This was the beginning of the New Year.

All the Fire Keepers would fast, meaning no food, no water, constant prayer, drinking the Black Drink (a diuretic plant used to cleanse the body from inside), and numerous other ceremonies and rituals.

All the Clan Mothers went to each home and had the head woman of the house put out the hearth fires and remove all the ashes and clean it all up. The Fire Keeper's helpers would extinguish the Sacred Fire of the town, city, or village, and remove all the ashes and old refuse that had built up for the past year. Every person, young, old, male, and female fasted. This was a time to purify, to cleanse the Spirit of each person.

Certain Clan Mothers, who were chosen for their wisdom

and justice, served to hear everyone's old complaints of wrongs done to them. This is under the Blood Laws for justice and peace to be restored. Their clan representatives then escorted to her those who had to appear before the Clan Mother for doing wrongs. Then the Clan Mother would decide the fate or fates of those who did wrong. If someone had crippled or injured a party that kept the family or clan from prospering or unable to take care of the family needs or clan needs, the Clan Mother would order the one who had caused this to now leave their clan and take on the responsibility of the one who was injured or crippled. And they would have to do so or be put to death by their own clan or family member for dishonoring them.

If a person was responsible for someone's death, then they might have to give their life to replace the loss of the one that had died. They might have to become a son or daughter to another mother or father, or they might have to die for what they did, but that was very, very rare.

The Blood Laws came from the Stars with us. They are designed to maintain Beauty, Love, Harmony, and Balance with all life here. If someone accidentally did something that cost a person, say a good catch of fish, then the Clan Mother would order that this be repaid seven times over. This way all bad feelings would be removed from the hearts of the People before the Sacred Fire was re-lit and a new year began. Young maidens would pick specific green corn which was to be used in the Green Corn Ceremony. The Beloved Women would seek special guidance from Spirit and their relatives from the Stars, and connect to the Sacred Skulls to see and know all that was to be given to the People.

Young boys, who were waiting to pass their final test to be initiated into the war societies as warriors, began their final ordeals. The War Leaders and War Clan Leaders conducted this test. Young boys would first be prepared using the Black Drink, and then they would run, being driven faster and faster by the War Leaders. They ran all day, all night, and into the next day. Then they were taken to the spring and ordered to stand in the ice-cold water all day. If any one of them moved, or moaned out in pain, or let their pain show in a facial expression, he did not pass, and would have to wait until the following year to try again, which brought shame upon his clan and family.

Now, with all this running and no food and water, the body is racked with pain. Standing in the cold water causes muscles to cramp and spasm, but it also makes you think of the refreshing cold water to drink. If you lost your concentration of prayers, it would cause you to fail. After standing in the cold water all day, you would be ordered out and to stand again to take the Black Drink.

A Holy Man comes now, and using a leg bone or a fire-hardened stick, which would have claws or teeth protruding from it, the Holy Man would say the prayer asking the boys to sing their power song. While you were singing, the Holy Man took the cutting stick and raked your body with four claws and teeth diagonally across your chest. There were four cuts with each stroke, crossing from shoulder to hip on both sides, first the front and then the back, then your arms, and then your legs.

After all of this was done to all the boys, the Holy Man led them all in Spirit Calling Songs. Then, they were ordered to run again all night long and through the next day. Then back into the ice-cold water. This time though, they were submerged completely. While they lay on the bottom, noted and respected warriors stood on top of them.

While they were lying on their backs, they talked to Mother Earth, since they were in her womb. They prayed for her help, her love, her gifts, and they made a vow to love her, protect her, and honor her and all her children.

Then they are taken out of the water, given a special drink prepared by a Beloved Woman, and told to run to a secluded area. There you would find yourself all alone, so you would then lie down on Mother and seek your Spirit Helpers to grant you a vision. When you returned depended on the individual. They returned to a designated area to meet with the Holy Ones to discuss their vision, and were then taken to a special lodge.

While the young boys were doing this, the young maidens were going through their own ceremonies as well.

Those who were close to their moon cycle were given a special herb that would stop the moon cycle. This would work as long as they took the herb each day. It was always prepared by a Moon Woman, an elder woman who is in charge of all the women's moon things. While they were drinking the herb, they would dance naked under Grandmother Moon's power, doing moon and shadow dances.

There were also young maidens about to become women. Therefore, they were preparing themselves to become a True Woman, learning all of the mysteries, power, and secret knowledge that are passed on to them by the Beloved Women. A woman's life is very important. Her heart must be of pure love. She is a giver of life. She is a protector of life, and she is the mother to all life. Only a woman can have True Power, for her heart is the only one that can use Power in True Love.

That is why the women are the ones that make the decisions for the people. They pass their needs, requests, and desires on to the Clan Mothers. The Clan Mothers consult with the Beloved Women, and then the council is informed by the Clan Mothers of the People's needs, requests, and wants. No war could ever be started without the Clan Mothers saying so. All warriors obeyed the wishes and commands of the Clan Mothers. Why? Because men are temperamental, full of egos, pride, jealousy, and such. They are easy to insult and easy to rile to anger. Many times they do foolish things. So it is women who provide good judgment, reason, and logic, because their hearts are for the good of the People.

The maidens were taught at this time how to use herbs to help get pregnant, how to ease childbirth pain, how to please a man, and how they are the keepers of True Love. They are taught that they are the mothers of the next generation and that they have duties and responsibilities to all the People to make sure that all was as it was intended to be. That is the reason that all of the Sacred things were given to women, not to men.

Now, while these things were going on, the Fire Keeper

led the ceremonies for the young Fire Keepers. This was an intense ritual. They purified in a lodge that was dug into the ground and built upwards in a spiral round dome. Inside were the Sacred Items of the Fire and the Fire Crystals, for these would be used to light the Sacred Fire.

The Fire Keeper would lead the young ones in prayer songs and purification, for they all had to become one with the Fire, using the Spiral Dance to become one with Spirit. You dance the Dream and the Dream becomes the Dance. The fire keepers are in the Spirit world and in this world at the same time, but all illusions are removed. They dance with power. They are the power.

Hot coals and hot rocks are passed to all. Each is to hold them in his hands. If he is true to his heart, true to Spirit, and one with Spirit, he can do this. When he gets to the state of mind where all is Beauty, and all is Love, the golden lights shimmer in him, through him, and all around him. He must not try to control the power, but just let it flow. Then he can take hot coals and hot rocks and rub them all over his body, with no burning and no blistering, until he puts the hot coal or hot rock in his mouth as he swallows the spirit of fire.

After Dancing with Spirit, it is easy not to want to come back. Many don't, and become trapped in the dance. It is not wrong. It is a choice, as all is a choice. But to come back means that you will now use this knowledge, this gift, to help all of your relatives.

When the young fire keeper comes back he is exhausted physically, yet vibrating with energy. Now the Fire Keeper lights a fire in the lodge. The fire is about six or seven feet in diameter. The logs burn hot and hot flames shoot up. The Fire Keeper sings a fire Song and enters the Spirit Dance, and then dances himself into the flames. The flames flow with him, into him, and around him, but do not harm him in any way. He is one with the Fire. All the young ones now start the Fire Song, and dancing with Spirit, they too now enter the Fire and Dance with Fire. They are now one. For four days this goes on day and night, inside the Fire Keeper's Lodge. There is no time. Nothing exists but the Dance.

Finally, at predawn, a Beloved Woman comes to the door. She enters and in the Sacred Language, she touches the Fire Keeper's and the young one's minds to come and follow her.

The Clan Mothers have been busy. They have the special wood that was chosen and blessed by the Beloved Women placed in the Sacred Fire area. It is now ready for the Fire Keeper. Every member of the People is present, all in accordance to their position and status with the People.

The Fire Keeper comes, being led by a Beloved Woman, who falls into step with all the Beloved Women as they lead the way to the Sacred Fire area, in the center of the town or village. The Beloved Women lead the procession around the area four times. Then all are stopped in the exact position. All face the east. Every eye is upon the rising of Grandfather Sun. The Beloved Women begin the Sun Song, an honor song, calling Grandfather Sun to come and bring his powerful love to Mother and to help all of her children. Every voice of the People joins with the Beloved Women. They are all singing in Love and Harmony for Grandfather to bless us all with his love. Slowly, slowly, we see him rise. Brilliant lights streak the sky inch by inch, moment by moment.

The Fire Keeper reaches into his Sacred bag and brings out the Sacred Fire Crystals. They are beautiful Power Wands. He holds them up for all to see, then sings the Fire Song - now joined by all the young Fire Keepers. Then he turns and faces Grandfather Sun and holds up the Fire crystals to the Sun, who we all love. Grandfather Sun rejoices in our love and fills the Sacred Crystals with his power. Beautiful, flashing light sparkles all around the Sacred Crystals. The crystals begin vibrating, as does the Fire Keeper. His hands and arms are trembling with the vibration of power that the Sacred Crystals are absorbing.

The Fire Keeper cries out and directs the Sacred Crystals at the Sacred Wood in the Sacred Fire area. He crashes the two Sacred Crystals together and directs the energy from them toward the wood. Sparks fly, and beams of powerful light pour from the Sacred Crystals into the wood. Smoke starts coming up, then the wood begins to glow hot red, and then flames shoot up. And all the People shout with joy. As the Sacred Fire begins to burn hotter and hotter, the Fire Keeper places the Sacred Crystals back into the Sacred Bag and hands it to the Beloved Woman. He then sings a special spirit song and starts his spirit dance. He dances with Spirit, and all the young Fire Keepers also start to dance and sing. They dance around the Sacred Fire again and again, getting closer and closer all the time, until the Fire Keeper steps into the fire itself. The People all rejoice for they know that Spirit has blessed them with a new life, a new year, and a New Sacred Fire. They will have life and all will be well.

Now each Clan Mother and each Beloved Woman takes a hot ember and gives it to every woman of each home, so that they will have a piece of the Sacred Fire in their home. This fire will now bring life, light, cook foods, cook teas and medicine, and bring warmth to each and every home. The ceremony is now complete. It is a time of feasting, games, courtship, and dancing for the next three to twenty-one days depending on the size of the town, city, or village. Visitors are welcomed and allowed to enjoy and participate now in feasting, dancing, games, etc. This is the way of the Ancient Ones, and the old ones, about the Sacred Fire. And it is all good!

Remember to Walk in Beauty and Love Always!

Chapter Twenty-two

The Purification Ceremony
(Sweat Lodge)

It has come to my attention that many today do not believe that the sweat lodge is important, necessary, or an integral part of Native Religion, Culture, and Traditions!

My name is Ghost. I am an enrolled member of the Muskogee Nation of Florida. I am a Red Stick member. I am a member of the Wind Clan and have practiced Traditional Religion all my life. I have learned from my own grandfathers and elders, and have learned and been taught by Lakota, Dakota, Nakota, Paiute, Arapaho, Iroquois, Ani-yun-wiya (Cherokee), Navajo, Apache, Cheyenne, Blackfoot, Crow, Pima, Tewa, Wasco, Nez Perce, Ojibwa, Menominee, Anishinabe, Aleut, Tlingit, Shoshone, Comanche, Yucci, Chumash, Eskimo, Hawaiian, Carib, Aztec, etc.

Every single teaching of every single traditional belief, of every single nation, clearly requires "purification", not only of the body, but also of the mind and spirit! I have personally conducted ceremonies on the outside as well as in prisons, and I have done this for many, many years! Every single true Holy Man or Holy Woman who practices traditional religion will tell you the same thing. You must "purify" yourself, sacrifice your body (give up the flesh), and endure pain, to meet the spirits to be reborn.

The purpose of the sweat lodge is many-fold!

1. To purify our bodies, mind, heart, and spirit
2. To pray and offer ourselves to the spirits for their help
3. To offer ourselves to the spirits for our people and our loved ones so that they do not suffer
4. To heal ourselves and those we pray for
5. To purify ourselves to prepare for other Sacred Ceremonies

6. To be reborn and let go of all of our past that we have done wrong
7. To connect to the spirits by meeting them halfway and showing them that we are sincerely trying; by truly humbling ourselves as how pitiful we truly are

There is not one single person I know that has not done something wrong. Your thoughts, words, actions can all have hurt someone, somehow or another. So no one is clean.

I know the Medicine Wheel. I was taught the Ancient Power Wheel by true Holy Ones. There is no way that anyone is allowed to go into a Medicine Wheel without purifying themselves first. A True Medicine Wheel is a Sacred, Holy Place. It is designed and prepared by those who have fasted, prayed and purified themselves the old ways.

Each stone is carefully asked if it will help. They are not randomly chosen. Each spirit, each element, each plant, animal, color, planet, star or moon is carefully asked by a person or persons who have purified themselves first. Offerings must be made. Offerings of these peoples' own flesh, blood, and spirit are made. There is no way an unclean person should ever be allowed on any Medicine Wheel.

By doing so, that unclean person will invite bad things to come, not only to that person, but loved ones, family members, and even others who may go to the Medicine Wheel.

Native Religion is not for just anybody. Native Religion is not propaganda nor does it solicit or recruit anyone to practice it. It is not an easy path to walk, but it can be walked by those true in spirit and in heart! You don't shortcut or modify the Tradition by excluding something as important as purifying yourself.

Now maybe some of you say that your tribe doesn't use a sweat! Well, those that didn't use a sweat lodge had a lot tougher ways to purify themselves: by fasting, drinking decoctions that make you (puke, have diarrhea, sweat, pass out from the poisons, etc.), by fasting and running all day and all night for three days-four days; by fasting (no food, no water, no sleep) and dancing with hot coals in your hands and dancing on hot coals; by being bitten by poisonous snakes and made to run; being cut with sticks that have claws and teeth in them all across your body; by using poison to kill the flesh, then having hot coals placed in your mouth; by making you run all day at full speed and being hit with sticks, then at night making you stand still in ice cold water not allowed to move. So, if your tribe didn't use the sweat lodge, they still made you purify!

I would strongly recommend each of you to use the sweat lodge as much as possible, because you most surely will have bad things on you, in you, every single day. Negative thoughts, emotions, words, physical actions around you in your environment, will surely contaminate you. This must be cleansed. Drinking, cursing, using drugs, fighting, arguing, even watching TV, will contaminate you.

We, those who do use a sweat lodge, know the importance of purification, and of the healing prayers being answered, being reborn, the total peace and connection that we share. The sweat lodge is very, very important, and it teaches you as well. When a small rock (grandfather), can make a strong man get on his knees and beg for pity, mercy, and make you scream; yes, you will be humble. You must understand that these grandfathers have sacrificed themselves to help you; just as the wood does; just as the water does; just as the air does. Everything is sacrificing itself to help you.

But the Spirits can't help you if you don't try to meet them halfway, at least. Only when you forget yourself and are concentrating in prayer for all your relatives (family, friends, plant people, animal people, water people, winged people, two-legged people, rock people, those that crawl and live in the ground, even your enemies, all the universe) will you reach the point that you no longer feel pain in your body. Cold chills will cover you and you will find the spirits waiting to help you.

The sweat lodge is not used as a contest to see who is the strongest or who can stand the most pain. No one is to judge you. The spirits will do that.

Since I have been taught by many elders and many

tribes, I use what was taught to me. Using the word "inipi" is to attach it to the Lakota people. "Inipi" means home of the inner breath of Spirit. It is called a "sweat lodge" in modern times as it is the sweating out of negative energies brought through the use of the steam, formed by pouring water on hot stone people that helps bring the purification. It has always been a purification lodge, called so in each language description by each tribe that uses it.

The symbolism of the lodge itself is the womb of the Earth Mother. We go into her for the gifts of purification we will get to be reborn, purified.

The sixteen willow saplings represent the Tree people, a part of the earth. These are the ones that go into the ground. They typically grow near water, a symbol of cleansing itself have healing properties first used as what we now use as aspirin. (Sometimes I make tea during the ceremony of willow bark).

The other 12 poles represent all the planets and star people, which gives you the complete sacred number 28, as in the 28 days of an actual month with 7 days per phase of each moon, and there being 4 moons, so four times seven is 28, and there are 28 ribs in a buffalo as well. Also the inner bark is shaved off from the poles to make casha, the medicine that is added to the tobacco to use in the cannupa.

The lodge (**EARTH**) is covered in traditional times with hides/today with blankets and/or tarps signifying the dark black of the night sky or the skin and body holding a not yet born baby.

The fire (**SUN**) represents Great Mystery/God/Creator. (The fire is always built in a symbolic way. See The Sacred Fire chapter.)

The stones that are heated are considered our elders, meaning grandfathers. The stones were here long before people. (Some stones are female. These are the ones that have hollow insides or pockets. As a woman has a womb so too do grandmother stones. These stones once they are seen to be female are placed to be in the south so they will feel better and can help us men feel the power of women's love more). We welcome the stones into the lodge with a prayer or song. Stones are male energy.

Water, used to make the steam, another symbol of purification, is seen as female energy. (When male and female are united, balance or harmony in the universe occurs.)

The resulting heat and steam is the ancestor spirits, which when combined with the stones and water create the breath of life for all the people in the home of the Creator, signified by the womb of Grandmother Earth.

There is a pit for the hot stones dug in the center of the lodge floor and this removed earth is used to build the <u>altar</u> (**MOON**), just outside the entry door (the **fire** pit is usually east of the altar) this round fireplace in the center of the lodge is the center of the universe (and our galaxy).

Lodge/Earth   Altar/Moon Fire/Sun   east   Layout of a lodge

We enter the lodge on hands and knees in humility as entering the womb of the Earth Mother. All participants enter in sunwise or clockwise order. After all have entered it is completely dark signifying our ignorance, the darkness from which we will seek the light.

Typically the ceremony is done with four rounds or doors of prayer and song. After each door is complete, the door covering is raised signifying the end of that door.

My symbolism of the four doors or rounds of prayer and endurance are:

<u>First Door</u> is for the East and the Spirits of the East. This door is for you to purify yourself and get your mind right, release whatever you have in you or on you that is holding you back from being cleaned, if you have something you need to say this is the door for that. You will pray for others until your

heart, your spirit, your body, and your mind are one with spirit, and clean, ready to help everyone with their prayers. This door is for all children because we come as a child to our Mother, for help and guidance, we are a child ready to receive, and get pure in heart. This door is very long and intense because you must be right within yourself, before you can help others. If you aren't then there is no telling what could happen to all the other peoples' relatives. You are messing with their safety and wellbeing. Also this door we sing calling for the spirits to come in and be with us. We sing also for each participant's personal spirit helpers to come. We also sing for the grandfathers and grandmothers who were just brought in (First 7 stone people to enter).

Door Two is the South door and represents all our females, this for their love as they give birth and suffer for us, they heal our hearts and comfort us as mothers, sisters, aunts, grandmothers, girlfriends, wives, daughter, etc. This door represents the South spirits and songs and dance, which are given to us from this door, it is known to us as the door of love and for all females. It also teaches us gentleness, songs for the women are usually sung, thank you songs, love songs, healing broken hearts, and forgiveness songs for those we may have wronged. Also this door is for the adolescents (teenagers).

Door Three is to the West and represents the West spirits and the sacred things that we have been given: air, water, fire, and earth, our medicines (plant people and stone peoples) eagle feathers, cannupas (Lakota word for pipes), all feathers and medicine from all life, foods, and shelter). It is called the door for adults, magic, seeking power and spiritual knowledge, songs for all Sacred items are sung, cannupa songs, prayers songs for the ones in need of special prayers, prayers for those who walk the walk of the sacred path and carry our Sacred items for us, all holy people and elders, and for the earth medicine (stone peoples).

Door Four is for the spirits of the North and represents the enlightenment and wisdom, of all things spiritual and mysteries. It represents inner reflections of yourself, and new beginnings, new ideas and goals. It has songs of thanks for all we've been given, learned and experienced. It is for all elders, grandmothers, grandfathers, it is a place where now you can ask for things you need for yourself in your life. It is to tell the spirits goodbye for now and to take our prayers and add your prayers together with ours and take it up to the Creator.

These are the things I instruct and tell all who enter the lodge when I conduct this ceremony. For each door I make sure all know what each door is, because at the beginning of each door I explain what the door is for. So everyone is on the same thought, same mind frame and all have those prayers together with each other now work as one.

Now, I'll give you a glimpse into the MOUND BUILDER'S WAY!

When I was growing up and learning my Peoples' ancient ways, it was nothing like today's ceremony!

The mound builder's range was far and wide, it was very similar to ancient Egypt, Sumerian, Inca, Mayan, Olmec, Toltec, and Anasazi. All the mounds are linked in connection to Mother Earth, the Stars, and the Universe, and all were in alignment with certain grids and energy points. All were and are powered by the elements of the universe, and the use of Sacred Stones. As I have said many times the power and effects of these stone people are enormous.

All technology today is based upon these facts. But what science never as yet learned is how to harness that energy and focus it. They are just now entertaining the truth of the effects of sounds and acoustics in the ancient sites, something every mound builder already knows. These truths are just now starting to come out by science, but like so many before me, I have taught this all my life, and have told all of you this numerous times over the years. And many of you thought that I was fantasizing, or just nuts.

So let me tell you how I conduct a Mound Builder Ceremony.

The mound is already waiting for me to enter. I have

prepared myself for this way in advance. I have been asked to help someone and the family and friends will also come to help as required, for we are all one. (Most all illness comes from the body or parts of the body out of tune so to speak. It is like your car running sputtering, missing and backfiring. Well something is wrong and you must get it fixed to run smooth again. It is the same with our bodies.) I walk the spiraling stairs down, down deep into our Mother, every step is a prayer, every step is on a stone person and I ask for forgiveness for stepping on them.

The walls and the seats are all made with the stone peoples. All have agreed to help and was asked before being brought and placed to be used in the building of the mounds. This is done in complete love, as we go into the Mother's womb to build this mound. And only then after asking her and asking for her forgiveness. We are all her children and must all respect her. (By the way the size of the mound above the ground is small compared to how big it is underground, because it gets bigger the deeper you go.)

Once I'm down in the circle of the center of the mound, all that have come to assist me, after I requested their help and offered them the gift offering and respect for their assistance in this ceremony, now take their places, except those outside who will assist as they are instructed by me. Then those at the top near the entrance also who are to assist me take their places as well! Drums, rattles, and other instruments, such as the flutes and whistles are also present. Incense is used to smudge us before we entered and is used again now that we are all in.

The person needing help is brought in and helped to lie down on a red cloth that has special herbs all covering it. The person who lies down did so at an exact place in the mound, and is on top of stone people who are there to help. Once I start to pray all go quiet as I invite the spirits to assist us. I ask for the water and stone people to be brought from those above, and begin to sing as my assistants all join in as well as those family members who are there as well. We call to our Mother to hear us as we are in her womb waiting for life, waiting for her to hear us. The drummers, those at the top and those at the bottom, beat the drum in a heartbeat rhythm. We sing of our love and we sing for all to help us reunite this person's body back to the heart beat of all.

The voices, the drums, the vibration is echoing and bouncing to the stone people and they let it come into them and add their energy and love, and those stone people who have the gift to magnify and amplify (crystals) send these sound vibrations through all of us. Those above have brought the water and hot stones and place them in the center as directed for the directions (seven) and I place the sacred herbs on them as they fill up and begin to smoke, as we fan the smoke over the person needing help.

We now sing and drum louder and the rattles and flute also begin to join in, until the power is building and vibrating all within Mother's womb. Drums are beating all over the top and around the person lying down, and from above the big drums send their booming sounds down and spiraling through us all.

I pour water from a gourd dipper over the hot stones and let the heat intensify everything as we continue singing and drumming and pouring water. A young maiden is summoned by me, and she approaches and kneels at the person needing help's side and begins to sing a solo song of love and life, filled with beauty.

Now a small child who is a member of the family comes as I motion. This child kneels down too and places its hands on the person's heart, and joins the maiden in singing as we all pray silently and send and direct our energy to the person laying there. I signal for more water and hot stone people, and we now all sing in harmony as second singers to the maiden and child.

Those of us who are stone people now use our stone helpers and direct our thoughts and our energy into the stone helpers to send directly to the person laying here. One of my assistants now pours the water over the new hot stone people and we all shout and sing as one getting our voices in harmony with the pitch of the drums and flutes and rattles.

Now I signal and we all stomp our feet into the Mother's

womb and Mother responds by vibrating and shaking as she sends her power back at the person laying there and at all of us. And now we shout out in pure love for our Mother and all our relatives. And we get more and more water and hot stones as we drum louder and louder. The person now sits up and is vibrating with the rhythm of the sounds and power.

Drums are in front and back of the person being healed, on both sides and above him. Then I place my stone person on his body as does members of his family with their stone people. We sing louder and drum louder as we pour more water over the hot stone people. He now stands up and begins to dance the dance of life, with the rhythm of life, because he is now in harmony again. His body is right in its frequency. The items that he had laid on are removed and burned.

There are four parts also to this ceremony too, because, four is a sacred number. There are four elements, four stages of life, four kingdoms, four seasons, four colors, four inner spirits of the body, four outer spirits of the body, and we use everything in fours to heal and make power, to bring balance. These ceremonies are a lot longer and more intense due to the design of the mound which has such an enormous amount of power to use and direct through the stone people.

This is the Mound Builder's Way

I hope and pray that what I have said can help you, and I pray that you all come to know and use the sweat lodge the right way: in love, respect, humbleness, prayer, truth, and in spirit.

Remember to Walk in Beauty and Love Always!

Chapter Twenty-three

The Medicine Wheel

Where has the way of the old ones gone? I know much has been lost by some Nations and Tribes, but some things are pretty much the same amongst all the Nations and Tribes. For instance, how many actual (real) Medicine Wheels are in existence today? How many really know how to build one the way our ancestors did? For the Medicine Wheel was, and is, one of the most important parts of every Nation and Tribe's way of life.

Every stone was not only selected, but each stone volunteered to be the one used at that exact point of each spoke of the wheel. Each was specially smudged, and worked in harmony with each of the other stones at that point of the spoke. Each spoke of the Wheel was a path, a power source, a teacher, healer, guide, helper, etc., for the purpose it was placed there. The Wheel was and is a direct map of ourselves, all of our relations, and all that is or is not. The reason so much is lost today, forgotten, is that the Medicine Wheel is not in use. The reason there is so much sickness, disease, alcoholism, drug addiction, child abuse, domestic violence, sexual abuse, etc., is because the Medicine Wheel is not being used.

Many people now days say, "Oh, we don't need those things they can be replaced with these other things." No, they can never replace a true Medicine Wheel. And no, a Medicine Wheel is not symbolic of something. A real Medicine Wheel is TRUE Medicine. A true Medicine Wheel is more than healing, it is healing plus power, knowledge, understanding, growing, touching, hearing, seeing, feeling, smelling, tasting; everything that exists; the past, present, and the future; of all that is or is not. Male, Female, infant, elder, child, adult, positive and, negative, all that is, is part of us, as we are part of All.

The old ones knew this; that is why it was used. When the Wheel was not used, the Power of the Nations was broken. The true Holy ones of the Old Times knew this, and it was why they had that power that all others today want to have, but haven't found it. The only way the Power will ever come back to the Nations is when the Medicine Wheels are built and used by the People again.

What is written in the following pages is something that might help you or someone you know. It is something that is vitally important to anyone who is truly seeking the Sacred Path and wishes to truly Walk the Path.

What follows is only a beginning to help you get started. If you truly wish to learn more, then you must seek those who will help you. But most important, seek the help from the Spirits and Creator, for only Spirit is the True Teacher.

What I have written is what I know personally, and what I was taught by my Grandfathers and Great Uncles who began teaching me when I was a child. One Grandfather was Ani-yun-wiya, the other Grandfather was Muskogee. Great Uncles were both Ani-yun-wiya and Muskogee. Other Elders taught and shared with me their knowledge. Many were of different Tribal Nations. However, most or all of them that I knew have gone on to the Spirit World.

I hope what you find within will stir a memory or a part of you to remember, through your Ancestors, the Truth.

Design of the Ancient Ones

These Sacred teachings have been forgotten and lost by most Tribes and Nations. They are truly Sacred, and I cannot and will not put all that you need to know to actually create one. For this knowledge is to be protected. I hope it will be enough though that it might inspire you to seek the Spiritual Guidance you need to learn more.

To begin, you must first find the right place to begin the creation. Once you find the spot, you must make sure it is on a hill, plateau, mesa, mountain, or bluff: a place that no one goes to, or would violate or desecrate. Once you have found that place, then you must begin the purification of the area.

This is done by smudging the area, saying prayers, and using a power shield to protect the area. Also there should be offerings of tobacco, cedar, corn meal, corn pollen, juniper, sweetgrass, and sage. If there is grass, brush etc. you must pray for these relatives, because you will have to burn them off. The reason it is burned off is for purification.

Your area will have to be 40 feet by 40 feet. Once it is marked off, you must make some marker sticks. You will need a total of 25 of these.

When you start, you must use the Sun and the Stars to make the <u>exact</u> alignments.

Start at Sunrise and place the markers for the East.

Then at high noon, stand in about the center and check for your shadow. You must find the exact center, using the Sun and your shadow. Now face the Sun and the East, lining up your body, hold out your right arm, walk out 20 feet from the center and place your marker stick for the South.

At Sunset, stand in the center and line up with the East at your back, facing the Sun, walk 20 feet from the center and place your marker stick for the West.

Make sure you stand back and look at the West marker stick, aligning it up with the center and the East stick.

At midnight locate the North Star, walk to the center, walk 20 feet to the North, and place your marker stick. Make sure to stand back and look, align the sticks with the center stick and the South stick.

At Sunrise, go to the center and watch the Morning Star. When it reaches halfway between the East and the South, walk 20 feet from the center and place the SE marker stick.

At Midnight, go to the center and face the North, locate the North Star, now turn sideways so that you face the East, place your arms straight out, turn left until you are halfway between West and North. Your right arm should be lined up with the center stick and the Southeast stick: walk 20 feet out and place your stick for the Northwest.

Go back to the center, then place your arms out to the

sides, with your right arm facing the SW, your left arm should be lined up halfway between the North and the East.

This is a simple way for you to get your locations of directions. If you have knowledge of Stars and Planet Alignments, then use the Stars and Planets for your alignments.

As a beginner, you will learn this as you grow on the Wheel. As you work on the Wheel, you will come to know the Stars and Planets, for they will line up with the Sacred Stones.

Now you must start the process of selecting the right Sacred Stones. You might think this is impossible, but no, it is not. Each of these stones is and can be found here on Turtle Island (North America). These Sacred Stones are to be handled and protected as such. Red Agate, Yellow, Red Jasper, etc., is easily found in many locations here in the United States. The best place to find the Quartz Crystals is in Arkansas, the Mt. Ida or Hot Springs area. You will need to learn about the different types of Quartz Crystals and what to look for.

The Phantom Quartz is the hardest to find, but it too, is in Mt. Ida, Arkansas. Bloodstone, Obsidian, Rose Quartz, and Rainbow Opal can be located in Oregon, Idaho, and Colorado. Like Arkansas, many places are available for you to find them yourself, or, owners will let you dig on their land for a fee. Hematite, Black Onyx, Jet, and Snowflake Obsidian are easily located in Arizona; also Rose Quartz, Quartz Crystal, and White Chert.

Remember this, for it is very important in selecting Sacred Stones: you must ask the Sacred Stones if they will help. Always touch, hold, and feel the Sacred Stones with your left hand while you ask and explain your purpose. If the Sacred Stone agrees, believe me you will know this. You will feel the vibration of energy flow into your hand. It will tingle, get warm to hot, vibrate, and pulse to let you know yes. If the answer is no, you will feel nothing.

Be very direct and precise in your prayers, and always give thanks whether the answer is yes, or no. Each stone must be selected this way. Each stone must agree to be used. Each stone must be smudged and recharged for purification. You must place each stone in the Sun, then in Salt Water, then in Spring Water. Place them in the Sun to swim in the water.

This may sound ridiculous to you, but you must learn that each stone has energy, power, electrical flow, and a vibration that is charged through Salt Water, Sun, Moon, and Spring Water. Once you have let them all charge in the Sun, you must let them charge in and under the moonlight. Yes, there is a vibration, energy, and frequency in this too.

Once they are all charged, then you must smudge them all again. Now you <u>must</u> tune these Sacred Stones to yourself. When I say tune, I mean just that. Energy flows and pulsates. It is constant and never ending. Energy is in the stones and energy is inside of you.

You must hold each stone in your left hand and talk to the stone with love, respect, truth, and humbleness. Understand these are our Relatives. They are the First People, the First Children of our Mother. Now <u>sing</u> from your heart to the Sacred Stone. Why? Because, as I said energy is a force, a motion of vibration.

This energy in you, in all things, has a musical scale. The vibration of the energy in your body will have a certain musical note. This <u>note</u> of vibration will then be picked up by the Sacred Stone and will harmonize with yours. It is a wonder to behold, feel, and experience this beautiful effect. It is even common, once you and all the stones are attuned, for all of them to sing together with you.

Sometimes, if you have done things right, they will give you an experience of a light show as well. By this I mean the energy of each stone has a color, just as our energy has a color; even multiple colors. When the Sacred Stones choose to do this it is such a beautiful sight to behold: dancing lights of all colors flowing around you, all over you, through you, until you too dance with light.

Get used to these things. Do not be frightened. This is their show of love, respect, power, and healing for you. In Ancient Times of Old, this is where the Truth of the Song, Truth of the Dance, Truth of the Dream, all came from. As time went on, generations forgot these Truths and they shortened and changed, until now they just sing and dance. But they know not where this all came from.

True Holy Ones, those that have <u>Power</u> and <u>Medicine,</u> all know these truths. For they sing things to come, to go, to be healed, and to make things happen. They Dance with This Power. They Dance with Energy of Love, of Life, Dance for Healings, etc. They Dream these Truths to make them happen; to heal, to come, and to see.

Understand this - a reminder has always been given to us: the Northern Lights, The Rainbow, the Sunrise, the Sunset, the Thunderstorm, the Lightning, the Moonlight, the Comets, the Solar Eclipses, the Lunar Eclipses, etc. Even our own Emotions show these dances, these Songs of Truths. Everything in existence has energy - a force, a vibration - and therefore all things are connected to each other.

What happened to us? Well, we just sort of short circuited, our batteries ran low and we tuned ourselves out of the frequency of all other things. Our reception, or our antenna, does not pick up all these things because we are on the wrong station. We are running an interference of static and haven't fixed it!

Now that you are attuned to these Sacred Stones, it is time to begin the creation. That is right. We are creating a Life Force of Truth, Love, Power, Respect, Humbleness, and Oneness with All that Is, All that is Not, All that Ever Was, All that will Ever Be, All that is Seen, and All that is Not Seen.

To begin with, study the diagram I have provided. You should see where and in what order the stones will be placed. At each place where you are to place a stone, you *must put an offering of tobacco, corn meal, cedar, and sage, and make your prayers by offering these items one at a time.* Using your left hand, offer them to that direction, to the element of that direction, to the Spirits, Animals and Plant Spirits of that direction. Then place the offerings on the ground at that exact spot. Then pick up the exact stone to that direction with all the Spirits, elements, and all that is in that direction.

Then with your back to that exact direction, face the center and say your prayers, place the Sacred Stone on top of the offerings and always say thank you. Do this in the exact sequence as the diagram shows.

Remember this: <u>You must always enter from the East</u> and <u>you must exit from the East.</u> No matter which direction of the Wheel you wish to experience, you must <u>always</u> start and enter from the East, then go to the center, then go to the direction you wish. When entering, always remember to greet the Spirits, Elements, Plants, Animals and Energies. Be respectful and truthful with <u>Love</u> in your <u>Heart</u> and <u>Humbleness!</u>

Once all the stones are placed, now you must have the <u>Elements!</u> Start in the East with a <u>living flame</u>, a flame that has been made the <u>old way</u> (either by using a crystal and the Sun, or by flint and iron). You <u>sing</u> to the Sun. You offer your love, spirit, respect, and humbleness, and you sing to the <u>Fire</u>. You will then walk barefooted, with the fire in your left hand, into the Wheel, placing each foot, one at a time, upon each stone and sing as you go all the way to the center, and stand in the center and sing from your heart. Then walk back to the East and place the Element Fire outside, but next to, the outermost stone of the East.

Next you must go to the West, but remember you must enter from the East, saying your greetings and prayers all the way to the center, then follow the stones, <u>always barefooted</u>, all the way to the West. Once there, you must <u>sing</u> to the West, Spirits, Animals, Plants, and Mother Earth. Make your prayers as well. Then reach down with your left hand, pick up a handful of soil and holding it in your left hand, sing to the soil and all the spirits. Then, with your back to the West, walk back to the center while touching each Sacred Stone with your bare foot, <u>singing</u> all the time as you go. Once in the center, stand and sing from your heart. Then walk back to the West and place the Element, Earth (mineral) outside, but next to, the outermost stone of the West. Now go back to the East, by way of the center (follow your stones), and get your Spring Water for your journey to the South.

Now get your Spring Water, enter from the East and say your greetings and prayers all the way to the center then follow the stones, always barefooted, all the way to the South. Once there you must sing to the South, Spirits, Animals, Plants, and Moon. Now sing to the Water and all the Spirits. Now walk to the center, holding the water and touching each stone until you are in the center stand there with the water and sing and pray from your heart. Then walk back to the South and place the water outside, but next to, the outermost stone of the South.

Now go back to the center and then to the East. Pick up a feather, Eagle or Hawk, a white feather is best if you have one, then use it; if not, substitute. Now entering from the East, greeting and singing to the Spirits, go to the center, stand there singing and praying, then go to the North. Now sing and pray to the Spirits of the North, then take the feather and fan the Air from the North towards the center. Sing to the Spirits of the North, Element Air, Buffalo, Elk, Caribou, Plants, etc. Now walk to the center, touching each stone along the way with the feather, while you sing to the Spirits. Now stand in the center, fanning the Air and singing and praying from your heart, then walk back to the North, touching each stone with your bare foot, singing all the way. Now take the feather and fan the Air down to just outside the outermost stone of the North. Now walk back to the center and exit through the East.

Now come back to the East with prayer offerings, (this is a person's choice of items, that is "what they wish to offer"), and while greeting and singing to the Spirits of the East, walk to the center. Then walk all around the circle of stones, around the center four times, while singing prayer songs from your heart to the Creator, to the Star People, Cloud People, and to all your Relations, touching each stone while you walk. Then go to the center and offer all your offerings, and yourself, to the Creator.

Speak from your heart about the thing you need in your life, what you wish to learn, understand, and how you can help all of your relations. Then sit down and listen with your heart, body, and all your senses. Become one with all that is. Feel it, taste it, smell it, touch it, hear it, and come to love all.

This is just a beginning of a long journey, but at least you have a path now to begin. How you walk and how far you go is all up to you. This is all I will write about now. Maybe I shouldn't have, maybe I should write more. All I know is that this is all that Spirit has let me feel comfortable with putting down on paper.

Maybe you can find some reading materials on these things. There are many good books about this. For example: Gemstones, Crystals, The Crystal Skull, Love is in the Earth, the Way, etc., by numerous authors. I was not taught by a book, so I wouldn't know how they would relate to these Ancient Teachings. I do know that in the Smithsonian Museum, Serpent Mounds, Cahokia Mounds, Eagle Mountains, Rockwood's Cavern, Moundsville, Alabama, Ruby Falls, and numerous sites all across this continent, there are actual relics of these Ancient Teachings. A few years ago they uncovered the one in Miami, Florida. I can only encourage you to seek for yourself.

Remember to Walk in Beauty and Love Always!

Medicine Wheel Design of the Ancient Ones

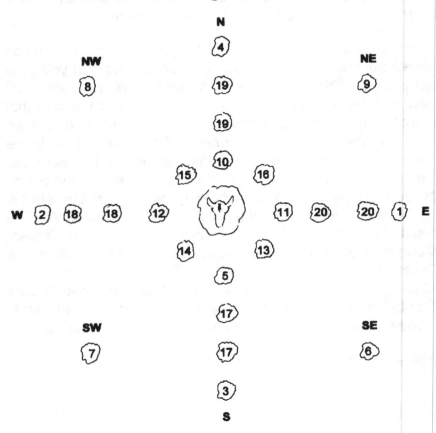

Details: The center consists of a base of bloodstone (approx. 24") with a skull set on top. A quartz crystal generator is placed on the top of the skull. The inner ring of stones is placed 2' from the center of the bloodstone to the center of the numbered stone. Going out in each of the cardinal directions, the distances from the center of the bloodstone will be 6', 10', and 14'. Numbers 6, 7, 8, and 9 will be 14' from the center of the bloodstone and exactly centered between the two cardinal direction stones on each side of it. This diagram uses numbers instead of the ancient markings so that you will understand the pattern which must be followed.

Legend of Proper Stones to Use

1   Amber

2   Obsidian

3   Red Garnet or Red Jasper

4   White Onyx

5   Red Agate

6   Quartz Crystal - Power Wand

7   Quartz Crystal - Healing Phantom

8   Quartz Crystal - Tabby

9   Quartz Crystal - Twin Power Wand

10   White Chalky Quartz - Key Crystal

11   Rainbow Opal

12   Smokey Quartz

13   Quartz Crystal - Teacher

14   Quartz Crystal - Double Terminated

15   Quartz Crystal - Record Keeper

16   Quartz Crystal - Shovel

17   Red Coral (inner) and Rose Quartz (outer)

18   Hematite or Jet (inner) and Onyx (outer)

19   Snowflake Obsidian (inner)
      and White Chert (outer)

20   Gold Filled Crystal (inner)
      and Yellow Agate (outer)

Medicine Wheel Directions

EAST

Called: The Farsighted Place

Color: Yellow

Element: Fire

Kingdom: Human

Human Aspect: Spirit

Season: Spring

Heavenly Body: Sun

Manifest: Spiritual Power, Oneness

with All, Enlightenment

Sacred Number: One

Spirit Helper: Eagle

Spirit Guides: Deer, Bobcat, Meadowlark, Canary, Robin, Hummingbird, Buzzard, Flamingo

Medicine Wheel Directions

WEST

Called: The Looks Within Place

Color: Black

Element: Earth

Kingdom: Mineral

Human Aspect: Transformation, Intuition, Physical Body

Season: Fall

Heavenly Body: Earth

Manifest: Magik, Magical Powers, Spirit Powers

Sacred Number: Two

Spirit Helper: Bear

Spirit Guides: Grizzly Bear, Black Bear, Coyote, Spider, Horse, Badger, Frog, Crow, Thunder Beings, Owl, Mink, Bat, Roadrunner, Grasshopper

Medicine Wheel Directions

SOUTH

Called: The Close to All Place

Color: Red

Element: Water

Kingdom: Plant

Human Aspect: Emotions

Season: Summer

Heavenly Body: Moon

Manifest: Singing, Dancing, Music, Speaking

Sacred Number: Three

Spirit Helper: Mouse

Spirit Guides: Rabbit, Squirrel, Red Bird, Red Tail Hawk, Groundhog, Snake, Fox, Turtle, White Crane, Lizard, Redheaded Woodpecker, Alligator, Manatee, Catfish

Medicine Wheel Directions

NORTH

Called: The Place of Knowledge

Color: White

Element: Air

Kingdom: Animal

Human Aspect: Mind, Wisdom, Knowledge

Season: Winter

Heavenly Body: Stars

Manifest: Spiritual Knowledge, Philosophy, Wisdom, Universal Knowledge, Quality Listener

Sacred Number: Four

Spirit Helper: Buffalo

Spirit Guides: Wolf, Elk, Wolverine, Caribou, Moose, Cougar, Mountain Sheep, Beaver, Goose, Reindeer, Salmon, Trout, Loon, Duck, Killdeer, Whale, Raven

Chapter Twenty-four

Sacred Stones

Clear quartz crystal-activates pineal or pituitary glands; stimulates your brain; directs and collects energy; stores energy; power stone; brings the power of the stars, can draw power, knowledge and wisdom from the stars, a very powerful stone.

Snowflake obsidian-helps the digestive organs; helps reduce emotional stress; helps ground a person; *all obsidian reflects what is in you!*

Rose quartz-induces love in the heart and passion; helps the kidneys and circulation in the body.

Aventurine-stimulates muscle tissue; eases anxiety attacks; helps a person see beauty.

Tiger eye-strengthens spleen, pancreas, colon; helps you find your center; grounds you from illusions.

Rhodonite-helps your nervous system, thyroid, and pituitary glands; has a calming effect.

Amethyst-strengthens your immune system and endocrine system; helps also in romance and loving yourself; known for its ability to enhance abilities; to ward off drunkenness; a conductor and collector of energies; usually used together with quartz crystals.

Moonstone-helps heal your stomach, spleen, pancreas, lymph nodes; also helps with drawing the power of Grandmother Moon.

Lapis-strengthens your skeletal system (bones) and activates your thyroid gland.

Black onyx-strengthens your bone marrow; relieves tension and stress; helps connect you to Mother Earth.

Leopard skin jasper-a powerful healer: helps your liver, gall bladder, and bladder; helps you produce antibodies to fight infection, disease and sickness; also known for its ability to protect a person who is spirit traveling and during trance states; helps a person take on duties, commitments and vows.

Citrine-helps your heart, liver, colon, gallbladder, and kidneys; it helps in acquiring wealth because it enhances your creativity and intuition, and stimulates your mental capacities; it will also help in making you alert.

Malachite-strengthens heart and circulatory system; helps a person heal themselves; can help bring true love to a person; helps protect a person from bad relationship thinking; it is also known to help protect children and animals.

Coral-helps with colds, digestive problems, asthma and fever; also known to protect against violence and accidents.

Opal-known to enhance your memories; helps increase your creativity and imagination.

Red jasper-known to help a person remember and recall instantaneously their dreams and memories of all they see, hear, feel and experience; powerful healer; liver, bladder, gallbladder.

Moss agate-an important stone when one is learning to communicate with animals and plants, even your spirit animals and spirit plants that come to help you; often called the farmer's stone; helps fertility and growing of plants, protection of the Earth; gives strength and confidence; help to be successful, healing, bringing rain, and finding the right mate.

Hematite-activates the spleen, stimulates the blood; draws the spirit of wolf and Grandmother Moon's power to you.

Carnelian-energizes your blood; helps your kidneys, lungs, and liver; helps prevent anger, jealousy and fear; also known to help people calm themselves about death and rebirth, helps to find harmony in the Circle of Life.

Sodalite-helps your pancreas, and helps balance your endocrine system.

Agate-tones your body; strengthens your body and mind; all agates help in love, creating appreciation for all of nature; helps your emotional balance.

Black agate-relieves stress, gives protection, and increases your courage.

Blue agate-creates hope, positive thinking, and truth; opens your heart to love and gentleness towards others.

Turquoise-a vision stone; helps bring clarity to all things; will enhance your intuition; will help you energize your inner beauty to radiate outward; absorbs negative energies to keep them away from you.

Garnet-helps you to learn to love yourself and to love others; inspires romantic love, sexuality, sensuality, and intimacy; helps you in learning your past life readings.

Jade-helps you in wisdom, balance, long life, and stability.

Chrysocolla-helps bring inner spiritual strength; helps in speaking; helps a person be more spiritual rather than material.

Chrysoprase-helps with courage and to get rid of negativity

Now I wish to help you learn even further with the knowledge that you have just read concerning the Sacred Stones. I did not list all of the stones, not because I don't know, but because they are not as commonly used or were not used by the Ancient Ones. Different geographical locations made some only used in one place exclusively. Some were used only in a few places. Shells, such as abalone, mussels, oyster, etc. were used many places but only a select few knew the way to use them for healing and psychic abilities, so I did not include them. I only listed what was most commonly used among the Ancient Ones.

This next part deals with the stones, your body, colors, planets, and purposes, so please study this closely to understand yourself and all that is connected to you.

Chakra	Planet	Color	Stone	Purpose
First	Pluto	black	obsidian	awakening your hidden potentials of power
First	Pluto	black	smoky quartz	balances your Spirit on Mother Earth
Base	Mars	deep red	blood stone	cleansing, energizing your physical body
Second	Pluto	red	garnet	using your creative Energy
Second	Pluto	red	ruby	creating energy to manifest your highest self
Creative	Mars	orange	carnelian	grounding your energy into physical
Third	Sun	orange	sulphur	creates physical radiance
Navel	Sun	yellow	citrine	develops discipline to live in higher awareness

Navel	Sun	blue	topaz	confidence in expressions creative power
Solar Plexus	Saturn	yellow	malachite	creates balances
Solar Plexus	Saturn	green	peridot	regenerates your body
Solar Plexus	Saturn	green	tourmaline	strengthens your body for spiritual force
Fourth	Moon	clear	rhodochrosite	moves energy from the heart to your navel
Heart	Moon	clear	moonstone	harmonizes you and balances your emotions
Heart	Moon	clear	opal	conscious intentions of emotions
Heart	Venus	green	rose quartz	develops love of ones self
Heart	Venus	pink	kunzite	activates heart chakra
Heart	Venus	pink	tourmaline	activates love in life through acts of sharing
Fifth	Mercury	blue	amazonite	helps in personal expression
Fifth	Mercury	blue	turquoise	clarity in communication and love

Fifth	Mercury	green	chrysocholla	helps in speaking our own truth
Throat	Uranus	blue	aquamarine	expressing universal truth
Throat	Uranus	blue	celestite	helps attune one to the higher mind
Throat	Uranus	blue	gem-silica	helps to channel higher realms and dimensions
Sixth	Jupiter	indigo	sodolite	understanding your connection to the universe
Sixth	Jupiter	indigo	lapis	penetrates through Illusions of the mind
Sixth	Jupiter	indigo	azurite	destroys limited concepts
Third eye	Neptune	purple	sugalite	understanding the divine purpose
Third eye	Neptune	purple	fluorite	using your visionary insights
Third eye	Neptune	purple	amethyst	surrender mind to the highest part of one's self
Seventh	Pluto	white	selenite	clarity of mind
Seventh	Pluto	white	quartz	activates crown chakra
Crown	Pluto	clear	diamond	identifies you with your immortal self

This will give you a good study guide to start learning about the stones yourself, how to use them, and where to use them on your body. I was advised not to do a crystal layout by Spirit for it is not easy and the person has to be trained in using the stones and has to have a pure heart.

Remember to Walk in Beauty and Love Always!

Chapter Twenty-Five

Simple Things You Should Know About Crystals

I wish to tell you some very simple facts about crystals that many people just don't know. That will help you and the crystal(s) you have or may have in the future. Now this will include all stone people, whether they are crystal, amethyst, aventurine, jade, or any and all stones. Yes even your diamonds! They are stones too you know. These simple little things, if you do them, will cleanse them, energize them, help you in using them correctly, and make you and your stone person(s) a whole lot happier with each other. It will also start you on a new and fulfilling adventure into being, with a stone person. So please read the following closely and start practicing these things and you will truly be rewarded by your stone person and those that you help.

Now it is important to cleanse your stone person. This is done by smudging. Smudging is when you take sage, either white, plains, or northern sage, and start it burning then blow out the flame and let it just smoke or smolder and blow the smoke over the stone person completely several times, then yourself as well. If you have more than one, then do all the stones you have in this same way. Cleanse them separately, unless they are all the same stone person type, for instance: all are crystal power points, or they are all pieces of the amethyst, or they are all diamonds of the same original stone. Once you have them cleansed, it is very important to recharge or energize the stone or the stones, but once again it is always best to do them each separately.

First you need a clear container such as a glass jar or drinking glass if it is large enough to hold the stone person inside. If you happen to have a large stone person, be sure the container is large enough to contain the stone person completely submerged. (If it is really large it is best to just place it in the ocean, or spring, or river and let it sit under the water with the sun shining down on it.) Now once you have your container, place your stone person inside and fill the container with natural spring water, mineral water, or tap water that is good. Now sprinkle in sea salt or Epsom salt, and table salt will also work. It is important that you make sure it mixes well. Then place it in the sun all day if possible. An hour will help, but if they haven't been cleansed in a long time they need a full charge. I try to take my crystal friends to the beach all the time to let them enjoy themselves as they play in the water and absorb the sun. Now once again if you have more than one stone person you need to cleanse all of them.

Once you have energized them in salt water and the sun, then you need to put them in the natural spring water, mineral water, or bottled water. Again, if you have large ones take them to a spring or a river that is fast moving and has good water, and do it that way. And again place them in the sun. This will also help cleanse and energize them for you.

Now you need to know how to attune yourself and your stone person to be one. And this is done by opening your heart with love for the stone person and holding it in your LEFT hand. The stone person then can draw the love from you and return it as one to you much stronger. Now while sending your love to the crystal, it is important that you either sing or hum, so the vibration of your spirit is picked up and amplified by the stone person. See we all have our own unique frequency that runs through our body. This frequency is what the stone person will identify with. All stone people operate on vibration and frequency energy, the vibration is then magnified and amplified 10,000 times stronger than it received, and for more powerful stone people this becomes 100,000 times stronger. What energy vibration it receives, it sends back as it is focused and directed to. This will be your signal to the stone person that it is you. You will be identified and therefore able to use it.

Now once you have your vibration and energy all as one now, you place the crystal or stone person in your RIGHT hand. This is the hand you send energy from, so when you are ready to send energy directed at something, you hum or sing and channel your energy into the stone person and focus your mind and intent at where it is to go and what it is to do, and it will release your energy combined and amplified and magnified directly as your intention was. Remember it is your energy, it is your concentration, and what you feel and are focused on that will receive this. Now also every time you use your stone person you need to cleanse and reenergize it. Especially if you are doing healings, if you don't have access to any springs, rivers, and oceans, then you need to make sure you get good bottled water.

Also you can use your stone people to make tonic, teas, and washes, and to cleanse and energize your body, or heal, or strengthen, someone else's body as well. This is done by sending your intentions and asking the stone person for its help, and placing it in the water, or tub. Now I would recommend that you learn more about healing with stone people before you try this. And always remember to ask your stone person friend before you do something. If you truly listen, you will learn the answer. It is also important that when attuning your stone person to you that you wear it or sleep with it touching your skin. This gives you better connections to each other.

Remember to walk in Love and Beauty Always!

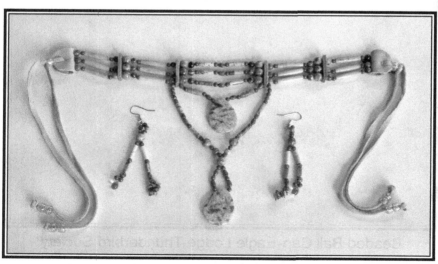

Jasper Choker and Earring Set
(All jewelry and beadwork in photos by Ghost Dancer)

Beaded Ball Cap-Eagle Lodge-Thunderbird Society

Peyote Stitched Wrapped Over Wire
Obsidian Center and Turquoise Nugget Side Sets

Turtle Medallion, Hairpiece, and Earrings

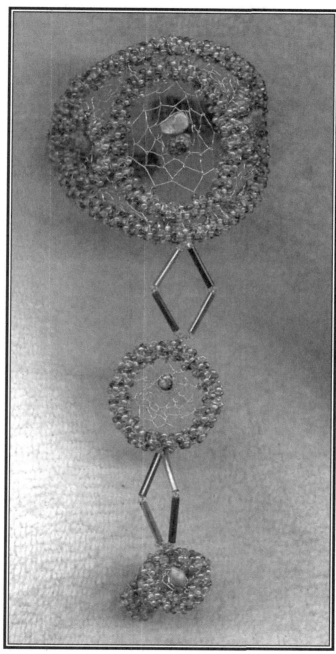

Dreamcatcher Slave Bracelet-Ring, Dreamcatcher, Bracelet
Peyote Stitch Wrapped Wire

Section 4

Commentary

Chapter Twenty-Six

The Way of the Old Ones

Spiritual knowledge, beliefs, practices, and understanding is an individual experience. For each individual must come to know Spirit on a one on one basis. The living Spirit is in all that exists, and the only true teacher is Spirit.

Once an individual sits still and silent, and empties oneself of everything, until they feel, hear and know the heartbeat of Mother/Grandmother upon which they sit, then, and only then can they start to know and see how everything is connected. The more they open themselves up to what is truly real, the more they will see, experience, and understand.

With this knowledge and understanding comes true power, the power of choice. For each and every moment there will always be choices. Living is true experience. For in life in the physical existence, we will experience every form upon our senses.

Never will the spiritual Teacher, who is a true one, give you an answer to any question, because each person must find the answer himself. Once the person finds the answer, then there are a lot more questions, for more things have opened up to that person.

Many people seek the power and knowledge of the universe through books, teachers, guides, etc. But, Spirit teaches us the truth. He who seeks the universe will know nothing. While he who seeks to know his true self will know everything. For within him is everything in the universe that exists.

For knowledge can never be taught. It must be experienced. For a person who tries to teach you knowledge will only sound foolish. When a person truly knows his true self, then he will see how he is connected to all things and what part he has in the Circle of Life. For each has a purpose and responsibilities and has a part in the Sacred Circle.

Each day of life is a true blessing, for it allows us to have another day to experience and learn more about the Sacred Circle of Life and about ourselves. Most people live in a world of illusions, caught in jobs, television, money, society, how they look, who they can impress, and even rushing everywhere because they don't have time to do other things. I ask you to ask yourself: Is that truly living? Is it real or just another illusion?

When was the last time you hugged a tree and thanked the tree for its beauty, the air you breathe, for the shelter it provides, for the food it provides, and all the things you take for granted? When was the last time you sat down and talked to one of the Stone People, one of the Animal People, or any other?

The old ones always used to send the children to learn about each and every thing, to learn firsthand about the life of rabbit, squirrel, bird, frog, tree, plant, deer, fox, etc. They learned how they lived, what they ate, where they slept, what they liked, what they feared, who were their enemies, who were their friends, etc. until they understood and knew all these things. They learned to feel the flow of life and to blend and become one with it and all that exists. Their Spirits touched the Spirit of all things.

These are the ways of the old ones, when all lived in respect, honor, and truth with our Mother/Grandmother, Father/Grandfather, and all of our relations. When we truly seek the Spiritual Path, then we will make the choice and seek these ways of the old ones, no matter where we are, nor how old we are. Remember, it is always each person's choice.

This is the way of the Old Ones.

Remember to Walk in Love and Beauty Always!

Chapter Twenty-Seven

For The Women and The Men

This is a lesson for you to teach the other ladies, the Beloved Women, who are now remembering who they are, and as a teacher, everyone else.

First it is also very important that you <u>believe</u> in yourself, your power, and your gifts. If you truly believe then things will begin to come easily to you. You are like a rose who has many petals. Each layer that is peeled back will reveal more inside. That is why in the old days a woman's vagina was referred to as a flower. For each petal held a secret. Each petal peeled back leads to another secret, until it goes to the center and is one with pure Love!

Today women have been programmed by society, religious dogmas, parents etc. not to understand their bodies; even not to find their hidden pleasures. Why? To keep them from their true power! A woman's body is totally, completely sensitive. Every single area is filled with nerve senses that ignite the essence of a woman. Very few women have experienced a touch, kiss, stroke, massage to every single cell of their bodies.

That is why the sweat lodge ceremony, is described as the womb of Mother Earth. Every single pole, every part of the structure is alive and has messages, spirits, and pleasures there. The hot rocks are love pouring into the passage of the womb to the center of Love! That is why it is so important not to have bad thoughts or feelings in the lodge. A lodge is of Love! This is why a woman cramps, menstruates, and pure pleasure are all in the same place, in the core of herself. It is your connection to the universe.

A man penetrating a woman's womb is not making love! There is a difference in that, as there is a difference in right and wrong. Making love is when two people give their love totally and completely with no strings attached. They do what their heart wants them to do with no expectations or limits. Making love could just as well be touching her cheek with love in the heart. When a person does anything with pure love, then it is a power that is beyond anything else. The key to all life is Love. Being a Beloved Woman is very special, for the person must have a heart of pure Love for the people, all people whether they are tree people, four-legged people, or two-legged people, and that love helps all that it touches whether one knows it or not.

If you have had a lot of pain in your life, and have had your struggles with many different problems, a heart of love has helped many, many people in this situation. This is especially important when a person is praying. If a person prays with true Love in their heart for what they are praying for, with total true Love to whom they are praying to, then that prayer is sent forth on True Power, the Power of Love that connects everything in the universe. This applies to everything they do, say, think, feel, touch, smell, and taste in life. If we do it in True Love, then it is a Power. That is why the old ones say you must "touch your Power."

Even our conscience is Love. Our true Spirit, which is part of Creator, is Love. Our conscience tells us when we do something wrong, because it is Love, and Love only wants good things for us. We can be anything we want. We can create whatever we want if we do it in True Love.

These are important lessons that if you practice them, you will become more gifted and will see the results. We must walk our path in True Love and teach others to truly love, for when you give love, you receive love.

Please share this with friends and family, for it is their choices in life that they must make. No one can make their choices for them.

Remember to Walk in Beauty and Love Always!

Chapter Twenty-Eight

Our Circle of Relatives

In understanding the Native psyche a person must understand all that is. Some, or even many of you, always have heard or seen Native People dancing in attire that is animal parts, or a whole outfit that is animal or bird parts, or even plant parts. Some of you may have heard of the Eagle Dancer, Buffalo Dancer, or Deer Dancer etc. But, what does it mean? What is it for? Where did it come from? Maybe some of you have heard of a Dream Stone, Spirit Stone, Medicine Bundle, or Stone Effigies or plants and trees that are used in ceremonies or rituals? Now what is their purpose? What could it do? Where did it come from? These questions few ask these days, including most Native Americans, because very, very few truly live this way anymore. Yeah, some of the old ones know. It breaks their heart with sadness that none of the younger ones understand, or take the time to learn these things.

But, let's go back, back in time, back to when the Mother was young, full of life, back when everything was simple. Go back to when man lived as one with his Mother and all her children. Man prayed every single moment, because life could be gone in a moment. Death was part of life. Plants could kill you. Animals could kill you. All types of dangers were there. Mother told her children that they should come to know one another. So, the children all started learning about each other. Time passed. Man, the two-legged, was weak. He deviated from the Circle. He wanted to be better.

After a time, man forgot the True Teachings. Man even forgot the language of his relatives. Man forgot that many of his relatives always helped him. Grandfather was sad. Grandmother was sad. Mother was sad. Man started killing and doing things without purpose of life. Grandfather hid his face from man for a long time. It got real cold. Man had no fur. Man did not have skin like a stone person. Man had no way to burrow into the ground. Mother pleaded to Grandfather, begging him to take pity upon man, the weakest of the children. Grandfather came back! And man started populating the earth again.

Spirit visited old ones in all parts of different Nations of the two-legged children, telling them they must love all the other children. They must love them completely as Spirit loves us all. They were told that the children of man must learn about all the other children again. They must watch them; learn how they live, how they think, what they do, what they eat, where they sleep, everything about every one of them until they become one of them. So, all of the two-legged men began becoming the oak tree, a frog, a rabbit, a duck, an eagle, a bear, a buffalo, a spider, a snake, etc. They even became a tiny pebble. They learned everything until they believed they were all of these.

Now love is a power and the more they loved all of the other children, the more love they had for them and even themselves. They saw how wrong they had been in the past, and now wanted to make amends for their past wrongs. So, they told all the other children that from now on they would honor them always in songs, dances, prayers, etc.

The other children were moved by this and told the two-leggeds: "You have touched our hearts with your love. Now, we too shall honor you. If you call upon us for help in any matter we will help you."

So, it began. Time passed further, but still honor was kept by all the children. Men and women would take on the spirit of the frog, wolf, deer, buffalo, snake, etc. and speak directly to the People of those children. For instance, a village may be hunting for meat, because people were hungry. A Buffalo Dancer would take on the Spirit of the Buffalo. He would go into the Spirit World and talk to the Buffalo People and call them to him, making offerings and prayers and songs to the Buffalo People. This would please the Buffalo People who loved the two-legged people. It was the same for the Corn Dancer, Eagle Dancer, for all dancers, songs and dreamers. Even the Stone People would help and dreamers took on the Spirit of the stone, and the Stone People would help them.

Many of you still do not understand the importance of

this. But let me give you an example for today's time so you can understand it better. Let's say you were driving out in the wilderness. You have a blow out and you have a wreck. You are flung from your vehicle and go rolling down a hill. Your vehicle catches on fire and explodes. It is freezing outside. Snow is four feet deep and there is no town or anyone for miles and miles around. Your coat was in the vehicle, so all you have on is what you have, which isn't much good in this weather. Your cell phone is in the car. It is gone. No one knows you have wrecked, so here you are all alone in the wilderness with no help, no warmth, no food, and no water.

Now, if you knew how to call the spirit of the wolf, you could become the wolf. You can smell like a wolf, and be warm, since a wolf has hair that keeps him warm regardless of the weather. You can hear as a wolf, and can run like a wolf. If you called the Spirit of Grandfather Sun, you would feel the heat, and would glow with his warmth. If you called the Spirit, say of the eagle, then you would have his sight, his feathers, etc. Everything that exists in this universe is part of you. If you tap into any of them, you can become them.

Back about a hundred years ago this was still very much taught, less taught fifty years ago, seldom taught twenty-five years ago, and almost non-existent today.

Let's discuss what you may have heard or seen concerning a True Dreamer, or a Spirit Stone, or Stone Effigy. A True Dreamer is one that creates the Dream, dances with the Dream and brings it into being. A True Dreamer can summon a herd of deer to walk right to their death, because a True Dreamer has given love to the Deer and asked them to do this. And, out of this love, the deer love the People and give their lives willingly.

After explaining all of this to you, many of you still are saying "how?" How can I do this? Well it is simple, but it does take practicing this. It is like physical exercise. The more you do the easier it gets. Well, it applies the same way here. So, if you do this, it will open you up to more; more abilities and understanding.

First I want you to start breathing the Ani-yun-wiya Way. (Also noted in Spiritual Exercises)

Breathe in deeply through your nose and exhale through your mouth.

Remember to find a chair or someplace that is comfortable to you.

I want you to start relaxing your body, one part at a time. Start with your left toes and continue to breathe the Ani-yun-wiya Way.

Do this relaxation part with your entire body.

Now empty your mind of all problems, worries, doubts, fears, etc.

Just relax and breathe the Ani-yun-wiya Way.

Now, in your mind, I want you to picture an animal, any animal you know.

How does it look, every detail?

See its eyes, nose, face, hair or fur, legs, feet, ears, tail, every single part of it.

I want you to see this animal completely.

Now, I want you to open your heart and send this animal pure love, telling it in your mind how beautiful it is, and all of the character and traits it has and how honorable they are.

I want you to thank this animal for all it has done for you and all of your people.

Keep sending your love until the animal looks into your eyes. See its eyes. See the love there in its eyes. Feel its power. Feel its thoughts. Feel its heart.

Now send your mind into the animal. Become the animal you see, feel, hear, taste, and smell. Become one!

And then you see yourself! You are now that animal with all that it is.

You are all that it knows, does, feels, hears, tastes, everything.

Stay this way for a while. Enjoy yourself. Learn! Learn all that is you!

When you are ready, come back.

For seven days do this every day. Then pick a different animal and continue. Then do birds, trees, plants, insects, fish, and stones. The more you do this, the more easily you can, and the more you learn. Now a Spirit Stone or a Stone Effigy is based on this. It is where the Spirit of the Stone is invoked plus other spirits have been called to it. Usually these are painted or carved or with other spirit designs on the stone. This is a powerful stone that the user has made this way by invoking the Spirits for help.

The same applies to a Stone Effigy, Bone Effigy, or Wooden Effigy. It is made by invoking the Spirit of the animal or bird, plant, etc. and calling it to the stone. This is for helping the user for the purpose of dreaming, healing, transportation etc. It is not done for art, but they are created in Beauty and Love, and it is an art and a talent but not for what art is for today.

Well, I hope this helps you in walking the path, and learning more about the path as you walk, because you are the path and the path is you.

Remember to Walk in Beauty and Love Always!

Chapter Twenty-Nine

The Power Of The Drum

I want to talk to you about the drum. Many of you see a drum and hear a drum, but do you truly know the power of the drum? Think of the different types of drums. Each of them has power; purpose.

First let me explain how a drum is made. In the old times, the drum maker always fasted and prayed as he chose the wood, bone, shell, etc., for the base of the drum. The drum maker called his spirit helpers to him as he began making the drum. The hide that was used was also prayed over and thanked for its help in the creation. The hide was stretched over the base, while calling the spirits to come inside. Mother Earth was called to put her heart in the drum. When the drum was finished, it was placed over a fire to purify it, and to dry the hide so it stretched tight.

The drum would then be prayed to and asked to let the spirits come forth while offerings of smoke were covered over it. A song for the drum was sung and played on the new drum then. It would loosen the hide so it would be pulled tighter and made stronger. Now it would be blessed again using tobacco, cedar, sage, corn pollen, and corn meal, which were then poured over the fire to be blessed by the fire, and to dry it out to tighten it real tight.

Now, do you know the purpose of the drum? Why is a drum used in so many ceremonies? It was not designed for music! It is a healing tool. That is right, by using the power of sound and vibration.

As I have told you previously, everything that exists has its own vibration and frequency. The drum is played (or drummed you might call it) to attune our bodies to align with the frequency and vibration of life.

Many times our bodies get out of frequency, which can be caused by injury, sickness, or blockages that throw us out of whack. A prayer for the spirit of the drum is made while it is being smudged and purified. This prayer activates the spirit of the drum to help you.

Then, while the drum is being played, the spirits cleanse with the power of sound, which sends vibrations through you and around you, again and again. This pulsating vibration touches your nerves, your senses, your organs, and every cell of your body and spirit as well.

This is the principle purpose of music. Music is a Power of Sound. It can make you cry, make you laugh, make you dance, slow you down, speed you up, put you to sleep; and yes, it can heal you.

Many people don't see the connection but it is real. This power is right around you always, but most don't know it exists. A drum is Sacred, and always to be respected and treated as such. I've drummed for most of my life. I have used it for all types of ceremonies and I know its power. Maybe you will come to see the Beauty and Love of this wonderful Power. A drum is a connection to the heartbeat of Mother Earth, the Universe, and your Spirit.

Remember to walk in Beauty and Love Always!

Ghost Dancer Sitting in at a Powwow Drum 2007

Chapter Thirty

The Mounds

Many people look at the ancient mounds and wonder, "Why are they built round?" First, all mounds are not all round, some are in rectangles, or they are round on the sides but come to a flat top and they are either rectangular or square. But for the answers to these questions you have to go into the spiritual understanding of the People, and the practiced knowledge given to them by their relatives such as the alligator, eagle, turtle, the sun, the moon, etc.

Now I know many of you still don't understand, so I'll try to explain this so you can finally realize the simplicity of this knowledge. Let's go back in time, many thousands of years ago, to a time when the animals and reptiles ruled the world; a time when giant beasts walked the land, when man was small and was food for all these relatives. Man paid attention and learned the behavior patterns of all his relatives.

He watched the alligator build huge mounds as a nest, to lay its eggs and then cover them up, and then lay on them. He watched the giant birds of prey build their nest in a circle, lay eggs, and find shelter against the elements. He watched the giant mammoths form a circle with the herd to protect the young and provide protection from the elements. He watched the giant turtles dig holes and lay eggs and form a mound over them to protect them. He saw turtles dig holes to make a den to live in. He watched the huge wolves dig holes for a den for protection of the young and protection from the elements.

He watched the Sun and saw its power in the circle and how it radiated outwards in all directions. He watched the moon in its power being full and new. The power of it was in the circle. The Mother that he walked on, that gave him life and created life every moment, he knew was round. He watched the stars and the planets and knew them as being round.

You may think ancient man was ignorant, but he was smarter than you think. In his simple reasoning he saw the power in the circle of life. He saw the protection it would provide, the power that could be accessed, and he did it out of respect and honor to all that had taught him. For all of these relatives were greater than a mere man. And man wanted to attain the power to become better than he was.

Most people today don't recognize the characters and behavior patterns of animals, plants, birds, reptiles, planets, stars, etc. Much less do they recognize some of these traits inside of themselves! Yet ancient man accepted the simplicity and gave honor and respect to all of these, and strived to make these characters, strengths, knowledge and power his own.

Not one of you ever connected your own head to the mounds. Your head is round, yet inside is the greatest power of computers that exists: analysis, programs, thinking, etc. Not one of you connected the power of the nerve signals in your brain to the energy of the nerve centers of the universe, to the mounds. Yes, everything in the universe has energy and is connected. The mounds are connected directly to the Mother Earth. All on Mother Earth connects directly to the mounds.

As I've stated before, the mounds, working with the vibrations of energies, songs, musical notes, harmonize to the universe, to the individual, and is magnified and amplified by the sacred stones designed in them.

Also understand the location of the mounds. The mounds are all in places where storms come frequently. Now what about the design in accordance with the storm? Let's look at a tornado. How is a tornado shaped? How does it draw power and how does it move? Ancient peoples knew all of this. Yet still people today do not connect these things. No tornado can harm a mound. Why? Use your brain. How is the mound designed? When a strong force comes into contact with the mound, it moves freely to either side and goes on, because it is designed so that no resistance allows the force to continue; to glance off or roll to either side.

But there is more. Did any of you know that the ancients used the power of the tornado and hurricane to use as time portals for teleportation? Well, it's true. All ancient records in

Egypt, Peru, Central America and here, all document this in stone records, and today's scientists still don't understand. I just wanted to share that fact with you. The knowledge of using the tornado and hurricane I cannot disclose, for I would be responsible for any who use that knowledge in a wrong way.

But back to the mounds! Now let's examine the Cahokia belief systems. The mounds were an important part, but what else is involved? The Sun, Moon and the Universe! Many others called them Sun worshippers, but they are wrong. The Sun was honored, paid tribute to, in respect for the power and energy it provided to all of them. They used its energy quite well, using the crystals and other sacred stones to energize the mound and heal themselves and to delve into the mysteries. Their bodies would radiate with the Sun's energy. Many could use this power to send fire or start a Sacred Fire. They could send this energy into a person's body to heal a specific area. They used it for their agriculture as well.

Another aspect of their beliefs and practices was the Spiral Dance, better known as the Dance with Sister or Mother Datura. Datura is a very powerful deadly plant that was used to go to the Spirit World for help in knowledge, in power, to guide one's life, in healing, and even for teleportation. Unfortunately, some even used it to take control of other people's minds. For mass ceremonies, a drink was prepared for all the people to drink. The High Priestess and the Sacred Sisters' Priestesses then used their power to show all the people the visions they saw themselves. That way everyone shared in this vision, a personal connection to the Sacred Priestesses and the High Priestess. Sometimes this was done in a wrong way by one who had a personal agenda of their own. Power can corrupt even the purest of hearts!

In private, the Holy People, (men and women) all used the Datura, but they purified themselves first in a Sweat Lodge. That's right. They had sweat lodges long before the Lakota. Then totally naked, and either with a Spiral Bowl, Spiral Stone, or any object that was specifically designed for the journey to First Woman (Mother Earth) to the center they followed the

Spiral to the Spirit World. They were easily recognized by the gray paste that covered both sides of their head in the temple area. Guards were always posted to watch over those who were making this journey.

Many different Nations sent envoys to this place. This later on cost the Cahokians dearly. The Aztec had been sending envoys and trading with Cahokia for many, many years; so had the Mayans. But it was the Aztecs who finally got control by marrying into the royal families; having their priests and priestesses also brought with them. They slowly took over. Now problems really began when a young Aztec man became Micco (The King).

This man craved power and knowledge and he hated the power of the High Priestesses and the control the Sacred Women had in all decisions. He slowly planned their downfall. He had his royal guards, all who were loyal to him, increase their numbers, and he began to demand sacrifices. The sacrificed were all the young priestesses. This caused chaos in the Cahokian Nation.

Disasters started happening: drought, then later flooding, then earthquakes, locusts, and other disasters came as well. The populace felt and knew it was the energy of the King that was causing this to happen. His energy was bad; therefore he was causing an imbalance with the mounds. By killing the Sacred Women he was destroying the Power of the Mounds. For the Sacred Women used their knowledge and power to work in harmony with the mounds.

Civil wars broke out. The population was fighting against the King's guards and army. The Sacred Women had soldiers that were loyal to them. A great war took place: massacres of whole families. Survivors fled the area; believing it was cursed.

If any of you ever saw inside the mounds, you would see the stories of the history of Cahokia. You would also see the artifacts from the Aztec, Mayan, and even Incas that are still there. You would find the Spirit Bowls and Sacred Bundles, including the Pipes. But this knowledge is kept from all of you.

See, most academics in the mainstream don't want you to know the truth and the whole facts. Knowledge is Power, and even today those in power don't want to share that knowledge or power with the general population. It's all about control. The mounds are still powerful if a person knows how to activate them.

Forget what you think you know. For you do not know what is not experienced and lived. What you seek can't be found by studying work or written words by someone who does not experience or live the way of their words. No scholar can teach you about things they truly do not know or understand.

Scholars in science, theology, geology, anthropology, pathology, physics, and even acoustics, know almost nothing about the true ancient civilizations. They only guess, theorize, and confuse each other. I've thought long and hard about what I am going to say here and I have prayed numerous times on these matters. The answers I sought for my heart have been given so I will relay some things to you. Maybe with this information you will find some answers to the questions that have bothered you.

My name is Ghost. I am half Muskogee, one quarter Ani-yun-wiya (Cherokee), and one quarter Irish. I was born and raised in the swamps of Florida. I was taught and lived the Ancient ways of my people the Muskogee. My Ani-yun-wiya grandfather also taught me the ancient ways of the Ani-yun-wiya. All of my young life was spent learning, participating and experiencing these ways of life. After I was older, I spent time with many elders of other tribal nations. Mostly I've always been a loner, and always sought the spirit world for answers and help. I was born with the gift of the stones (crystals, rocks, catlinite, etc.), meaning I was given a gift to use with all these different stone helpers. The stones will talk to me, show me things and give their strength and power to add to mine. I mention this because of what I will say later; so you can understand better.

Many of you have heard of Serpent Mounds, Cahokia Mounds, Etowah Mounds, Aztec Pyramids, Inca, Mayan and others. Yet not one scholar I have ever heard of even came close to knowing what these are, just as they are ignorant of the Egyptian Pyramids or even why they are built where they are built. Technology, even today, cannot duplicate any of those. Yet these same scientists and scholars claim they know, and want you to take their idea as your own. That is not only ignorant, but is a waste of your time, for there is not a spiritual understanding in them; they do not believe in nor practice these ways of life.

I am not an educated man. I will tell you that so you can better understand my words. I have a hard time even speaking in this language, much less explaining things in your words. So bear with me, for I don't know big words or words that you would probably use. I will try to explain it as it was meant to be taught. As a grandfather would teach a grandchild or a grandmother would teach a grandchild. For it is in the simple mind of a child that true knowledge can be planted and will grow. And when you come with the heart and mind of a child, you come in anticipation, open-minded, full of wonder and hope.

I will only tell you what I feel comfortable speaking about, for I was brought up with responsibility. I am responsible for what I say, do, teach, or give in life, as each person should be brought up. With all this said, I pray that Spirit will guide me in doing this. Muto (thank you).

When you go to Cahokia, go with an open heart and mind. Go at sunrise or sunset. Then go at each time. Take off your shoes and socks; remove all watches, rings, earrings, necklaces. Do not have metal of any kind on you. I tell you this so the metal does not interfere with the energy of this place.

Now feel the Mother Earth beneath your feet. Taste the wind upon your tongue. Smell all the aromas coming from everywhere. Listen as the wind, trees, birds, all sing. Feel the rhythm of Mother Earth beneath your feet. Close your eyes: feel, taste, smell, and hear all that is. Let your heartbeat match to the rhythm all around, until you feel inside the beat of life. Sing, hum, or chant as you walk towards the mound. Hold your left palm out in front of you. Feel the energy flow into your hand and course through your body.

You see, Cahokia is a place of powerful energy, perfectly aligned to connect the stars, planets, moon, and all the other mounds and pyramids everywhere. It is like an amplifier of energy. When it was built, it was designed to a perfect key to all the others throughout the world. It is also designed with the acoustic vibrating energy of a musical note. See, even all mathematics, physics, energy, music, and sound, travels in waves of patterns.

That is why I say you must sing, chant, hum, etc., for you put forth an energy which the mound can relate to. Every mound, pyramid, was designed to help the people and all life in each of their areas. It was a place of worship, to harmonize our bodies to the flow of the universe, life, and all things. It was a place of great healings, great teachings, and song and dance. Cahokia is just one of many places. All are connected. Each one is important. Inside the mounds are many things: gifts from other nations: Mayan, Aztec, Toltec, Natchee, Muskogee, Etowah, Inca, and Polynesian.

There are many things that historians and scientists do not want known because it destroys their ideology, the history and record they want to be, and it is against religion and government wishes and policy for any of you to know the truth. They can't tell you of a Welsh harp found inside. They can't tell you of the mica tiles inside, or the hieroglyphics that match many of the artifacts found in pyramids in countries across the ocean. Ha! Ha! Why? Because all of your life, you have been lied to. They won't tell you the truth. It's under the National Security excuses! Ha! Ha! They surely won't tell you about the crystal talking skull. So what makes you think they will tell you about these mounds, their different purposes and how they are connected? They don't want you to know about these things because it is a knowledge they want to keep for themselves.

You think Cahokia just disappeared? No! You think the Etowah just disappeared? No! What about the Aztecs,

Maya, Inca? No! No to all you think which are gone forever. In each of these places, things happened: famine, earthquakes, tornadoes, disease, etc. It happens all over the world.

When something like a catastrophe happens, people leave and scatter from the area. When many lives are lost, people instinctively breed more, even with other nations. For a nation to be strong it requires plenty of warriors to guard and protect the nation. It requires plenty of hunters to provide for the people. It requires different people to fill all the necessary professions and skills every civilization needs to meet the needs of its people. No, these people didn't disappear. They scattered in all directions and joined other nations and intermarried and interbred with these people.

Now many noted scholars of different specific professional fields will prove and have proven many facts. Yet mainstream academic societies try to discredit these scholars. Why? It is a matter of power, control and money. You see, you have those that are in established positions and they will never let anyone present facts that contradict their own beliefs.

Now, back to Cahokia! Many of you may have plenty of doubts about what I have said here. Okay, I can understand that. Are you ready to test your doubts? What is sound? Is it energy? Can it destroy? Can it heal? How does it travel? Can you see it with your naked eyes? Can you touch sound? Please bear with me now and try a little experiment.

How many of you listen to and enjoy music? Okay. One at a time, listen to your music with your eyes closed. Music each one of you likes or prefers. As each different one is listening to their particular music, everyone else should observe and note on paper any different postures, movements, feelings, emotional displays of the person that is listening to the music. When each of you has taken his or her turn listening to the music and taking notes on everyone else, compare your notes. I know you all will note and observe differences in everyone.

You see? Music is energy! It is a vibrational force that can soothe, energize, hypnotize, mesmerize, heal, destroy, and change anyone or anything. Your own body has vibrations within it because your body has energy all inside of it. This frequency of vibration can be altered at any time by outside vibrations. By feeling these vibrations, you can quite easily understand that power is in the energy. Now with that in mind, let's truly look at Cahokia Mounds.

Cahokia is designed in an ancient design to help amplify and harmonize all the different energies - those of all the planets, sun, moon, stars; all with the directional forces, Mother Earth's electromagnetic force, and most important <u>water!</u>

Water is a conductor. It is an element true enough. And most of our body is water. And we were in our mother's womb and lived in water then. Every mound/pyramid is built on top of or near this water, for the water is a conductor of energy and it has its own energy force, and its own vibration of sound.

Water gives us nourishment. It is vital to our life in our bodies. It bathes us, soothes us, and cools us and everything on Mother Earth. Just as we have arteries, veins and capillaries, so does the Mother-oceans, lakes, rivers, streams, etc. If you went under the water and lay on the bottom, you would not only hear this, you would feel this power and vibrating sound easily.

I would ask that you all conduct another little test. Each of you would take turns while the others would take notes of the subject's answers afterward. Go outside. Choose anyone to be the first two participants. Have one lay with their head on the ground with their ear touching the ground. The other one goes 50 yards away and stamps their feet upon the ground. Continue with this until all have experienced this. Now pick two participants and have them lay down on the ground a half a mile apart. The rest of you split into two groups. Go between the participants and each group and go in opposite directions from each other.

Group 1

Person 1 ←1/2 mile → Person 2

Group 2

Now group one should stomp the ground with one foot all together. Group two should jump up and down stomping the ground with both feet. Then write down the responses of person one and two. Choose two more participants and repeat the test. Keep doing this until everyone has experienced this.

As you now all have experienced sound and vibration transporting through the earth and felt it also in your body, you can now look at Cahokia Mounds in a new light. The Mounds are above ground as your eyes can tell you, but the mounds are also below ground level.

As I mentioned earlier, the mounds have chambers, just as the pyramids do. Each chamber is designed in specific dimensions and designed for acoustic sound. A musical note is the key for each chamber, just as those in Egypt's pyramids are. Each stone is tuned for that: a musical note. Each of our bodies has a musical note in our voice. Each voice is different.

A person harmonizes with the musical note vibrations of the stones and the chamber's. This is an amplifier of energy. The vibrational force causes the body to vibrate and resonate to this. This is the power that has always been: chants, prayer songs, hymns, and musical instruments used in these places and all ceremonies. Because the vibration from sound can and will heal a person's mind, heart, body, and spirit, many have in history called this alchemy, necromancy, sorcery, etc. But it is not. It is the power that has always been and always will be. Most people have just forgotten all they experienced in the world as a small child.

I now would like for you to try another experiment. This requires a drum and drum stick. Have someone lay down flat on their back while someone beats the drum. Start with a slow rhythmic beat near the center of the body. And moving clockwise, continuing around the body with the drum near the body. Each person takes notes about what the person laying down felt. Then take turns drumming and laying down. Yes, you will feel things going on in your body. Now try this experiment with a flute.

By personally experiencing these different experiments you each will find answers to how ancient civilizations and Traditional Native Americans understood the mysteries that elude most people, including scholars.

Now, with all these things in mind, use the alignment of planets, stars and moon to experience different forces in your body. Go to Cahokia at different times, when different planets are in alignment, an eclipse, during the equinoxes and solstices, different seasons, etc.

These techniques will work at the mounds and pyramids around the world, such as Serpent Mounds, Moundville, Cahokia, Window Rock, Devil's Lair, Eagle Rock, Jiharda Rock, Stone Mountain etc. All over this continent there are these places designed this way. Most you may not know, but they are known.

I would like each of you to get a copy of "Ancient Americas" magazine. Also contact the Smithsonian Institution in Washington D.C. at the Natural History of Man in North America. In these you can find many reports on these ancient sites, which can give you a more overall view of the vast number of sites located all over. And you will see that very little research or understanding is known about any of them.

You will also come to realize that the understanding of these places and what their true purposes are elude most scientific minds, because they don't view it as spiritual, with the knowledge of being connected to all things and of the power of energy that connects us all. Nor do they understand the importance of crystals, sound, vibrations, exact design with planetary alignments, and water conductors.

By missing all the understanding of how we are all connected to all things and the energy all things have, they fail to have knowledge even of themselves. They can't even figure out where these people went from all these different civilizations. As I have said earlier, when things happen, people will scatter. They are then absorbed into other tribes. They bring to each of these tribes their people's knowledge, skills, and history. That is why many legends are similar among so many tribes.

The old stories that tell the history and lessons of life are loaded with information. These are not what you call fairy tales, but lessons of life for the young to understand about their history, their culture, their connection to all life. This is why you must understand this connection to truly begin to understand yourselves.

I mentioned the crystals and stones, because these are vital to truly understanding the power of energy. Having the knowledge of the stones and gift of the stones allows one to see, feel, hear and experience all that the stones have seen, felt, heard, and lived. That is why all important events, knowledge, history, and prophecy is recorded in stone, and the stones will speak to you, if and only if you allow yourself to open up to them.

You have been programmed to look at them as nothing. You don't see their beauty, their energy, their knowledge or gifts, so they don't speak to you. Every civilization back in time has recognized the importance of the stones and used them accordingly. They worked with them in all things. Modern man has lost these valuable brothers and sisters, grandfathers and grandmothers in their quest to be supreme above all things. What they fail to realize is that they are lost without them!

The stones are used today as lasers, in computer chips, telecommunications, satellites, weapons, surgical instruments, and all aspects of your lives. Yet you, along with all the others, don't even see how important they are. Even the ones who use them to design their inventions, for their power, don't understand. That is why scientists today don't even understand what a meteor or a comet really is. They only guess.

How many of you have held a crystal in your hand, saw its beauty, felt its warmth and power, talked to the crystal, asked for its help, or asked it to heal or teach you? Or is this beyond your supreme minds?

To be wise one must first recognize and understand themselves, and all that is a part of them, to see how they connect to all things in existence. To teach, one must first learn. If you don't seek knowledge, you surely will not find it.

Only when someone is not closed minded but open to learn, can one find answers. Just as a child is so open, easily seeking wonder and full of questions, full of exploring all around, so must you become if you want to find truths for yourselves and understand the universe in which you live. And then you can truly learn, not only the past, but the present as well. And eventually you will know the future.

Remember to Walk in Beauty and Love Always!

Chapter Thirty-One

Walking the Path

Many times I get asked about medicine! Who has medicine? Who doesn't? How do you know who has medicine?

First, let's clarify what the question is. Are you asking about medicine to heal, or medicine referring to power? There is a difference. Also, many times breeds, mixed bloods or others are told they have no medicine or power due to the color of their skin, or the amount of blood quantum one has.

Let me be very plain. Anyone and everyone have power if they truly seek the true spirit within them. If at any time a person of any descent, mixed blood, breed, or even of a another totally different race of people, who enters a Sacred Circle, humbles themselves, prays sincerely, and asks Spirit for help, particularly in a ceremony, the spirits will help them, and will always give them medicine.

Only people who try to hold power or are ignorant of the true Red Road, would ever attack either verbally or physically anyone who is truly seeking the Red Road in the most humble way. They would go so far as to try to insult a person or person's right to seek Spirit!

I, Ghost, a member of the Muskogee Nation, who has met numerous true Holy Ones, Teachers, and Spirit Leaders from all over, know that these True Ones who truly walk the Red Road would be shocked to know that some of the People would conduct themselves this way!

Many times I have seen this. I also know that sometimes it is a test to see how sincere a person is, to see if they truly are seeking this way. Or can they be easily deterred, or give up? Then they were truly not seeking. If I saw that this didn't deter them, then I would always speak to them and advise them to stay strong and listen to their hearts, or introduce them to someone to help them or help them myself.

Brothers and sisters NEVER let anyone deter you from

your path. You would not be in the Circle unless Spirit moved you to be a part of it. Never feel less in the presence of a full-blood. Most full-bloods, who would act in this ignorant way, truly are insecure in their own self and truly do not walk the Red Road. MOST full-bloods are not like the few.

Spirit looks at your heart and knows. If a person ever says negative things to you, remember this: that person doesn't have medicine or power otherwise they could see your heart and spirit, and they truly are lost and haven't found the Red Road or even Spirit.

I pray my words will touch your hearts, and Spirit will speak to you, to help you know that what I said is true. I am a simple man, one who has walked this Red Road all of my life, and have had Spirit Leaders, Teachers, and Holy Ones teach me these things all of my life. Spirit has shown me that this is true. I am very comfortable in who and what I am. Hopefully, one day you will be too.

Remember to Walk in Love and Beauty Always

Chapter Thirty-Two

Volunteers

Aho, all my Brothers, Sisters, and all my Relatives!

First I wish to say: May Spirit bless each and every one of you, and fill your heart with love, true love, and your lives with beauty.

I pray that each of you will be filled with Spirit and given energy to continue to stride forward. In walking the Red Road there are many obstacles sometimes in the way. Sometimes things or events are put in our paths to see how each of us will respond. Many times it is to test our Spiritual strength, or to teach us how lacking we are. Other times it will not reveal the purpose at first, but will cost a valuable lesson in life. Spirit wants all of us to learn and experience all of the beauty and love that was created for us to learn True Love, True Beauty, the pure essence of Spirit.

I have battled to protect our Traditional Sacred Ceremonies, and our Religious Freedom all of my life. Now many of you get upset about what government authorities do to deny Native People these Sacred Practices; ways that were given to all of us by Spirit. But most feel they can't do anything and feel helpless in battling such powerful forces. But let me tell you that each one of you is important in doing these things. Each one is just as powerful in your prayers as needed to make a circle.

Your voices need to be heard. Speak out in writing to your State legislators about the atrocities against Human Rights, Religious Freedoms, about violating Federal Laws, and Constitutional Laws. Your elected officials in state governments must listen to you, for in truth, they are employed by you. It is your tax dollars that pay their salaries. You must speak out to them. Write them letters. Send them emails, phone them, or speak to them in public. This applies to the federal levels of government as well: to Congress, Senate, US Attorney General, whoever you feel needs to be awakened.

If you remain silent or do nothing they will continue to violate the laws and your rights. It is as in life; if you can't protect and stand up for those that can't stand up for themselves, then you have not learned the most basic of truths about being loved. For it is known throughout eternity; to love is free, love is given freely.

To love others sincerely is a blessing. Every circle is only as strong as the weakest member. Every member should want to help and volunteer. Why? How otherwise do you learn sacrifice, humbleness, generosity, compassion? If you don't give of yourself, then you are only taking of others. How can you learn if you do not participate or experience it? I realize you all have busy lives, demanding schedules, bills to pay, and personal matters, each and every day. But what you put into your beliefs and practices is what you get out of them as well.

Never should only a handful have to repeatedly do all that needs doing. If everyone helped, put forth the effort, all kinds of things can be done, and each will be rewarded by doing so. If you give to the circle, the circle will give unto you. If you help others, others will be there to help you. This is the Law of Spirit. Spirit gives to us each and every moment. Do we?

In life we have a choice of either being a taker or a giver. True spiritual ones, (those that walk the Sacred Red Road) know you must give to ever receive. And you must always be generous with your life, your time, your energy in helping others. Many different religious groups and individuals go to hospitals, nursing homes, schools, mental health institutions, as well as jails, and prisons. Why? Because they don't judge or look down on anyone no matter the condition of that person's life. No one knows what another person's path is, or what they have to learn or endure to experience or balance something from the past or past life even.

Being Native American, and practicing the old time traditional beliefs as I do, I have been to hospitals, nursing homes, retirement homes, assisted living homes, mental institutions, handicapped schools, jails, orphanages, and even prisons. I have learned and experienced many wonderful times and seen some of the most tragic atrocities as well. Many people are quick to judge anyone, or accept the judgment of others or a person. I do not and will not! Be careful of doing such things because who knows what may happen to you, or someone you love, a friend, or a relative?

One of the most beautiful memories I have had is seeing the reaction of the autistic children when the wolves (Shungamanito and Montaseetha) went with me to the Morning Star school for the handicapped. The place had children with all types of diseases: cerebral palsy, multiple sclerosis, autism, and numerous others. Yet the wolves knew instinctively that these were special people and they used their selves as healing tools to help these children express their love.

Just seeing the joy in their eyes of someone coming to see them, play with them, listening to them, even though maybe not in words or sounds, but in their energy, you could see remarkable reactions. Some so much so, that staff members, such as doctors and nurses, were astonished at the responses that never before had ever occurred from the child or children. Many tears of joy and love were shed and shared. It would tear anyone's heart out to see such things and you want to do so much more. Yet all you can do is, make the effort and pray. Events like this in my life have been all that I have needed to keep me going no matter how hard or how difficult life might be.

Conducting ceremonies inside of a prison of maximum security, or lesser, is still the same no matter which one you are at. You see and feel the problems that face anyone who is doing time and trying to practice a religion that is not readily acceptable by the majority. You experience the pain, suffering, and frustration of trying to get those in charge of the prisons, to just be fair and allow everyone to pray as they choose and to practice whatever their religion is.

You see and feel the joy of people coming together even through all the obstacles that "authority" may try to use to frustrate, or even stop these ceremonies. You feel the energy and love that comes from every one and all that have ever suffered together and endured. And it is for that reason I wish to speak on these matters.

People on the outside of prison enjoy a freedom that is given to them many times by the suffering of others who fought and won those freedoms and rights for everyone. The Native American Religious Freedom Law came into law August 11, 1978 after the sacrifice of many Native American brothers and sisters in prison. What they suffered and endured would make most cry out and beg for mercy, and give up. What they gave can never be paid for in money or material things. And still prison authorities tried to frustrate and persecute the religion and those that practice it. And still the suffering went on.

Finally in 1994 the Free Exercise Law for Native American Religion was passed into law and still the prison authorities do their best to circumvent, and frustrate, persecute, and harass the Native American prisoners as they try their best to practice their traditional religious beliefs. I tell you this because it is the truth and needs to be said.

No other religion has ever had to endure the persecution, suffering, and harassment that all Native Americans face each and every day in this country. It was illegal for Native Americans to practice their religion in this country until 1978. And many ceremonies were so hated that laws were in place under penalty of death if convicted for practicing them.

It is now 2012 and still everyday Native American prisoners face these same problems and must endure this suffering and frustration just to practice their beliefs and religious ceremonies. Now with that being said I would like to thank some very moving, remarkable men who stay true to their beliefs and practice their religion every opportunity they get to conduct ceremonies and participate in them as well.

These men are my brothers and I'm very proud to call them my brothers. We have prayed together, suffered together, fasted together, sang our songs, and have shared our lives and our hearts for all of our people, and as we say, all of our relations. These men are still in prisons, carrying on the struggle for religious freedom for all.

Many do not understand that what we fight for is for everyone. For if we lose then everyone loses. Then if you allow the minority Native Americans to fade away, then who is next? It must have a balance. So I say to each of you, go to a prison or jail and visit those who are there. Listen to their story. Hear their heart, their beliefs. Share your time on the Path! To give of yourself is always a true blessing. Then you will see! All who visit those in prison, hospitals, nursing homes, special handicapped places, schools, and orphanages will truly be blessed with love by the Creator, and all those they see as well!

May you all feel the Voice of Spirit inside of your Heart!

I pray these words may touch your hearts and motivate you to always be involved in giving. Oleha, Mvto (At Last, Thank You)

Remember to Walk in Love and Beauty Always!

Chapter Thirty-Three

Earth Changes and Prophecy

The Earth changes will affect everyone. As the Earth changes so must we. Her magnetic energy lines will change, which affects us as well, because our bodies are attuned to her more than most even have a clue about. Just as it affects her, it affects the moon and the moon's pull on our bodies and all life here on earth. All the tides, plants, animals, and all will be affected. Seasons will become nonexistent. Why? The chaotic shifts in magnetic fields and lunar effects which change the weather and then the shift in the sun's flares will bring totally uncontrollable freak weather that rips and tears up everything. Storms will have such mass that they will pop up totally unexpected. And at any time!

People are truly running out of time to readjust their conscious thought which is a powerful energy, and they must readjust their way of thinking. If they don't learn to live in the flow and balance, then what is out of balance will crash and be destroyed. When the ancient ones talk of the world ending, it doesn't mean the earth will be totally destroyed, it means the world as we know it will be gone forever. And we either change or pass into oblivion.

Most people will panic. Most people don't know how to readjust. They have lived so long in total isolation from life that they could not survive the first week of total blackouts and no power. Because when people panic they become afraid, and people who are afraid always attack and strike out at all around them. Those that attack will do anything for your clothes, food, water, and weapons, whatever you have, because they don't know how to live with the land. They don't know what to eat, what can be eaten, and what we can't eat. They don't know how to find water. They don't know how to keep from polluting the area around them. Even if they find a place that had clean water and there was food, they could contaminate it in less than seven days.

Very few left alive know how to make, design, store, preserve, find, grow, organize, and everything else they need to live, with only what the Mother Earth has to offer. It is because of these irresponsible choices that they now are all in this predicament, the choice to separate yourself from Nature or Mother Earth. Understand, the universe has a cycle too, just as all that is created does. It is time for the cleaning to be done and start fresh again! Now you either get your mind made up to be a survivor or just give up and die.

Even at my age I'll be perfectly fine and those that come and ask for help will get it. But understand this. This is not one of your restaurants. You can't have it your way! It is either the right way with you learning and helping or, no way, so hit the highway! You won't be able to go somewhere and get what you need.

You will be on the menu of a lot of animals as well. Understand old Fido there. You haven't fed him and he's hungry. He'll learn to hunt or starve. Which do you think he will do? And if he finds some friends well that is only Nature taking back what is natural to her. He will hunt you with his pack and attack you. Why? Well because he senses in you an easy meal. If you are hurt, or weak or scared, he'll know it! Just as all those you have allowed to be put in zoos and other fenced in areas. They are content as long as they get the free meal, but let them get hungry and see the difference. Just as you will.

Let's see how you will do when you are so hungry that you think your backbone is busting through your rib cage. And you would do anything I mean anything to eat. What will you do for your kids, or your spouse, or poor old mom and pop, or grandpa, and grandma? Don't try to tell me you'll be civilized and ask people for help.

Walking around and there is nothing left, what do you choose? It depends on your mind, your spirit, your determination whether you live or die, and will power alone won't get it. So get prepared people! Don't say you haven't been warned. I've been telling you and others have too, to get ready but you wouldn't believe, and didn't listen. Well I hope and pray that you start paying attention now and start learning things and how to do things, make things, and prepare foods from the raw resources! And if you don't know how, you better learn.

And plan for making your area sanitary, otherwise you'll have a plague starting fast in the area, and you can bet there will be plagues in every single city, and yes it will spread. It will bring more and more death when you allow others who just wouldn't listen and now have fled the cities and want to bring their walking death with them to you and yours!

What will you do now? Are you really mentally, physically, and emotionally preparing yourself? Look around you! Look at the changes that have been right in your face every day but you were always too busy. Did you pay attention to the weather changes, or the water situations around the world including your own area? Did you notice all the destructive storms, earthquakes, tsunamis, tornadoes, hurricanes? All kinds have been increasing at an alarming rate!

Well, I hope and pray that you have, because the change is coming. And when the cycle begins to increase and the Blue Star comes, understand it is too late for you to change then. And just as all the ancients have written in stone: "It is coming. The Blue Star always comes in this cycle and with it comes the changes and others that is always in its trail and follows closely."

The Blue Star is the second sun spoken of in the ancient Mayan and other prophecies. And it brings "others" means it is bringing a lot of asteroids, and meteors with it. Now it also means that the government has to surely already know about it, using the space telescopes.

It is time for the Beloved Women to come forth and be united again with the Crystal Skulls to usher in this time of Change, Balance, and Peace!

Yes it is time! It is time for all Beloved ones to answer their calling. The Crystal Skulls cry out to them to open their hearts and they will come to them. They will be directed to where they must come and where they should go. It is a time for all those who are guardians to come forth and protect the

Beloved ones and the Crystal Skulls! Because only with these can change truly come to those that seek. For the Crystal Skulls have the power and only with the Beloved and their True Hearts can all of those hearts and minds be uplifted!

I will continue to hope and pray you pay attention and make the changes each in your own self!

Remember to walk in Beauty and Love Always!

Section 5

Medicine Stories

Introduction

The purpose and importance of the medicine stories in my life and for all native peoples and especially the young is the messages! Yes the messages that each story has and is teaching you about life, about the experience of something that you may relate to your own life. Or maybe some time in your future? Every story ever told has this purpose. It isn't so much about the specific character, as it is about the messages that lay within the story of the character!

See, growing up we are taught many lessons of life, each and every moment of the day, whether by nature, or someone in your family, or a friend, or even an enemy. There are lessons in everything.

Even in the worse situation you can find a valuable lesson. You just have to look for it. Many times people have laughed and made fun of our native stories, saying "oh that is some BS" but that is only that person's lack of perspective. I would ask them, "okay well explain to me in the Bible, there are many parables, and stories about certain things, so what are they? Are they BS, or do they have a purpose?"

My answer is this: each has a message to teach you, just as the medicine stories of my people. Yes we use animals, and birds a lot, but then so does the Bible, in the new and old testament. And for you who do read the Bible, look in Job 12: 7-9 KJV "But ask now the beasts and they shall teach thee, and the fowls of the air, and they shall teach thee, Or speak to the earth, and it shall teach thee. And the fishes of the sea shall declare unto thee"!

Now we native people study nature every way possible, and all of nature. And we learn everything from them. The medicine stories teach us character, honor, truth, love, laughter, sadness, courage, gentleness, compassion, and humbleness, what today's society calls morals.

Each story may have more than one message in it. Some are very true and in fact did happen. Others are what they were designed to be "a tool used to help you"! In my life, the stories were something I sat in anticipation and anxiously waited to hear. Why, because they were filled with wonder to me as a child. As a child we see the world in purely magical wonder at everything in existence. We sit and wonder "wow how could that have been made"!

You look at a butterfly and are struck with the awe of beauty and magic that this beautiful being is. You stare at a flower and try to imagine just how did Creator do this? It is so delicate, so filled with scents, and beauty in the design. As children, your eyes and all your senses are bombarded with magic in everything. You want to be that pretty little humming bird, or that beautiful hawk, or that bumble bee, or you look at the clouds and want to go lay on them.

And when you listen to these medicine stories, they come to life inside of you. You become the rabbit, or the wolf, or the bear, you want to be them because you feel in your heart, and mind that part of you is really them.

So to all native peoples, we know that we are part of everything in existence. Nothing and I mean nothing, is not part of us. We know that we are all related, and we feel everything that is felt by all. The medicine stories touch that part of you; that is the character that is experiencing that lesson in life. Just as those who watch television are getting a story told to them, no matter if it is a movie, or reality, or sitcom, or even the news, a story is being told that has a message in it for you, and you choose to hear the message, or not!

Just as the stories that I have told you of my life and those around me, there are many messages there for you. I know many will say "well not me, I live in the city; or I wouldn't do that; or it just does not apply to me". Well it doesn't really matter if you live in the city, the projects, the country, or suburbs, or wherever. There is a message in everything. And yes it would apply to you. You just have to see it for what it is.

True it is my life, true it is my experience, and what I felt or had to deal with, but it is also YOU! Because whether you believe as I do, or as any native, or of any belief, we are all related. And being related means just that; we all have the same Creator and everything is created as part of the whole.

So if you had a piece of pie and cut it from the whole, would not that piece be the same as all of the pie? Was it not created as one pie? One hair on your head is just one part of the whole. Now in the stories, just one part is still a part of the whole, and the story has only one purpose and that is to teach and share that experience with you, because it is in you just as it is in the story. You are the story, because that is life, a never ending circle. Stories are never ending in life, and life is never ending. They are just new beginnings!

Remember to Walk in Love and Beauty Always!

Chapter Thirty-Four

Why Skunk Has a White Stripe

My grandfather told me this story when I was a small boy and now I will tell you!

In the old times when all the children of the land were one, all could understand and talk to one another. The birds love to talk, except the owls, who like to always have an audience first. The fish loved to show off their speed and agility. Some of them loved to perform their feats all day. The wolves always loved to play and have games. The bears, oh they only wanted to eat, sleep, and play. They didn't talk much unless you offered them food first. And any good hunk of honeycomb would keep them telling you of all the medicine plants they knew. Now the rabbits, oh they would keep you entertained for hours on end. We two-leggeds loved the rabbit people. They loved to laugh and once they started they could tell you their jokes forever if you let them. Have you ever seen a rabbit put his foot in his mouth and blow on it? HA! HA! His ears jump straight up, his eyes get real big like they will blow up, and his face is so ridiculously funny that he'll have your ribs hurting with laughing so much.

Now the snake people, oh they were a whole different attitude. They were about no nonsense. They would talk to you but they never started any conversations. They would just sit and listen, but when they spoke everyone paid attention. Because snakes were said to have the wisdom and secrets of the underworld, they knew of healing techniques that few ever dreamed of. And it was said by the real old ones that snakes used to walk and run, but they are best known as the guardians of the Sacred Places!

The mouse people, they were always up to no good. They would steal from you in a second. Raccoon people were marked for stealing the eggs from the one of the Thunder Beings. It is why he has the mask on now forever marking him. They can't help themselves, just as weasel and mink are marked for their uncontrollable thievery. Now skunk people they were unhappy now but they didn't use to be. Back when they were all black, and some of the best furred four-legged friends you could want, they were everywhere. They got along with everybody, not like today.

See, it all happened when Grandmother was going to have a big celebration. And all the children of the land were going to be there, so all kinds of foods were gathered and the best dishes were prepared for all. Some were made for every species of life. Now Grandmother knew that these foods and desserts, and dishes could not be left unguarded but who could she trust to truly watch over these day and night that would not be scared by any of them? She interviewed some of every group of her children. The eagle people couldn't, even though they were worthy, because they couldn't guard at night. The bear couldn't be the guard because they admitted that they couldn't control themselves. The wolves too said they were sorry but their bellies would make them tempted. She had just about interviewed all of them when the skunks came and begged to be given this opportunity to show everyone their strength and courage.

Grandmother asked them were they sure, because you know you don't have the claws of bear or of panther. You don't have the speed and teeth of wolf or alligator. "Can you really do this" she asked?

They all jumped up and said "yes, you can trust us. We will protect everything for you". Grandmother said "very well, but be sure that you do this. It is my time to celebrate my spring equinox and it better be all right when it's time."

Now all the skunk people were happy as could be, they loved this new status they had amongst all the children of the land. They scattered out and formed a big circle around all the foods, and desserts. And every time any more was brought they opened a way for the new dish to be let in. They loved all the respect they were being given. Other children brought the skunk peoples all kinds of gift offerings for their devotion and respect for everyone.

Oh the skunk people's hearts swelled with pride. They took the scented waters that were made from the flower people and covered themselves in it. They smelled so good and they looked so pretty! Others brought the skunk people gifts that came from the stone people, shell people, and the bird people. The skunks knew this was their most important time for them, and they relished it.

Now during this time, more and more foods were coming, more and more desserts, gifts for Grandmother, coming from all her children, until the place was piled high as a mountain. One night two days before the big day, the bears and others were having a hard time. The smells that filled the air was driving them mad. It was so painful, for the bears had to eat, and they could not help themselves. It was the same with the alligators, weasel, minks, raccoons, opossums, coyotes, ferrets, and all others that needed their natures eased with the food.

They could not help themselves. They surrounded the skunks and charged as one, screaming at them in the night. The skunks were terrified. They just knew they would be killed. It scared them so bad they messed on themselves and fled into the night and hid. The bears and all the others went for the food and desserts.

But Grandmother had heard all the commotion and she came a storming in. All the children froze and realized they had made a mistake. Grandmother seeing all that had gone on regained her self-composure and said "come gather around my children", and they did; all except the skunk children.

This really upset Grandmother so she called out in her powerful voice and said "I said come here to me, yes, you too my skunk children!" Slowly they came out of hiding and came to her. All the other children got out of their way opening up space for them. They smelled really bad. When they messed themselves they hadn't even cleaned themselves up!

Grandmother was furious. She said "since you failed me and ran in fear I will mark you for all time for all to see. Since you hid from me even after I came to help you, you will keep your stink to you for all time, and because you are still scared, every time you are in fear, you will release your rotten smell so all will know you for your fear". She lifted her hand and lightning came from her hand and burned a white stripe down the backs of all the skunks, and until this day all skunks are marked this way and if they get frightened they spray a stinking smell that just stays and stays.

Remember to Walk in Love and Beauty Always!

Butterfly Barrette

Chapter Thirty-Five

Butterfly

A long time ago when it was the old, old times, the old ones told the story of the caterpillar. Now in the story you have to know certain things, things like we all could talk and understand each other and we all were created by the same Creator so truly we were all brothers and sisters and we all had the same Mother. So sit there now and I'll share with you what I was told when I was a small person and as it was told to the one that told me.

In the old days of time when all was beauty and all lived in peace and harmony, the small ones who crawled were all given different gifts that were hard to see, for some that is. Some of the gifts to the ones that crawl were very obvious. Such as the beetle who had the shell of armor to protect him, or the ant that was so strong and had weapons of claws too. While some such as the slug left a trail of slick slime, or the stink bug who releases a terrible stink in the air all around him when threatened. The snakes were given their poison because they felt others just wanted to step on them. The lizards (ground puppies as we call them) were given their abilities to climb, or perfect camouflage.

But the caterpillar was given only his colors and some had spines that held some poison, but most just happened that their only ability was to remain motionless. All the other species of life all came together on a regular basis and spoke of their problems and to settle any that had disputes that might cause difficulties. And always Mother sat and listened, especially when she was asked for help because of this or that, and if any had dishonored her, she issued out her punishments.

Always it was the same ones constantly complaining about what they had or what they wanted, until it got to be annoying to Mother. Finally she said the ones that could go without complaining about their life, their problems, or wanting this or that, she would grant them a wonderful gift. Now everyone was excited, because Mother's gifts were truly wonders as it was, but for her to call it wonderful it surely would be.

As time wore on, meeting after meeting, each came and complained about this or that, or how rough and miserable was their plight. Why weren't they given this? Why couldn't they have that because the other had it? Only one people remained uncomplaining, always just quietly going about life as it was given to them.

Mother then spoke and said "caterpillars come to Mother", and they all came and sat around to see what Mother wanted.

Mother said "why don't you ever complain or want this or that like all the others? Are you afraid to speak to me"?

All was silent until the leader of the caterpillars rose up and said "no Mother we aren't scared to talk to you. We love you, but we feel if you wanted us to be any other way you would have made us that way. We are what you made us and we accept that as a gift as it is".

Mother smiled as she usually does when she is pleased and said "for that my children I will give you a special gift that no other shall have for your trust in me and my judgment of things. From this day forward let it be that when your life as a caterpillar is near its end you shall ball up into a cocoon and be born again. And as you are born again you shall wear wings and fly around tasting the best of the flowers, nectars, and pollens as your feast. You'll fly upon the winds as a symbol for all to see, that eternal life is a gift that comes to all, but only those who go through life and don't complain to me, and live their life as it was meant to be, shall become butterflies in the next world they see."

So every time you see a butterfly remember it could be someone you knew who lived without complaining about all the things that were given so freely, and one day you too might become a butterfly.

Remember to Walk in Love and Beauty Always!

Chapter Thirty-Six

The Story of The Cedar Tree

My Ani-yun-wiya Grandfather, Edgar Beaver, told me this story when I was a little boy. It was one of many he shared with me and I thought maybe some of you would like to hear it.

I can't talk like he did. I'm not that talented, for he was totally blind, yet he saw all things and when he told the story, his whole body talked the story. His power was great, and he used it to let you experience it just as if you were there. I will do my best though, and hopefully you will enjoy it.

In the times of the old, old ones, this story begins. I was a little one when my grandfather told me this story. He said that when he was a little one, this is what he was told: It was in a time long, long ago, longer than ten generations of trees lives when the world was still young and the people hadn't been living here that long - not long after coming from the stars on the clouds that moved through Spider Woman's web which kept the people in the air.

The people had lived on the ground here a few generations. First Man and First Woman, Kaniti and Selu had long passed. Our home was in these mountains that had been created by Buzzard when he flew down to see if the land had dried out; land that water beetle had brought up on his back. It was after the long battle with Giant Serpent and the Great Eagles. It was after the days of darkness when the sorcerers had tried to kill Grandmother Sun and had killed her daughter by mistake. It was after the days the youngest had brought the Sun's daughter back from the land of the dead and became Red Bird, and Grandmother Sun showed her love again by blessing us with her glorious light and warmth. It was right after brother skunk got his stripe down his back for falling asleep. That's when this story truly began, so sit there and listen closely, for this is very important and there is a message in it for you, as it is for every one of us.

At this time our People were doing well once again. Food was plentiful and the People were having celebrations, for at last we weren't warring with any other tribes. The land was peaceful all around. The People were multiplying and the Nation was growing. Happiness filled everyone's heart.

We were blessed with a powerful Healer who was very wise and was respected by even those who at one time were our enemies. Many people whispered he was a Spirit man, one who had once been a powerful Spirit who came here in the form of a man and walked as one of the people.

No, he was not born to our People. No one knew where he came from. Even the Little People whispered that he was one of the Blessed Ones. Some even claim he came by way of Spider Woman, as did our ancestors. Anyway, he was full of power, and he was with us and lived with us. His heart was pure and everyone loved him.

Anyway, during this time, a young boy child had been born of a bad marriage arrangement. The boy was afflicted by the Spirits. His body was not right, and as he had grown, everyone began to see his problems with speech and understanding. Other children began poking fun at him and always picking at him. His mother had run away and left the town. Now the boy was alone, living like one of the town dogs. During this time, the boy grew more and more skittish of the people, as a wild wolf pup. No one ever offered him any love, nor even a kind word. No one gave him food or even clothes.

Finally, right before Sacred Ceremony, one of the members of the Holy Ones said that he had a dream and that the boy who was strange must be driven from town or bad things would happen to them. Now the people grew upset. None wanted the wrath of the Spirits to befall the people or the town. No one spoke up for the boy, so the council had the boy brought before them.

While they were informing him of his fate, the wise and powerful Healer came upon the gathering. He had been out gathering herbs and knew nothing about what was happening. So he stood and listened to what was going on and was shocked. He parted the people in front of him and made his way before the council. The council acknowledged him and asked if he wanted to speak. He said yes, and he began giving them a tongue lashing about not one of them taking care of the boy or willing to adopt him, or even speaking up for him.

Then he spoke directly to the group of Holy Ones, particularly to the one who claimed the dream. He stated that he too had dreams all the time, but not once in his entire life had he ever known the Spirits to single out a boy who was no harm to anyone, who was simple-minded and who was unfortunate enough to have been born with his physical impairments, to be banished and surely to die.

No, he said, Spirits protect ones such as this child and have always instructed the people to treat these children with special care, for they are blessed by always being in the Spirit World. Furthermore, he said he would take the boy raise him as his own son, and would adopt him right here and now. And that if this banishment was still to be enforced then he too would be banished.

Now the People and the council were stunned. First, they needed the Healer since he was known by all the other Nations and none of the people would want him to leave them and go to another Nation. Also they felt hurt in their hearts; for they knew what he said was true.

And they knew that they had failed to live by their own code of love, respect, honor, humbleness, and generosity. So the council ordered that the boy would not be driven away and furthermore that an adoption ceremony would take place as soon as the Healer could arrange all the matters that must be observed.

Then he began the teaching of the boy and how he learned the plants, remedies, and the secret mysteries that the great Healer knew. The boy was given new clothes, bathed and purified. He was as happy as a puppy with a new plaything.

The boy went with the great Healer everywhere, helping

him in all the ceremonies. As years went by, the boy was allowed to do many of the healing ceremonies himself. His confidence grew, and so did his heart. Where in the past his heart had turned hard towards the People, it now had nothing but love, and especially loved the great Healer who had changed his life so much. To the amazement of everyone, the boy developed a beautiful singing voice; a voice that vibrated with love, emotions and power as he sang the powerful healing and prayer songs.

The years went on and on until the boy was an elderly man. Still the Healer looked the same. One day he told the boy that he must go elsewhere. The boy didn't understand. Why must the great Healer leave? The great Healer told the boy that his work was done here; that he was needed somewhere else.

The boy said, "What about these people here, who will help them, heal them, teach them if you leave? We still need you."

The great Healer told him "You will. That is your place and duty now. You have learned all I can teach. Now you must do these things for the People."

In the morning the great Healer was gone. Scouts, hunters, and trackers tried to find him, but he left not one trace or trail to where he had gone.

Now the one-time long-ago boy was an elderly man, all on his own again. So it came to pass now that the People, who long ago had no compassion for a small boy, called on the elderly man for his help. He loved his work. He loved helping people. He loved seeing them happy and removing their pain. Now he too became known far and wide. His skills and knowledge were nothing compared to his heart of compassion. His love was felt and seen by all the People in everything he did.

And years had passed and the old healer now had a student he was teaching, for he was getting older and older and his body was not as strong as his heart. The years passed on and the old healer now was faced with a fear. The People were dying and no cure he had tried had helped them. No matter what he did, it could not defeat the sickness that was spreading amongst the People.

That night the young man who was learning from the old healer was shaken awake by the old man, and was told that he must follow him. The old man gathered some things and told the young man to come. They traveled all night and all of the next day, stopping only long enough for the old man to rest his tired body, until they finally had reached a very remote and isolated area in the mountains.

The old man told his helper to build a fire, for they would camp here awhile. The old man wandered off and sat in silent prayer all that day and into the night. He refused to eat and even drink. Still he sat in silent prayer and thought. For three days this went on until the fourth day. The old man was very weak and the young helper knew that he was dying and his heart cried out for the old healer.

That night the old healer asked for help to sit next to the fire. He wanted the young man not to worry, that a visitor was coming. Later that night a very powerful man appeared and walked up to the fire. Greeting them as friends and in peace, they offered him food and drink. Later they lay down for the night.

The old man prayed long and hard for he knew he was dying. He prayed for his People. He prayed that a cure would be found to heal the new sickness. He cried for his people and he cried for his failures that had not saved the ones that were sick, until he felt his spirit leaving his body. As his spirit left his body, a Spirit spoke to him and asked him if there was one thing he wished he could do for his people.

He said, "Yes, let there be a plant that would cure the sickness of his People."

The next morning the young man woke up and was scared because the old man was gone. His bed disappeared and where he had slept was a large green tree. He looked around in fear and realized that the visitor was gone too. He called out for the old healer but no answer came. He sat down and wept until he felt a hand on his shoulder. He looked up startled to see the visitor there smiling.

The visitor told him not to worry, that the old man had not left his People; that he would always be with his People, who he loved. The visitor told him that the old man had one final wish that the Grandmother had granted because of his love. There, that tree was the cure for the sickness that was killing the People. For the young man was to pick the green leaves and boil them and have the sick ones to drink it. Have others boil the leaves and wash their bodies with it, so that the sickness would not spread.

He took the young man over to the tree and explained that Grandmother had seen love in the old man's heart and had rewarded him by turning him into this tree. That this was a special tree, that inside the tree was the heart of the old man, so he would always be with the People he loved, that this tree would never wither even in the winter, that it would always be green so that the People would be reminded of the gift of life and the old man's love; that this tree would spread its seed so that the old man's love would spread all over the land. The visitor now told the young man to gather some leaves to make the medicine teas and return to his People. The visitor then disappeared.

To this day the old man's love is with the People, and the People revere this beautiful tree. This is the story of the cedar tree as was told to me.

Remember to Walk in Beauty and Love Always!

Chapter Thirty-Seven

Why Buzzard Has No Feathers on His Head

This was first told to me by my grandmother when I was about the size of a watermelon. I hope I can tell it to you as good as she did for me! She was a very gifted story teller.

In the old, old times, the two-leggeds were very proud of themselves. They started out being the youngest of all of Grandmother's children, and were so pitiful that all their brothers and sisters felt so sorry for them.

Many of them saw that the two-legged ones had no fur to keep warm, had no feathers either. They had no claws or teeth to protect themselves. They were not very big. They could not run very fast. The two-leggeds couldn't camouflage themselves to hide. They were not hard like their stone brothers and sisters. They were not tough hided like the alligator, or turtle. They didn't have bark on them like brother and sister tall peoples (trees). They didn't have scales, and were very slow in the water. They didn't have gills either, so they were stuck on the land, and since they didn't have feathers they could not fly.

They were getting burnt by Grandmother Sun, and they did hide from her. Many of their siblings asked them "why were they getting burnt?" They didn't know, so some of their brothers and sisters offered them help! Giving them bark, stone, furs, feather, leaves, hides, from themselves. Turtle even offered his shell, just to help the pitiful two-legged ones.

Now the two-leggeds saw that all loved them and they survived at first, being the youngest, and all their relatives always looked out for them. Now they had covering on they would go out and greet Grandmother Sun every day. And she naturally loved them all.

After time went on the two-legged felt they were better than their relatives and smarter. They started tricking them into doing all kinds of things for them, while the two-legged sat back and smiled and encouraging them on with their praises of how good that was. And they learned to exploit the love of their relatives even farther. They started asking them to give up their bodies so they could grow stronger. And many of their relatives did.

They tricked the deer, rabbit, buffalo, fish, bird, and even turtle into giving them their lives and in return they would name their children after them, to always honor them. Boy did one after another offer their lives to the two-legged ones.

It got worse and worse because the two-leggeds began making weapons now that would kill many of their relatives. More and more were killed and the two-leggeds got to boasting of how smart they were and how dumb their relatives were. Day after day the two-legged now just took who they wanted without asking.

Their greed and arrogance sickened their Grandmother and she came out and told them how evil they had become, and so greedy to kill without asking, to take but never give, and by taking more than they needed that she would turn her back on them and never shine her warmth on them again.

Grandmother Sun fled from their view and everything grew dark. It became so dark so fast, that storms started brewing. First, the lightning people began pounding the sky, then the thunder beings began rumbling, and shaking the ground beneath their feet. The two-legged ones threw their heads up and screamed they didn't care. They weren't scared! Grandmother Earth began crying and the Cloud people, emptied their hearts of water out, as the wind people began howling and pushing hard at everything. Time stood still. No light of day came.

On and on the storms of the children raged, then suddenly the rain turned to snow and the wind people blew it hard and everywhere. Colder and colder it got. Ice began forming everywhere, and did not melt. It became so cold that the thunder beings went and hid, as did all the children. Now many were more able to withstand the cold, but others could not so they went and hid or tried to find somewhere else to live. The two-legged children now scattered, and covered Grandmother Earth everywhere, all trying to survive. The two-leggeds saw that they had caused this so they cried out to Grandmother but she ignored them.

Finally after a long, long time, the children all gathered to discuss how to get Grandmother Sun to show her face again. Many argued, all trying to put themselves in the Grandmother's place. They all agreed that it would take one of great courage to fly that far and hope to find her. Eagle said he'd try but he did not think he would make it, as did many of the bird people's representatives. Finally Buzzard said "I think I can find her, because I use a glide and rest practice of flying and I can fly that high as well."

So Buzzard went and after many days had passed, he found Grandmother and begged her to please come back, that all was dying because it was so cold. She was crying and said I'll come but the two-legged and the others can never be as they were before. Buzzard said that would be fine, just come.

Grandmother followed Buzzard back. All the children looked up and shouted to her their love. And as Buzzard came down they sang songs about him and shouted out praises for bringing Grandmother back. Now Buzzard loved attention as everyone knows and he shook out his feathers ruffling them up showing off how beautiful he was. And as each day came all the children raised their heads up and shouted their love to Grandmother Sun, and the land grew warm again.

All the other children now looked up to Buzzard and he marveled at all the attention, and soon he was overwhelmed with the glory, as more and more children came to hear him tell his story of his glory. Then he started asking for food to be brought to him before he would tell the story and it got bigger and better as the food and gifts grew. Buzzard's ego grew as well and one day he dared to disrespect Eagle and tried to make him out as a coward for not flying to find Grandmother. Now we all know you never disrespect Eagle because Eagle will fight really fast and he is good too.

Anyway, Eagle challenged Buzzard but Buzzard refused

to fight. And a huge argument began between the supporters of Eagle and those that supported Buzzard.

Grandmother Sun heard all the commotion and came closer and asked "what is going on here?"

And it was explained to her. She had been watching Buzzard for some time now hoping he would settle back down and just be himself but no, he wanted to be different. He got used to his new status and he wanted more. Why should Eagle be the leader of all the winged? Why couldn't he be the leader? Didn't he prove he was better than Eagle? Eagle should have to clean up after him. Eagle should have to clean up after everyone! He shouted and shouted until it hurt her ears.

Grandmother, being as wise as she was, proposed a race. The one who could fly the fastest from that mountain there in the east to this mountain here in the west as she pointed, shall be declared the winner and shall be the leader of all winged ones. And the loser shall clean up after all of my children! Now this statement really got everyone's attention because no one liked having to clean up the remains of food carcasses of their own, and others that were where they lived.

Buzzard was worried but his supporters all shouted their encouragement, and he puffed himself up big and proud throwing out his chest and screamed I accept the challenge and the agreement! Eagle said he'd accept but didn't feel the loser should have to clean up after everyone.

Buzzard reared up tall as he could and called out "why are you such a coward?" Eagle put his head down and shook it and said "I accept. I was only thinking of you brother, but remember you asked for this not me".

So the race was set. And everyone was ready, many wagering this or that with Grandmother as the judge. She asked "are you ready?" and looked at Buzzard and he said "yes" and then she asked Eagle and he said "yes".

She said, "On my signal you go there and back. The one that does this first shall be the winner." Everyone was tense and waiting. Grandmother shouted "go", and off they flew, with their wings pumping up and down as fast as they could. Eagle was out in front and Buzzard was screaming at him calling him names. Eagle said nothing just continued to fly, and when he reached the mountain he touched his claws to the ground never even slowing down and dragged his feet and spun himself around in seconds and was headed back when he flew by Buzzard.

Buzzard couldn't believe what he saw, and he tried it himself but not with the speed and grace of Eagle. He finally got himself turned around and was headed back screaming his fury because he knew he would lose. Eagle touched down on the other mountain and waited for Buzzard to finish his flight. But Buzzard was mad and humiliated and he flew up at Grandmother screaming at her.

This surprised her and made her mad. And as Buzzard was mad too he flew right straight up at her. Suddenly his head was burning. He tried to dive as fast as he could but not fast enough. All of his feathers on his head were burnt off and his head was reddish pink as he then went head first into the lake. His shoulders were smoldering and smoke was coming up from the water when he raised his head. He saw his reflection in the water and screamed out his fury.

Grandmother using her powerful voice called out to all to listen and they did. She looked at Buzzard and said "you have lost the challenge and the race. Therefore for all time you will be cleaning up after all my children, and because of your disrespect to me you will remain bald with no feathers on your head to show you and remind all of your shame. You brought this on yourself, when everyone was looking up to you for your great deeds. But you let that go to your head, and turned on your greatest friend Eagle here. Now go cleanup all the messes that are everywhere."

And that is why Buzzard has no feathers on his head and why he still has to clean up all the messes of the land.

Remember to Walk in Love and Beauty Always!

Section 6

Spiritual Exercises

Spiritual Exercise 1

Breathing the Way of Spirit
The Ani-yun-wiya breathing technique

Now we must breathe the way of Spirit, and the way we've been taught to harmonize our entire beings into relaxation, so we can let go of this world.

You must breathe in slowly through your nose deeply and then exhale through your mouth.

Now, beginning with your left foot, relax your toes and foot, letting your muscles, aches and pains totally relax. Then relax your left calf muscle and knee, relax your left hamstring and thigh.

Now do the right foot, leg and thigh, just as you did the left. Relax your left bottom, and your left side, now your right bottom and your right side, now your lower back and lower stomach.

Now relax your shoulders and your chest, then your neck. Now relax your left hand and fingers, moving up to your shoulder.

Now relax your right hand and fingers moving up to your shoulder. Now begin to relax your face, your eyes, and then relax your mind.

Release all thoughts you had. Empty your mind. Picture a hole in the top of your head and all your thoughts, worries, problems, and fears pouring out of your head like water pouring from a faucet.

Now picture in your mind a large bowl with spiraling designs going down to inside the bowl. This bowl is the universe and you are in the universe.

You are totally safe here, and are loved. Now with your crystal, touch it to your spirit eye and hold it there and feel it harmonize with you and the universe.

(This method of meditation of the Ani-yun-wiya is a traditional method used in many ways, such as for healing, for hypnosis, spirit travel, training a little person to enhance their memories, etc. Sometimes a spirit bowl is used, sometimes a secret place; using mountains, trees, waterfall, etc. In the old days, the Ani-yun-wiya knew this technique.)

Spiritual Exercise 2

Opening the Spirit Eye/Mind's Eye/Third Eye

Get a comfortable chair and sit in it.

Practice breathing the Ani-yun-wiya way. Do this with your eyes closed.

After doing this slowly and as deeply as you can, take your left hand, place two fingers over your eyelids, holding them down.

Now, with your eyes still closed and held down by the two fingers of your left hand, look up - moving your eyes up only. Your eyelids will still be closed and held down by your fingers.

You are looking up to your forehead, still be breathing in as deep as you can through your nose, and exhaling slowly though your mouth.

Clear your mind. Don't think about anything. Do not try to see anything. Just relax.

Now, still doing this at the same time, use another finger of your left hand and start tapping a triangle in the center of your forehead while you breathe in slowly. Now hold your breath as long as you can while you are still tapping the triangle.

Then exhale. Repeat this for seven minutes.

While you are tapping the triangle on your forehead and breathing in through your nose as deeply as you can, hold it, and tap four times in the center of the triangle you have been tapping into your forehead.

Example: While holding your breath and looking up toward your forehead, tap the triangle onto your forehead to the count of 12 taps, then tap your forehead 4 times, open your eyes slowly, and let out your breath. You will need to practice multiple sets like this to work up to the seven minutes. Your arm will get tired! Be patient! All of these exercises take time and practice!

Then, open your eyes and notice the difference in your sight.

While you were doing this, you saw things as well. Write them down as best you remember them - whatever you saw, where it came from, where it went, shapes, and colors. Everything has meaning.

Try to do this two to four times per day if you are able.

This will help you start seeing the energies and vibration of all objects, life, life forms, etc., and will open you to seeing spirits.

This is a muscle! So exercise it and work to make it stronger.

Also, while you are exercising this new sight, ask questions of Spirit, very simple direct questions. Never ask two questions in a single question, nor do you ask a question that has multiple answers. Be very precise in your question.

Then, also you must let the Spirit know if you don't understand, and ask, "Please show me so I will understand."

These techniques will open up new discoveries for you if you practice and exercise them.

Spiritual Exercise 3

Searching Your Past

First find a large vase-type bowl: wide at the top, lessening at the bottom.

While it is dry, paint a spiraling design all the way to the bottom.

The spiral must go around this bowl and be clearly visible, so use a color you can see, and make sure it is water permanent so it won't dissolve.

After the bowl is finished and dry, fill it with water from a spring or clear stream.

Look and make sure you can see the lines spiraling down inside of it.

Once you are finished with that, then use the Ani-yun-wiya breathing technique and gently empty all of your problems out of your mind.

When you are focused and clear of all problems and thoughts, then starting at the top, gently look at the lines spiraling down.

Picture in your mind becoming one with the water and you are actually swimming down, down, to the bottom.

When you get to the bottom, it is dark, so let your spirit call your helper, bird, animal, etc. and become one with your helper, and fly, swim, walk through the darkness and emerge in your past lives.

Each trip will lead to another, but take it slow and only learn one lifetime at a time so you won't get confused.

Use all of your senses in each journey, to experience it - let your mind reveal all of it using your senses.

When you come back, use a crystal by placing it on your forehead to help clarify your memory and enhance your memory cells.

Spiritual Exercise 4

Who Am I

Get a red candle. Turn out the lights. Light the candle and let it burn way in the back of the room. Make sure there is very little light in the room, but enough to see.

A moonlit night is best! Sit comfortably in a chair. Get a mirror and begin looking directly into your own eyes in your reflection.

Keep doing this. Now repeat – "Come, come, come show me my true self." Repeat this seven times. Now ask yourself to change into your animal form.

Look real close. Keep the mirror close to your face. Watch yourself change. During all of this, you will see yourself change and see spirits coming from the side of your image and into your image. You will see your true self. This is something else that must be practiced.

Spiritual Exercise 5

Circle of Love

I want to talk to you about conducting a Circle of Love. This is a technique that was used by the Old Ones of long ago. It was here for millions of years, until it has all been forgotten except for a few. It is time now for the Circle to come back, for the women must pick their hearts up off the ground and restore Love back into this world.

Only women can be trusted with power, otherwise the world you live in now will get worse until Mother calls her relatives and the world as we know now will cease to exist. Only those that live for Spirit and live the life of the Old Ones will survive. You have a choice to make. Only you can make it. If the women of this world unite and use their power, they can change this world, for a woman's heart is full of love, and only in love can forgiveness, peace, joy, and happiness return everywhere.

I tell you this because I have been given this message to give to you. Many of you can see the world as it is now: full of wars, disease, jealousy, hatred, murder, rape, starvation, pollution, no honor, no families, no truth, and no love. Look all around you. Is this what you truly want? Life wasn't meant to be this way. Life isn't life now. It is only existing in illusions of sufferings.

Women outnumber men in every country of this world. You must speak out, use your hearts, and use your vast numbers to make changes. Now many of you will think, yes, I believe this too, but what can I do? What can I do? No one will listen to me. Well, you can make a difference. Each one of you can, but first you need to get your heart right. You must believe you are a Woman!

Believe you are a woman who is given the gift of True Love by the Spirit, Creator, or whatever name you wish to use. You must know inside of your heart that you are Love, you want Love, you will freely give this Love, and you will not see negative or bad things. You will only see the beauty that you have, the love that you have. You will find this in everything you see, hear, feel, taste, and smell. You are Beautiful. You are True Love. You are Powerful, and you are making the choice of Truth.

Once you have done this, now gather other women to you to join a Circle of Love. You speak to each other with only love in your hearts, and beauty in all that you see. You give them your love and they give you their love. Each one of you will send this energy of pure love to each other. Each of you now makes the choice to start more Circles of Love, and you lift your voices up together to get changes started in your immediate areas.

Each of you has a power over men. You know this, for it is truth, and only you need to decide to seek the proper position of power to make the changes.

For example, in this country, women can vote. Unite all the women in your area, to vote for one of you for each political office. Then do it for your counties, then your state, taking over the positions of the town councils, mayor's office, judge's offices, state legislature, county commissions, state commissions, state attorney generals, county attorneys, sheriff's office, US Congressional seats, US Senate seats, Governor's office, Lt Governor's office, etc.

Then go further and take over the cabinet positions, president's office, ambassador's office, etc. You do this by using your voice on concerns of your heart, for education, pollution, employment, salaries, cost of living, living conditions, health care, food programs, housing, safe environment, elder care, etc. Since you outnumber men in most places ten to one, you can do this.

Some of you might think "I'm not qualified." I've never known any woman who isn't qualified for this. You are born with a heart of love, beauty, and happiness; you all have a good sense of responsibilities, character, and values. You all know how to organize your homes, and how to manage on a budget. You do these things every day. You know how busy you are, all the different things you have to do.

Why is it difficult to realize how important you truly are? Why continue to let men dictate your lives to all these messes behind their thirst for power, egos, jealousy, and pride. Why let them start wars, let children suffer, cause disease by biologically engineering it themselves, and experimenting on you, your families, and your loved ones?

Each of you knows in your heart that what I'm saying

is true. Listen to your own heart. It will tell you. Now many of you have been enslaved by society's dogmas, government brainwashing, and religious hogwash that tell you that you are here to serve men, be silent, etc. In your own hearts you know that you have been lied to.

Men were never supposed to be in power. Men were never supposed to make decisions for you. Men were never supposed to be in control of you. Men were never supposed to abuse you, disrespect you, hurt you, or own anything. Men should live at your commands, your decisions!

Your power was for all, not like men who only think of themselves. Men are lost. They don't have true power, so they make power by physical force over women, yet women have allowed this. That is why the world is as it is. You have the Power by Birth. It belongs only to you. You have the power to heal a man's heart, if you only will.

I give you this message because, as I said, if you don't pick up your hearts then only death and destruction will come.

I am a man, but a true man. I live by the Ancient Code. I listen to the Spirit and I know the Truth. Love is the only Answer, and only women have True Love in their hearts. Start with yourself today. Start others today. Make the changes. I say this with love in my heart.

Men can participate in a Circle of Love but they must ask forgiveness from the women of the Circle and give up their egos, pride, and past way of thinking, and only give love and support to the Circle. The Circle can heal the men's hearts and show them the error of their ways.

Spiritual Exercise 6

Salt Crystal Water Bath

Using rock salt, or preferably, sea salt (that's now available in the grocery stores in the baking aisle) run water in a tub mixing the salt up real good in the hot water.

Then add the pure quartz crystals. Crystals love to bathe and it energizes them as well.

Next add yourself.

Turn the lights out after lighting some candles, put on some good meditation music, and just relax and meditate while your body gets energized by the crystals, salt, and water.

Try to do this bath two times a week. After you've finished, rinse yourself off with clear water.

It is important that while you soak that you meditate, to free your mind and attune yourself and your vibration to the crystals.

Spiritual Exercise 7

Protection When Calling Forth Spirits!

I thought I would speak on a subject for I have to help people all the time, because they do things which they do not know of and wind up having problems because they didn't know! This is calling forth spirits either unintentionally or intentionally.

Many times throughout my life I have been asked to help someone who has problems because they messed with things that they didn't understand the consequences of, or were not told of these things, or were just playing around. When you do things that have a mere chance of calling forth a spirit or spirits, you must be protected.

And this starts with using sage to smudge and using cedar. Then you can either mark a circle around you, or invoke a "magical circle" as some have termed it now days, using salt, or with something that is copper.

I have used and tried these ways to make sure that they would work for those who like to play with things that they shouldn't. The only reason I'm even doing this, is for those who are going to get in trouble no matter what because they just never will listen. This is why they always have so many problems in their lives. I have had people who have no experience in these things do this with me supervising them to make sure it would work for anyone. If you want to play and get your lives turned upside down and have things messing with you day and night, it is all bad.

First, realize that you should never do these things, second after you realize you really screwed up and you need help, well do what I now tell you. Smudge yourself and all around you with sage, either white sage or plains sage, or northern, (no not the sage you cook with) any herb, stone, or metaphysical shop will have these.

Second, get some salt, either a box of salt or a large saltshaker, and make a circle around you on the ground, next place pieces of copper or copper wire in a circle around you on top of the salt, use the salt again to cover it up. Take one drop of your blood and sprinkle it on the salt.

Third, call forth the spirit or spirits that have been messing with you. Once the spirit is there, command it to leave from you and never return.

Use these words, "I (then state your name) command you to leave and never return. You have no power over me. You have no power to use against me."

Now pick up the sage and light it so it is smoking, blow the smoke out and around you and say "only those spirits that are good are welcome around me, I command all bad spirits to leave and never return. You are not welcome here".

Do this seven (7) times and then smudge yourself and say "I command this and so shall it be."

Now step out of your circle and scoop it all together and now burn it. No not the copper, just the salt and the blood you have used or you may go bury it somewhere away from everyone, and place a piece of copper over it. The copper will bind all that was there.

Now I did this for those who have played with their Ouija boards, tarot cards, pentagrams, et cetera so that people will stop when they don't know what they are messing around with.

Don't play with spirits!

Spiritual Exercise 8

Learning What's Inside

When I was a small person my grandfather taught me a way to learn things. Now I know some people have a hard time learning some things while others just absorb it like a sponge.

This way of learning was shown to me to help me learn what a stone person (a stone or rock), an old sea shell, a tall person (a tree), an old broken piece of pottery, etc. knows. But during my life I have come to learn that this works for anything and everything.

My grandfather told me: "Everything has a spirit. Everything that is in existence has life. We may not see it, but it doesn't mean that it doesn't exist.

"So to learn what is hidden from most people, you must open your mind to everything. You must listen to the spirit that is in everything. And if you do listen and ask that spirit it will tell you what it knows. All spirits like to talk, so just remember this and you will learn many things that others miss in life."

Now I was a small person when he first told me this, but I found out myself that what he told me was true. And all we have to do is open our minds and heart up to everything. By doing this you will learn from the spirit of whatever you ask what it knows. I will give you a simple way to start learning this way. The more you practice it, the more developed you get at doing it. I know many of you might be thinking I'm full of it, that's okay, but what do you have to lose huh? Just try and you might be surprised at yourself.

This is just an example for you to try.

Find a book one that you have not read, one that you would consider hard for you to learn. It could be a school text book, a language book, a math book, any book that you know nothing about.

Once you have chosen your book, I want you to just relax with the book in your hands, empty your thoughts of anything else. And just let your mind and heart relax.

Breathe slow and deep to help calm yourself. Breathe through your nose only! Use your belly to breath, breathing in push your belly out and expand yourself, exhale slowly letting your belly suck in. Do this until you have relaxed yourself and your breathing is slow and steady, but taking long and deep breaths.

Once you have your breathing and body relaxed, take your book and holding it in your hands, do not open it. And begin talking to the spirit of the book, telling the spirit how much you really want to learn what the book knows all that is inside the book. That you need help in learning what is in it. That you would truly love for the spirit of the book to teach you and tell you all that was inside the book.

Now once you have asked that, either hold the book to your head or lay down your head on the book. (I usually do this at night while I'm ready to go to sleep.)

Make sure your head is really lying flat on it. And just relax. If you go to sleep that is okay, because sometimes it is easier for you to learn this in your sleep. Because many people have a wandering mind, and their minds are constantly working, it causes them problems even to go to sleep because their minds are steadily jumping around from thought to thought.

Once you have opened your mind to the spirit of the book, the spirit can begin to work on you. Now if you go to sleep usually the spirit will either teach you in your sleep or fill your mind with the memories of all that it knows inside of the book. Once you awaken or you have received your information, thank the spirit of the book for its help and generosity.

If for some reason you didn't get anything, try again, but this time, really relax yourself first. For some people it works better at their bed time, because they are going to relax as they sleep.

Now for those who are trying to learn from stone people, do the same thing. Make sure you sleep with the rock or stone touching your head. If it is a small stone person you can even tape it to yourself. I have even filled the bath tub up with natural spring or creek water and placed the crystals or other stones in the water and climbed in (naked of course) and relaxed myself in the tub and went to sleep asking them for their help, their knowledge, the information they have seen and lived through! I have done this with about everything you could imagine talking to.

I really love talking to the ancient ones, for they have lots to tell you. And you can learn about things first hand. I enjoy talking to and learning new things, such as languages, and histories from these ancient ones. I do also love to learn the customs and beliefs of these other peoples. What do you have to lose?

Nothing, because even if you really don't learn, well you can always use the relaxation! I hope you all have a great time doing and learning this way. I know that we never stop learning and always need to expand our knowledge in all areas.

Remember to always ask with respect and love in your words and in your heart.

Spiritual Exercise 9

Making a Medicine Bag

Many times I have people, even native brothers, ask me to make a medicine bag for them. I would like to explain something to you that most people don't know and most have no clue about. Making a medicine bag must be done by the individual that is making his or her own medicine bag.

Now when a person asks me to do this, I explain that I cannot do that. What I can do is just make you a bag, but you have to make your own medicine to go in it, but it is best that you make the bag yourself. Why? Well because, to make medicine you need something that is for you and for you only.

What I make wouldn't be your medicine. Now there is a difference between medicine that is to cure a sickness, injury, spirit sickness (when a bad spirit or spirits have entered the body) then yes, I can make something or do something to help that person. But to make a person's personal medicine (power) bag is something that person needs to do themselves.

As I said earlier, you need to put your heart, your prayers into this bag when making it. You are putting your time and energy into designing this, and the love and prayers add more power to it.

Then it is the item or items that you put in there that also gives it power. It could be a special stone that called you to pick it up, or a piece of broken bone, or a piece or a whole shell, or a feather. It could be anything that you saw in a dream that came to you or you could have fasted and something called you to it, or a spirit told you to get this and put this in your bag. It could be many totally different things or just one thing. But it would be yours and yours alone. And no one else should ever touch or open it. Only you should do that.

Many times people tell me: well so and so said this, or so and so sold me one before, and I was told this or I saw this on a show, etc. Understand this. If it is Sacred it can't be sold. If it is bought then you got ripped off, because medicine does not work that way.

Even when I must do a healing and I have to gather certain things (herbs, stones etc.). I have to be asked first, then, I have to ask the herbs, the stones, for their permission and why I need their help. Then, even then, I must still use and work with things that are the sick person's personal things to draw that energy and spirit from them as well. I don't do healing or talk to spirits for money. I only do and use what was given to me to use in a Sacred way.

Yes I have been paid to do things, but I did not charge for it. People give me things if they chose to out of respect. I'm allowed to accept gifts of respect and gratitude, or to pay for my expenses to travel to do something, or perform a ritual etc.

Yes I am very thankful for the things, and knowledge I

have been blessed with, and it is appropriate for me to receive gifts for these things. But I never charge anyone for doing these things, and I have never denied anyone if they didn't pay me, or didn't have the money to pay for my traveling to come, or didn't give me a gift.

I help when I can and how ever I can, because that is what I was given to do. None of the power or knowledge, or gifts that were given to me was paid for in money or materialistic things. I was given these things in love and respect from Spirit and I use them in love and respect. I chose and made a commitment with Spirit, and I live to that code and those requirements always. It does not mean that others do!

Then you will always have those who do things only for money or personal gain. Those you should know are not real. No Sacred Ceremony will ever have a charge for sale. You cannot buy Sacred anything!

It is just someone who is cheating you, for their own gain. Always stop and think before you ask for anything, and always be careful of what you ask for because you just might get it. And if you find yourself not wanting it because everything that you ask for comes with something else, remember always there is Balance.

So when you make yourself the bag, be careful of what you say and what you ask in your prayers and before you put anything in the bag always ask that spirit of that item, if it will or would like to be a help to you. And always place cedar and sage inside the bag for the item(s) to have protection as well.

Spiritual Exercise 10

Drawing in Energy to Heal and Release

Many times I have been asked to help someone by doing a healing. Now some healings just need to be done with making a special type herbal tea, or by using a certain stone, or even needing a drum to use the power of sound. But many times all that is required is the drawing of energy and directing it to the specific part of the body that needs to be healed.

Don't try any type of healing unless you are properly trained in doing this, under the guidance of someone that is, or unless your heart is a heart of love and you wish to truly heal with no explanations or returns for doing so. Then you should follow your heart. Bad intentions will not accomplish anything!

Now working with energy requires good concentration. You must be able to focus on something and not be distracted. You must be asked for your help to heal, or a family member or friend must ask for your help. That is the Rule!

First you must draw nothing but pure love in your heart, fill it completely up in you. You can do this by seeing everything around you as love, see it, feel it, smell it, taste it, hear it, and believe it.

Once you have all this love focused you draw it all into yourself, starting at your toes, then your feet, feel it draw into you. Now draw it up your legs, and into your waist area. Pull as if you are drawing yourself up like a giant balloon, and instead of air it is pure love energy you are pulling up inside of you. Keep pulling until you are completely full, your eyes, ears, and head feels like it is about to explode.

Now look at the person, animal, plant, or whatever it is that needs your help in healing. They have asked you for that help! Even a plant or animal will be drawn to those that can help them! Place your hands on the area, or areas, and say a prayer of love for that person.

Let the love energy that you have for that person, and all that was around you, now pour forth from you like a water faucet; that the water pours from as you turn on the handle. See it, smell it, taste it, hear it, and feel it as it flows from you into that person.

When you believe in all that you do in love, will help that person, it will. The person doesn't necessarily have to believe in what you are doing. But you must believe in what you are doing. It can help if the person believes but it isn't necessary.

If you have others there who also wish to help then have

them do the same things at the same time with you and it will increase all that energy as well. If there is a small child that is a relative of the person, or is a relative of yours, that child's energy will be more powerful than yours and you should always ask the small person if they would like to help. It must be their choice, and done with free will. These rules must always be followed.

The more you work with energy the better you will get at it. And never hold energy within you. Hold it only as long as necessary to direct it towards or at something, and then you must release it. Energy must always be released otherwise you will have an explosion of energy, instead of the gentle flow that heals and helps.

Once again this is not something to play with. What I mean is playing like "wow did I just do that?" Then drawing energy and slinging it at something just to play with your new understanding of energy. This is only discussed here to help others who have hearts of love for healing, not for those to try to use it in any type of bad way. There are consequences for those that do!

Section 7
English/Muskogee Dictionary

English/Muskogee Dictionary

Muskogee Alphabet

A	always broad as in far, as aha
C	che for ch as ceme, cesus
E	long as in meat, eat, beet-line over the e when written E e
E	short as i in spin, bin tin
F	as in English
H	as in English
I	always long as in spine, time
K	as in English
L	as in English
M	as in English
N	as in English
O	always long as in boat, note
P	as in English
R	hle, for hl as rvro for hvlvhlo
S	as in English
T	as in English
U	always sounds like oo as in boot, cool
V	always as u as in tub, rub, but
W	as in English
Y	as in English

Diphthongs

AE	as in Aeha, aela
AU	as ou in out
EU	euchee
OU	as in bout, stout
UE	as in ue-wu is oo-ee-woo (water)

English	Muskogee	phonetic
abdomen	nvr'ke	nurhle-kee
about here	yv'mv	yu'mu
accuse, to accuse	vta'wetv	uta'wetu
accuse falsely	oh-la'ksetv	oh-lak-setu
afternoon	fvtcvlik-hoyanen	fut-chuli-hoyanen
air, wind	ho'tvle	ho'tulee
alligator	hvlpv'tv	hulpu'tu
always	emu'nken	e-moon-ken
Americans	Wacenvlke	Wa'chenul-kee
amulet	tvkhv'ketv	tuku-ketu
ancestors	purke-tate	poorhlkee-ta-tee
Ancients	Hofunv'lke	hofoonu-lkee
around, all about	hvmecicet	hu'mechi'chet
any, any one	e'ston	e-ston
Beloved Woman	Vnokec'ke Hok'te	unoke'chkee hok'tee
Beloved Ones	Hvm'ken Vnokec'ke	hum-ken u noke che-ke
bird	fuswv	fooswu
black snake	cetto-lvste	chetto lustee
Black Water Swamp	Opelo'fv Uewv Lvste	o pelo fu oo-e wu lus-te
bless-verb-to bless	oh-mekusvp'etv	oh-mekoosup-etu
blue eyes	tur'wv hola'tte	toohle-wu-ho-latte
boy	capa'ne	che-pa-nee
boy, little	capa'nuse	chepa-noosee
butterfly	tvffolupv	tuf-foloo-pu
cedar	vcenv	uche-nu
chicken snake	apv-yakv	apu-yaku
Children of the Stars *	Hopu'etake Ekococumpu	hopoo-etakee ekochochoompa
clan	mvliketv	muleketu
come here	yv'mvnahtes	yu-mun-ahtes
conjure-verb-to use magik	por'retv	pohlr'hlretu
corn	v'ce	u'che
corn meal	vce-enfulotkv	uche-enfoolotku
corn silk	vto'klope	uto-klopee
corn cob	talvpe	talupee
dance-verb-to dance	opvinketv	opu-nketu
dance-noun	opvn'kv	opun-ku

death cry	hakih'ketv el'kv	ha-kih-ketu el-ku
dream-verb-to dream	pussvl'etv	poossul-etu
dream-noun	pussvl'kv'	poossul-ku
eagle	lv'mhe	lu'mhee
east	hvsos'sv	husso'su
fast-verb-starve	elauwe'cetv	ela-oowe-che-tu
oneself	elauwetv	ela-oowe-tu
feather	tafv	tafu
fire	totkv	tot-ku
foreign people	tvlepo'rv este lke	tule-po thlu-este-lkee
friend, my friend	vnhesse	unhessee
ghosts, spirits	puyvfe'kev'lke	pooyufekchu-lkee
giant, large	rak'ke	rak'kee
gift-noun	nak-emkv or nak-emtv	nak-emeku or nakemetu
girl	hoktuce	hok-too-chee
give-verb	hoyetv	ho-yetu
good morning	hiyvt'tke here	hi-yu-t-kee hee-rhlee
grandfather	puca	poo-cha
grandmother	pose	po-see
half-breed	ha'tv-ha'yv	ha tu-ha-yu
hawk	ayo'	a-yo'
heart	feke	fekee
help, assist-verb	vnicetv	uni'chetu
help-noun	vnickv	uni-chku
helper	vnicv	uni-chu
hello	hen'sci	henschee
holly leaf	es'se fv'ske	es-se fu-skee
how?	estome'cet	esto-me-chet
how much?	esto'musen	esto-moo-sen
I or my	vne	unee
journey	a'yetv	a-yetu
long time ago	hofune	hofoonee
love-verb-to love	vnokecv'keto	unokee-chu-ketu
love-noun	vnoke'ckv	unokee-chku
man	este-hunv'nwv	estee-hoonu-n-wu
Master of Breath Master of Life	Pucase Hesuketu	poo-cha-see he-sa-ke etu
me	vnen	unen
medicine	heleswv	he-les-wu

moon	hvre'sse	huhlre'ssee
new moon	hvresse pvlokse	huhlre-ssee pulok- see
Mother Earth	Et'ske Ekv'nv	et-skee eku-nu
noon	fvtcvlike	fut-chulikee
north	hunera	hoone hlra
not much	esto'musekon	esto-moo-see-kon
old customs	hofune-nak-afvstv'lke	hofoonee-nak-afustu-lkee
panther, swamp tiger	katcv opelofv	katcu opee-lo'-fu
pray-verb-to pray	mekusv'petv	mekoosu-petu
rattlesnake	cetto-mekko	chetto mekko
religion	mekusv'pkv	mekoosu-pku
Sacred Stones of Power	Vcake Cvto Eyek'cetv	uchakee-chuto-e-yek-* chetu
shaman, wizard	por'rv	po-thle-thu
sing	yvhiketv	yu-hi-k-etu
singer	yvhikv	yu-hi-ku
soul, spirit, mind	puyvfekcv	pooyufek-chu
south	wahv'llv	wahu'llu
snake	cetto	chetto
Snake Dance	cetto-hayv	chetto-hayu
spider	acuk-rv'nwv	achook-hlru-nwu
Star People	Kococu'mpv Estv'lke	kocho-choompu estu-lkee
suffer-verb	estemer'retv	este-mehlr-hlretu
sun	hvs'e	hus-ee
sun eclipsed	hv'se-teyvpos'ke	husee-uha-kee
Sunday	net'tv-cako	net-tu-cha'-ko
sundown	hvs'e-aklat'kv	hus-ee-aklat-ku
sunrise	hvs-e-vhake	hus-ee-uha-kee
	hvs'e-aos'sv	hus-ee-aos-su
sunset	ak-hu'se	ak-hu-see
talk, tell-verb-to talk, tell	punayetu'	poona-yetu
talk, language-noun	punv'kv	poonu'ku
thanks	mvto	mu-to
thing, also means what is it?	na'ke or nak	nakee or nak
thorn trees	eto-fv'ske	eto-fu-skee
tobacco	hece	hechee

turtle	lo'ca	loca
Turtle Clan	mvliketv lo'ca	mu-like-tu lo-cha
vision	nakheciho'cat	nak-he-chi-ho-chat
war clan	kepayu	kee-pa-yu
water	ue'wv	oo-eewu ? oo-eewoo
water moccasin	ue-ak-cetto	ooee-ak-chetto
west	hvs-aklatkv	hus-aklatku
white man	es'te hvtke	este-hu-t-kee
which way?	estv'min	estu-min
wife	hiwv	hi-wu
wild pig	suk'hvce hon ece	sook-huchee hon eechee
What is your name?	Cena'ke hocefkv estome os	Che-na-kee ho-chef-ku esto-mee os
where, why, what?	esto'men	esto-men
woman	hokte	hok-tee
young guardian	ahecicv mvnet'te	a-he-chi-chu mu net-tee

About the Author

Lynda M Means PhD teaches Native American Studies at a private university in Missouri, where she has taught for eighteen years. She is a mother and grandmother both by blood and tradition. Lynda was an elder in the Thunderbird Society, Eagle Lodge until its dissolution December 2007. She is a Pipe carrier in the Native Tradition for seventeen years and practices that spiritual way of life daily. Lynda teaches wherever she is needed, especially enjoying teaching teachers in primary education.

The Turtle Jewelry Lynda is wearing was designed by Ghost Dancer and photographed separately within this book.

The photograph was taken by Denyse Walton in 2010.

.